PUPPETMASTERS

PUPPETMASTERS

The political use of
terrorism in Italy

PHILIP WILLAN

CONSTABLE · LONDON

First published in Great Britain 1991
by Constable and Company Limited
3 The Lanchesters, 162 Fulham Palace Road
London W6 9ER
Copyright © 1991 Philip Willan
The right of Philip Willan to be
identified as the author of this work
has been asserted by him in accordance
with the Copyright, Designs and Patents act 1988
ISBN 0 09 470590 9
Set in Monophoto Sabon
by Servis Filmsetting Ltd, Manchester
Printed in Great Britain
by St Edmundsbury Press Limited
Bury St Edmunds, Suffolk

A CIP catalogue record for this book
is available from the British Library

Treason doth never prosper: what's the reason?
For if it prosper, none dare call it treason.
Sir John Harington, 1561–1612

CONTENTS

ILLUSTRATIONS

INTRODUCTION

The manipulation of Italian terrorism is a complex and highly controversial subject. Many of the most interesting insights come from highly suspect sources: terrorists, common criminals and members of the secret services, who, if they are not licensed to kill, are certainly expected to lie in the interests of the state. Nobody's word, therefore, should be taken on trust. Wherever possible, I have identified the sources of my information and I believe that the many fragments go to make up a plausible overall pattern.

Italian magistrates constitute one of the most reliable sources. Many of them are highly intelligent, courageous and independent-minded people, who have generated hundreds of thousands of pages of written reports to describe crimes of politically motivated violence in their country. Much of what is known about Italian terrorism today is the result of their skill in threading a path through the innumerable traps and obstacles that have been laid in their way. Until 1989, a judicial investigation had to be initiated by a public prosecutor. He would then work in tandem with an examining magistrate. At the end of the investigation, the prosecutor submitted his written recommendations to the examining magistrate, who responded with a written report of his own, and the prosecutor then took the case forward to the actual trial. The result of this somewhat laborious process is a vast fund of documentary evidence about Italian crime. Following a judicial reform introduced in October 1989, the role of the examining magistrate has been greatly reduced and the length of the pre-trial investigation has also been curtailed.

Paradoxically, while some practitioners of Anglo-Saxon law have been impressed by Italy's success in defeating terrorism and have been advocating a move towards the Italian legal system, the Italians have decided to change theirs to something closer to the British or American model. As we shall see, the efficacy of the Italian judicial system was by no means the only reason for the country's ultimate success in eradicating domestic terrorism.

The Italian secret service played a crucial role in both the rise and the fall of Italian terrorism. The military intelligence service has been through a bewildering series of name changes as a result of the political scandals and conspiracies in which it has been involved, each new name supposedly indicating that the service has been changed and reformed. The Servizio Informazioni Militari (Military Information Service) or SIM was established in 1925 and disbanded in 1945 at the end of the Second World War. Only in 1949 did the Allies allow the service to be re-established as SIFAR (Servizio Informazioni Forze Armate – Armed Forces Information Service). SIFAR was succeeded, from 1965 to 1977, by SID (Servizio Informazioni Difesa – Defence Information Service). In 1977 the current system was established, with SISMI (Servizio per le Informazioni e la Sicurezza Militare – Military Information and Security Service) taking over from SID and a new domestic intelligence service, SISDE (Servizio per le Informazioni e la Sicurezza Democratica – Democratic Information and Security Service), being created. The two services report to the Defence Minister and the Interior Minister respectively, as well as to a co-ordinating committee presided over by the Prime Minister. Despite these many reincarnations, the creature does not seem to have changed its spots and has frequently been accused of collusion with terrorism.

Another useful source of information comes from the obscure hints and blackmailing messages uttered by some of the protagonists in the story. These do not necessarily provide reliable guidance but they can cast an interesting light on events in the absence of more concrete evidence, and they are an established feature of Italian political life.

For the purposes of this book I have accepted the conclusions of the Parliamentary P2 Commission that the lodge membership lists found in the possession of Licio Gelli are an accurate guide to the lodge's adherents. Many of the people named in the lists disagree.

This book is dedicated to those who helped and to those who wouldn't, whatever their reasons.

[1]

IN DEFENCE
OF DEMOCRACY

A T 10.25 a.m. on 2 August 1980, a powerful bomb exploded in the second-class waiting room at Bologna railway station. It was the height of the summer holiday season and the station was crowded with tourists and Italians heading for their holidays by the sea. Eighty-five people were killed and 200 injured in one of the worst terrorist atrocities seen in Europe since the war. Seven of the victims were children under the age of fifteen, one of them a girl of three. Ten foreigners were killed in the blast, including a young English couple and a twenty-year-old student from Japan, the victims of a conflict they can have known nothing about. More than a decade later very little is known for certain about the bombing. What is clear, however, is that the Italian secret services worked hard to prevent judicial investigators from uncovering the truth. Partly for this reason, the process of justice has followed a pattern set in previous terrorist bombings, with initial convictions being overturned on appeal and mystery ultimately shrouding the identity of the bombers.

If the genesis of the Bologna bombing remains obscure, the political background to the earlier bombings has become increasingly plain. Eight indiscriminate bomb attacks on the Italian public, from the bombing of a bank in Milan on 12 December 1969 to the blowing up of a train near Florence on 23 December 1984, cost 150 lives and injured 818 people over a fifteen-year period. Magistrates now attribute much of that violence to a strategy of terrorism fostered by Italian and foreign secret services and designed to prevent the Communist Party from achieving power. The Bologna station bombing has also been attributed to that strategy, following a seven-year judicial investigation. On 11 July 1988, after a trial lasting more than a year, a Bologna assize court convicted four right-wing extremists of planting the bomb and sentenced them to life imprisonment. But two years later, on 18 July 1990, an appeal court in the same city overturned that verdict. There was widespread consternation as yet another terrorist outrage went unpunished. Amid all the uncertainty, alarming new hypotheses have begun to emerge as to the motivation of the Bologna bombing.

A constant feature of right-wing bombings has been the deliberate muddying of the waters by representatives of the Italian secret services. On occasion, the secret services have had prior knowledge of terrorist attacks but have done nothing to prevent them; they have protected from prosecution people suspected of involvement in terrorism; and they have laid false trails for investigating magistrates. Repeated scandals have prompted repeated attempts at reform and the removal of so-called 'deviant' elements, but the secret services have remained true to their central objective, even when this has involved complicity with terrorists. The result has been a confusing series of name changes but little real change. Since the war, the acronym by which the military intelligence service is known has changed three times, from SIFAR, to SID, to SISMI. According to Felice Casson, an examining magistrate from Venice who has probably done more than any other to lay bare the roots of right-wing terrorism, the reforms have made little impact on the secret services. 'The situation has not changed at all. They did not collaborate before and they don't collaborate now. The law has changed, but not the men and the structures.'[1]

One possible explanation for why the secret services should act as guardians of the terrorists is offered by a philosophy professor from Brescia, Emanuele Severino. In an article in the *Corriere della Sera* newspaper (16 January 1985), he drew attention to the fact that terrorist violence in Italy has been administered in small doses, with left-wing terrorists taking a rest while the right-wing are active and vice versa. He also pointed out that while the bombers were capable of destroying ten trains in one night, in practice they would only blow up one at a time and that once every few years. 'Terrorism does not unleash a destructive power capable of overthrowing our social system, but enough to maintain it under constant pressure,' he wrote. Given that terror increases people's desire for security at the expense of their desire for change, Severino observed that the ideology that has suffered the most from the consequences of terrorism in Italy is that of the Communist Party, 'because it proposes the renewal of society in the most radical and unpredictable way'. This, in a nutshell, is the 'strategy of tension': destabilizing in order to stabilize. It has been applied in Italy with considerable success, bolstering the mainly centre-right governments that have ruled the country since the war whenever their electoral support showed signs of faltering.

In the two decades since 1969, Italy has suffered the most protracted and traumatic terrorist onslaught of any developed Western country, with the exception of Britain and Spain. By 1987, 356 people had been killed and more than 1,000 wounded as a result of Italy's domestic political terrorism. This in a country bordering on communist Yugoslavia, with a strategic position dominating the central Mediterranean, and containing the largest Communist Party in Western Europe. In June 1976 that party came close to taking over from the Christian Democrat Party as the largest party in the country and thus bidding for the right to form a government. A period of violent activity by left-wing terrorist groups, which began in 1974 and climaxed in 1978, helped to create a climate of fear in which wavering voters were unlikely to be tempted by the adventure of change, and ensured that the unthinkable did not happen.

The violence in Italy pales into insignificance in comparison with the sectarian slaughter seen in Northern Ireland. In the equivalent period between 1969 and 1987, 2,618 people were killed and more than 33,000 injured in the disjointed British province. Though the Irish Republican Army (IRA) may have succeeded in laying siege to Ulster society, its violence, perhaps surprisingly, has had relatively little impact on politics and society in mainland Britain.

In his maverick book, *Of Terrorism and of the State*, Gianfranco Sanguinetti divided all terrorist actions into two categories: offensive and defensive. He described Irish and Palestinian terrorism as offensive and Italian terrorism as defensive. 'The desperate and the deluded resort to offensive terrorism; on the other hand it is always and only states who resort to defensive terrorism, either because they are in a deep social crisis, like the Italian state, or because they fear one, like the German state,' he wrote. In his rare, privately published book, which is written in a frequently truculent style, Sanguinetti suggested it was easy for secret services to take control of genuine 'offensive' terrorist groups and manipulate them to their own advantage. 'All secret terrorist groups are organized and run by a hierarchy which is kept secret even from their own members, and which reflects the division of labour typical of this kind of social organization: decisions are taken at the top and carried out by the bottom. Ideology and military discipline protect the true leaders from any risk and the base from any suspicion.'[2]

Those with an interest in seeing that the Communist Party did not come to power were not only the secret services, the armed forces, and the conservative politicians who controlled them, but also the United States, Italy's most powerful NATO partner. The US government was understandably unenthusiastic about communist electoral advances in Italy in the mid-1970s, and since Italy's defeat in the Second World War American intelligence agencies have exercised a strong and abiding influence over their Italian counterparts. A parliamentary commission investigating illegal spying on people in public life by the Italian secret services found that much of this activity was carried out on behalf of the United States and the Vatican. The minority report of the commission, submitted by the Socialist Party (PSI), described the situation as 'contrary to the Constitution, an open violation of national sovereignty and of the principle of the liberty and equality of citizens, and a constant threat to the very democratic equilibrium of our country.'[3]

Italy's strategic importance to the Western Alliance should not be underestimated. Until 1988 the country did not possess an aircraft carrier. This was not just because of its studiedly unaggressive foreign policy stance but because its geographic position, jutting into the central Mediterranean, enables it to project air power throughout the Mediterranean basin. On 5 June 1967, the decision was made to base the NATO Mediterranean naval command in Naples. At about the same time the NATO Defence College was moved from Paris to Rome and the US Sixth Fleet from Villefranche to Gaeta following the decision by General Charles de Gaulle on 7 March of the previous year to withdraw his country from full membership of the Atlantic Alliance. The importance of Italian naval bases was further increased after Dom Mintoff came to power in Malta, in June 1971, and promptly closed Maltese ports to Western warships as part of his country's new policy of non-alignment. With a total of 10,000 personnel in nine military bases, including a submarine base in Sardinia and air bases scattered throughout the Italian peninsula, it is not surprising that the US government were not keen to see the communists growing in electoral strength and knocking on the door of government.

The growth in the electoral support for the Italian Communist Party (PCI) was accompanied by a progressive distancing of the party from Moscow, as it spearheaded the development of Eurocommunism and sought a middle way between Soviet-style Marxism-Leninism and Western free-market capitalism. In elections for the Chamber of Deputies, the PCI's share of the vote moved from 26.9 per cent in 1968, to 27.2 per cent in 1972, to 34.4 per cent in 1976, tailing off in 1979 to 30.4 per cent. Over the same period, the Christian Democrat Party's (DC's) share of the vote remained stable at around 39 per cent, making it the largest party in the country, followed by the communists in second place and then by the PSI with under 10 per cent. The tendency of the PCI to perform better at regional elections, where control over the national government was not at stake, made this trend seem all the more alarming to those who were ideologically committed to keeping the PCI out of government. The parabola of electoral support for the PCI was shadowed and paralleled by the amount of terrorist activity in the country. There were 398 terrorist attacks in 1969, the figure rising to 595 in 1972, and to 1,353 in 1976. The peak period for terrorist activity came in the following three years: 1,926 attacks in 1977, 2,379 in 1978, 2,513 in 1979. After 1980, with 1,502 attacks, the figure began to decline steadily, to 634 in 1981, 347 in 1982, with a return to double figures in 1984. It is hard to believe that the increase in the communist vote and the matching increase in terrorist violence were pure coincidence.

The PCI was founded in 1921. Its first major step away from its revolutionary roots came in March 1944, when party secretary Palmiro Togliatti told a meeting in Salerno that the party was going to change from being a small revolutionary vanguard to a mass party operating within democratic rules and institutions for the transformation of Italian society. For many years the PCI leadership maintained an ambivalent attitude towards the revolutionary aspirations of many of the party rank and file. This policy of double-bluff, known as *doppiezza*, was as much designed to keep the militants quiet by leading them to believe that the party was in the process of penetrating the bourgeois citadel in order, eventually, to overthrow it, as it was intended to deceive conservative political rivals into lowering their guard. The inherent dishonesty in it, however, would provide opponents with ample material to justify their claim that the PCI was not a genuinely democratic party. More ammunition was handed to

[17]

critics in 1956, when the party defended the Soviet suppression of the Hungarian uprising. After this one hiccup, the gulf between the party and Moscow would grow steadily wider, with the pace of divergence increasing noticeably in the 1970s. In 1968 the PCI condemned the Soviet invasion of Czechoslovakia, by the mid-1970s it had accepted Italian membership of NATO, in 1979 it criticized Soviet deployment of SS-20 missiles. It was also critical of US plans to deploy equivalent missiles in Europe but did not forcefully oppose the scheme. And in 1980 it condemned the Soviet invasion of Afghanistan. Under the leadership of Enrico Berlinguer in the 1970s, the party came to espouse positions on foreign policy and defence which many would consider took it to the right of the British Labour Party. But there is no indication that any of this was recognized in Washington or that it made the PCI any less obnoxious to American eyes.

In 1988 the US embassy in Rome told me that the US government's attitude to the Italian Communist Party remained that expressed in 1981 by Assistant Secretary for Political Affairs Lawrence Eagleburger. In answer to a question on the Reagan Administration's view on possible communist participation in a future Italian government, the US official told *Il Tempo* newspaper (1 May 1981), 'We and our allies stand for freedom and democracy. We do not believe the communists share our values.' While insisting that the US would not interfere in the democratic choices of its allies, Eagleburger said the US government had an obligation to them to express its views clearly. 'The US in both Republican and Democratic administrations has been opposed to Communist Party participation in governments of our allies. We would like to see communist influence in any Western European country reduced. That policy has been consistent and clear. It spans the post-war period. It is not under review.'

The importance of keeping the communists from power in Italy was not merely dictated by the presence of NATO military bases or the strategic geographic position of the country. The Yalta Agreement in 1945 had laid the basis for the division of Europe into two geopolitical blocks. Whether the maintenance of those blocks depended more on the agreement or on the realities of military power is open to argument. Many Italian commentators attribute the tacit understanding between the superpowers that each should have a free hand in their own sphere of influence to what they call 'the logic of Yalta'. Just as, according to this interpretation, the Americans were unable to intervene when Russian tanks rolled into Czechoslovakia or Hungary,

[18]

so it was unthinkable that a Communist Party could be allowed to come to power in a country of the capitalist West. It followed then that the Soviet Union would have accepted that outright communist rule in Italy was out of the question and that, if necessary, American tanks would move to prevent it. When, in the late 1970s, a coalition government including both the Christian Democrats and the communists was proposed, the Soviets would have been almost as alarmed as the Americans at the prospect. It was far preferable for them to have the Communist Party in opposition and, they hoped, loyal to Moscow, than in a centrist coalition government and aligned with the West.

It is not easy to determine exactly who was responsible for the political decisions that gave rise to the strategy of tension. Those decisions would be taken in secret and frequently outside institutional frameworks. It is unlikely that intelligence agencies in the United States and Italy kept their governments fully informed about the more unsavoury of their clandestine operations. But there can be no doubt that the rising strength of the Communist Party was perceived as a major threat and that the relevant agencies did not just sit and watch. CIA Director William Colby has described in his memoirs how he was sent to Italy in the 1950s to run 'what was by far the CIA's largest covert political-action program undertaken until then, or, indeed, since.' The man who was CIA director from 1973 to 1976 explained how his task was 'to prevent Italy from being taken over by the communists in the next – 1958 – elections and thus prevent the NATO military defences from being circumvented politically by a subversive fifth column, the Partito Comunista Italiano.'

Colby went on to point out that it had been anxiety at the possibility that the communists might win the 1948 elections in Italy that led to the formation of the Office of Policy Coordination, 'which gave the CIA the capability to undertake covert political, propaganda, and paramilitary operations in the first place.' The Italian Communist Party has clearly been singled out for the special attention of the CIA since the end of the war. It is a good indication of the priority it was accorded that Colby recalled his own covert action programme in Italy in the fifties as being the largest undertaken during his career with the agency, and therefore until his retirement in 1976. He described his job in Italy as 'an unparalleled opportunity to demonstrate that secret aid could help our friends and frustrate our foes without the use of force or violence.'[4] It can safely be assumed that if Colby was aware of the CIA using violence in Italy he would not consider the information as suitable for publication in his memoirs.

Colby had no regrets about the programme when I questioned him about it in 1989. 'There were some negative consequences but not many. The assistance was not given to the right wing but to the centre. It went to build institutions such as trade unions, which would otherwise have been under the total control of the Communist Party,' he said. Colby claimed that the PCI was at that time receiving massive aid from the Soviet Union, running at $50 million a year according to CIA estimates. These claims have never been independently confirmed. 'It helped to match the activity supported from Moscow.' He did not believe that the aid had been more damaging than beneficial in the long run because of the perceived corruption of many political leaders and resulting public disenchantment with them. 'You don't have an issue that Christian Democrat politicians were personally rich as a result of stealing from the public till. You did have corrupt leaders but there were also some prosecutions.'[5] Colby's view is over-optimistic, as we shall see.

According to Ray Cline, former deputy director of the CIA, the first numbered document issued by the new National Security Council, on 14 November 1947, was NSC 1/1, a top secret report entitled 'The Position of the United States with Respect to Italy'. United States concern for the outcome of the 1948 elections was borne out by a cable from George Kennan, director of the State Department's Policy Planning Staff, quoted by Cline in his book *The CIA under Reagan, Bush and Casey*. On 15 March 1947 Kennan wrote: 'As far as Europe is concerned, Italy is obviously key point. If communists were to win election there our whole position in the Mediterranean, and possibly in Western Europe as well, would probably be undermined.' For Kennan, the stakes were high indeed. Cline was in no doubt that the creation of the Office of Policy Coordination and a permanent covert political action capability for the CIA was 'intended to include paramilitary operations as well as political and economic warfare'. Cline traced authorization for covert action to the National Security Act of 1947. 'An elastic, catch-all clause was included, referring to the CIA's performance of "such other functions and duties related to intelligence affecting the national security as the National Security Council may from time to time direct," and this clause was later cited as giving authority for covert actions,'[6] he noted. The Senate Committee on Intelligence, chaired by Senator Frank Church, found in 1976 that the CIA had been involved in activities that the committee considered to be unethical. 'The Committee has found that certain covert operations have been incompatible with American principles and ideals and, when exposed, have resulted in damaging this nation's ability to exercise moral and ethical leadership throughout the world,' it reported.[7] The committee was not in the business of making damaging revelations about the CIA's use of violence, in Italy or anywhere else, but the report makes specific mention of the agency's activities in Chile in 1970. The payment over the years of millions of dollars by the CIA and American multinational companies to centre and right-wing political parties and individuals in Italy has undoubtedly helped to swing a number of close-run elections. However, the public perception that these parties were venal and corrupt gave rise to strong popular disaffection for them and to the view that real political change could not be achieved through the democratic process: both elements that contributed to the rise of terrorism, particularly the terrorism of the left.

It would be absurd to claim that no pawn moved on the chess-board of terror without the hand of the CIA or the Italian secret services behind it. The conservative forces with an interest in the strategy of tension were often divided by fierce personal rivalries, they were sometimes seeking different and incompatible goals and they operated within a kaleidoscope of constantly shifting alliances. Relations between intelligence agencies and terrorists are rarely candid or straightforward. Often they are based on reciprocal blackmail and a secret service may find that granting protection for a small crime leads it into covering up for a bigger one later. The motives of the terrorists themselves are not easily fathomed and their own convictions do not provide a reliable guide to understanding them. Giovanni Tamburino, an examining magistrate who investigated a major right-wing conspiracy in the early 1970s, warned that a terrorist is liable to 'say he is something different than he believes he is; believe he is something different than he is; be something different than the organization to which he belongs and which conditions him.'

It is often argued that the inability of the Italian secret services to combat terrorism was not the result of a deliberate policy of protecting terrorists but of incompetence: the secret services were in disarray following repeated scandals and attempts at reform and were unprepared for the terrorist onslaught. There were undoubtedly difficulties and instances of incompetence, but the presence of secret

[21]

service informers in virtually every terrorist organization of note belies this argument. 'Few statements, measured against experience, are as unwise as the statement that the secret services are inefficient: if there is an area where the secret services have been present, active and informed, this is the area of terrorism,' Tamburino told a 1984 magistrates' conference.[8]

Despite the partial and contradictory nature of the evidence, there have been two constants in the story of Italian terrorism since it flared up at the beginning of the 1970s: the attitude of the Italian secret services and the consequences of the terrorism. From 1969 to 1974 the secret services nurtured certain right-wing terrorist groups. After 1974 they stood back and watched while left-wing terrorism flourished, largely of its own accord. The effect of both right- and left-wing terrorism was to damage the electoral prospects of the Communist Party.

The early phase of right-wing terrorism, which lasted until 1974 and was characterized by the tactic of indiscriminate bombings directed against the public, can only be understood in conjunction with a series of right-wing coup plots. The plots were supported by conservative figures from the spheres of politics, industry and the military, and on several occasions they came close to achieving power by the overthrow of the elected government. The threat of a military coup and the constant pressure from terrorism were enough to exercise an intimidating influence on left-wing political parties and to increase the public's demand for security, both of which bolstered the centre-right components of the coalition governments. This was all along the intention of the more sophisticated political leaders who were prepared to make use of the radical right-wing elements in the conspiracy but were unwilling to go all the way with them in a violent seizure of power. The more cautious of the conspirators were also well aware of the difficulties they were likely to encounter if the powerful Communist Party and trade unions were to mobilize popular opposition to a *coup d'état*: they could almost certainly have made the country ungovernable, even by a military regime.

The principal purpose of the bomb outrages was to provide the excuse for military intervention. The perpetrators of the bombings frequently tried to attribute responsibility for their attacks to left-wing or anarchist groups and police and secret service investigators eagerly followed up these leads. One right-winger seriously injured himself when a bomb he was handling blew up in a train's toilet on

7 April 1973. Before attempting to set the timing device going, he had walked up and down the train displaying a copy of *Lotta Continua* (Continuous Struggle), a newspaper of the extreme left.[9] It may well have been decided that there was more to be gained by falsely blaming the left for terrorist attacks than by risking such potential political capital on the uncertain outcome of a military coup.

The bloody right-wing bombings often came as the culmination of a series of bloodless demonstrative bombings against political or economic targets. It is possible to see this as a kind of dialogue within the right-wing camp: those who promised to move after our demonstrative bombings have done nothing so we will give them a bombing that will force them into action. This interpretation is supported by the testimony of a right-wing terrorist, Sergio Calore, to a Florence public prosecutor in 1984. Calore said the bombing of the Banca Nazionale dell'Agricoltura in Piazza Fontana in Milan, which inaugurated the series of right-wing bomb massacres, was a message to the organizers of a projected military coup. 'When, in December 1969, it was decided that the coup would not take place, various young extremists, loosely linked to the youth groups of the Fronte Nazionale (National Front), decided to force the situation by carrying out the December 12, 1969, bombings in order to provoke the stabilizing intervention of the armed forces.'[10]

By 1969 the theorists of the strategy of tension had already elaborated their doctrine. It is spelt out in graphic terms in an anonymous document entitled 'Our Political Action', which was sent from Italy to the Aginter Press, a Lisbon-based agency that gave cover to extremist political activity throughout Europe, in November 1968. The document recommends the promotion of chaos throughout the structures of the regime and the undermining of the economy. 'This will lead to a situation of strong political tension, of fear in the industrial world, of hostility towards the government and all the parties. In our opinion the first action to be embarked upon is the destruction of the structures of the state, which should appear to be the action of the communists and the pro-Chinese.' It then goes on to recommend working on public opinion and the armed forces to highlight the inadequacies of the legally constituted government and 'to make us appear as the only ones capable of providing a social, political and economic solution suited to the needs of the moment.'[11]

It is hard to imagine the secret services being accomplices in such a direct attack on the constituted order which it was their job to defend, particularly when it was the police and armed forces, their colleagues in arms, who were most exposed to terrorist violence. Many terrorists, especially those on the left, forcefully reject suggestions of such complicity. Yet in one particularly cynical instance, officers of the *carabinieri* paramilitary police granted protection to the terrorists who had used a booby-trapped car-bomb to murder three members of their own force.

The career of Ievno Azev, the agent of the tsarist secret police who infiltrated a socialist revolutionary group with such gusto that it is almost impossible to tell whether his true role was that of terrorist or informer, shows just how difficult it is to determine loyalties in the murky world of intelligence and betrayal. Azev's terrorist associates were at first unable to believe that he was an agent because he was an accomplice in so many political assassinations, including the murder of the head of the political section of the secret police and the Interior Minister. Azev, born the son of a Jewish tailor in 1869, became the head of the 'Battle Organization' of the Social Revolutionaries following the arrest of the group's original leaders. But the fact that an *agent provocateur* was in charge did not bring an end to the high-level assassinations. On 17 February 1905, Azev's group murdered Grand Duke Sergei Alexandrovitch, the tsar's uncle and head of the Moscow military region, and it appears the tsar himself was a target for assassination. In 1909 it was revealed that Azev had been an informer of the secret police since 1892, on an annual salary of 14,000 roubles. His life is one of the most extreme examples of how the role of terrorist and secret agent can be combined within the same person.

By 1974 it was clear that the original strategy of tension was not working. Investigations by independent-minded magistrates were establishing that it was not the left but the right who had been behind the bombing campaigns, and electoral support for the communists was continuing to grow. After years during which the authorities tried to lay the blame for terrorism falsely on the left, a generation of genuinely left-wing extremists was about to take up arms and begin attacking magistrates, police, politicians and industrialists in the vain hope of bringing about a revolution. Their 'attack on the heart of the state' would far more effectively discredit the Communist Party than anything the secret services had hitherto been able to devise. In September 1974 General Vito Miceli, the head of military intelligence, made a fateful prediction during the course of an interrogation by Judge Tamburino: 'Now you will no longer hear people talk about black [fascist] terrorism, now you will only hear tell of those others.'[12] This forecast that left-wing terrorists would dominate the headlines in the coming years shows anything but incompetence on the part of the secret services, rather an uncanny prescience.

It is ironic that one of the factors that gave rise to red terrorism was precisely the fear of an imminent right-wing coup. This was frequently cited by left-wing millionaire publisher Giangiacomo Feltrinelli as the reason for his financing of armed revolutionary groups. His followers, he said, would stage a latter-day Resistance when the military seized power. The secret services could not have been more pleased at the eventual activities of his acolytes, many of whom ultimately joined the Red Brigades. Feltrinelli was killed in an operation of old-style terrorism, trying to blow up an electricity pylon near Milan, on land he himself owned, in 1972. Given the reputation that the secret services had by then acquired, it was suggested, inevitably, that they were in some way involved in his death.

Relatively little reliable evidence of collusion between the Italian secret services and left-wing terrorism has as yet emerged. There can be little doubt that left-wing terrorist groups enjoyed widespread popular support, at least in the early 1970s, and that they sprang up as a spontaneous response to genuine social problems. There is no suggestion of their having been as thoroughly or as blatantly manipulated as their right-wing counterparts. Many Italians, and particularly those who once sympathized with the ideals of their 'erring comrades', hotly contest any suggestion whatsoever that groups like the Red Brigades may have been working, perhaps unconsciously, for their political enemies. Nevertheless, some former Red Brigades leaders now suspect that they were in fact used by the secret services to prevent or slow down political change in Italy.

In *Of Terrorism and of the State*, Sanguinetti claimed that nothing was easier for the secret services than to infiltrate and take control of spontaneously arisen terrorist groups 'either through arrests made at the appropriate moment, or through the killing of the original leaders, which normally occurs in a shoot-out with the police, tipped off by their own infiltrators'. He added that the original terrorist group, 'born of its supporters' delusions about the possibility of carrying out an effective strategic offensive, changes strategists and becomes nothing more than a defensive appendage of the state'.[13] In 1974 the *carabinieri*, acting on a tip-off from an infiltrator, arrested most of the leadership of the first generation of Red Brigades. Several of those who subsequently took over from them have been suspected of collusion with the secret services. The truth about the manipulation of left-wing terrorism will never be fully known. It is particularly hard to be sure of the real motives of the left-wing extremists since many of them shared with the secret services a passionate hatred of the Communist Party. They considered the party to be revisionist and a traitor to its original Marxist ideals as it slid progressively, throughout the Seventies, towards an accommodation with the Christian Democrats. Paradoxically, both the secret services from their conservative standpoint, and the Red Brigades as hardline Marxists, had a common interest in thwarting such an alliance.

As with right-wing terrorism, it is sometimes possible to get an idea of the truth, when there is a lack of reliable factual evidence, from the coded messages sent out by some of the protagonists. They often contain a blackmailing intent and there is no guarantee as to their accuracy, but they can provide persuasive indications that the truth is somewhat more sinister than the official versions would have us believe. The Moro kidnap is the single episode that has generated the greatest doubts about the real nature and purpose of the Red Brigades. The precedent of secret service dealings with right-wing terrorists, now well established both judicially and historically, should at least convince us to keep an open mind about what may also have happened on the left.

On 31 October 1974, General Vito Miceli, then head of Italian military intelligence, was arrested on a charge of conspiring to overthrow the government by provoking an armed insurrection in order to provide an excuse for military intervention. The warrant, signed by Judge Tamburino, referred to the existence of a so-called security organization, which 'in fact acts as an obstacle to particular changes in domestic and international politics'. Tamburino said the organization resorted to 'illegal, secret and violent acts' in order to restrict popular sovereignty. Miceli defended himself by arguing that he had always remained faithful to his institutional duties, which he could not discuss as they were covered by state secrecy laws. He did, however, indicate that the incriminated organization, which became known as the 'Parallel SID', was formed under a secret agreement with the United States and within the framework of NATO.

One of Miceli's co-conspirators, a lieutenant-colonel in the military secret services by the name of Amos Spiazzi, was slightly more forthcoming. He told magistrates he had joined the 'Rosa dei Venti'

(Compass Rose) right-wing conspiracy on the orders of a SID officer. Asked whether he had received an order in June 1973 to put the irregular 'support groups' of the armed forces on standby, Spiazzi answered: 'I received an order from a military superior belonging to the security organization of the armed forces, which does not have a subversive purpose but aims to protect the institutions of the state against Marxism. This organization is not the same as SID but in large part coincides with it.'[14] Spiazzi added that the membership was not made up purely of military personnel but also of civilians, including industrialists and politicians. Miceli himself offered a slightly more detailed account of the secret, Parallel SID in 1977, during a trial for a 1970 coup attempt. 'There is and always has existed a certain very secret organization, which the highest authorities of the state know about. Seen from outside, by the profane, this organization could be incorrectly interpreted, it could appear to be something outside official policy.'[15] Miceli said the organization fell within the frame-work of SID, that its activities were 'fully institutional', but 'far removed from information gathering'.

It is at this secret level of intelligence co-operation between Italy and the United States that the men responsible for the strategy of tension are likely to be found. The existence of secret NATO protocols committing the secret services of the signatory countries to work to prevent the Communist Party from coming to power first emerged in 1966 when President de Gaulle decided to pull France out of NATO's combined command structure, denouncing the protocols as an infringement of national sovereignty. According to Giuseppe De Lutiis' *History of the Secret Services in Italy*, Italy signed the protocols in 1949 when it was first admitted to the Atlantic Pact. He said the protocols provided for the creation of an unofficial organization 'charged with guaranteeing Italy's international alignment within the Western Block by any means, even if the electorate were to show a different inclination'.[16] In Italy, with the largest Communist Party in the West challenging to become the largest party in the country, there was clearly plenty of work for such an organization. Given the secret and illegal nature of the protocols, De Lutiis commented, they were not destined to leave much trace in official archives. The rigour with which they were applied would depend on the attitude of the head of the Italian secret service towards his American counterparts.

A Top Secret Memorandum of the US Joint Chiefs of Staff dated 14 May 1952 reveals the existence of a plan code-named 'Demagnetize', designed to reduce the influence of the Communist Party in two European countries. The document states that the fundamental objective of the plan is to lessen the influence of the communists over government and trade unions in Italy and France so as to reduce the risk of communism becoming established in either country and thus damaging the interests of the United States. To that end a series of 'political, paramilitary and psychological operations' were to be employed. The Italian and French governments must not be made aware of the plan's existence as it 'may interfere with their national sovereignty'.[17] The man charged with implementing the Italian end of the plan, without informing his political bosses, was the then head of Italian military intelligence, General Giovanni De Lorenzo. He would later be accused of having plotted a military coup in the summer of 1964.

It is by no means easy to determine who was responsible for day-to-day tactical decisions in the running of the strategy of tension. But there can be little doubt that overall responsibility for the strategy lay with the government and intelligence services of the United States. The rise of communism in Italy naturally posed a security problem for NATO and ultimate responsibility for solving it inevitably rested with Italy's most powerful NATO ally. It is hardly surprising that the United States should have been concerned by Italy's lurch to the left in the 1970s and that it should have taken steps to bring it to a halt. Some might argue that clandestine intervention in Italian politics prevented the communists from gaining power and thus sparking off a full-blown civil war, or worse, war between the superpowers in Europe. Nevertheless, questions will remain about the adoption of methods that brought violent death to hundreds of innocent victims. The United States has consistently refused to recognize the Italian Communist Party's increasingly wholehearted commitment to the principles of Western democracy and its validity as an alternative to the generally corrupt and incompetent political parties that have governed Italy since the war. Had it done so, much of the bloodshed resulting from the strategy of tension might have been avoided.

Notes

1 Felice Casson to the author, 1987.
2 Gianfranco Sanguinetti, *Del Terrorismo e dello Stato*, Milan, 1980, p. 28.

3 *Commissione parlamentare d'inchiesta sugli eventi del giugno-luglio 1964, Relazione di minoranza*, Rome, 1971.

4 William Colby, *Honourable Men*, Hutchinson, London, 1978, p. 109.

5 William Colby to the author, 4 December 1989.

6 Ray S. Cline, *The CIA under Reagan, Bush and Casey*, Acropolis Books, Washington, 1981, pp. 122–5.

7 Senate Select Committee to study governmental operations with respect to intelligence activities, Washington, 1976.

8 Giovanni Tamburino in *L'Eversione Nera: Cronache di un Decennio, Atti del Convegno, Brescia 25–26 May 1984*, Franco Angeli, Milan, 1985, pp. 138–42.

9 Gianni Flamini, *Il Partito del Golpe*, Vol. 3, Tome 2, Bovolenta, Ferrara, 1983, p. 318.

10 Quoted in Pietro Calderoni (ed.), *Servizi Segreti*, Tullio Pironti, Naples, 1986, pp. 109–10.

11 Quoted in Gianni Flamini, *Il Partito del Golpe*, Vol. 1, Italo Bovolenta, Ferrara, 1981, p. 174.

12 Investigation of Judge Giovanni Tamburino, in Giuseppe De Lutiis, *Storia dei Servizi Segreti in Italia*, Editori Riuniti, Rome, 1984, p. 137.

13 Gianfranco Sanguinetti, op. cit., p. 28.

14 Quoted in *L'Espresso*, 16 March 1975.

15 Giuseppe De Lutiis, op. cit., p. 129.

16 Giuseppe De Lutiis, op. cit., p. 126.

17 Quoted in *Il Malaffare*, Roberto Faenza, Mondadori, Milan, 1978, pp. 313–14.

[2]

THE ORIGINS
OF TERROR

IN order to understand the origins of the strategy of tension and the directions that terrorism would take in later years, it is necessary to go back to what happened during the Second World War and in its immediate aftermath. The identification of the vast majority of the Italian people, and in particular the establishment and middle class, with Benito Mussolini's fascist regime was to pose serious problems after its fall, when the majority of Italians discovered overnight that, at heart, they had supported the Resistance all along. The problem, for those embarking on the reconstruction of a stable, democratic society in Italy after the war, was that one of the largest groups with the most convincing anti-fascist credentials was the Communist Party. Because of their ideological distance from Mussolini there had been no question of the communists becoming his accomplices. They had instead established some of the most active and effective Resistance units to harry the German and Italian fascist forces ahead of the advancing Allied armies. But even before the liberation of Italy was completed the first signs of tension between communist Resistance forces and their more conservative Resistance allies were beginning to emerge. Agents of the American Office of Strategic Services (OSS) and the British Special Operations Executive (SOE) who parachuted into Italy behind German lines often faced a delicate task in convincing the left- and right-wing Resistance fighters to finish the war against Hitler before starting to settle scores among themselves. Many Italians were already moving into the East–West Cold War before the shooting war was over. All this against a background of widespread lawlessness and considerable controversy over the tactics of the Resistance, which inevitably sparked German reprisals against the civilian population. There was a certain bandit element in many of the Resistance groups, a fact that has tended to be glossed over in the post-war mythification of the movement: this tendency was fuelled by the guilty consciences of those who had failed to make a stand against fascism at the time.

Another bandit element recruited by the United States to support the Allied war effort was the Sicilian Mafia. Mafia boss Lucky Luciano was released from prison in America so that he could activate his contacts in Sicily to prepare the ground for the Allied landings there. The Mafia was also drafted in to provide the backbone of post-war local government in southern Italy. It was a natural choice, since Mussolini's ruthless crackdown on the criminal organization meant the conservative-minded Mafia could be relied upon to be both anti-fascist and anti-communist. This set a precedent for the years to come, as the Mafia would provide a useful secret conduit between the United States and Italy and an effective instrument for exerting influence in Italian politics. Not being too fussy about one's friends during the prosecution of a world war is understandable, but continuing to use those unpresentable friends in peacetime is less so. Unless, of course, one believes the peace is really just war by another name. The Mafia's support would later be sought in the right-wing coup season of the early 1970s. Another victim of Mussolini's persecution, Freemasonry, would be called upon to stand alongside the Mafia in the conservative anti-communist alliance. It too would constitute a secret, transatlantic channel of influence and play a role in the strategy of tension.

The first major challenge for the Allies in their attempt to ensure a stable democratic future for Italy within the Western orbit came with the 1948 general elections, which became a fierce tussle for the country's political soul. In practice, it was a challenge for the United States, as Britain, one of the three Yalta signatories, was already slipping away from its pre-war superpower status. As we have seen, it was these elections which called into being the CIA as a peacetime successor to the OSS and with the same covert action capabilities that had gone without question during the war.

With the elections scheduled for 18 April, the full extent of the threat was made apparent on 15 February, when the Popular Democratic Front made up of the Communist Party (PCI) and the Socialist Party (PSI) won municipal elections in Pescara with a 10 per cent increase on their 1946 showing and with the Christian Democrats

(DC) coming in a poor second. Document 1/2 of the United States National Security Council, dated 10 February 1948, urged 'actively combating communist propaganda in Italy by an effective US information programme and by all other practicable means'.[1] NSC 1/3 on 8 March recommends the United States should as a matter of priority take 'further measures designed to prevent the communists from winning participation in the government'. These were to include urging members of Congress 'to announce immediately that the attitude of the American people is such that they would never support economic assistance to Italy if its government included parties inimical to the United States'. For a country still recovering from the devastation of war this was an argument liable to carry considerable weight. The document also recommended the initiation of a campaign of speeches by government officials and private individuals and of letter-writing by private citizens, 'regarding the political issues in Italy'.

Form letters, provided for the use of the less articulate members of the Italo-American community, got the message across with admirable bluntness. 'A communist victory would ruin Italy. The United States would withdraw aid and a world war would probably result,' they read.[2] Or alternatively, 'If the forces of true democracy should lose the Italian election, the American government will not send any more money to Italy and we won't send any more money to you, our relatives.' The State Department let it be known that anyone who was known to have voted communist would not be allowed to enter the United States and it was urged that this information be emphasized in letters to Italy.[3] *Time* magazine made its contribution in an article shortly before the election in which it supported the notion that the US 'should make it clear that it will use force, if necessary, to prevent Italy from going communist'.[4]

The United States found an enthusiastic ally in the Catholic Church, which was understandably opposed to the spread of atheistic communism and threw itself into the task of mobilizing support for the anti-communist parties. Pope Pius XII himself lent a hand with a Christmas radio address in 1947 in which he warned that 'whoever gives his support, his services or his talent to those parties and those forces which deny God is a deserter and a traitor'. The conservative Cardinal Giuseppe Siri of Genoa followed his example with an eight-point message to Catholic voters in which he made it clear that 'not voting in itself constitutes a mortal sin,' and that 'the materialistic and consequently atheistic doctrines and methods on which communism is based can in no way be reconciled with the Christian Faith'.[5] On 8 February 1948, Professor Luigi Gedda, the president of Catholic Action, founded an organization known as Citizens' Committees with the intention of getting out the anti-communist vote and with the blessing of the Vatican and the CIA. The organization was able to call on the support of 300,000 activists from 22,000 parishes. With slogans such as 'You're a rabbit if you don't vote,' the Citizens' Committees were remarkably successful in drumming up the electoral support of the devout and ill-educated peasant class. A CIA report on Gedda's organization said it was undoubtedly one of the decisive factors in the elections and that it had been decided to keep it in existence even after they were over, 'as an exemplary and permanent unit for anti-communist propaganda'.[6]

Well-timed acts of generosity on the part of the United States also played their part. A month before the elections President Harry Truman announced the decision to transfer twenty-nine merchant ships to the Italian government, as 'a gesture of friendship and confidence in a democratic Italy'.[7] Four days later the House Appropriations Committee approved payment of an additional $18.7 million of 'interim aid' funds for Italy. In the lead-up to the elections the CIA channelled $1 million directly to Italian 'centre parties'.[8] A survey by United Press showed that the anti-communist parties spent seven and a half times as much as the Popular Democratic Front on all forms of propaganda, with the Christian Democrats alone spending four times as much. The Soviet Union did little to help the Front. The communist seizure of power in Czechoslovakia in February was an object lesson in what could happen if you were on the wrong side of the Yalta divide and helped to justify US intervention on its own side. What's more, the US, France and Britain urged the Soviet Union to agree to the return of the Adriatic port city of Trieste to Italy from its status as a 'free city' under the terms of the peace treaty. In order not to antagonize its ally Yugoslavia, whose border passes close to Trieste, the Soviet Union rejected the Western proposal. Its decision, announced five days before the Italian vote, was a severe blow to the electoral hopes of the Front. The Christian Democrat Party emerged as clear winners with 48 per cent of the vote, the left-wing Front trailing in with a mere 31 per cent. Italy had been saved for democracy.

After this resounding success it was safe to admit Italy as a member of NATO and allow it to have its own military intelligence service, which had been disbanded at the end of the war. It was not thought prudent to allow Italy an autonomous intelligence agency after 1944 until its future political alignment had been resolved by the 1948 elections. The contemporaneous joining of NATO and reinstatement of an intelligence capability was more than mere coincidence and gives an insight into the fundamental purpose of the post-war Italian secret service in the intentions of those who sanctioned its rebirth. While the Central Treaty Organization, which grouped the United States, Britain, Turkey, Iran and Pakistan, provided specifically for the creation of an anti-subversion committee, NATO preferred to resort to secret bilateral agreements in this area, out of deference to the left-wing oppositions in Italy and France.

Given the widespread Italian support for fascism it was almost inevitable that the administrative personnel of the new Italian republic should in large part be made up of people co-opted from the former fascist regime. In October 1946 there were 40,000 fascists in Italian prisons, but a few months later this figure fell to 4,000. An attempt to purge the state of those people most closely identified with fascism was brought to an end by an amnesty signed by Justice Minister Palmiro Togliatti. Togliatti, the leader of the Communist Party, was a member of a series of post-war coalition governments, from 1945 until 1947, in recognition of his party's contribution to the defeat of Mussolini. The failure to remove fascist sympathizers from the state bureaucracy would have important long-term consequences for the country. Their retention in the police and later in the re-established secret services would prove particularly significant. The OSS made contact with leaders of the fascist secret police in Mussolini's last-stand Republic of Salò (named after its capital, a small town on Lake Garda) before their surrender. After the fall of Salò, secret police chief Guido Leto was provisionally confirmed in his post by the Allies. He was subsequently cleared of all war crimes charges and in 1946 became director of Italy's police schools. It has been suggested that his lenient treatment may have had something to do with his role as custodian of the sensitive OVRA (secret police) archives at the end of the war, which subsequently passed into the hands of the Allies.⁹

Another fascist to achieve sensitive office in post-war Italy was *carabiniere* General Giuseppe Pièche. He had served in fascist military intelligence, co-ordinating the supply of military assistance to General Francisco Franco in Spain in 1937. Later he served as head of the

Italian military mission in Yugoslavia, liaising with the bloodthirsty leader of the anti-communist Ustascia forces, Ante Pavelich. Despite having been investigated for his activities under Mussolini, Pièche was put in charge of the Interior Ministry's fire department, which he combined with a secret political police role. He oversaw a new purge of the police under which ex-members of the Resistance were compulsorily retired at forty while former fascist policemen were taken on up to the age of sixty. In the run-up to the 1948 elections he infiltrated his agents into left-wing organizations and encouraged the creation of armed right-wing groups such as the Anti-Bolshevik Front, which was financed by the CIA and British intelligence service.[10] While Western intelligence agencies elsewhere were recruiting Nazi war criminals such as Klaus Barbie to work for them because of their anti-communist dependability and experience in the intelligence field, it is hardly surprising that a similar process should have been set under way in Italy. Italian fascists could also be relied upon for their anti-communism and they were the only people with recent experience of government.

The first major scandal involving the Italian secret services came to light on 11 May 1967, when *L'Espresso* magazine published the first of a series of revelations about preparations for a military coup which had been set in motion in the summer of 1964 but had never actually been brought to completion. Inquiries by a Defence Ministry commission and a later parliamentary commission showed that the *carabinieri* had drawn up a secret plan known as Piano Solo, which, as the name implies, provided for the paramilitary police to intervene on their own in order to restore public order. In investigating the background to the coup the inquiries discovered that the secret services had embarked on a massive programme of surveillance of Italian political and business figures. This was partly intended to identify left-wing suspects who, under the plan, would be rounded up and then imprisoned in concentration camps on the island of Sardinia. The investigators' findings gave an idea of the subordination of Italian intelligence agencies to their US and NATO counterparts. But a full understanding of this was made impossible by the imposition of state secrecy. The whole episode provides a good illustration of the uncomfortable position Italy was in, with a large left-wing component to the electorate, a political system frozen in immobility and conditioned from outside by secret military and intelligence accords.

According to the report of the Defence Ministry commission, the creation of personal intelligence dossiers on prominent and less prominent citizens began in 1959 and expanded over the years until the secret services had amassed 157,000 files, including '34,000 devoted to members of the business world, politicians and other categories of people of importance to the life of the nation'.[11] The commission reported a tendency on the part of SIFAR (military intelligence) not only to gather information potentially damaging to their targets but to distort the information so as to emphasize its unfavourable significance. Attention would focus on 'business operations of doubtful legality and even frivolous manifestations'. It also found the secret services had resorted to spreading false rumours and then recording them in their files: 'the information was created and then gathered in.' According to General Giovanni De Lorenzo, head of the *carabinieri* at the time of the projected coup, this unsavoury activity was a matter of NATO security. De Lorenzo told the commission that the intelligence-gathering was carried out by the *carabinieri* at the request of the Atlantic Pact Security Office to check on the reliability of state officials before granting security clearance. 'The matter of the dossiers is therefore a question of the security of the Atlantic Pact,' he said.

This interpretation is supported by Roberto Faenza, who claims in his detailed account of US influence in Italian domestic politics,[12] that a copy of the SIFAR dossiers was routinely deposited at CIA headquarters in Langley, Virginia. He quotes an unclassified CIA cable acknowledging receipt 'from our contact in the Italian secret services' of reports on political leaders 'under observation'. To illustrate the wide range of SIFAR's interests, Faenza cites a 1960 order from General De Lorenzo inviting his secret service subordinates to extend their dossiers to cover 'prelates, bishops and priests of the various dioceses'. This snooping does not appear to have unduly antagonized the Vatican, given that the minority report of the parliamentary commission found that much of SIFAR's intelligence-gathering was carried out on behalf of 'countries of the Atlantic Alliance and the Vatican State'.[13] Pope John XXIII was, however, furious when it was discovered that SIFAR had planted microphones in the papal apartments to monitor his conversations and those of his staff. SIFAR also planted bugs in the offices of the Italian President's official Rome residence, the Quirinale Palace. This operation, which continued over a number of years, at times with the approval of the President himself, was ordered by De Lorenzo at the request, according to Faenza, of CIA station chief William Colby. That such an operation could be contemplated is an indication that SIFAR did not ultimately owe its allegiance to the Italian head of state.

It is of course possible that the generals implicated in Italy's various secret service scandals claimed falsely that they had acted in accordance with NATO agreements when, in reality, they had broken the law entirely on their own initiative. This was indeed the conclusion of the Defence Ministry inquiry presided over by General Aldo Beolchini. 'Direct responsibility for the deviations, which were due to an excess of zeal and personal ambition, falls on the heads of SIFAR from 1956 onwards,'[14] it said. However, NATO has never publicly distanced itself from the excesses of Italy's right-wing generals and Beolchini's reductive view is hard to square with the repeated imposition of state secrecy on investigations into their misdemeanours. Beolchini's own findings were censored: it was decided that Parliament could be trusted with only half of his eighty-one-page report. A later report by the deputy commander of the *carabinieri*, General Giorgio Manes, was peppered with seventy-two deletions. Beolchini subsequently stated that had his report been made fully available to Parliament and the judiciary he believed it would have prevented the recurrence of such scandals.[15]

The man responsible for concealing the results of these inquiries through the imposition of state secrecy, and whose thoroughness in the task earned him the sobriquet 'Signor Omissis' (Mr Deletions), was Prime Minister Aldo Moro. But this display of Atlantic loyalty and responsibility would not be enough to remove Moro from the spotlight of suspicion. Some years earlier Rome CIA station chief Thomas Karamessines had asked General De Lorenzo, then head of SIFAR, for dossiers on politicians who favoured the formation of an alliance with the Socialist Party and, in particular, for detailed study of Moro's circle of collaborators.[16] Moro would again come under suspicion in the 1970s as he attempted to bring the communists into a government of national unity.

Virtually any politician of note was liable to come under the scrutiny of the secret services, whose job on occasion included developing a photographic chronicle of the subject's 'extra-conjugal or otherwise irregular sexual relations'. An idea of their conscientiousness can be gathered from the size of the dossiers they generated, as described in an interview with *Il Mondo* by Beolchini. 'Some of them were enormous. For Deputy [Amintore] Fanfani, for example, there were four volumes, each twice as fat as a dictionary.'[17] The intimidatory nature of such spying was emphasized in a speech to Parliament in 1967 by socialist Deputy Luigi Anderlini. 'I'm thinking of the SIFAR dossiers. In somebody's mind it could have been the net into which the entire ruling class of our country could be made to fall.' Anderlini likened the 1964 crisis to the military coup that had just been staged by the Greek colonels. A third Defence Ministry inquiry into the SIFAR scandal, presided over by General Luigi Lombardi, concluded that there had been no coup attempt in 1964. It did, however, concede that General De Lorenzo had instituted illegal measures to enable the *carabinieri* to take control of Italy's main cities, which is close enough to a coup for most people. It also revealed the existence of 'support units' made up largely of retired *carabinieri*.

The recruitment of irregular 'support units' is a recurrent theme in the succession of secret service scandals. They provide an ideal opportunity for the arms-length use of *agents provocateurs* and for the manipulation of terrorism. One of the men involved in this recruitment was Colonel Renzo Rocca, director of SIFAR's office of industrial counter-espionage, the Office of Economic and Industrial Research (REI). The parliamentary commission of inquiry into the SIFAR scandal found that Rocca used secret service funds and other money provided by wealthy industrialists to recruit members for these paramilitary forces, who would be paid as secret service 'informants'. 'The recruitment concentrated primarily on retired *carabinieri* and naval personnel but it also included other groups of adventure-seeking youths, who were to act above all as *provocateurs*,'[18] the minority report stated. Rocca's activities were closely monitored by the CIA. According to Faenza, Rome station chief William Harvey urged the colonel to try to destabilize Moro's attempts to reach an understanding with the socialists. Harvey suggested Rocca use his 'action squads' to 'carry out bombings against Christian Democrat Party offices and certain newspapers in the north, which were to be attributed to the left'.[19] Faenza also claimed that Harvey was in possession of lists containing more than 2,000 names of right-wingers belonging to paramilitary groups, who were available for use against the communists.

Rocca committed suicide in 1968, shortly before he was due to be questioned by the parliamentary commission. His death is one of a series of mysterious suicides and accidents which befell people who were privy to the sensitive secrets of the Italian intelligence service.

Rocca was found dead in his central Rome office on 27 June, having apparently shot himself in the head with a small, pearl-handled pistol. He had left the secret service a year earlier in order to work for the Fiat car manufacturer but the close collaboration between the secret service and Fiat meant that the change was merely cosmetic, despite official statements to the contrary. The Turin-based industry in fact made extensive use of SIFAR agents to spy on its own unruly workforce. Rocca's continuing links with intelligence made it worthwhile for secret service agents to visit his office and remove certain documents before calling in a magistrate. According to some accounts, they removed a file concerning Rocca's illegal 1964 recruitment campaign.[20] The rest of the documents were removed from the office on the orders of the public prosecutor, Ottorino Pesce. So alarmed was the head of the secret service, Admiral Eugenio Henke, at the prospect that they might contain information harmful to the security of the state that he requested that they only be examined in the presence of one of his officers, who would be able to identify any papers covered by state secrecy. Pesce refused the request and was subsequently relieved of the case, which passed into the hands of a more malleable magistrate, who duly concluded that Rocca had indeed shot himself. Forensic tests, however, failed to pick up any traces on Rocca's hand that would indicate he had himself fired the pistol. Bloodstains on the floor beside the body appeared to show that, if Rocca had shot himself, he must have lain down flat on the floor before doing so.[21] The minority report of the parliamentary commission emphasized Rocca's anxiety at the prospect of having to testify before the commission about his knowledge of delicate secret service activities. 'Certainly, responsibility for the most obscure and secret and also the least lawful operations, had fallen to him,'[22] it observed.

Rocca was not the only person with inside knowledge of the SIFAR scandal to meet with sudden death. On 27 April 1969 the former head of the *carabinieri*, who had been responsible for commissioning an investigation into the events of 1964, died in a car accident. General Carlo Ciglieri was driving alone on a straight stretch of road outside Padua when his car suddenly ran off the road. Unusually, no personal identity documents were found on him. Photographers who came to the scene took pictures of the car boot which showed it contained a bag. The bag subsequently disappeared. The man from whom Ciglieri commissioned the report was General Giorgio Manes. He collapsed and died of a heart attack on 25 June 1969, while waiting to give evidence to the parliamentary commission.[23] His assistant, Colonel Remo D'Ottavio, who actually wrote the report for him, attempted suicide in July.[24] D'Ottavio shot himself in the region of the heart, but miraculously survived. Many people who had assumed he was dead were astonished when he was called to give evidence by Venice magistrate Felice Casson more than twenty years later.

One of Rocca's delicate tasks on behalf of SIFAR was to finance the Alberto Pollio Institute, a right-wing think-tank founded in 1964 with the purpose of developing a strategy and tactics for combating the communist menace. He prevailed upon a number of companies which were interested in winning defence contracts to subscribe to the institute's newsletter: a conveniently discreet way of subsidizing its activities. Rocca also contributed to the costs of a conference held by the institute in Rome's Parco dei Principi Hotel from 3 to 5 May 1965. The conference speeches[25] offer an illuminating insight into the thinking of the unreconstructed fascists and other conservative figures who attended. Among these were Guido Giannettini, a journalist and secret service informer, who would later be charged with involvement in the 1969 Piazza Fontana bombing. Also present was a group of right-wing students from Rome University, including Stefano Delle Chiaie, the future terrorist leader. When he was asked during the Bologna bomb trial in 1987 about his presence at the conference, Delle Chiaie's memory was hazy but he thought he might have looked in on it briefly. The reason for his amnesia became clear when he said he was well aware that the conference had been branded as the 'momento zero' of the strategy of tension.

The subject of the conference was 'Revolutionary War', seen as the undeclared war waged on a global scale and without respite by world communism. The meeting endorsed the view that 'the Third World War is already under way, even if it is being fought at a low level of military intensity'. Ex-fascist and founder member of the institute Enrico De Boccard told the meeting that the communist onslaught aimed at the 'general disintegration of society' through the use of 'subversion backed by terror'. 'We say therefore that we don't accept communism and we publicly express our desire to fight it, returning in full measure to the communists the terror that they have imposed on the world,' he said. Many of the speakers stressed the need to move from the theoretical to the practical in the counter-revolutionary war. Right-wing journalist Pino Rauti, founder of the terrorist organization Ordine Nuovo (New Order) and later to be another of the suspects in the Piazza Fontana bombing, highlighted the propaganda value of the conference. But he added that it would be up to others 'to draw the concrete consequences from all this' and ensure that it was followed up by a 'complete elaboration of tactics for counter-revolution and defence'.

De Boccard took a similarly firm line, warning that any violation of the 'sanctuary' of the state by the communists, 'even if it were only by obtaining an under-secretary in the Post Office Ministry', would constitute 'such a grave attack on the vital "political space" of the state as to necessitate the implementation against them of a total defence plan. That is to say the direct, determined and decisive intervention of the armed forces.' Another speaker, Eggardo Beltrametti, urged the creation of 'permanent self-defence groups' to oppose communist penetration, which 'would not hesitate to take up the struggle in the most unorthodox conditions, with the necessary energy and ruthlessness.' Beltrametti described the blocking of the communist advance as a task 'which the Atlantic Alliance implicitly confers on us'. In order to carry out this task he called on both fascists and former Resistance members to unite their forces. All were invited to bury their differences in the common vision of the conference, which was forcefully summarized by Beltrametti: 'It is a struggle to the last drop of blood and our aim is to eliminate the communist threat by whatever means. We would prefer non-violent methods but we must not refuse to consider other forms of struggle.' He concluded rather lugubriously by pointing out, 'without being too optimistic', that violent conflict would reveal how many true communists there were in Italy. 'Perhaps then we will find there will be less of them than we believed.'

A more practical approach was offered by Pio Filippani Ronconi, a university professor, in his outline of a plan of defence and counter-attack. After discussing two categories of passive supporter of the anti-communist struggle, he went on to recommend the creation of a third level, made up of 'élite units with very few members, trained for counter-terror tasks', who would be used to destroy the precarious balance and bring about a rearrangement of the forces in power. 'These units, possibly unknown to one another, but well co-ordinated by an executive committee, could be made up in part of those youths who currently exhaust their energies, their time, and worse still their anonymity, in noble but sterile demonstrative enterprises which do not succeed in shaking the indifference of the masses in the face of the deteriorating national situation.' This was the sort of subversive planning which was being carried out with the money and the blessing of the Italian secret services and would later be faithfully reflected in the organization and methods of neo-fascist terrorism.

The practical application of the ideas discussed by the Pollio Institute can be seen in the activities of Ordine Nuovo. ON had been set up by Pino Rauti in 1956, officially as a centre for the study of Italian fascism and German national-socialism. In practice it became the rallying point for many in the extreme right who were dissatisfied with the excessive moderation of the official neo-fascist party, the Movimento Sociale Italiano (MSI). A letter from the National Directorate of Ordine Nuovo dated 3 June 1970 gives details of the subjects to be covered in a series of summer camps scheduled for July and August of that year, which mirror to a remarkable degree the content of the Pollio Institute's discussions. 'Lesson 1: The Third World War has already begun. Characteristics of the Third World War: psychological, revolutionary, ideological, total war. Lesson 2: The theory of revolutionary war. Technical aspects of revolutionary war. Revolutionary war in advanced industrialized countries. The problem of response to revolutionary attack. . . . Lesson 7: Organization of an operational revolutionary group. . . . Lesson 10: Techniques for the organization of self-defence groups. . . . Lesson 13: Strategy and tactics for the struggle in universities and schools.'[26] A reading list for the course recommended Giannettini's book *Techniques of Revolutionary War* along with Adolf Hitler's *Mein Kampf*. The letter also outlined the timetable for a typical day. Having started with coffee at 6 a.m., the aspiring Ordine Nuovo cadres would move on to gymnastic exercises, karate and self-defence lessons from 6.15 to 8 a.m. From 8.30 to 12 they would be walking in the mountains and taking part in the uninformatively vague 'various exercises'. After lunch there would be more karate and self-defence, political discussion and lessons, and the day would be rounded off by bucolic 'songs and drinks around the camp-fire', before bed at 11 p.m.

A flavour of the kind of people Ordine Nuovo sought to attract can be gathered from one of their questionnaires, which begins by asking, 'Why are you in ON?' 'Question 3: Do you want ON to impose dictatorship on the country? Why? . . . Question 5: Are you capable of supporting a completely unpopular thesis at a public meeting? Why? Question 6: Do you respect public opinion? . . . Question 8: Are you anti-semitic? Why? Question 9: Can you demonstrate that men are not equal? How? Question 10: Do you consider yourself bound by common morality? Why?'

On 21 November 1973, a Rome assize court sentenced thirty members of Ordine Nuovo to prison terms of up to five years for reconstituting the banned Fascist Party. By then forty-three members of the organization had been accused of minor acts of violence and criminal damage but in later years ON affiliates would go on to commit some of the bloodiest crimes perpetrated by the right. Among the documents confiscated from ON members before the 1973 trial was one that gave a vivid idea of the organization's potential for violence. 'Behind the proud axe [symbol] of Ordine Nuovo have gathered men who have no fear, whose violent force will descend implacably upon the filthy, bleating herd, led by Christian-communist jackals,' it read. This is just the frame of mind required if one is to plant bombs in crowded public places. The prosecutor at the 1973 trial was Vittorio Occorsio. He was shot dead by Ordine Nuovo members on 10 July 1976, in the first assassination of a magistrate carried out by a right-wing group.

One of the principal influences on the ideology of Ordine Nuovo, and of the neo-fascists in general, was the philosopher Julius Evola. Evola rejected what he saw as the decadence of the modern world in favour of the nobility of 'tradition', based on a blend of mythology, occultism and esotericism. It has even been suggested that the remarkable control exercised by the leaders of the extreme right over some of their teenage followers could in part be explained by their dabbling in black magic and esotericism. Evola puts forward an idea of aristocratic élitism as a basis for society and an alternative to the despised concept of democracy. One of the subjects for discussion at the 1970 ON summer camp was 'The ideological and existential identity between the concept of Western neo-capitalism and Marxism-Leninism'. Evola in fact rejected American capitalism as wholeheartedly as he did Marxism, since he considered that they were both based on a materialistic vision of life. This was reflected in ON's policies: in favour of a strong Europe and virulently anti-Soviet and anti-American. This may make it hard to imagine ON playing a role in a wider conservative conspiracy ultimately manoeuvred by NATO secret services. But the use of apparently hostile forces to further one's own intelligence aims provides an excellent opportunity for plausibly deniable covert operations. The extremists of both right and left were, in any case, frequently divided by fierce ideological and personal differences. The public prosecutor at the Bologna bomb trial described the relationship between terrorists and representatives of the Italian state as one of 'constant alliance and conflict based on reciprocal manipulation'.[27]

One characteristic of extremist right-wing groups that would be of interest to the secret services, if it was not originally instigated by them, was their eagerness to acquire intelligence about the communist enemy. Attempts to infiltrate anarchist or left-wing groups have been a constant feature of rightist extremism. A notebook confiscated from Clemente Graziani before the 1973 trial showed that ON had devised its own 'secret service' in order to learn 'how the enemy is organized'. It made use of people whose politics were not known to their friends and who were not members of the neo-fascist MSI party, who were to compile 'secret dossiers' for the organization. Infiltration of left-wing groups was not only useful for intelligence-gathering but could also be used to lay the blame on the left for right-wing terrorist actions.

In 1959 Stefano Delle Chiaie, formerly the secretary of a Rome branch of the MSI, founded a rival organization to ON known as Avanguardia Nazionale (National Vanguard). The group would go on to distinguish itself for its participation in violent clashes with left-wing students at Rome University in the 1960s and would later develop into a fully fledged terrorist organization. Throughout its existence, AN has been dogged by rumours of secret contacts between some of its leaders and senior officials in the Interior Ministry. A document published by AN itself hints at potentially embarrassing collusion between the terrorist group and members of the Italian political establishment. The document, published in the National-revolutionary Counter-information Bulletin of 30 June 1975, was a response to a decision by the Interior Minister to ban the organization, accusing it, like ON, of reconstituting the Fascist Party. The bulletin warns that the organization will resist the ban and then adds menacingly: 'If it comes to a trial, Avanguardia Nazionale will call to the witness stand ministers, politicians, party secretaries, secret services and all those who, in one way or another, first sought the "friendship" of Avanguardia Nazionale and then, having seen their advances rejected, decided to put an end to an organization that cannot be fitted into the game-plan of the regime.' It is possible, of course, that these were merely empty threats and Delle Chiaie has never spelt out exactly what he meant. But the evidence suggests otherwise. Delle Chiaie has continued to drop similar hints over the years and is doubtless well aware that blackmail cards are only valuable while you keep them up your sleeve.

In the years following the meeting at the Parco dei Principi Hotel, the counter-revolutionary strategy devised by the Pollio Institute was progressively put into effect in Italy, often involving close practical collaboration between the secret services and members of the extreme right. One particularly scandalous instance of this was the training of rightists at a secret NATO base near Capo Marrargiu on the west coast of Sardinia. According to Giuseppe De Lutiis,[28] the base was set up in 1963, just as General De Lorenzo was laying plans for his coup of the following year, as a school for saboteurs to be run by Italian military intelligence. In 1968 the base was expanded and modernized under the guidance of American 'technicians'. Its purpose was to train 'stay-behind units' who would organize resistance and sabotage behind enemy lines in the event of an Eastern Bloc invasion of Italy. More realistically, the units were to carry out sabotage and terrorism in peacetime Italy to ensure that Italian communists never got their hands on the levers of power. Those trained at the school came from a similar background to Colonel Rocca's recruits: former military personnel and right-wingers who could be relied on for their passionate anti-communism. The school was at its most active between 1969 and 1975. During that time, which coincided with the early years of the strategy of tension, between 1,000 and 4,000 potential terrorists were trained at the base. Many of the students were flown in by military aircraft from Ciampino military airport just outside Rome and then taken out to the base, which was inaccessible by road, by helicopter. At the end of the course, Capo Marrargiu graduates would be allowed to keep the weapons and explosives with which they had been provided on arrival at the base. This may go some way towards explaining why the explosives used in right-wing bombings very rarely turned out to be stolen. According to one account, Arab guerrillas and members of left-wing groups also received training at the base.[29] De Lutiis' account of the base bears a remarkable similarity to a training camp for CIA special agents described in *L'Espresso* magazine (18 January 1976): 'It's in Sardinia, in an inaccessible location, and the trainees are almost all destined for the countries of Eastern Europe and the Middle East.' Clearly, not all Capo Marrargiu's graduates went so far afield.

A meeting of Ordine Nuovo held in the town of Cattolica on the north-east coast of Italy between 28 February and 2 March 1974 gives a further indication of the close relationship between the secret services and members of the far right. Despite the fact that ON had been officially banned by the Interior Minister in November 1973, the group decided to stage its meeting at a hotel run by a secret service informer. Subjects for discussion were the clandestine reorganization of Ordine Nuovo and weapons procurement. The hotel was the Pensione Giada, run by Caterino Falzari, a fluent speaker of Slavonic languages who had worked as a translator for the police, the *carabinieri* and the secret services. 'It is at the very least unusual for the leaders of an illegal group to choose to meet in a place where they know they may be under surveillance,' commented Vito Zincani, an examining magistrate from Bologna. 'The only explanation is that that was the one place where they knew they were safe.'[30]

Whatever the Italian secret services were doing, it is unlikely they were acting entirely on their own initiative, if one bears in mind the comments of the minority report of the parliamentary investigation into the SIFAR affair. It found that the Italian government had allowed the establishment of a secret service office 'at the disposal of the secret services of other countries, to gather information on entire categories of citizens, particularly those of a certain political persuasion, but also on the whole political class of our country'. The report said that the foreign secret services (its authors fight shy of openly naming the United States) had as a result been able to influence Italian government appointments. It warned that the provision of this information 'makes the interference of foreign secret services far more penetrating; the propensity of some of them to intervene, even violently, in other countries' political affairs, is known through past experience. The activities of such agencies have constituted, and still do, a latent threat to the democratic stability and the prospects for progress of our country.'[31]

Notes

1 Quoted in Ray S. Cline, *The CIA under Reagan, Bush and Casey*, Acropolis Books, Washington, 1981, p. 123.
2 William Blum, *The CIA: A Forgotten History*, Zed Books, London, 1986, p. 25.
3 Ibid., p. 27.
4 Ibid., p. 27.
5 *La Repubblica*, 5 April 1988.

6 Roberto Faenza and Marco Fini, *Gli Americani in Italia*, Feltrinelli, Milan, 1976, p. 276.
7 William Blum, op. cit., p. 29.
8 Ibid., p. 29.
9 Giuseppe De Lutiis, *Storia dei Servizi Segreti in Italia*, Editori Riuniti, Rome, 1984, pp. 48–9.
10 Ibid., p. 50.
11 Quoted in Pietro Calderoni (ed.), *Servizi Segreti*, Tullio Pironti, Naples, 1984, p. 4.
12 Roberto Faenza, *Il Malaffare*, Mondadori, Milan, 1978, p. 318.
13 Quoted in Pietro Calderoni, op. cit., p. 14.
14 Quoted in Gianni Flamini, *Il Partito del Golpe*, Vol.1, Italo Bovolenta, Ferrara, 1981, p. 136.
15 Massimo Caprara, 'La verità sta negli omissis', in *Il Mondo*, 25 July.
16 Roberto Faenza, op. cit., p. 317.
17 Massimo Caprara, op. cit.
18 Marco Sassano, *SID e Partito Americano*, Marsilio Editori, Padua, 1975, p. 76.
19 Roberto Faenza, op. cit., p. 369.
20 Marco Sassano, op. cit., p. 80.
21 Ibid., p. 85.
22 Giuseppe De Lutiis, op. cit., p. 73.
23 Ibid., p. 87.
24 Ambrogio Viviani, *Servizi Segreti Italiani 1815–1985*, ADN Kronos Libri, Rome, 1985, p. 137.
25 *La Guerra Rivoluzionaria, Atti del primo convegno organizzato dall'Istituto Pollio*, Giovanni Volpe Editore, Rome, 1965.
26 *Atti del processo a carico di Graziani Clemente ed altri*, Rome, 1973.
27 Quoted in Pietro Calderoni, op. cit., p. 19.
28 Giuseppe De Lutiis, op. cit., pp. 133–7.
29 Corrado Incerti and Sandro Ottolenghi, *L'Europeo*, 21 May 1976.
30 Quoted in Pietro Calderoni, op. cit., p. 39.
31 Ibid., p. 15.

[3]

THE MASONIC
CONSPIRACY

Ahi, Pistoia, Pistoia, chè non stanzi
D'incenerarti sì che più non duri,
Poi che in mal far lo seme tuo avanzi?

(Ah, Pistoia, Pistoia, why do you not decree your
own reduction to ashes so that you endure no
longer, since you surpass even your ancestors in
evil-doing?)

Dante Alighieri, *Inferno*, Canto 25.

In 1967 many of the most sensitive files from the SIFAR archives
passed into the hands of the man who would later become Venerable
Master of the Propaganda Two (P2) secret masonic lodge. They were
given to him by General Giovanni Allavena, director of SIFAR until
his dismissal in June 1965, on the general's joining the lodge. The man
who received them and whose discreet use of them would make him
one of the most influential power-brokers in Italy was Licio Gelli. The
son of a Tuscan miller, Gelli was born in Pistoia on 21 April 1919. By
the early 1970s he was firmly established as the head of a lodge which
numbered among its members senior officers from all branches of the
military (including the secret services), parliamentarians, civil
servants and members of the judiciary, as well as prominent figures
from the worlds of finance and industry. At the height of his power,
Gelli and his associates were able to influence government appointments and policy, help to advance the careers of P2 members in all

fields, and enrich themselves by converting political influence into material wealth on a grand scale. This period coincided with the most radical implementation of the strategy of tension and an upsurge of terrorist violence in Italy. It is unlikely that US intelligence agencies would have allowed the SIFAR files, which were created at their instigation and at a time when they exercised tight control over the Italian secret services, to fall into unauthorized hands.

There are a wide range of conflicting views as to the real nature and purpose of P2. Some people maintain it was principally an association of thieves, others that it was a mutual aid society for ambitious careerists, and others that it was primarily a political organization. There is also considerable disagreement over its political aims, whom it served and who was damaged by its activities. The first accurate insight into the nature and dimensions of the lodge came in March 1981 when two Milan magistrates ordered a search of Gelli's Arezzo home and of his office at the Giole mattress factory in nearby Castiglion Fibocchi. The latter yielded up membership lists containing 962 names, along with other documents relating to the lodge. The discovery that four cabinet ministers, three under-secretaries and thirty-eight parliamentarians were members of P2 precipitated the fall of the government led by Arnaldo Forlani, and for the first time since the war a Prime Minister was appointed from outside the Christian Democrat Party. A commission of legal experts decided the lodge was a secret association and therefore illegal under the terms of the constitution. An all-party parliamentary commission then spent three years investigating the activities of the lodge. Its report, couched in cautious and at times ambiguous language, reflected an attempt to gain the widest possible political support for its conclusions and embarrassment at the extent to which the Italian establishment had identified with Gelli's political project.

The commission was presided over by Tina Anselmi, a Christian Democrat deputy, whose independent-minded direction of the investigation effectively scotched her chances of achieving ministerial office. Its report, published in 1984, described P2 as 'a neutral instrument for operations of conditioning and control' of Italian political life. It likened P2 to a pyramid with Gelli at the apex, but suggested that above Gelli there was another, inverted, pyramid containing the people responsible for the overall strategy and who passed their orders down to the lower pyramid through Gelli. For understandable reasons of political expediency the commission chose not to point an accusing finger at Italy's powerful ally, the United States. It claimed that it had been unable to identify the forces present in the upper pyramid 'other than identifying the nature of the relationship linking Licio Gelli to the secret services'. In a first draft, the report described Gelli's relationship with the military as having the objective of 'maintaining a political framework congenial to the traditional forces of power'.[1] This passage, which could also be applied to his relationship with the secret services, was dropped as part of the process of toning down the original version of the report. The final document gives no clear and unequivocal account of the purpose of Gelli's partnership with the secret services; it does, however, drop the hint that interpretations of P2 'should not be restricted to narrow domestic horizons, but should look realistically at the problems of our epoch and the role our country plays in it'.[2]

Despite the overwhelming evidence of P2's role in a wider conservative conspiracy, the accounts of the lodge are as varied as the diverse political parties that care to put them forward. One version popular among the conservative parties is that Gelli was an agent of the KGB or some other Eastern Bloc secret service. Gelli being a complex character, there is some evidence to support this view, at least with regard to the early years of his career. But the first public manifestation of his political leanings came with the Spanish Civil War. At the age of seventeen, Gelli enrolled as a volunteer in the 735th Black Shirts Battalion and went to fight in Spain, where his brother Raffaele was killed at Malaga in April 1938. After returning to Italy Gelli enlisted in an infantry regiment in 1940. A year later he volunteered to join a parachute regiment but was invalided out after an accident in training. In 1942 he was sent to the small port of Cattaro in Yugoslavia as aide-de-camp to a Fascist Party official. There he is reported to have worked for SIM, the wartime secret service, and come into contact with representatives of the British and Soviet secret services.[3] At the time the Italians were holding the Yugoslav national gold reserves in the town before transporting them to Rome and were warding off attempts by the British, Germans and Yugoslav Resistance to 'liberate' the gold. The fact is sometimes cited as a possible explanation for Gelli's subsequent wealth. His boss, Piero Parini, was reportedly involved in putting out secret feelers on behalf of Mussolini to both Soviet and Western representatives.[4] If Gelli was involved in these negotiations it may have given him his first opportunity to enter into contact with secret services from both sides of the future Iron

Curtain.

In 1943 he returned to Italy to become liaison officer for the German forces in his home town of Pistoia, with the rank of sergeant-major in the Hermann Goering Division of the German SS. It was during the closing stages of the war that he began to show the talent for deviousness and double-dealing for which he would later be renowned and which would make it so difficult to identify him in his true political colours. Overtly committed to the fascist Salò regime but facing the certainty of an imminent Allied victory, Gelli had to resolve a further dilemma: with which partisan camp should he throw in his lot? Given the hostility between the communists and the other anti-fascist forces, having collaborated with one group would not necessarily guarantee protection from the other. As a natural survivor, Gelli appears to have hedged his bets. His biographers cite descriptions of him as a ferocious torturer of Italian partisans and deserters. But other accounts have him leading German troops on fruitless searches of the Italian countryside having first tipped off the Resistance about their plans.

A document dated 4 October 1944, and signed by the communist president of the Pistoia National Liberation Committee, Italo Carobbi, states that Gelli, 'despite having served the fascists and the Germans, made himself useful to the cause of local patriots'.[5] Pending further examination of his activities, it said, he should not be interfered with in any way. It stated specifically that Gelli had warned partisans that they were about to be arrested, driven supplies to two non-communist Resistance formations on six occasions, and participated in a raid to free political prisoners from jail. The curious thing about the document is that it is signed by a communist Resistance leader, but the specific instances of collaboration that it cites were carried out with non-communist partisan groups, who do not appear to have been consulted before the document was drawn up. It is possible, however, that Gelli also collaborated with the communists through one of his sisters, who was married to a communist Resistance member.

One of the groups with which Gelli worked was led by an anarchist, Silvano Fedi. Fedi was betrayed to the Germans and killed in an ambush on 29 July 1944. Rumours at the time suggested that it was Gelli who had betrayed him. According to Marcello Coppetti, a Florentine journalist, expert on UFOs and the paranormal, and a self-professed 'enemy' of Gelli's, Gelli may have betrayed Fedi as a favour to the communists, who viewed him as a dangerous and unruly rival. It was this favour, according to Coppetti, that would enable Gelli to blackmail the Communist Party in later years. Coppetti claims the destabilization of Italy may have been the fruit of a secret pact between the CIA and the KGB, working together to a common goal. Although he was at times close to both Gelli and the Italian secret services and excessively well informed, he does not appear a particularly reliable witness. We will meet him again.

The confusingly ambivalent communist attitude towards Gelli was well illustrated by an article in the neo-fascist newspaper *Il Giornale d'Italia* (3 February 1982). The paper published a letter, dated 29 January 1952, from a former mayor of Pistoia and Communist Party senator, Giuseppe Corsini, requesting Gelli's assistance in speeding up the payment of a pension to one of Corsini's relatives. The letter opened 'Dear Licio' and concluded 'with sincere thanks and cordial greetings'. Another letter followed from Corsini, this time to an old friend of his, the freemason Menotti Baldini, who had written to him to inquire about Gelli's wartime activities. The letter, dated 30 April 1972, described the fascist Gelli as 'the organizer of all the reprisals' and responsible for 'the most ferocious torture' of suspected partisans. Either Corsini had gathered new information on Gelli in the intervening years or he had known this all along and was a man of remarkable cynicism. Alternatively, he may have considered that it was necessary to preserve Gelli's persona as a fascist torturer as cover for someone who was, in reality, a faithful servant of the communists. The lukewarm denunciation of Gelli by the communists in later years and their acceptance of a soft-soaping P2 Commission report would square with the view of Gelli as a communist spy or in some way capable of blackmailing the Communist Party.

Communist Party representatives argue that their delay in denouncing Gelli was the result of ignorance about him, caused by their exclusion from government and its confidential sources of information. Their acceptance of a weakly worded parliamentary report was prompted by the desire to see it endorsed by as many parties as possible and, according to their friends, by a long-standing inferiority complex when it comes to criticism of the United States. Gelli himself offered a possible clue in a defensive memorandum he sent to the commission in 1984. In his inimitable style, he complained of the distortion of the facts and the false charges laid against him 'in the hope, which I intend to disappoint, that I may have forgotten what I learned in my multifarious contacts, which spread in every direction, in absolutely every direction'.[6]

The author of a 1950 secret service report on Gelli, published by the P2 Commission, had no doubt about his political leanings. 'The above-mentioned is one of the most dangerous elements operating in the 8th Zone under the direct orders of the Communist Party,' he wrote. In short, Gelli was ideally cut out to be a communist spy 'because of his qualities as a traitor, because of his skills as a delinquent and because of his mobility'. According to the report, entitled Cominform, Gelli went over to the communists in 1944 'to save his skin'. He had been put up against a wall and was about to be shot by partisans 'when the timely intervention of the communist Giuseppe Corsini saved him from his just deserts'. He began his intelligence-gathering work in 1947, making full use of the fact that he was considered to be a fascist sympathizer. The report noted that he appeared to spend far more money than his probable earnings would allow and said he was suspected of involvement in arms trafficking with members of a communist revolutionary cell.[7] Another secret service report written about the same time stated that Gelli was 'continuing his suspect activity, masked by his work for an American typewriter company: Remington Rand Italiana', whose representative he had become. Gelli had opened a shop in Pistoia's Corso Gramsci, it said, where 'a portrait of General MacArthur dominates one wall'.[8] Neither report however offers any concrete evidence of Gelli's espionage activities and rather than pursuing him and bringing him to trial for spying, the secret services subsequently appear to have lost all interest in him. In 1956 his name was removed from the Interior Ministry's register of potential subversives. By 1974 he was being described as politically to the right and 'highly regarded in influential circles in Arezzo', where he then lived.[9]

Thus far, it would appear that Gelli may have worked for communist partisans in the closing stages of the war and for communist intelligence after it. Having been discovered by the Italian secret services he then changed his allegiance again and agreed to work for them, after which the secret service archives have little of interest to offer on him. There is, however, no concrete detail on what he may have done for the communists and it would be wise to view any secret service report on him with considerable scepticism. The parliamentary commission suggested as much when it said the letters accompanying the Cominform report appeared to be 'more the formal pretext' for acquiring the document than a genuine correspondence between secret service offices.[10]

Gelli's reported contacts with Western intelligence go back just as far as those with the communists. It is of course possible that for a while he worked for both. A note accompanying a list of fifty-six Pistoia fascists betrayed to the police by Gelli after the war's end reported that he began collaborating with the Counter Intelligence Corps (CIC) of the American Fifth Army in October 1944. And an article in *La Nazione* newspaper (1 September 1981) described Gelli's capture by communist partisans on 8 September 1944, as he acted as guide to a patrol of South African soldiers. In this version he was saved from a firing squad by Osvaldo Gori, a nephew of Corsini, who confirmed the account. 'I knew that Licio had been a fascist but I also knew that he had later collaborated with us, although, after all these years, I couldn't say how,' he told the paper. It is also interesting that amid correspondence predating the Cominform report was a note requesting information about Gelli following a tip-off from 'an allied agency' that he was a suspected communist agent. And a covering letter accompanying the report, dated 29 September 1950, actually attributes Cominform to 'the noted informant at the American embassy' from whom it had been received some time earlier.[11] So it would appear that Gelli may owe his communist credentials, true or false, to American intelligence.

The P2 Commission was in no doubt about Gelli's relationship with the Italian secret service. 'There is no alternative but to recognize that Gelli belonged to the secret service, since it is the only logical explanation for the protection extended to him, both passively, by not acquiring information on him, and actively, by not supplying information to the political authorities who requested it,' it wrote. The commission cited two reports from the office of military intelligence in Florence which related that, prior to June 1971, Gelli told a number of people that he was a secret service agent operating under the cover name of Filippo. The commission considered that he had offered convincing evidence to back up his claim. Among other things, the reports said, he used to give the telephone number of the Florence secret service office to people who needed to contact him. The commission also cited an incident in which the director of counter-espionage 'flew into a fury' on learning that the head of the Florence office of military intelligence had initiated an investigation into Gelli. He later personally reprimanded the officer for his action, describing Gelli as 'someone influential and useful to the service'.[12] In later years Gelli had a secret service office in Rome at his personal disposal. On 1 July 1978, he wrote to members of the P2 lodge to inform them that they could call a number in Rome, 4759347, during office hours if they wanted further information about 'our institution'. Even years later, according to Bologna prosecutors Libero Mancuso and Attilio Dardani, the number corresponded to a secret service office in an annexe of the Defence Ministry.[13] It is unlikely that at this stage the secret services can have suspected Gelli of having secret communist leanings.

Controversy persists, though, over the nature of Gelli's political loyalties. His biographer Gianfranco Piazzesi describes him as someone always open to the highest bidder. 'Rather than a secret agent, Gelli was a trader in information . . . He discovered that a collection of photocopies can be more valuable than the most prized stamp collection and he acted accordingly. In the field of international espionage he was more a depository than a divulger of secrets,'[14] he wrote. But what made Gelli's photocopy collection really valuable was its blackmail potential, and it was this that conferred on the P2 boss his astonishing power. Piazzesi cites the opinion of masonic Grand Master Lino Salvini that Gelli was a pragmatist whose greatest satisfaction would be to make peace between Communist Party Secretary Enrico Berlinguer and the Pope. 'Gelli is a man without ideals,' Salvini said. 'With hindsight I realize that he never really wanted a strong government. With a strong government there is no space for mediators.'[15]

Communist P2 commissioner Antonio Bellocchio takes a different view. 'We have identified, above all, the American secret services as the occupants of the upper pyramid,' he told me.[16] 'We have come to the definite conclusion that Italy is a country of limited sovereignty because of the interference of the American secret services and international freemasonry. If the majority of the commission had been prepared to follow us in this analysis they would have had to admit that they are puppets of the United States of America, and they don't intend to admit that ever.' It is possible that both Piazzesi and Bellocchio are right. It is unlikely that Gelli was the originator of the political projects he pursued. For a start, he was only semi-educated, having been expelled from school at the age of thirteen for striking the headmaster. His role was simply to follow instructions. It is a sad reflection on Italian political life that a man of Gelli's modest intellectual abilities, for all his shrewdness and cunning, should once have wielded such influence. There can be little doubt, given his talent for timely shifts of allegiance in order to ensure his presence on the winning side, that from an early stage he had thrown in his lot with the conservative forces that have dominated post-war Italy and who had the ultimate guarantor of their power in Washington.

This did not preclude him from engaging in profitable trading relations with Romania while, according to one report, P2 members in the finance police turned a blind eye to customs irregularities. Gelli's involvement in the clothes and textiles trade with Romania in the 1970s is frequently cited by those who claim he was an East Bloc agent. Given the independent foreign policy line pursued by President Nikolai Ceausescu and the favour, including an English knighthood, that it won him in the West, the argument is not entirely convincing. The Italian secret service can hardly expect to be believed when it generates a report describing Gelli as a potential communist 'sleeper' at a time when he is on intimate terms with the heads of the service, who also happen to belong to his masonic lodge. In order to understand the complex and elusive character who was Venerable Master of P2 it is necessary to appreciate the nature of the lodge, its relationship to the secret services, and the patrons who promoted Gelli's remarkable masonic and political career. There is plenty of evidence available.

Gelli himself has offered plenty of clues, in numerous interviews, in memoranda to the P2 Commission and in his autobiography, modestly entitled *The Truth*. His utterances are undoubtedly self-serving but can sometimes be illuminating, particularly if one manages to decipher his coded messages to powerful former friends. I went to speak to him in the summer of 1989 at his luxury villa surrounded by vineyards and cypress trees on a secluded hill near the Tuscan town of Arezzo. Gelli was happily holding court to members of the foreign and Italian press who wished to make the pilgrimage to hear his tale of the political persecution of innocent men. He gave the impression of a mild-mannered provincial banker, with grey hair, a grey suit and a slightly bulbous nose in a placid-looking face. There were no visible signs of the heart disease that had secured his early release from prison for an urgent bypass operation, which many months later had still not been deemed necessary. Nor did his judicial position seem to be causing undue preoccupation.

Gelli began our conversation with a solemn and somewhat sanctimonious disquisition on the abuse of media power and the iniquities of the twentieth century. The P2 lodge, he was happy to explain, was a regular lodge owing obedience to the Grand Orient of Italy but with special rules of confidentiality because it contained important personalities and others whose ideology ostensibly precluded them from becoming masons. It was therefore inappropriate for their identities to be divulged or for them to be expected to meet all the other members of the lodge. 'And anyway it was impossible as there was nowhere large enough for 1,000 or 1,500 people to meet.'[17] This was reassuring news. Listening to Gelli's bland words and observing his mild demeanour, one might have started to believe that he really was an inoffensive old man, the victim of judicial persecution. But here, already, was one of the blackmailing messages for which he is renowned. So there are 500 people who have still not been identified? 'I don't know. There are those who speak of 1,000 members, others speak of 1,500, others of 2,000, some have even reached the figure of 3,000.' Gelli had handed over the membership list to the Grand Master before leaving the country in 1981 and it was up to that official's successor, he said, to reveal the true figure. There have been repeated claims that the P2 membership was well over 1,000 and this implicit confirmation from Gelli himself would indeed be worrying for members whose identity had not yet publicly emerged.

Gelli continued in similar vein. What was his reaction to claims by Clara Calvi, widow of Banco Ambrosiano chairman Roberto Calvi, that the real head of P2 had been Giulio Andreotti, followed at the top of the organization by Francesco Cosentino, secretary general of the Chamber of Deputies, and businessman Umberto Ortolani: according to this hierarchy, Gelli was only fourth in the pecking order of the lodge? 'Really? I was the Venerable Master, so if those others were members, and I am not free to say, they were only ordinary members.' This is a curious lapse on Gelli's part. The names of both Ortolani and Cosentino were on the Castiglion Fibocchi lists; Andreotti's was not, something one might have expected Gelli to point out.

Gelli began his masonic career in 1965 when he joined the Romagnosi lodge of the Grand Orient of Italy. Italian freemasonry is divided into two principal groupings, commonly referred to by the name of their Rome headquarters. The Grand Orient, with between 15,000 and 20,000 members, had its headquarters in Palazzo Giustiniani, while its chief rival, with 5,000–10,000 affiliates, was based in the central Piazza del Gesù. The revival of freemasonry in Italy after the war was encouraged by both the British and the

Americans and lodges sprang up in the wake of the advancing Allied armies as the period of fascist persecution of masons came to an end. A secret service report on 'Freemasonry in Italy' highlighted the influence of British and American freemasonry on Italian lodges. 'Washington's policy is to direct European states towards interests and objectives that fall into the United States' orbit, concerned as it is not to lose Western Europe and to counteract Moscow's attempts to engineer the break-up of NATO,'[18] it observed. The masonic influence of the United States coincided with its military presence. According to Giuseppe D'Alema,[19] American lodges have been set up for every NATO base in Italy, beginning with the Benjamin Franklin, established in Livorno on 25 July 1959. Palazzo Giustiniani owed a particular debt of gratitude to US freemasonry as it only recovered its headquarters, which had been confiscated under Mussolini, after American pressure on the Italian government. A key role in the negotiations was played by one Frank Gigliotti, a former OSS and then CIA agent. The agreement to return the building to the Grand Orient was signed in 1960 by the Italian Finance Minister and Grand Master Publio Cortini. Witnesses at the ceremony were US Ambassador James Zellerbach and Frank Gigliotti.[20]

Also in 1960, Palazzo Giustiniani received official recognition from the powerful North American masonic district. Part of the deal was that the Grand Orient should agree to merge with a small Scottish rite lodge headed by the right-wing Sicilian Prince Giovanni Alliata di Montereale. Despite its diminutive size, Alliata's lodge, based in Via Lombardia in Rome, already enjoyed the recognition of the North American district. It is a good indication of the political complexion of US-sponsored freemasonry that Alliata would later be implicated in both the Borghese and Rosa dei Venti coup plots, as well as being linked to the Mafia.

This was exactly the milieu in which Gelli's career would thrive. After a year in the Romagnosi lodge he was transferred to P2, a lodge where the membership was known only to the Grand Master and to the lodge secretary, in order to protect its influential affiliates from the importunate demands for assistance of their less fortunate 'brothers'. The lodge was named Propaganda Two to distinguish it from another, regular Propaganda lodge based in Turin. In 1969 Gelli was given the task of working for the unification of the various Italian masonic groupings and to improve relations with the Catholic Church, which until 1983 explicitly excommunicated any Catholic who became a freemason. In 1971 he was made secretary of P2. This accelerated masonic promotion was personally instigated by Grand Master Giordano Gamberini, who has been dubbed 'the travelling-salesman of anti-communism'. On his retirement in 1970, Gamberini was given responsibility for contacts with foreign masonic lodges and with the CIA.[21] Gelli was asked about the reason for his rapid masonic career by the left-leaning mason Ferdinando Accornero at a meeting of the Grand Orient's governing council in 1967. 'He told me he was a member of the council as a representative of a foreign Grand Lodge the name of which I don't remember,' Accornero told Bologna magistrates in 1977.

In order to understand the purpose of P2 one has to bear in mind the nature of its membership. Politicians in the lodge were recruited from every political party except the Radical and Communist Parties. The membership lists discovered in 1981 showed that 195 high-ranking officers from all branches of the military belonged to the lodge. There were fifty-two officers from the *carabinieri* paramilitary police, six from the police and thirty-seven from the finance police; nine belonged to the Air Force, twenty-nine to the Navy and fifty to the Army. Most significantly, the heads of both the domestic secret service (SISDE) and military intelligence (SISMI) were affiliates. 'As can be seen at a glance, the membership lists reveal a map of the highest levels of military power, with individuals who have often played a central role in particularly significant moments of the recent history of our country, as well as in events of a subversive nature,'[22] the P2 Commission commented.

One of the most significant names on the list was that of General Vito Miceli, the head of military intelligence arrested in 1974 on a charge of subversive conspiracy. Miceli's membership of the lodge is particularly illuminating, given the sensitive nature of his military career. Before becoming head of military intelligence Miceli had been responsible for the Atlantic Pact Security Office, vetting government officials for their security clearance: not a job that would be entrusted to someone who did not enjoy the full confidence of the NATO intelligence establishment. American confidence in Miceli was illustrated in February 1972 when Ambassador Graham Martin made him a secret payment of $800,000 to be used on political propaganda. Miceli joined P2 in October 1971, in the same month as he was appointed director of SID. Gelli was at first coy about his relationship with members of the secret services when I spoke to him. 'If there was an officer who was a member of P2 I wasn't in a position to know it because I wouldn't ask him whether he belonged to the secret services and if he did belong, he shouldn't tell me, or what sort of secret services would they have been?' But he quickly recognized the manifest implausibility of this explanation coming from the head of a masonic lodge whose members numbered among them the highest ranks in both branches of the intelligence service. 'I knew masses of them, what do you expect? I knew whether or not they belonged to the secret services,' Gelli said, while insisting that he had never himself worked for either the KGB, the CIA or the Italian intelligence services. A more accurate impression of his influence emerges from a claim he made to Florence Prosecutor Pierluigi Vigna. He boasted to the magistrate in 1974 that he had actually engineered Miceli's appointment as director of SID through his own political contacts.[23] The claim is by no means implausible. In June 1976 Miceli was elected to Parliament as a representative of the neo-fascist party, the Movimento Sociale Italiano (MSI).

Gelli's overt political activity has always been right-wing, despite the secret service disinformation about his Eastern Bloc contacts and his complex relationship with some members of the PCI. Clearly, a man of Miceli's political outlook felt quite at home in the P2 lodge. Gelli himself has made no secret of his anti-communism, while preferring to classify himself as a political moderate in his conversation with the author. 'I can tell you that we [in the P2 lodge] were always anti-communist. We were above all political ideology but we wanted nothing whatever to do with the two political extremes, with the far right and the far left. All the others were acceptable.' Gelli claimed he had never had any contacts with the PCI, other than with Italo Carobbi, an old family friend, and with Osvaldo Gori, a distant cousin and the man who had saved him from a partisan firing squad. 'I have no respect for the PCI. There are those who are born mediocre and those who become mediocre by joining the PCI,' he quipped.

For all his claims that he and his lodge were above politics, there is considerable evidence that both were actively involved in the politics of the extreme right over many years. As early as September 1969, a freemason from the Umbrian town of Grosseto referred in a letter to Gelli's involvement in the secret masonic initiation of 400 senior army officers in order to prepare a 'government of colonels, always preferable to a communist government'.[24] But there is more than mere hearsay to go on. On 15 July 1971, Gelli sent a copy of the minutes of a

P2 meeting held in Rome on 5 March to those members who had been unable to attend. 'As you can see, philosophy has been banned, but we thought, and still do, that we must tackle solid and concrete questions concerning the entire life of the nation,' he wrote in a covering letter, thus reversing the usual masonic embargo on politics. The subjects discussed at the meeting included: 'a. the political and economic situation in Italy; b. the threat of the Communist Party, allied to clericalism, attempting to seize power; c. the inadequacy of the forces of law and order; f. our position in the event of the clerico-communists coming to power.'[25] At a meeting of the governing council of the Grand Orient on 10 July 1971, Grand Master Salvini warned that Gelli was organizing a coup. At about the same time, the left-wing mason Ermenegildo Benedetti was receiving reports that Gelli had written to senior military officers belonging to P2 inviting them to consider the possibility of forming a military government.

Gelli's publicly professed political ideas can be gathered from an affidavit he swore for Michele Sindona when the Sicilian financier was fighting extradition from the United States to Italy following the 1974 collapse of his transatlantic banking empire. In his testimony Gelli described himself as someone who had spent all his life fighting against communism. 'As a businessman I am known for being anti-communist and I am aware of the communist attacks on Michele Sindona,' he declared. 'The hatred of the communists for Michele Sindona is due to the fact that he is anti-communist and has always been in favour of a free enterprise system in a democratic Italy.' He rounded off his affidavit by emphasizing the deteriorating situation in Italy caused by the 'infiltration of the left' and warning that Sindona would not get a fair trial in the country but that his very life could be in danger.[26]

The political project elaborated within P2 is spelt out in detail in two documents confiscated from Gelli's daughter Maria Grazia at Rome airport on 4 July 1981. The documents, written for Gelli around 1976, advocate a government by technocrats and reform of the constitution to allow a presidential system of government based on the French or American model. Some of the proposals, such as the civil responsibility of magistrates and other constitutional changes, have since been introduced or are currently under discussion. The overall package was unquestionably right-wing – restricting the political influence of trade unions was a prime objective – but it contained a number of perfectly reasonable and moderate proposals that could hardly be seen as a denial of the principles of Western democracy. More objectionable, though, were the methods by which the plans were to be implemented.

In one of the documents, a 'Memorandum on the Political Situation in Italy', the author speculated about the possibility of civil war in Italy, which would justify the formation of a military government 'as the only alternative to a communist regime'. The author observed that the international situation 'does not seem to allow exceptions to the logic of Yalta, not even for Finnish-style frontier experiments, and if that may seem comforting on the one hand, in another respect it is not, because the dominant power (USA) does not appear to be inclined, despite its experiences in South-east Asia, towards patient British-style therapies.' The memorandum referred to the PCI as 'hiding its true Hungarian and Czechoslovak face behind a mask of respectability' and voiced the suspicion that Italy's terrorist bombings were the work of Soviet or East German agents. The second document, a 'Plan for Democratic Revival', specifically ruled out the overthrow of the system by force but recommended corruption as a suitable alternative. The author suggested that 'figures of not more than 30 or 40 billion Lire [£20–26 million] should be enough for well-chosen men of good faith to win the necessary key positions' in order to control the political parties, press and trade unions. If it was decided that the existing political parties were not so discredited as to be useless, 'adequate financial instruments' would be made available to buy their control. If they were not salvageable, two new political parties would be created. With regard to the press, a couple of campaigning news magazines were to be bought, as were individual journalists, two or three per publication. 'Once acquired, the journalists must be given the task of "supporting" selected politicians,' the author noted. Though the season for coups passed without the feared military takeover ever occurring, the 'Democratic Revival' of Italy was well under way before Gelli's disgrace in 1981.[27]

Given its membership and the political project it pursued, it seems clear that the true function of P2 was that of an anti-communist security organization, operating to prevent the PCI from achieving power in Italy and to reduce its influence in the country. Gelli himself did not quarrel with this definition when I spoke to him. Until 1976 a number of its members played a leading role in a succession of right-wing coup plots, though opinion was divided over whether the coup should really be enacted or whether the mere threat of it would be enough to shift the political centre of gravity to the right.

Over the years various judicial investigations have uncovered evidence linking P2 to right-wing terrorism. One of the earliest, the investigation into the bombing of the Italicus express train on 4 August 1974, in which twelve people were killed and 105 injured, concluded that the P2 lodge was at the time 'a powerful arsenal containing the most dangerous instruments of political and moral subversion and as such in irrefutable contrast with the professed statutory aims of the institution'.[28] The Bologna assize court acquitted the defendants for lack of evidence but it put on record the opinion of the injured parties that the accused had been 'inspired, armed and financed by freemasonry, which made use of subversion and right-wing terrorism in the framework of the so-called "strategy of tension" to create the conditions for a possible *coup d'état*.' The verdict stated that the implication of P2 in the crime had met with 'grave and alarming corroboration', despite the fact that the evidence was insufficient to secure a conviction. It also noted that P2 showed 'evident leanings towards coup plotting' and had financed right-wing parliamentarians and youths belonging to rightist extra-parliamentary groups.

In December 1987 a Florence assize court sentenced Gelli to eight years' imprisonment for financing an armed band, whose activities included planting bombs on railway lines in Tuscany between 1973 and 1975. The court found him guilty of making a payment of 18 million Lire (£11,000) to Augusto Cauchi, the co-ordinator of 'black' terrorism in Tuscany, in the spring of 1974. The verdict stated that Gelli was aware that 'the money offered would be used to buy arms and explosives' and that it was likely to be used for terrorist acts 'aimed at blocking the movement to the left of the political order; he could not but be aware of that because that was his aim too and because in those years a terrorist bombing was neither an exceptional nor improbable event'. According to ex-terrorist Andrea Brogi, Cauchi told Gelli the money would be used for training and for minor bombings in the lead-up to that year's referendum on divorce, which was expected to result in a victory for the left. Cauchi's group feared that the defeat of the Christian Democrats by a vote for the retention of the divorce law would be followed by a further victory of the left in subsequent general elections. 'In practice we would have become partisans in reverse and would have taken to the hills,' Brogi explained. He said that Gelli agreed to make the payment provided a representative of the *carabinieri* was present at the handover and that the money was used exclusively for the purposes Cauchi had indicated to him. The surprising insistence that a member of the paramilitary police should act as guarantor for the transaction is less strange when one remembers the frequent collusion between members of the armed forces and right-wing terrorists and coup plotters.

In July 1988 Gelli was convicted of aggravated calumny at the Bologna bomb trial and sentenced to ten years' imprisonment. The unusually harsh sentence was because Gelli was held to have been involved in an attempt to disrupt the investigations by fabricating evidence against innocent people. The court acquitted him for lack of evidence on charges of subversive conspiracy. Since Switzerland has refused to extradite him for these 'political' offences, the sentences remain a dead letter. On 15 September 1987, Gelli brought to an end a period of six years on the run in South America by giving himself up to the Swiss authorities. He had previously been arrested in Switzerland in 1982 for using a false passport but had avoided extradition to Italy then by his timely escape from Champ-Dollon prison on 10 August 1983. Though he cannot be tried for terrorism-related crimes, the Swiss did agree to extradite him to face charges of calumny against two Milan magistrates and for his alleged involvement in the fraudulent bankruptcy of the Banco Ambrosiano. He was finally extradited to Italy on 17 February 1988, and released on grounds of ill health a mere seven weeks later. Since then, his role as invalid and victim of judicial persecution has not prevented him from travelling freely within Italy, accompanied everywhere by a police escort, and reviving many of his old political and business contacts. His decision to return to Italy via Switzerland was clearly taken on excellent legal advice and effectively protects him from prosecution for the most serious crimes of which he has been accused. The Italian Justice Ministry has shown no particular eagerness to see him tried for his political crimes, repeating its extradition request to Switzerland in terms it already knew were inadmissible under Swiss law.

More recently, the courts appear to have been working diligently to rehabilitate the P2 boss. In July 1990 Gelli was acquitted of calumny in connection with the 1980 station bombing by a Bologna appeal court. Later the same year, in October, the Court of Cassation ruled that Gelli could not be tried for financing the Tuscan railway line bombings because the Swiss had not granted his extradition for that offence. Nevertheless, the court decided that Gelli was entitled to a fresh trial in order to give him the opportunity to prove his innocence. Effectively, the new trial could reach only one verdict: Gelli's innocence. At the end of the day, the only defendant to be found guilty, and sentenced to eight years' imprisonment, was Gelli's accuser, Andrea Brogi. This extraordinary state of affairs was the result of much complex legal argument concerning the terms of various extradition treaties, but anyone believing Gelli to enjoy the protection of very powerful friends could only have their suspicions reinforced by the verdict.

Notes

1 'Il Complotto di Gelli', *L'Espresso* Special Supplement, 20 May, 1984, p. 37.
2 *Relazione della Commissione Parlamentare d'Inchiesta Sulla Loggia P2* (Report of the P2 Commission), Rome, 1984, p. 154.
3 Giuseppe De Lutiis, *Storia dei Servizi Segreti in Italia*, Editori Riuniti, Rome, 1984, p. 180.
4 Gianfranco Piazzesi, *Gelli*, Garzanti, Milan, 1983, p. 74.
5 Ibid., p. 266.
6 'Il Memoriale Gelli', *L'Espresso* Special Supplement, 10 June 1984, p. 15.
7 P2 Commission, *Allegati alla Relazione*, Vol. 3, Tome 2, Rome, 1984, pp. 74–88.
8 Ibid., p. 90.
9 Ibid., p. 119.
10 Report of the P2 Commission, p. 63.
11 P2 Commission, *Allegati alla Relazione*, Vol. 3, Tome 2, Rome 1984, pp. 312–13.
12 Report of the P2 Commission, pp. 64–71.
13 Quoted in Pietro Calderoni (ed.), *Servizi Segreti*, Tullio Pironti, Naples, 1986, p. XI.
14 Gianfranco Piazzesi, op. cit., p. 212.
15 Ibid., p. 214.
16 Antonio Bellocchio to the author, 1984.
17 Licio Gelli to the author, 27 June 1989.
18 P2 Commission, *Allegati alla Relazione*, Vol. 3, Tome 2, Rome, 1984, pp. 134–5.
19 Giuseppe D'Alema, in *La Resistibile Ascesa della P2*, De Donato, Bari, 1983, p. 54.
20 Report of the P2 Commission, p.11.
21 Ibid., p. 13.
22 Ibid., p. 77.

23 Ibid., p. 80.

24 Gianni Rossi and Francesco Lombrassa, *In Nome della Loggia*, Napoleone, Rome, 1981, p. 44.

25 P2 Commission, *Allegati alla Relazione*, Vol. 3, Tome 1, Rome, 1984, pp. 456–60.

26 P2 Commission, *Allegati alla Relazione*, Vol. 1, Tome 1, Rome, 1984, p. 136.

27 P2 Commission, *Allegati alla Relazione*, Vol. 7, Tome 1, Rome, 1987, pp. 187–207.

28 Report of the P2 Commission, p. 93.

[4]

GELLI AND AMERICA

THERE is much evidence that Gelli, like numerous of his P2 colleagues, enjoyed the complete confidence of the United States intelligence establishment. He attended the inaugural ceremonies of Presidents Ford, Carter and Reagan, and was, as General Giuseppe Santovito, head of military intelligence in the late 1970s and a fellow lodge member, told the P2 Commission, 'the only Italian invited to Reagan's inaugural lunch'.[1] According to his own account, he was seated in the front row for at least two of the ceremonies. There is not a great deal of information available, however, as to who Gelli's contacts in the United States were. One of them was Philip Guarino, an Italo-American ex-priest who in 1979 was director of the Senior Citizens Division of the Republican Party National Committee, and who had been introduced to Gelli by Michele Sindona. In a letter to Guarino dated 28 August 1979, Gelli wrote: 'I would also like you to let me know as urgently as possible whether the candidate you support is General Alexander Haig: as you know, we are able to help both through the Italian press, to influence Italo-Americans and Italians resident in your country, and through other channels, as well as economically.'[2] The letter could perhaps throw light on the minutes of a Pike Committee hearing of 14 July 1975. '(State Department official) said that one of the problems he had in dealing with (deleted [Italian]) affairs is that people like (international businessman) have excellent access to higher echelons of our government and there was no way of knowing their information input. He said that (international businessman) had very good relations with (deleted) of the White House. (The international businessman conducted foreign fund-raising activities for a US political party.)'³ Of course the 'businessman' could equally well be Michele Sindona or somebody quite different. However, it does appear that the United States authorities have reason to be embarrassed about their relationship with Gelli. A spokesman at the US embassy in Rome told me that the subject was 'too delicate' when I requested 'information on contacts between Licio Gelli and the US government or US individuals', in 1988.

Gelli's collaboration with American intelligence, as we have seen, dates back to the end of the war, when he worked for the Counter Intelligence Corps of the US Fifth Army. At about the same time, in Germany, US Army Intelligence was enlisting the services of Nazi war criminal Klaus Barbie. After the partisans had handed Gelli over to the Americans, he was held for a fortnight in the Pistoia region before being moved to the tiny island of Maddalena off the north coast of Sardinia. 'They gave me 10 Lire and a kilo of bread a day for my family,' he told me. But why? 'I don't know.' Could he be useful to them? 'I think so, but they never asked me anything. I have always had a great admiration for the Americans.'

A number of people have testified to the existence of political links between Gelli and the Americans in subsequent years, a subject about which he is not himself forthcoming. Some accounts might appear implausible if they were not made less so by the overall context of Gelli's relationship with the United States. P2 member Arrigo Molinari told magistrates that, following communist advances at regional elections in 1975, Gelli had attended a meeting at the US embassy in Rome between representatives of the American and Italian secret services, and multinational companies, to discuss ways of halting the communist electoral surge. It was decided to make money available to buy control of the press and use it for propaganda purposes. According to Molinari, the money was collected and deposited in the Banco Ambrosiano but when the PCI vote fell back the following year, the funds were returned to their original contributors. He said the source of this information was Professor Lorenzo Acquarone, a P2 member and former head of the law faculty at Genoa University. Molinari, an official in the Genoa police, claimed that he had joined P2 on the orders of his superiors in order to investigate possible links between the secret lodge and the Red Brigades. His testimony was first published in L'Espresso magazine (3 June 1984) and was commented on by US Ambassador Maxwell Rabb in a now declassified cable to the State Department. Rabb opened his report by informing the Secretary of State that *L'Espresso* was carrying a story 'which purports to link the US embassy in Rome to Licio Gelli and the financing of the P2 masonic lodge' and went on to observe that the story was 'far-fetched and has aroused little interest here'. The embassy cable summarized Molinari's central allegations and then commented on some of his other claims:' "Gelli and his friends" were invited to a number of US presidential inaugurations (which ones were not specified by Molinari).' Despite Rabb's disparaging parenthetical comment, this is now an established fact and should have been known to the ambassador at the time. 'Gelli and his associate, Umberto Ortolani, "introduced" current Italian Foreign Minister Giulio Andreotti to US and Argentine presidential circles. Though it is not explained why Andreotti would have required Gelli's help to make such contacts.' Again Rabb sought to minimize Molinari's claim but Gelli's close relationship with Argentine President Juan Peron is another well established fact and the ambassador was presumably aware of whatever relationship existed between Gelli and 'US presidential circles'. The cable ended by dismissing Molinari's story as 'confused and contradictory. It lacks dates and specifics with regard to most of the alleged events he describes and appears to have been discounted by most serious journalists here.' Rabb noted, with obvious satisfaction, that 'the embassy has received no inquiries about it'. But most telling of all was his final comment: 'The embassy has no record of contacts with either Molinari or Acquarone.' The ambassador denied the existence of contacts with the author of the allegations or his source. He did not deny the existence of contacts between the embassy and Gelli; a curious omission![4]

Another witness, prison health administrator Matteo Lex, told an examining magistrate from Bologna of a meeting held in Livorno in the autumn of 1980 to reassure P2 members in the aftermath of a lengthy interview granted by Gelli to the *Corriere della Sera* (5 October 1980) in which he discussed the activities of the lodge. A representative of Gelli 'reassured us about our cover, given that there were personalities in the lodge whose names would never emerge and he told us that the names of all P2 members were held in code by the Pentagon'. Lex also related how a colleague, a consultant psychiatrist at a military hospital in Florence, had told him that the destabilization of Italy was not the work of two groups, 'red' and 'black' terrorists, but of a single organization, working to a single purpose. His colleague had claimed that both the United States and Libya were involved in this activity. Lex said he had been introduced to Philip Guarino by Gelli and had attended a party given by Guarino in Washington, where General Vito Miceli was among the guests.[5]

There are also numerous documents alleging links between Gelli and the CIA. The journalist Marcello Coppetti handed over a series of his own handwritten notes about Gelli to magistrates in Florence. One of them read: 'P2 is the [lodge] which maintains contacts with the CIA under the cover of "international relations." '[6] In another of his notes Coppetti had scrawled, '(USA: Gelli), (British: Salvini).'[7] In a letter to two Florence magistrates following his expulsion from P2, Gelli's long-standing opponent Francesco Siniscalchi suggested that many masons 'would be able to testify to the links to the CIA (or to known members of this American espionage organization) of Messrs Salvini, Gamberini and Gelli'.[8] Even an anonymous letter sent to Examining Magistrate Luciano Violante in 1975 when he was investigating a coup plot instigated by Gelli's P2 partner Edgardo Sogno, declared that Gelli 'appeared to be linked to Allied intelligence services' since the time of the Liberation of Italy. More specifically, it added, 'he appears to be in touch with the intelligence services of the United States', and it correctly drew attention to his links with Sogno.[9] In contrast, the director of SID, Admiral Mario Casardi, replied in 1977 to a request for information about P2 from magistrates investigating the Italicus bombing by saying that his organization had 'no particular information about the P2 lodge' and 'no information about Licio Gelli as regards his membership of the lodge other than what has been widely reported in the press'.[10]

The documents confiscated from Gelli's office in 1981 serve to cast further light on the Venerable Master's contacts and interests. Among them was an index for Gelli's archive, with 426 dossiers dedicated mainly to leading Italian public figures. Other titles dealt with SID (the Italian secret service), CIA – disposition other countries, US policy, Report on international communism, Communist cells in the armed forces, Italian Communist Party, Extremist groups; many of these were based on the original Italian intelligence service files.[11] The dossiers themselves were not found but had already been safely transferred abroad. Another illuminating document is Gelli's office address book. Along with a sprinkling of admirals, generals and secret service personnel, were the names of nine politicians who had already reached cabinet rank or would do so later. Of these, three have held the office of Prime Minister: Giulio Andreotti (address, home and office telephone number), Emilio Colombo (address only), and Francesco Cossiga (telephone number only), who was elected State President in 1985. Given that the addresses and telephone numbers of important people are not easy to come by in Italy for security reasons, Gelli was clearly well connected. Another of his addresses was that of a certain Colonel Rocco Cannizzaro, to be found at the offices of the Western European Union, the political association grouping European NATO members, in Paris.

Given Gelli's familiarity with members of the Italian political and military establishment, his US and NATO contacts and the unequivocally right-wing political complexion of P2, it is significant that the disinformation practised about him has not been restricted to the Italian secret services. British intelligence also played its part. Not long after the breaking of the P2 scandal a British intelligence source was repeating the myth about Gelli's Eastern Bloc contacts to author Stephen Knight. Knight's 1983 book on freemasonry, *The Brotherhood*, relayed the NATO line: 'According to an impeccable source within British intelligence, Gelli was recruited by the KGB soon after he set about the task of building up . . . P2. Britain's intelligence service (MI6) has closely monitored P2 since its inception. It detected KGB involvement in the affair at an early stage.' Knight's informant claimed that P2 was 'a KGB-sponsored programme aimed at destabilizing Italy, weakening NATO's southern flank, sweeping the communists into power in Italy and sending resultant shock waves throughout the Western world.'[12] An eloquent 'error', assuming Knight's source really was as 'impeccable' as he claimed.

The Bologna bomb trial prosecutors cited numerous accounts of the close relationship Gelli enjoyed with many of Italy's most influential public figures. In their written indictment, they referred to the testimony of Gelli's two secretaries describing how the chairman of Fiat, Italy's most powerful industrialist, Gianni Agnelli, had presented their boss with a 'golden telephone', as a gift. They also cited the account by P2 Commission functionary Giovanni Di Ciommo of a meeting with Gelli's Rome secretary Nara Lazzerini. 'The sense of what she said was this: Gelli had such widespread connections that he was in constant and not merely superficial contact with people ranging from Agnelli to Delle Chiaie.'[13] Lazzerini was never formally interrogated by the P2 Commission. When a communist commissioner suggested that she should be, his proposal was rejected after objections from Christian Democrat Deputy Bernardo D'Arezzo pertaining to 'the witness's morality'.[14] Lazzerini had been Gelli's mistress, but it was what she might have said, rather than her sexual morality, that seems to have caused D'Arezzo's embarrassment.

An early indication of Gelli's connections with the Italian military establishment came in 1964 when the Permaflex company, of which he was a director, won a contract to supply 40,000 mattresses to all branches of the armed forces. The following year he opened a factory in Frosinone, the political fiefdom of Defence Minister Giulio Andreotti. In 1966, it was Andreotti who, as Industry Minister, recommended that Gelli should be made a *commendatore* (commander), a state honour given to outstanding figures in business and public life.

The Bologna magistrates were in no doubt as to the nature of his relationship with the secret services. 'From the trial documents the figure of Gelli emerges clearly as the "dominus" of the secret services (and not a mere "source" of information . . . as his affiliates tried to describe him in various depositions to the P2 Commission and the judiciary). He is, in fact, a "dominus" whose will cannot be questioned, given the relationship of masonic subordination to him that the official directors of the secret services had accepted from the outset.' The prosecutors wrote that Gelli 'conditioned secret service careers, indicated subjects for investigation and the line to be followed' as well as personally enjoying the protection of the intelligence service bosses, who were responsible for 'omissions, lies and the sidetracking of the most delicate terrorism investigations' in order to shield him.[15]

Gelli's relationship with the American authorities is illuminated by a curious document filed at the Bologna trial by Francesco Pazienza, a businessman and collaborator of Italian military intelligence who was accused of attempting to sidetrack the investigation into the station bombing. It is a letter from Paul Goldberger of the New York law firm Goldberger and Dubin to Gelli's Rome lawyer Maurizio Di Pietropaolo discussing ongoing negotiations with the US Justice Department aimed at securing some kind of immunity from prosecution or protection against Italian extradition requests. In the letter, dated 3 September 1985, Gelli is referred to by the pseudonym Maurice III. 'I am now in a position to obtain a written agreement with the United States Justice Department executed at the highest level which would absolutely guarantee the items which you and the client feel are required,' Goldberger wrote to his Italian colleague. 'There will be absolutely no chance of any double dealing – the agreement will be binding and enforceable in any court in the United States.' That these negotiations should even have been initiated is in itself highly significant and can only be explained by the existence of contacts between Gelli and the US authorities of a type that has never publicly emerged. Goldberger recommended that 'Maurice III' should only enter the United States on receipt of a written agreement from the government. 'All arrangements, including security, living accommodations, bail status, etc, would be made in advance so as to assure no possible inconvenience to the client,' Goldberger wrote. The letter gave the impression that the negotiations had made considerable progress. 'We are very close to concluding the matter,' Goldberger said and proposed holding an urgent meeting 'so that I can learn each of your requirements and present them to the US government and obtain further iron-clad approval.'

Pazienza, despite having collaborated over the years with various US intelligence agencies, was arrested by the FBI in the United States in March 1985 and extradited to Italy in June of the following year. But this discouraging experience should not be a cause for alarm, Goldberger told Di Pietropaolo. 'It is important that you understand that Pazienza's situation should not be looked at as [a] precedent for any situation regarding Maurice III,' the American lawyer wrote. The galling contrast between his own experience and what the letter indicated would be the likely treatment of Gelli may well go some way towards explaining why Pazienza made the document public by filing it at court. What is perhaps more likely, however, is that Pazienza knew something of the background to the negotiations and of Gelli's prior links to the Americans and wanted to drop a gentle hint about his ability to make embarrassing revelations on the subject.

The presence of senior military and secret service officers in the P2 membership lists goes a long way to defining the nature and purpose of the lodge. Other emblematic names help to take the process further. One such was that of Federico Umberto D'Amato. A Neapolitan bon viveur and sometime restaurant reviewer for *L'Espresso* magazine, D'Amato played a crucial role in determining the police response to political subversion. He has been accused in the media of fostering terrorism of both right and left but has only ever come under investigation by the judiciary for his alleged part in a relatively minor episode of illegal telephone-tapping, of which he was acquitted. He too is a man who unquestionably enjoyed the confidence of the American security services. D'Amato, like many of the people whose names appear on the list, has denied belonging to P2. Some have even gone to court to clear their names and in some instances civil tribunals have indeed decided that they did not belong to the lodge. The P2 Commission, however, concluded that the lists were authentic and that, if anything, they were incomplete.

In the summer of 1943 D'Amato contacted the Allies and became an OSS agent operating in occupied Rome, where he was responsible for winding up a spy network run by the German Air Force. For this and other achievements the Americans awarded him the Bronze Star and the congressional 'Medal of Freedom', the same award as was granted to Pope John XXIII and the first US astronauts. He joined the Italian police shortly before the end of the war and worked as a liaison officer between the police and the OSS. One of his more delicate tasks was as a member of the OSS mission which contacted Guido Leto, head of the fascist secret police, to negotiate the handover of the OVRA archives.[16] Feelers were put out to Leto in June 1944, before the war's end, and there has been speculation that the bargain that was struck may explain how Leto emerged unscathed from war crimes trials to end his career as the national director of police schools.

Like Miceli, D'Amato worked for NATO security, heading the Interior Ministry secretariat of the Atlantic Pact Security Office. He also represented the Italian security services on a NATO committee dealing with terrorism and subversion from 1960 to 1974 and was appointed head of the Interior Ministry's Office of Special Affairs in 1971. In 1968, he was the prime mover behind the creation of the Club of Berne, an association of European police chiefs providing a framework for regular meetings to co-ordinate anti-terrorist activity. Having been 'a protagonist in the battle against subversion and terrorism for thirty years', D'Amato was, according to his own curriculum vitae, 'one of the targets most exposed to the threat of attack by terrorists of all political colours'.[17] Despite these risks and despite his claims to have instigated police crackdowns on extremist organizations of every political hue, allegations that he had a less than limpid relationship with certain terrorist leaders have persisted. Secret service reports brought to light by the Catanzaro assize court[18] state that Stefano Delle Chiaie was being financed by the Rome police in 1968 and in 1975 was in contact with the Interior Ministry's Office of

Special Affairs. 'Certain of the media have often indicated that Delle Chiaie was an informant of the ex-Office of Special Affairs and in particular of Police Chief D'Amato. From our files, the individual appears generally to be considered as in contact with the aforementioned office,' a SID report, dated 24 April 1976, declared. It is even alleged that D'Amato used Delle Chiaie and his followers to daub Rome with posters attacking the soft line of the Communist Party from the standpoint of the extreme left. 'The ultra-left was created out of nothing in the Office of Special Affairs,' claim journalists Andrea Barberi and Nazareno Pagani.[19]

D'Amato was interviewed by *La Repubblica* newspaper shortly after his retirement (8 July 1984). Asked about his professional contacts with the Americans, he replied abruptly: 'Listen, I believe I have always worked in the interests and at the service of my country . . . What's more the Americans have always worked correctly here in Italy, in a correct manner according to the interests of their country, except for one period, under (Prime Minister Fernando) Tambroni.' His one quibble was that American intelligence had fed Tambroni with false information about the revolutionary intentions of the PCI in 1960. D'Amato's view of P2 was similarly reductive. Gelli, whom he admitted meeting five or six times, was 'basically a cretin'. 'Gelli's purpose in establishing this organization was not political but economic', he told the newspaper. 'Why should he have subverted institutions, planned a coup? He was doing very well as it was, scheming, making masses of money, finding people who would listen to him . . . He couldn't care less about politics.' This view contrasts starkly with the one expressed by the president of the P2 Commission, Tina Anselmi (*Corriere della Sera*, 12 April 1989). 'P2 was not a club,' Anselmi said, in an attempt to counteract Gelli's successful self-rehabilitation. 'It tried to influence and condition political life in our country, above all by acting through the secret services, which it controlled for many years.' She reminded her interviewer of the numerous military officers, politicians and magistrates who had been members of the lodge. 'These people did not attend to talk about masonic brotherhood or business. Besides, businessmen were under-represented in the lodge.'

D'Amato's coyness in admitting to no more than half a dozen meetings with Gelli caused the P2 boss some hilarity when I spoke to him. 'If he has spoken of those four or five occasions [that we met], it's obvious that he doesn't remember the others.' Gelli claimed that he had not discussed the detail of D'Amato's police work with him but had spoken of it in general terms. 'When we met for lunch or dinner, we discussed the situation in general, how these politicians could be improved, their need for a government that was, yes, democratic but with greater powers, how to provide the executive with much greater powers in order to save the republic and democracy. We never went beyond this.'

While D'Amato, according to his own account, would appear to have paid Gelli scant attention, only meeting him for the first time in 1976, studying him briefly after press allegations that he was implicated in right-wing terrorism, and taking no further action, Gelli seems to have been more conscientious in his scrutiny of the corpulent police chief. One of the files smuggled out of Italy before the police raid on Gelli's office but later obtained from Uruguay by the P2 Commission was devoted to D'Amato. 'D'A's financial holdings in Switzerland and at the Banque Morin in Paris (American payments) are very large,' Gelli's report said. It also suggested that D'Amato was himself in possession of an important private archive, which he used to describe to his friends as 'my powder keg'.

Delle Chiaie has reportedly boasted of his ability to ruin D'Amato and other Interior Ministry officials if he ever decided to talk.[20] The possibility that there may be more to D'Amato's career than meets the eye emerges from a curious exchange that began at the Bologna bomb trial in 1987. On 4 June, Francesco Pazienza, the SISMI consultant charged with subversive conspiracy, reiterated a request that the court should interrogate D'Amato. 'Federico Umberto D'Amato has been one of the CIA's men in Italy since the time of Angleton,' Pazienza said, in making his request. Like Delle Chiaie, Pazienza's defence tactic was to hint at the powerful people he might, if necessary, implicate in the affairs that had brought him to trial. A little over a month later it appeared that he had elicited a reply. D'Amato gave an interview to *Il Borghese* magazine (12 July 1987) about his long-standing friendship with James Jesus Angleton, the OSS, then CIA agent who played an important role in paving the way for the Christian Democrat victory in the 1948 elections and later rose to be CIA head of counter-espionage. D'Amato recounted a series of anecdotes about his professional association with Angleton to *Il Borghese*'s editor Mario Tedeschi, a neo-fascist ex-senator and member of P2. Among other things, he told how Angleton sought him out towards the end of 1946 to tell him that fascism was defeated and the new enemy was communism. 'I told him that I understood the new strategy perfectly: it was a historic watershed, as I had already begun to realize.' This was presumably a cryptic reference to the often unconfessable tactics with which the 'new enemy' had been fought. But the real purpose of the interview came in the final exchange. D'Amato remarked how Angleton, like any good agent, had taken his secrets with him to the grave. 'Aren't you tempted to speak out? To go beyond the stories you have told me today?' asked Tedeschi. 'D'Amato smiles. "Who knows," he says, "who knows . . ."' Those who were meant to will surely have got the message.

Despite this interview, D'Amato was still called to give evidence at the Bologna bomb trial, as Pazienza had requested. During his interrogation by the court, he was questioned in detail about his alleged contacts with Stefano Delle Chiaie. The police chief said he had never met Delle Chiaie before and that the Avanguardia Nazionale leader had never been an informer of the Office of Special Affairs. He said the rumour had been put about by SID agent Captain Antonio Labruna at the behest of his commanding officer General Gianadelio Maletti, the director of counter-espionage. 'At a certain moment, General Maletti initiated a series of operations which were directed against the Interior Ministry and against the intelligence services of the Interior Ministry, because there was a kind of dualism and rivalry as regards relations with foreign secret services,'[21] D'Amato said. His deposition reveals an extraordinary state of affairs: that competition between the military intelligence service and the Interior Ministry intelligence service was so fierce that the one was prepared to accuse the other, probably accurately, of collaborating with one of Italy's most dangerous fascist terrorists. It is significant that D'Amato attributes the conflict to rivalry over relations with foreign secret services. The foreign secret service he had in mind was the CIA, the most important Allied agency with whom the Italians had to deal.

During the session, D'Amato was questioned in detail by Pazienza's lawyer about obscure financial dealings with apparently little bearing on the subject of the trial. Presumably Pazienza was taking the opportunity to stir embarrassing memories for 'one of the CIA's men in Italy'.

In the summer of 1990 RAI1, the Christian Democrat-controlled channel of state-run Italian television, broadcast a remarkable series of allegations about Gelli's relationship with the CIA and his role in

the manipulation of Italian terrorism. The man making the allegations was Richard Brenneke, an American who claimed to have
worked for the CIA and to have first-hand knowledge of the activities
he described. The report, aired on 2 July, was the final programme in a
four-part investigation into allegations that P2 had been in some way
involved in the 1986 assassination of Swedish premier Olof Palme. It
unleashed a storm of political controversy, which was heightened
when President Cossiga wrote to Prime Minister Andreotti calling on
the government to investigate Brenneke's claims. In the event of the
allegations being unfounded, Cossiga wrote, legal action should be
taken against those responsible for their dissemination. It was not
clear from the President's letter which outcome he thought most
likely, or most desirable.

In the television interview Brenneke, a balding forty-eight-year-old
who runs a property management company in Lake Oswego, Oregon,
and who claims to have worked on covert operations for the CIA,
Mossad and the US Customs, said that he had first come into contact
with P2 in 1969 and that he had been personally involved in making
payments to the lodge on behalf of the CIA. The amount varied, at
times, from $1 million to more than $10 million a month. The money,
Brenneke claimed, had been used to finance drug trafficking and
terrorism. 'We used them to create a situation that would favour the
outbreak of terrorism in Italy and in other European countries in the
early seventies. These were very important activities, since certain
governments fell as a result of them,' Brenneke told the interviewer.
The American said he had worked for the CIA on a contract basis and
that Gelli did likewise. He claimed he had met the P2 boss on a number
of occasions, including one, in Colorado, when Gelli was a fugitive
from Italian justice. Brenneke also said he was aware of the existence
of an operational link between P2 and the American Mafia.

Gelli issued a swift and indignant denial, announcing through his
lawyer on 9 July that he would be seeking 'purely symbolic' damages
from RAI of 10 billion Lire (£5 million). The charges, Gelli said, were
'unfounded, crazy and highly defamatory'. Even the CIA was moved
to issue a formal denial that Brenneke 'was ever an agent of the CIA or
associated in any way with the CIA'. 'We repeat this public denial
because of the outrageous nature of his claims,' the aptly named CIA
spokesman Peter Earnest told American news agencies. 'Allegations
attributed to him regarding Agency involvement in terrorist activities
in Italy or the Palme assassination are absolute nonsense.'[22] Only a

month earlier, however, as we shall see, a court in Portland, Oregon, had chosen to believe Brenneke's claims that he had worked for the Agency rather than official assurances that he had not.

Gelli himself appears not to have been unduly put out at the idea that people might believe Brenneke's claims, at least to judge by the curious wording of some of his later denials. 'This Mr Brenneke, of whose existence I was unaware until now, must be a sleepwalker or a dreamer,' he told *L'Europeo* magazine (4 August 1990). 'However, I cannot refrain from pointing out the stupidity of making such statements. If he really had been a CIA agent he should know that certain revelations are forbidden. And if they were false, it would be forbidden even to think them.' Did Gelli mean to imply that Brenneke's claims were actually true? A similar impression might be gained from his statement to another news magazine at about the same time (*Panorama*, 5 August 1990). 'I'm a friend of the current President, George Bush. I met him in 1981, at Reagan's inauguration. We saw one another for an entire week . . .' Gelli was careful not to date his acquaintance with Bush any earlier, particularly not as far back as 1976, when Bush was himself director of the CIA. But what could the two men, who had only just met, have discussed for an entire week? It was certainly a bizarre choice on Gelli's part to claim such intimacy with Bush, especially as Brenneke had made extremely damaging allegations about the President and had linked him, in the process, to Gelli.

In the course of the television interview, and on other occasions, Brenneke had alleged that Bush had taken part in secret negotiations with representatives of the Khomeini regime to delay the release of the fifty-two US hostages then being held in Teheran until after the US presidential elections. According to Brenneke's claim, the Republican Party was worried that if President Carter succeeded in obtaining the release of the hostages before the vote it might be enough to win him a second term in office. Brenneke said that Bush, then vice-presidential candidate, campaign director William Casey who was later appointed director of the CIA by President Reagan, and CIA officer Donald Gregg attended a secret meeting in Paris at which the Iranians were promised arms in return for delaying the release of the hostages. Gelli too, Brenneke said, had attended the meetings.

The American hostages were released on 20 January 1981, the day of President Reagan's inauguration. Shortly afterwards the US began clandestinely supplying arms to Iran, in some cases with the assistance of Israel. These same secret supply channels would be used in later years in what became known as the Iran-Contra scandal, which involved the diversion of profits from arms sales to Iran to finance the anti-Sandinista rebels in Nicaragua, in order to get round a Congressional ban on such aid.

Brenneke had made similar allegations in a US court while giving evidence on behalf of a friend who also claimed to have worked for the CIA. As a result he had himself been taken to court, charged with five counts of lying under oath. A jury in Portland, Oregon, acquitted him on all five counts without a single dissenting vote in May 1990. 'It was 100 per cent,' jury foreman Mark Kristoff told journalists after the trial. 'There never was a guilty vote.'[23] Kristoff told a local reporter: 'We were convinced that, yes, there was a meeting, and he was there and the people listed on the indictment were there.'[24] Donald Gregg's personal credibility emerged somewhat tattered from the trial. He told the court that he could not have attended the secret Paris meeting because he was on holiday in Delaware at the time and produced photographs to prove it. Gregg, who became Vice-President Bush's national security adviser in 1981 and was later appointed ambassador to South Korea, was discomfited when Brenneke called up a meteorologist who testified that the photos could not have been taken in Delaware on the day in question because the weather was different (*Economist*, 12 May 1990). Brenneke's contention has also received support from former President Jimmy Carter. 'I chose to ignore the reports of backstairs deals by Reagan campaign officials,' he wrote in 1988 to two American journalists investigating the affair. He said he had subsequently learned from former Iranian President Bani Sadr that 'an agreement was made involving McFarlane, George Bush and, perhaps, Bill Casey. By this time the elections were over and the results would not be changed.' (*Wall Street Journal*, 20 October 1988.)

Brenneke elaborated on his allegations about CIA/P2 involvement in the destabilization of Italy in a number of interviews with Italian news magazines. He described P2 as a 'parallel NATO structure' dependent on Italian but above all American organizations and 'leading the attack on the political opposition'. He said the CIA at times made use of apparently hostile forces in order to prosecute its own campaigns. 'There are former CIA agents in prison accused of having trained terrorists in Libya, some of whom were active in your country [Italy]. The CIA has denied these agents ever officially belonged to the Agency, but you shouldn't be taken in: this is their classic *modus operandi*. Ostensibly hostile entities, such as Libya, are used to set up operations that cannot be traced back to their true originator.' (*L'Europeo*, 9 November 1990.) On another occasion Brenneke was asked whether he thought Eastern Bloc secret services had been aware of this CIA activity. 'Not to begin with. We duped them and used them. All the arms and supplies came from the countries of the Socialist Bloc. Then around 1980 they realized but they didn't intervene. It is possible that we were given a free hand as a result of a very high level agreement.' (*L'Europeo*, 18 August 1990.) A sensitive use of East Bloc weapons by the Italian secret services in the context of NATO security policy has recently been made public in Italy. Brenneke has supplied convincing evidence that he was personally involved in acquiring arms from Czechoslovakia. His suggestion that the destabilization of Italy may have taken place within the framework of informal secret service accords between the superpowers has been put forward by other informed sources, as we shall see.

In one of the magazine interviews Brenneke claimed that the CIA had used Michele Sindona's Banca Privata Finanziaria to channel funds into Italy. This assertion was supported by another witness interviewed in the course of the RAI television investigation. The man, who also claimed to have worked for the CIA over many years, was not identified by name and his face was concealed from view. He was later identified as Ibrahim Razin but is said to use numerous aliases, including Oswald LeWinter and George Cave. According to one account he was at one time the CIA's number two man in Europe. During the interview, which focused mainly on the background to the Palme assassination, Razin stated categorically that Sindona had been a CIA 'asset', or unpaid collaborator, over many years. In another interview, with the left-wing Italian magazine *Avvenimenti* (5 September 1990), Razin backed up Brenneke's claim to have financed P2 on behalf of the CIA. He said he knew that P2 had passed on part of the money to terrorist groups. 'It all served to increase the "red peril" and so to keep the communists out of government,' he said.

It is unwise to trust too blindly the word of anyone emerging from the shadowy world of secret intelligence and, at first sight, Razin and Brenneke appear to have spun a number of particularly fantastic tales. However, Brenneke's claims about P2 do fit into a plausible overall pattern of evidence. For the first time, someone claiming to have detailed first-hand knowledge of the relationship between P2 and the

CIA has decided to speak out. The CIA itself recently did its bit to bolster Brenneke's credibility. The Agency turned down a Freedom of Information Act request for documents about Gelli made by an American journalist in order to protect national defence and foreign policy interests as well as the Agency's own methods and sources.[25] The confirmation that Gelli had either been an asset or an agent of the CIA could hardly have been clearer.

Notes

1 P2 Commission, *Allegati alla Relazione*, Vol. 3, Tome 19, Rome, 1984, p. 679.
2 P2 Commission, *Allegati alla Relazione*, Vol. 1, Tome 2, Rome, 1984, p. 1102.
3 Report of the Pike Committee, in *Village Voice*, 20 February 1976.
4 Telegram from US Embassy, Rome, to State Department, No.013974, 'Italian weekly ties US embassy to P2', May 1984.
5 P2 Commission, *Allegati alla Relazione*, Vol. 7, Tome 20, Rome, 1987, pp. 535–8.
6 P2 Commission, *Allegati alla Relazione*, Vol. 7, Tome 18, Rome, 1987, p. 850.
7 Ibid., p. 1090.
8 Ibid., p. 978.
9 P2 Commission, *Allegati alla Relazione*, Vol. 3, Tome 3, Rome, 1984, p. 92.
10 Report of the P2 Commission, p. 75.
11 *Il Mondo* Special Supplement, 7 August 1981, p. 43.
12 Stephen Knight, *The Brotherhood*, Granada, London, 1983, p. 281.
13 Quoted in Pietro Calderoni, op. cit., p. 160.
14 Ibid., p. 161.
15 Ibid., pp. 125–30.
16 Umberto Cecchi, *Storia della P2*, Editori Riuniti, Rome, 1985, p. 41.
17 P2 Commission, *Allegati alla Relazione*, Vol. 7, Tome 22, Rome, 1987, pp. 527–8
18 Quoted in Gianni Flamini, *Il Partito del Golpe*, Vol. 4, Tome 1, Bovolenta, Ferrara, 1985, pp. 180–1.
19 Andrea Barberi and Nazareno Pagani, in *L'Italia della P2*, Mondadori, Milan, 1981, p. 80.
20 Norberto Valentini, *La Notte della Madonna*, Le Monde, Rome, 1978, p. 22.
21 Federico Umberto D'Amato to Bologna assize court, 19 October 1987, p. 58.

22 UPI, Rome, 23 July 1990, 'National furore mounts over television allegations linking the CIA with Italian terrorism.'

23 AP, Portland, 5 June 1990, 'Jury foreman says he never doubted Brenneke's innocence.'

24 *Willamette Week*, 10–16 May 1990, 'A question of treason.'

25 *La Repubblica*, 21 October 1990.

[5]

MINO PECORELLI

FURTHER light is cast on Gelli, and much else besides, by the writings of an unusual journalist, Mino Pecorelli, the editor of a scurrilous magazine called *Osservatore Politico* (Political Observer) and known by its initials, *OP*. Pecorelli began his career as a lawyer specializing in commercial work but he soon moved on to work in a very special kind of journalism, using inside knowledge of business and political scandals to write blackmailing articles couched in an allusive, hermetic style that could often only be understood by the inner circles of power or the person directly concerned. For those wishing to broadcast the blackmailing messages, *OP*, and a clutch of other publications like it, were viewed as 'taxis': you paid their fee and they took you wherever you wanted to go. Pecorelli's first job in journalism was for the magazine *Mondo d'Oggi* (Today's World), whose editor, Paolo Senise, was the son of the fascist regime's chief of police, Carmine Senise. Also on the staff was Nino Pulejo, who helped to hide the fascist Prince Valerio Borghese from the partisans at the end of the war as a favour to James Angleton, then director of the OSS in Italy. For a while, Pecorelli was flanked as editor of *OP* by Nicola Falde, a 'former' officer in military intelligence, was subsidised by SID, and ran a bitter campaign against the secret service clique headed by General Gianadelio Maletti on behalf of Maletti's boss and personal enemy, SID director General Vito Miceli. The rivalry within SID itself was just as intense as that between Maletti and D'Amato.

One of Pecorelli's early techniques for extracting payment, as explained to the P2 Commission by Federico D'Amato, was to show his intended victim an advance copy of his article. Pecorelli would explain that he would be forced to publish the story unless the subject could help the magazine out of a financial hole by agreeing to buy a painting from him, at a suitable price. 'It would appear not as a case of corruption but as the purchase of a painting. Thus the matter could be more or less resolved,' D'Amato told the commissioners.

One of Pecorelli's more spectacular unpublished scoops was entitled 'The Prime Minister's Cheques' and was to be put on the front page with a photo of then Prime Minister Giulio Andreotti to illustrate it. According to testimony to Rome magistrates by one of Pecorelli's journalists, Renato Corsini, the article contained proof of the existence of a financial relationship between Andreotti and Guido Giannettini.[1] Given that Giannettini had been implicated in the Piazza Fontana bombing and in the secret service manipulation of terrorism, Andreotti might well have preferred to buy one of Pecorelli's paintings rather than see such a relationship publicized. A close aide of Andreotti, Franco Evangelisti, received a copy of the prospective magazine cover through the post and subsequently prevailed upon a Rome property developer, Gaetano Caltagirone, to pay Pecorelli 30 million Lire (£20,000) in order to prevent publication.[2]

Andreotti was a popular target for Pecorelli's literary barbs. In one brief article he drew attention to the Christian Democrat politician's friendship with Michele Sindona by mixing up the two men's names. 'The well-known financier Michele Andreotti has decided he will soon move, lock, stock and barrel, to an unspecified locality abroad,' Pecorelli wrote, at a time when Sindona's financial empire was running into trouble. 'Meanwhile, Deputy Giulio Sindona is expected to return to Italy before Christmas.' (*OP*, 17 December 1974.)

On 2 January 1979, Pecorelli turned his attention to Gelli, publishing an article about him entitled 'Twice a Partisan', in which he apparently set out to dismantle media accusations about the Venerable Master's right-wing leanings. He began by pillorying the view expressed in four national newspapers that Italian freemasonry was 'nothing less than a tool of the perfidious CIA'. 'Businessmen, financiers, politicians, generals and magistrates, by swearing allegiance to freemasonry would appear to have put themselves at the service of the US intelligence agency, in order to prevent the PCI from entering the sanctuary of power. How absurd this theory is can easily be said.' He then recapitulated the media charges that Gelli was 'an ex-Nazi, agent of the Argentine secret service, personal friend of Lopez Rega and founder of the AAA death squads in Latin America, linked to the CIA, to [John] Connally and to the American hawks.' Having summed up the accusations against Gelli with rather more force and concision than the mainstream media, he then went on to rebut them by publishing anecdotes about Gelli's collaboration with the partisans and a copy of the document signed by communist Resistance leader Italo Carobbi to attest this. 'So it is not a fascist, pro-American and coup-plotting Gelli that emerges but a Venerable Master who is a sincere democrat and ex-partisan,' Pecorelli wrote and concluded with a dig at Gelli's well-known 'relationship with the People's Republic of Ceausescu'. It is, however, by no means clear whether Pecorelli expected Gelli to be more embarrassed about the revelation of his apparent left-wing contacts or at the eloquent summary of his right-wing associations. A favourite Pecorelli technique, and popular pastime of the Italian secret services, was to reveal an awkward truth and then scoff at it as though it were untrue.

On 20 February 1979, Pecorelli published another article in which he claimed to have been passed a copy of the Cominform report by a secret service officer, Lieutenant Colonel Antonio Viezzer. He even gave a secret service index number for the document. 'It's a long list of names that someone one day betrayed,' he wrote but promised that 'we will not betray them a second time. Because it is not our custom to reveal state secrets (and this certainly seems to be one).' The list Pecorelli was referring to was that containing the names of fifty-six fascists betrayed to the police by Gelli at the end of the war. However, Cominform was not the title of that document but was the name given to the secret service report detailing Gelli's alleged spying for the communists. Pecorelli's intention was, presumably, to let Gelli know that he had that too.

On 20 March 1979, Pecorelli was shot dead as he got into his car in the street below his office in a professionally executed, Mafia-style killing. His diary showed that he had an appointment for 'dinner Licio' on the following evening. He had so many potential enemies, though, that his killer and those behind his death have never been identified. For what it's worth, Gelli himself has suggested that the murder has not been investigated as seriously as it should have been. 'I don't think the police were really interested in clearing up the crime,' he told me. 'If I had been investigating it, I would have gone through all the back numbers of the magazine for the previous two years.' From the sound of it, Gelli clearly had his own idea of who, other than himself, might have been behind the murder.

An interesting light has been shed on the background to Pecorelli's assassination by the testimony of Angelo Izzo, a right-winger serving a life sentence for rape and murder. In 1975 he and two friends raped and tortured two girls in a villa at the beach resort of San Felice Circeo. Afterwards they dumped their bodies in the boot of a car abandoned in a Rome street. Only one of the girls survived the ordeal and the crime provoked great public outrage at the time. During his detention, Izzo was taken into the confidence of numerous imprisoned right-wingers and later passed on what he had learned to the authorities. In 1986 he told Bologna magistrates that Valerio Fioravanti, a right-wing terrorist who had been a television soap opera star as a child, had admitted to him that he was responsible for Pecorelli's murder as well as the 1980 assassination of Piersanti Mattarella, a Christian Democrat politician from Sicily who was shot dead in a Palermo street.

At the origin of this discovery was the tension that existed in prison between Fioravanti and another rightist, Roberto Nistri, both of whom were friends of Izzo's. Nistri explained to Izzo: 'We don't want Valerio in here because he's a killer for P2.' 'This seemed to me incredible, but Nistri added that they knew for certain that Valerio was responsible for the Pecorelli and Mattarella murders as well as for the murder of several French bankers, a couple I think, although I don't know anything more about this,'[3] Izzo testified. Izzo said he had offered Fioravanti his support if the latter decided to have the matter out with Nistri. Fioravanti had refused the confrontation, suggesting instead that they might attempt to poison his accuser. At this point Izzo asked Fioravanti for an explanation and Fioravanti admitted his responsibility for the Mattarella and Pecorelli murders. At first, Izzo said, Fioravanti gave a reductive account of the murder, claiming that he had carried it out in order to do a favour for a terrorist friend and to try out some new silencers. Fioravanti then went on to describe the details of the action, saying he had shot the journalist with a silenced 7.65 calibre pistol and that he had worn an elegant white raincoat for the occasion so as not to attract attention to himself. He had another terrorist to cover him and his brother, Cristiano, waiting for them nearby in a car.

What is particularly interesting in Izzo's testimony is his claim that Fioravanti admitted to him that the murder was commissioned by Danilo Abbruciati, a leading member of the Magliana band, a Rome underworld gang with links to the Mafia, to P2 and to the Italian secret services. Abbruciati was himself in contact with Cesare Valsania, described by Izzo as 'Gelli's intermediary for his relations with the Rome underworld'.

According to a magistrate who investigated Pecorelli's murder, the journalist was shot four times. Two of the bullets came from Italian-made Fiocchi cartridges and the other two were Javelots, a rare type of French munition. 400 Javelot rounds were subsequently found in an arms deposit concealed in the basement of a Health Ministry building in Rome. The deposit was jointly controlled by Egidio Giuliani, a right-wing terrorist who developed close contacts with members of the extreme left and who appears to have enjoyed the protection of the secret services, and by the Magliana band. A link between the Magliana band and Pecorelli's murder would be highly significant since, as we shall discover, members of the band later made use of his death as the basis for a series of blackmailing messages.

The Mattarella assassination was a similarly delicate affair. Izzo told the magistrates that he had originally been told of the background to the murder by Pierluigi Concutelli, the military leader of Ordine Nuovo and a notorious 'prison murderer': a man serving a life sentence who continues to kill behind bars because he has nothing left to lose by doing so. Concutelli told him that the murder had been carried out by right-wingers but commissioned by Stefano Bontade, a powerful Mafia boss and senior freemason. 'Concutelli told me that Mattarella had fallen foul of the Mafia because, being the son of someone who had been involved in rumours and scandals, he had distinguished himself through his extreme moral rigour in order to try and clear his father's name.' In earlier testimony,[4] Izzo had said that both Concutelli and Fioravanti had told him that 'the Mafia, business circles linked to freemasonry and Roman members of the Christian Democrat faction opposed to that of Mattarella' were all interested in the elimination of the Sicilian politician. Fioravanti had also told him that the people who had commissioned the crime had been prepared to trust him with the operation because they had received assurances about him from the Magliana group.

The extreme sensitivity of the background to Mattarella's murder is also illustrated by the testimony of Fioravanti's brother. Cristiano Fioravanti told Palermo magistrates in 1986 that his brother had privately admitted responsibility for shooting Mattarella. 'If he admits that while continuing to deny his involvement in the Bologna bombing, I will deduce that he is innocent on the latter charge. But if he also denies responsibility for the Mattarella murder, which, as I have said, I know he committed, I will deduce that it is possible that he really was involved in the Bologna massacre.'[5] It is remarkable that Cristiano Fioravanti, who had previously been close to Valerio, whom he had followed into a life of terrorism, should have made up his mind to level such serious accusations against his own brother.

The word of 'repentant' terrorists should be treated with great caution. Nevertheless, it is significant that two sensitive political assassinations such as those of Mattarella and Pecorelli should be attributed to right-wingers allegedly in contact with P2 and with the Magliana band. The Rome underworld gang increasingly emerges as a sinister force operating in the spheres of terrorism and political assassination as well as in the regular criminal fields of kidnapping and drug dealing. In particular, Pecorelli's murder can be seen as persuasive confirmation of the accuracy and importance of some of the revelations he published in *OP*. We will consider them in greater detail in a later chapter.

Notes

1 P2 Commission, *Allegati alla Relazione*, Vol. 3, Tome 24, Rome, 1984, p. 442.
2 Ibid., pp. 476–7.
3 Angelo Izzo to G. I. Vito Zincani and Sergio Castaldo, 8 April 1986.
4 Angelo Izzo to P. M. Libero Mancuso, Paliano prison, 25 March 1986, p. 10.
5 Cristiano Fioravanti to G. I. Paolo Borsellino and Giovanni Miccichè, Palermo, 23 March 1986, p. 2.

[6]

THE COUP SEASON

MINO Pecorelli was in an ideal position to gain access to the most sensitive information about Italy's political scandals. As his diaries show, he was in regular contact with senior figures in the secret services, the police and Parliament. He was also a member of P2 and at one point it was proposed that lodge members should supply *OP* with any information they considered suitable for publication, so that the magazine would become a kind of masonic in-house journal. Nothing came of the suggestion and Pecorelli eventually resigned from P2 but he continued to be a prolific fount of confidential information and remained in contact with Gelli. In January 1978 he published the secret service report which was the basis for the prosecution of the participants in a 1970 coup attempt led by Prince Valerio Borghese. The operation has gone down to history as a comic-opera coup staged by naïve incompetents, which posed no real threat to the state. Nearly fifteen years after the event a Rome appeal court acquitted all the defendants and newspapers dubbed the event 'the coup that never was'. It was no mean feat on the part of the conspirators to succeed in occupying the Interior Ministry, then return peacefully to their homes, and ultimately to evade the judicial consequences of their actions. Recent revelations of Mafia involvement in the conspiracy indicate that the threat may have been more serious than the Italian public has been led to believe. The coup attempt was one of a series of right-wing conspiracies which exercised an unquestionable influence over the direction and shape of Italian politics. The secret service report was sent to the Rome public prosecutor's office in July 1974 by Giulio Andreotti, then Defence

Minister. It reveals a detailed knowledge of the conspirators' activities, some of it gathered by the secret service before and during the coup attempt and some in its immediate aftermath, and it is clear that several of the protagonists regarded members of the secret service as their trusted confidants.

The coup leader, Valerio Borghese, was a renowned Second World War naval commander who founded the right-wing Fronte Nazionale (National Front) in 1968. It was intended to be, according to the secret service report,[1] a mass anti-communist organization and it advocated a *coup d'état* to overthrow the government. Its first members were recruited from the ranks of former fascists and its first public manifestation was a meeting at the Hotel Royal in Viareggio. Borghese addressed the gathering of about 200 people on the need for a moral and political revival of the country and called for unity in the battle against communism. The organization put into effect one of the concepts discussed at the Pollio Institute conference in 1965. It was divided into two basic types of organization: overt, public groups known as Group A and a secret, military wing known as Group B, which specialized in collecting weapons, recruiting people suitable for use in 'unscrupulous' activities, and the preparation of hideouts or refuges. It was also keen to recruit personnel from the armed forces and the Ministry of the Interior.

On the night of 7 December 1970, Fronte Nazionale members from all over the country gathered in Rome for the projected coup. The enterprise was codenamed Operation Tora Tora after the Japanese attack on Pearl Harbor, which took place on the night of 7 December 1941 and which brought the United States into the Second World War. Who knows, the conspirators may have hoped that their own Tora Tora might draw the Americans into the anti-communist struggle in Italy? They were supported by Delle Chiaie's Avanguardia Nazionale and a group of nearly 200 armed forest guards who arrived in coaches from the town of Cittaducale, a couple of hours' drive from Rome. They had been promised the support of three army regiments and units from the police and *carabinieri*. They also believed they had the backing of the Air Force. The plan was to seize control of the Interior, Defence and Foreign Ministries, Parliament, and the headquarters of the state broadcasting corporation, RAI, as well as other key sites in Rome. It was also intended that Police Chief Angelo Vicari should be 'physically eliminated' and the President, Giuseppe Saragat, captured. The plan called for the arrest of left-wing political and trade union leaders, who were to be shipped to captivity on the Eolian Islands, a tiny archipelago off the north coast of Sicily, a feature reminiscent of the De Lorenzo coup project of 1964, which had included plans for the detention of left-wingers on the island of Sardinia.

One group succeeded in entering the Interior Ministry through the complicity of the police guards on duty that night; they helped themselves to weapons and sent out a lorry with a consignment of 180 machine-guns for their associates. At around midnight, however, Borghese and the coup leaders received a mysterious order telling them to call the operation off and a desperate scramble ensued to catch up with the various groups before they went into action and to recover the weapons. One of the conspirators who entered the Interior Ministry took the precaution of keeping a Beretta machine-pistol as a souvenir. The weapon would later become a useful instrument of blackmail, proving that the enterprise had indeed taken place and that the plotters had achieved a degree of success that would not have been possible without extensive official collusion. As a result, the coup leaders were forced to have a replica weapon made and to substitute it for the original in the Interior Ministry armoury. Borghese subsequently explained that the decision to call off the coup was prompted by the last-minute withdrawal of the complicity which was to have made possible the occupation of the Defence Ministry, though not everyone found his account entirely convincing. Members of Avanguardia Nazionale became suspicious as to the true intentions of some of the coup leaders, particularly when they discovered that one of the protagonists, a doctor named Salvatore Drago, was a close friend of Federico D'Amato, head of the Office of Special Affairs at the Interior Ministry. They feared that the coup might be a trap, designed to eliminate the extreme right following the example of the Greek colonels, who arrested extremists of both left and right after staging their coup in 1967. Initially, both Miceli and Interior Minister Franco Restivo denied there had ever been any penetration of the Interior Ministry building. 'None of Delle Chiaie's followers ended up in prison and this fact confirms that D'Amato must have considered it prudent not to strike against people who could have revealed the disturbing background to emerge from the investigation of the Fronte Nazionale,' the secret service report commented.

There were moments on the night of the 7th which resembled a grotesque comedy. One group from Avanguardia Nazionale set off to kidnap 'an unknown personage'. Having gone to the wrong address, they then proceeded to get stuck in the lift and were only able to get out early the next morning, returning to base empty-handed. There was, however, a more serious side to the coup, which is also brought out in the secret service report. 'The Fronte Nazionale had established long-standing links with the USA, in the person of President Nixon, and with NATO units based in Malta, for the execution of the coup,' it declared. The contact between Nixon and the conspirators, according to the report, was handled by an American named Hugh Hammond Fenwich, who worked in Italy for the Selenia arms and electronics company. Four NATO ships were on standby in Malta, ready to support the conspirators if requested, the report said.

The source of the information about the US connection was Remo Orlandini, a wealthy builder and founder member of the Fronte Nazionale. He was approached three years after the coup by a SID operative, Captain Antonio Labruna, who recorded a number of conversations with him. The candour with which Orlandini discussed the coup makes it clear that he had no doubt that he was talking to someone sympathetic to the cause: not such an unreasonable assumption in the circumstances. Labruna told him he wanted to know exactly what had gone wrong so that the same mistakes could be avoided in the future. On 12 February 1973, the two men met in a secret service office in Rome. 'Labruna: And the outside support, from abroad? Orlandini: NATO and [West] Germany. At the military level, because we don't trust the civilians. Labruna: You must tell me the names, everything, because I know a lot about the international scene. Orlandini: Look, for America there's Nixon, as well as his entourage.'[2] At another meeting in June, Orlandini told Labruna that a phone call to summon international assistance had been made, as planned, from Rome to the NATO base in Naples, to be relayed via Malta to Nixon in person but that it appeared not to have been passed on from Malta. 'The NATO fleet had already started up its engines and was ready to depart and approach us . . . whatever happened, we had it in support. That's why I tell you you don't have the slightest idea of the scale and the seriousness of the thing.'[3]

A good idea of the outlook and policies of the coup plotters can be gathered from the text of a proclamation Borghese intended to read on radio and television once the coup had gone into effect. 'The political formula which has governed us for twenty-five years and brought us to the verge of economic and moral collapse has ceased to exist,'[4] the text ran. 'The armed forces, the forces of order, the most competent and representative men in the nation are with us and we can assure you that the most dangerous enemies, to be clear, those who wanted to enslave the fatherland to the foreigner, have been rendered inoffensive.' Borghese would have gone on to tell his listeners that there would be no special laws passed but to assure the members of the armed forces that he would no longer allow them to be 'ridiculed, insulted, injured and killed with impunity'. Another document confiscated from one of the conspirators in 1974 outlined the new government's policies. These included: 'Maintenance of the present military and financial commitment to NATO and the preparation of a plan to increase Italy's contribution to the Atlantic Alliance,'[5] and the appointment of a special envoy to the United States to organize an Italian military contribution to the Vietnam war.

One of the collaborators in the coup was a major in the *carabinieri*, Salvatore Pecorella, who led a unit of sixteen paramilitary police in the abortive attempt to seize the Defence Ministry. He was also the *carabiniere* officer whose presence was requested by Gelli to witness the handover of funds to right-wing terrorist Augusto Cauchi in 1974. According to a number of accounts Gelli played an important role in the coup plot and may have been in some way responsible for the last-minute decision to call the attempt off. Paolo Aleandri, a right-wing terrorist who was too young to participate in the coup but who was in contact in later years with two of its protagonists, the brothers Fabio and Alfredo De Felice, told a Rome magistrate that Gelli provided an obligatory channel of communication to supporters of the coup among the *carabinieri*. Aleandri also reported that the De Felice brothers had named Federico D'Amato of the Interior Ministry as one of the people who 'had pledged their support for the Borghese coup and to the strategy of tension in general', adding that D'Amato was on intimate terms with Alfredo De Felice. According to Fabio De Felice, there was a theatrical element in the Borghese coup but the real essence of the project was to provoke the implementation of an emergency, anti-insurrection plan held by the *carabinieri*, in what appears to be a remarkable rerun of General De Lorenzo's 1964 coup attempt. 'Fabio De Felice told me that the author of this substantial part of the coup was Giannettini,' Aleandri said.[6] Guido Giannettini was the right-wing journalist and SID informant implicated in the 1969 Piazza Fontana bomb atrocity. He provided an important link between the secret services and certain right-wing terrorists, a role we will consider in more detail in the next chapter.

Another aspect of the coup in which Gelli was active was the subsequent manoeuvring to ensure the protagonists escaped conviction in the courts. Aleandri liaised with him on behalf of several of the coup plotters who went into hiding abroad while Gelli exercised his political influence to encourage leniency on the part of the judiciary and to foster the view that the Borghese coup was a trivial blip in the history of Italian subversion. One of the coup exiles was Filippo De Iorio, a right-wing Christian Democrat and lawyer, who had been a close collaborator of Andreotti's in the early Seventies, before the coup scandal forced him to flee abroad. De Iorio, whose name would later appear on the P2 membership list, would telephone Aleandri using the pseudonym 'Marcelli'. Aleandri, in his turn, was able to relay encouraging news from Gelli: 'He told me to tell De Iorio not to worry because they were negotiating a general solution for everyone at a political level.'[7] At the same time, Gelli set out to diminish the seriousness of the affair by discrediting witnesses such as Orlandini. He warned secret service colonel Antonio Viezzer, who joined his lodge in 1977, that Orlandini was untrustworthy, when Viezzer sought Gelli's views on the attempted coup. Gelli described Orlandini as 'unreliable, a teller of tall tales, and that is what I put in my report,' Viezzer told a Bologna assize court in 1982.[8] It is understandable that Gelli should want to discredit Orlandini given the sensitive nature of the latter's revelations to Captain Labruna.

Gelli was also dismissive of the episode when I asked him about it in 1989. He denied that there had been a coup attempt or that he had had anything to do with the order to call it off. 'That wasn't a coup. If it was anything it was just a prank. I say a prank because it started to rain and they all went home.' The P2 boss claimed he had not followed the affair as it unfolded, although he admitted to being a close friend of Valerio Borghese. Curiously, he did leave open the possibility of US involvement: 'Certainly, the Americans follow everything. Do you imagine they wouldn't have followed this? And then it was at a time when there was a serious threat, that doesn't exist today. The PCI was very well organized, it didn't want to seize power because if it had wanted to, it could have done. At that time, the Americans kept Italy under very close observation.'[9] Gelli is hardly giving anything away here, but his hints appear to be based on the logic adopted by many of the right-wing conspirators: if I am guilty then everyone is guilty, right up to the top.

The public prosecutor at the Borghese coup trial chose to remain sceptical of Orlandini's claims about US support for the plot. 'As well as revealing many circumstances which have been amply confirmed by the judicial inquiry, Orlandini has made allegations that cannot be checked. Among them are those relating to the alleged collusion between the conspirators and the President of the United States, Nixon, and the leadership of the NATO fleet in the Mediterranean. Despite the manifest implausibility and vagueness of the claim, it has been investigated, but without producing any results,' Prosecutor Claudio Vitalone, a long-standing ally of Andreotti's and later to become a Christian Democrat senator, wrote in his indictment.[10] Vitalone might have been less convinced of the 'manifest implausibility' of the US President fomenting coups in foreign countries if he had read the memoirs of CIA Director William Colby. One of Colby's reminiscences concerns the CIA's efforts to prevent Salvador Allende from achieving power in Chile and to undermine him once he was elected. 'Certainly, in Track II in 1970 it [the CIA] sought a military coup, at the direct order of President Nixon,' he wrote.[11] Vitalone gave no account of the steps that had been taken to investigate the US connection in the Borghese coup. He acknowledged that Orlandini had been found in possession of secret documents on NATO and Italian troop dispositions 'that would have aroused the envy of the highest levels of military command as well as of the most efficient espionage agencies'. But he offered no explanation as to how Orlandini might have come by them. The case against the plotters was gradually whittled away: 145 people were originally charged but only seventy-eight actually brought to trial, forty-six of whom were convicted by a Rome assize court, before the final blanket acquittals on appeal. The investigation of the US role in the coup remained open for a number of years but was eventually laid to rest without any further inquiries being carried out. And the identity of a US company based in Switzerland which allegedly financed the conspiracy was never established.

Revelations by a number of Mafia bosses in the 1980s about attempts to enlist Mafia support for the Borghese coup have added a new and sinister dimension to the 'coup that never was'. Mafia supergrass Tommaso Buscetta was the first senior member of the Sicilian crime organization to break its fearsome code of silence, known as 'omertà'. He told Palermo Examining Magistrate Giovanni Falcone in December 1984 of Borghese's attempt to obtain the armed support of the Mafia for his anti-communist coup. In exchange,

Buscetta said, Borghese offered an amnesty for imprisoned mafiosi. 'Sectors of the government parties and other institutions were ready to provide their support,' he said. Despite the enthusiastic backing of some important bosses, the project eventually foundered. 'Someone very high up wanted to know the names of all the mafiosi who were to support the Borghese operation. Many bosses were against it; it could have been extremely risky. It would have given unequivocal proof of membership of Cosa Nostra,' he said. 'Nothing was done and the coup came to nothing, partly because there were a lot of Soviet ships cruising in the Mediterranean at the time.'[12]

Buscetta's revelations received authoritative confirmation in 1986 when the powerful boss Luciano Liggio told the Reggio Calabria assize court of an approach from Buscetta to elicit his support. 'They told me that the secret services and the Americans were in favour. I told them to get lost and as a result I was given a life sentence at Bari.'[13] Liggio's account was particularly significant because Buscetta's testimony had been kept secret until then. Further confirmation came in 1987 from Antonino Calderone, the brother of a Mafia boss who participated directly in the negotiations. 'There was considerable perplexity on the part of Cosa Nostra because they actually wanted the mafiosi to wear an arm band like the other conspirators. Furthermore they wanted a list of the mafiosi who would be used. In general the thinking was to guarantee a generic support for the coup but not to get involved in practice. These proposals were put directly to my brother by Prince Junio Valerio Borghese in Rome, where they met on a single occasion,' Calderone said.[14]

According to one of the coup's participants, a small contingent of Mafia men did actually take part in the operation. 'A column of mafiosi arrived from Sicily: about twenty men,' Gaetano Lunetta told L'Espresso magazine (20 January 1989). 'They were supposed to arrest Police Chief Angelo Vicari in his home, but they went to the wrong apartment and the action failed.' Lunetta's version is reminiscent of the secret service report about a group of conspirators who intended to kidnap 'an unknown personage' but went to the wrong address and ended up getting stuck in the lift. Also, according to the secret services, Vicari was to have been 'physically eliminated', and who better for that task than a squad of twenty mafiosi?

The main purpose of Lunetta's interview with L'Espresso was an angry rebuttal of the notion that the Borghese coup had been a figment of the conspirators' imagination. 'It's ridiculous when people talk about a "presumed coup". The Borghese coup . . . really happened: with comrades from La Spezia and the Liguria region we were the absolute masters of the Interior Ministry for about two hours, and I was there; we had the keys to all the rooms, the armoury, the telephone switchboards, telegraph, radio,' Lunetta, who spent a year in prison for his involvement in the enterprise, told the magazine. He said it was a mistake to consider it an 'attempted' coup. 'The political objective of those who organized the attack was achieved: the blocking of Aldo Moro's policy, the ejection of the PCI from the area of government, guarantees of a total loyalty to the Atlantic Alliance and to the Americans. The truth is that the coup took place and was a success.'

Lunetta claimed that on the night of the coup troops were on standby to occupy key points in the city, the *carabinieri* were on alert and NATO troops based in Verona had been moved south to encircle the capital. Like Orlandini, he was convinced that it had been a serious business. His description of the preparations for the coup also lend weight to that assertion. Lunetta said he had been given a private tour of the Interior Ministry by D'Amato's friend Salvatore Drago two months before the occupation went ahead. He claimed that representatives of SID, of the *carabinieri* and of the three armed services had attended preparatory meetings to discuss the coup. Also present was 'someone who was pointed out to me as the head of the CIA in Rome, a small but very energetic man'.

An explanation for the sudden decision to call the coup off, which coincides with the accounts of both Lunetta and Orlandini, was furnished by Sandro Saccucci, one of the coup leaders, in private conversation with fellow members of the MSI. Saccucci was a former parachutist and MSI deputy whose public appearances often degenerated into bruising political affrays. It was he who was sent to head off the column of forest guards after the order to call off the coup had come through. He succeeded in halting them at Ponte Milvio, a bridge only ten minutes from the broadcasting centre they were on their way to occupy. He told one party colleague afterwards that the counterorder originated with the US State Department, which had learnt of the coup at the last minute and hastily overruled the CIA, which had already given its backing to the project. Other accounts, however, have US Ambassador Graham Martin being kept abreast of developments by Orlandini's contact, Hugh Fenwich, and it seems unlikely that Martin would have omitted to pass on this information to the

State Department. Orlandini himself claimed that the military attaché at the embassy, James Clavio, had also been monitoring the conspirators' activities and sounding out the views of Italian officers on the possibility of military intervention in the event of a political crisis. There is little doubt that the plotters were a heterogeneous and divided group. Whether the coup was called off because of second thoughts on the part of some of its leaders or because someone was tipped off that the conspirators were about to be arrested and used as scapegoats to justify a more moderate, centrist coup, remains unclear. What is clear is that the plotters believed they enjoyed the support of senior figures in the US government and that they were never disabused. It is extremely unlikely that they would have pressed ahead with the enterprise if the Americans had set their face against it. The Borghese coup cost no lives, but some of the other subversive activities of the extreme right were not so bloodless.

While Rome magistrates were investigating the Borghese coup a parallel investigation in northern Italy was uncovering the activities of the Rosa dei Venti (Compass Rose) conspiracy. According to some accounts, the organization took its name from the compass rose, the star-like shape which marks the four points of the compass and which has been adopted as the symbol of NATO. Others suggested that it was a loosely knit association linking twenty, and later more, right-wing subversive organizations. What is certain is that the Rosa dei Venti was involved in coup-plotting in the early Seventies and was financed by a number of wealthy northern industrialists. It also appears to have enjoyed the usual support of the NATO security establishment. It was in the course of the Rosa dei Venti investigation that Padua Examining Magistrate Giovanni Tamburino took the unprecedented step of arresting the head of the Italian secret service, General Vito Miceli. The Court of Cassation ruled that the case should be handled in Rome and it was subsequently combined with the Borghese investigation. The more deferential Rome magistrates reduced the charge against Miceli from conspiracy to one of aiding and abetting a conspiracy and he was eventually acquitted.

One of the principal sources of information about the Rosa dei Venti was a young right-wing trade unionist named Roberto Cavallaro. Posing as a magistrate in the military justice system Cavallaro travelled the country contacting right-wing military officers to canvass their support for a coup. His high-level contacts in the secret services were sufficient to give him unfettered access to military bases without his being exposed as a fraud. He provided a detailed account of his activities to Tamburino and to other magistrates as well as in a lengthy interview to *L'Europeo* magazine (17 October 1974). 'Italians don't know that one fine morning they could have woken up with a coup already enacted,' he told the magazine. 'They don't know that everything had been prepared a long time in advance, that the technical means were ready, that operational meetings were held with American officers, that we had the agreement of NATO headquarters, that the army had been put on alert. They don't know that the "organization" was about to implement the plan. They can't know it. I know it because I was part of that "organization", because I had been working for a long time for a change in the management of power in Italy.'

Cavallaro claimed that what he referred to as 'Organization X' conditioned and made use of a number of right-wing groups including the Rosa dei Venti. 'It was headed by the secret agencies of the state, the secret services, including foreign secret services.' He claimed that the 'organization' had a legitimate structure whose purpose was the protection of the institutions of the state and described how it became operational to respond to disturbances and to restore order. 'What happened is this: when disturbances did not occur, they were artificially created by the "organization" through its parallel groups, which are all those right-wing extremist groups (but there are also some on the extreme left, you know) currently on trial.' Cavallaro traced the origins of the 'organization' to 1964, since when 'everything that happens (from the meeting of the Pollio Institute in 1965 to the most recent events) has been along its chosen course'. He claimed that two foreign powers were informed of the imminent coup, as well as NATO headquarters. 'If I am guilty then everyone in the pyramid is guilty, right up to the summit. Otherwise we are all innocent,' he said.

Cavallaro's account is one of the most detailed ever offered of the inner workings of the strategy of tension. His claim that left-wing groups were among those which, sometimes unwittingly, worked on behalf of the 'organization' is particularly significant. His view was endorsed by Tamburino in an interview with the socialist newspaper *L'Avanti* (16 July 1978). 'What do you think of the new "face" of subversion that has replaced the political bombings? In other words the Red Brigades and (Workers') Autonomy?' the magistrate was asked. 'I believe that the hypothesis of a two-pronged assault on our institutions headed by a single organizational structure may best explain what we are experiencing at the moment,' Tamburino answered. He went on to point out how fascist violence had given way to that of the Red Brigades just at a time when left-wing parties were close to assuming a role in government. The upsurge in BR activity naturally put the PCI under extreme pressure as well as tending to discredit the party in the eyes of the public. Tamburino also drew attention to the importance of Padua as a centre of political extremism; the city had been the home base of the right-wing terrorist cell implicated in the Piazza Fontana bombing before becoming a centre of operations for the leftists of Autonomia Operaia. It remains an important military base for the strategic north-eastern sector of the country.

Arrested with Cavallaro was Lieutenant-Colonel Amos Spiazzi, who revealed to magistrates the existence of the 'Parallel SID' or 'SuperSID', an anti-communist security organization made up of military personnel and civilians, which was not the same as the secret service but which in large part coincided with it. Spiazzi's co-operation with the magistrates came to an abrupt halt after a judicial confrontation with one of his superior officers, General Antonio Alemanno. 'You must say that everything you did was done as individuals. You must not involve others,' Alemanno, head of the SID internal security office, told him.[15] Nine years later Spiazzi told the P2 Commission how he received an order on the night of the Borghese coup instructing him to mobilize troops specially selected for their political reliability and take up positions in Sesto San Giovanni, a working-class suburb of Milan and a heartland of communist electoral support. As the fully armed unit approached Milan from Cremona, where his regiment was based, Spiazzi received a second order countermanding the original one and telling him to carry out a regular training exercise.[16] The coup was off.

One of Cavallaro's revelations to Tamburino concerned the involvement in the Rosa dei Venti conspiracy of the Sicilian financier Michele Sindona. At the time, Sindona was still a respected figure in the business world and Tamburino viewed Cavallaro's allegations with considerable scepticism. In later years it would emerge that Sindona's activities had led him into contact not only with conservative business and political figures in Italy but with the Americans, the Mafia and freemasonry. It was during an investigation into Sindona's affairs that the Milan magistrates stumbled across the P2 membership lists at Gelli's office near Arezzo. Sindona was born at Patti in Sicily in 1920. He studied law at Messina University and began his business career during the war, selling agricultural produce in a lorry bought from American forces who had landed on the island in 1943. He later moved to Milan where he worked as a tax adviser to wealthy Italians and laid the foundations of his own financial empire, which would eventually straddle the Atlantic when he added the Franklin National Bank to the two Italian banks he already owned. His prestige was greatly boosted when he became a financial adviser to the Vatican, counselling the Holy See on how best to transfer its considerable investments out of Italy.

Cavallaro told Tamburino of a meeting held at a villa near Vicenza in March 1973 and attended by Sindona, an important politician, an American General Johnson and three senior officers from the Italian Navy and Air Force. He said the villa 'probably belonged to Sindona'.[17] Further information about Sindona's participation in the coup plots emerged during a confrontation between Spiazzi and Cavallaro staged in the presence of Judge Tamburino. 'Spiazzi: Sindona's name was mentioned by [Dario] Zagolin, who told me the first time I met him that the Genoa connection [several of the Rosa dei Venti's paymasters came from Genoa] went very high, right up to Sindona. It is not true however that Cavallaro talked about an alleged coup by Andreotti. Cavallaro: I confirm that both [Giuseppe] De Marchi and Spiazzi talked about it.'[18] In another deposition Cavallaro claimed that Andreotti had been planning a coup, with money from Sindona, which was aborted after some of the conspirators began to suspect his intentions. 'Spiazzi told me that the coup was abandoned because he suspected that Andreotti would have dealt a blow to the right and one to the left, seizing power without sharing it.'[19] Investigators discovered that one of the principal financial backers of the Rosa dei Venti was a Genoa-based moped manufacturer, Andrea Piaggio, who kept a large portion of his secret funds in a Swiss bank (Finabank, Lugano) owned by Sindona.[20] The secret service report published by Pecorelli records a payment by Attilio Lercari, Piaggio's administrator, of 19 million Lire (£12,000) to three of the Rosa dei Venti conspirators in June 1973. Overall, Piaggio made 200 million Lire (£130,000) available to the group. Further evidence of Sindona's involvement in coup-plotting was offered by his general manager Carlo Bordoni in an interview with Il Mondo magazine. Bordoni claimed that Sindona had financed Italian military leaders planning a coup with the backing of NATO. 'In order to understand the purpose of the coup you must remember the relationship that Sindona had established in the United States with President Richard Nixon, with the ambassador to Italy, John Volpe, . . . and above all with David Kennedy, ex-Treasury Minister and President of Fasco, Sindona's holding company,' Bordoni said.[21]

Sindona's financial empire collapsed in 1974, shortly after the Watergate scandal had forced President Nixon from office, and only a year after being publicly hailed as 'the saviour of the Lira' by Prime Minister Andreotti. Despite his bankruptcy, Sindona, who joined P2 in 1977, did not lose his taste for bizarre reactionary conspiracies. The most mysterious occurred between 2 August and 16 October 1979, when Sindona disappeared from New York, where he was awaiting trial for the collapse of the Franklin National Bank. Following his disappearance, a number of messages were sent to his Italian lawyer claiming that he had been kidnapped by a left-wing terrorist group called Giustizieri Proletari (Proletarian Avengers), who were pressuring him to reveal sensitive information about his associates in Italian business and politics. It later emerged that the kidnap was a fake and that Sindona was actually in hiding in Sicily as a guest of the Mafia. Even stranger, a number of witnesses claimed that the purpose of Sindona's visit was to organize a separatist, anti-communist coup in Sicily. According to an FBI report: 'The uprising was intended to block what the conspirators saw as the spread of communism in Sicily. Following the secession of Sicily from Italy, the island would have been offered to the United States as a location for Mediterranean naval bases.'[22] According to the witnesses the enterprise had the backing of Italian freemasons, the Mafia and the American government. Antony Caruso, one of the people who accompanied Sindona on the trip, later told *Panorama* magazine (9 March 1981): 'Sindona's lawyers intend to prove that he left the United States and went to Italy on behalf of the American government.' The ploy was not enough to enable Sindona to avoid conviction in an American court for the fraudulent bankruptcy of the Franklin National Bank and he was sentenced to twenty-five years' imprisonment.

Sindona had returned to New York from Sicily with a deliberately inflicted wound in his leg which was supposed to pass as a gunshot wound. What exactly he was doing during his absence has never been clear, other than attempting to force his influential friends to rally round with a little judicious blackmail. The Italian magistrates who first investigated the affair viewed the secessionist plan with considerable scepticism. More recently, however, Palermo magistrates have highlighted the existence of links between the Mafia and right-wing terrorism and have begun to take a more serious look at Sindona's Sicilian activities. It is possible that his political scheme was in itself an attempt to blackmail the US authorities by reference to their backing for previous coup plots in Italy. Alternatively it is possible that some kind of Sicilian uprising could have provided an excuse for a military takeover in Rome. It is extremely unlikely that anyone in the US government would have backed a separatist coup in Sicily unless the rest of Italy had already fallen to the communists. Another possible interpretation is that Sindona may have been negotiating with the Mafia for the unimpeded construction of a cruise missile base later to be sited on the island near the town of Comiso.

Sindona was extradited to Italy in 1984 and in 1986 he was sentenced to life imprisonment for having ordered the murder of Giorgio Ambrosoli, the Milan lawyer who was the court-appointed liquidator of his Italian banking empire. Sindona died on 22 March 1986, four days after the court verdict, after drinking a cup of poisoned coffee. A magistrate's inquiry ruled that he had committed suicide. On 27 September 1984, Francesco Pazienza deposited with his American lawyer a curious handwritten document entitled 'How Sindona will be eliminated'. Written before Sindona's extradition, the document speculated that if Sindona was put in a normal prison he would be murdered by his fellow prisoners, but if it was a high security prison and he was kept in isolation (as he was), he would be given a poisoned cup of coffee by one of the two branches of the Italian secret services. 'If Sindona were to die in a "clean" and sudden manner it means that the Americans have entered the game.' Pazienza claimed that only the Americans could provide the Italians with sophisticated poisons capable of killing people without leaving any suspicious traces that might be detected at an autopsy. 'The Italians don't know, or don't have the chance of using, anything more than arsenic or cyanide.' Explaining why the Americans might be interested in Sindona's demise, Pazienza claimed that Sindona had not gone to Sicily in 1979 of his own volition. He said Sindona's son, Nino, had told him in 1983 that 'his father didn't go to Sicily for pleasure but on behalf of elements in the Carter administration'.

Pazienza was right in predicting that Sindona would die by drinking poisoned coffee. According to his argument, though, it must have been the Italian secret services, rather than the Americans, who were responsible for his death: the poison used was cyanide. In actual fact, the magistrates who investigated his death found persuasive evidence that Sindona had deliberately taken his own life. He had dissolved half a gram of cyanide in a large cup of coffee, a sufficient quantity to give the drink a repellent taste and odour. He had then drained the cup to the bottom, despite the fact that the drink immediately caused a burning sensation and traces of burning were found inside his mouth. There was no way he could have failed to notice the poison and yet he persisted in drinking it all. Though these facts reduce Pazienza's apparent powers of clairvoyance, they do not diminish the interest of his document or its effectiveness as an instrument of blackmail.

Another group interested in Sindona's elimination, according to Pazienza, was the Vatican. 'It would eliminate "the other one who knows". Calvi was the other "other".' The third 'interested party' was Andreotti. In a separate document entitled Andreotti Operation OSSA, Pazienza claimed that he had been sent to New York in 1980 by General Santovito, head of military intelligence, to ensure that Sindona was not about to talk about his relationship with Andreotti. OSSA, Pazienza said, stood for Honoured Society Sindona Andreotti. During his trip to New York Pazienza had two meetings with an unnamed interlocutor who assured him that Sindona had been 'convinced' to keep quiet. In another document called 'More on the possible elimination of Sindona', Pazienza suggested that Sindona's death might make Gelli either stronger or more vulnerable. He said that Gelli had acquired part of Sindona's sensitive 'material' in 1979. 'The elimination of Sindona would make Gelli the only possible blackmailer of Roman high society on the Sindona-Vatican-DC (Christian Democrat Party)-Andreotti affairs. We shall see,' he wrote. Pazienza deposited these documents at the Bologna bomb trial with the obvious intention of incorporating blackmail in his own defence. He refused to offer the court any further elucidation of them. Sindona too had not been averse to blackmail, frequently hinting that he was in a position to make revelations capable of damaging the relationship between the United States and Italy.[23] This had not kept him out of prison, either in the United States or Italy, but that does not necessarily mean that he was only bluffing. A first-hand account of United States participation in Italian coup plots would certainly have put a strain on bilateral relations. Whatever the truth, he took the secret of it with him to the grave, leaving some of his sensitive information, as

Pazienza suggests, to be inherited by Gelli.

The relationship between Giulio Andreotti and the coup plotters and, for that matter, his relationship with Gelli, have never been fully clarified. Several witnesses have testified that Gelli frequently spoke on the phone in their presence to someone he claimed was Andreotti. There is also an often-published photograph which shows the two standing together in evening dress and beaming smiles. Andreotti stated in a 1989 interview (*Panorama*, 22 October 1989) that he had met Gelli because of the latter's role as a director of the Permaflex mattress factory in Frosinone, which would mean their acquaintance dates from 1965 at the earliest, as the factory was inaugurated in that year. According to Gelli, however, the two first met in 1958.[24] Andreotti described how he had met Gelli later, in Argentina when Juan Peron returned to power, and was amazed at the deference with which Gelli was treated by the Argentine President, an observation that supports Arrigo Molinari's assertion, examined earlier, that Gelli may have been in some way instrumental in presenting Andreotti to Peron. 'Gelli also had one of the places of honour at Reagan's inauguration eight years ago,' Andreotti told the interviewer. He then added the barbed comment: 'Subsequently something must have happened inside the clique. This is an area in which I have no competence and I have no wish to acquire it.' Surprisingly, for someone who as Defence Minister held responsibility for the secret services over many years and at a time when the secret services were, in their turn, on intimate terms with Gelli, Andreotti declared that he had no reason to think that 'Gelli was someone to avoid'.

In contrast to this somewhat lukewarm testimonial, Gelli professes the highest regard for Andreotti. 'Everyone has an idol. Some people admire film stars, others sports stars like [the soccer player Diego] Maradona. I have a great admiration for this particular politician,' the P2 boss told the author.[25] Gelli rounded off his potentially embarrassing tribute by saying: 'I consider him to be very intelligent. He is able to turn negative events into positive events, even when these concern other countries.' Gelli showed no eagerness to explain these cryptic words, merely confirming that the 'other countries' in question were Western allies. It would perhaps be fanciful to take this as a reference to the negative events of terrorism, instigated by Italy's principal Western ally, which had the positive effect of propping up centrist governments, many of them presided over by Giulio Andreotti. Gelli said he had met Andreotti 'just as much as the other politicians', a claim that suggests considerable familiarity, given the numerous witnesses who have testified to the close relations the masonic conspirator enjoyed with many of Italy's most influential political leaders.

Andreotti was too shrewd a politician to share the views of the more reactionary of the coup plotters but it is possible that he may have played along with them in order to get them to show their hand and then have them arrested, at the same time as exploiting the coup threat to condition political parties on the left. Alternatively, he may have thought that if the United States decided that a coup along the lines of the Greek colonels' was the appropriate remedy for Italy's ills it would be preferable if he were the man to administer the medicine. He was undoubtedly one of the people best placed to keep abreast of the plots, having been Defence Minister, and therefore responsible for the secret services, from 1959 to 1966 and again in 1974, a crucial year for coup projects. He was also Prime Minister for most of 1972 and half of 1973 and is not a man who could be suspected of naïvety or incompetence.

According to Paolo Aleandri, it was a common rumour among rightists that Andreotti had been considered by the Borghese coup plotters to be a kind of beacon or reference point within the political establishment.[26] General Miceli offered a non-committal comment on this delicate subject during an interrogation by Judge Tamburino in 1974. 'As for the rumours about Andreotti's leanings towards a coup, I can say that there is a literature on the subject which has not been backed up by objective proof. Anonymous documents about it were in circulation in 1972 and I believe that D'Amato was in possession of a couple of reports which were passed to me and which I sent on to the Prime Minister [that is to Andreotti.]'[27]

One of the protagonists in a campaign for constitutional change very similar to that advocated in Gelli's 'Plan for Democratic Revival' and an associate of many of the supporters of the Borghese coup and other interlocking conspiracies was Count Edgardo Sogno. Sogno advocated a Gaullist-style presidency and a government of techno-crats to tackle what he saw as the moral and economic decline of the country. He became a member of P2 in 1979. Born into an aristocratic family in Turin in 1915, Sogno had been a hero of the Resistance, working with the forces of the British Special Operations Executive and winning an American Bronze Star for his bravery during the war. As such he was an ideal leader for the anti-communist struggle, being untainted by fascist associations. After the war he became a diplomat, serving at the Italian consulate in Paris before becoming director of the NATO Planning and Co-ordinating Group in London in 1954. He returned to Paris, to the NATO Defence College, which he addressed on one occasion on 'The communist menace in Italy'. It was during the 1950s that he made his contribution to the Cold War by founding the Peace and Freedom Association (Pace e Libertà), which became a vehicle for a rabidly anti-communist propaganda campaign. He was ably assisted in this endeavour by Luigi Cavallo, a former communist journalist and secret service *agent provocateur*. In the 1960s Sogno moved to the United States, where he served in the consulate in Philadelphia and then as a counsellor at the Washington embassy, before ending up as an ambassador in Rangoon, Burma. He returned to Italy in 1970, just in time to play his part in saving the country from chaos and communism.

In 1971 he formed a Committee for Democratic Resistance to promote his constitutional reforms, which included a change to the electoral system which he hoped would halve the number of communists in Parliament. According to a secret service report, Sogno claimed to have the backing of the Agnelli family for his project. The powerful Turin industrialists had been childhood friends of the count. One well-informed account stated that Sogno received financial support from Fiat, the Turin Industrialists' Union and 'probably from Michele Sindona and the CIA'.[28] A secret service report declared that the Milan office of the United States Information Service (USIS) 'appears recently to have made a payment of 3 million Lire (£2,000) to the Peace and Freedom Association for their anti-communist struggle, which is already underway'.[29] Pace e Libertà was an offshoot of a French anti-communist organization, Paix et Liberté, which was founded in Paris by a former NATO official, Jean Paul David, and financed in part by the United States. One of the principal activities of the Italian branch was spying on Fiat workers with communist sympathies and drawing up intelligence dossiers on them. This was the work of Cavallo, who was paid for it by both Fiat and the secret service Office of Economic and Industrial Research, run by Colonel Rocca.

If Sogno's was the respectable face of the coup conspiracies, Cavallo's was decidedly less attractive. He was born in 1920, the son of an agricultural labourer, and spent part of the war in Berlin, studying German. After the war he was sent to Paris as a correspondent for the Communist Party newspaper *L'Unità*. His behaviour in Paris was, according to a secret service report, ambiguous, 'raising suspicions that he was in contact with the British and American embassies to which he appears to have supplied information on the activities of the Italian and French Communist Parties'.[30] In 1949 he was sacked by *L'Unità* and on 1 December the paper published a note informing readers that Cavallo had failed to clarify certain aspects of his past relationship with the Nazi authorities and warning party members to steer clear of him. Cavallo then moved to New York as correspondent for the *Gazzetta del Popolo*, a Christian Democrat newspaper based in Turin. He remained in the United States until 1954, when he returned to Italy to assist Sogno in the running of his anti-communist Peace and Freedom organization.

The culmination of Sogno's plans was to have been reached in August 1974 with the seizure of the presidential Quirinale Palace. President Giovanni Leone would be forced to dissolve Parliament and appoint a government of technocrats headed by Randolfo Pacciardi, another non-communist Resistance hero and a former Defence Minister. The plan was never implemented as the secret services had got wind of it but, more importantly, because there was insufficient political and military support to guarantee its success. Sogno and Cavallo were arrested in 1976 and charged with trying to overthrow the government by violent means. The nature of their project was clearly outlined in a number of documents confiscated from Cavallo. The documents stressed the corruption and incompetence of Italy's current political leaders and recommended the retroactive abolition of parliamentary immunity so that some of them could be tried for their alleged crimes. The new military government aimed to divide its potential opponents with a right-wing coup accompanied by progressive left-wing policies 'to split the anti-fascist block and eliminate the fascists from the game'. The coup itself was to be staged 'with the criteria of the Blitzkrieg; on a Saturday during the holidays, with the factories closed for another two weeks and the masses dispersed on vacation'.[31] By 1974 the project had increased in sophistication; it studiously avoided being tainted by overt association with fascism and exploited the widespread perception that many of the country's rulers were deeply corrupt, just as the Red Brigades did in later years. Other papers confiscated from Cavallo included NATO documents marked 'secret' and 'confidential', relating to the years 1952–54. Like Orlandini, he does not seem to have lacked for friends in the Atlantic

Alliance.

Sogno and the other conspirators were eventually acquitted by Rome Examining Magistrate Francesco Amato. Investigators were unable to discover the full extent of Sogno's contacts with Italian and foreign secret services because Prime Minister Aldo Moro confirmed that a number of secret service documents requested by the prosecution could not be released since they were covered by state secrecy. Moro assured the magistrates, that they 'had no bearing on the present case' but 'might cause serious harm to foreign citizens'. In reaching his verdict Amato explained that the imposition of state secrecy had prevented him from establishing whether there was any truth in the allegation that Sogno's subversive activities were carried out in association with Italian and foreign secret services. He ruled that the withholding of the evidence could not be construed as proving guilt. Before the case passed to Rome it had been rather more energetically pursued by Turin Magistrate Luciano Violante. In November 1974 Violante informed the SID authorities that he would like to question Lieutenant Colonel Giuseppe Condo, one of the secret service's prime sources of information about Sogno's coup plans. He was somewhat surprised to learn that Condo had died of a heart-attack the week before. He was forty-two.

One informed source has suggested to me that of all Italy's coup plots, Sogno's was the one with the greatest chance of success. This is perfectly believable, given Sogno's high-level US and NATO contacts. It is also likely that the decision to call off the coup was taken at the highest NATO level. Only at that level would it have been known that the Western security establishment had a subtler alternative up its sleeve. In 1974, the Red Brigades were beginning to come into their own. As we shall see, their activities would bring about, in effect, a long, slow, secret, centrist coup; Sogno's coup under a different guise.

Yet another holder of the Bronze Star and a coup plotter in contact with Sogno and with members of the Rosa dei Venti was Carlo Fumagalli. During the war Fumagalli was the leader of a non-communist partisan group operating in the mountainous Valtellina region in north-east Italy and resupplied by American parachute drops. He was wounded four times in the course of the war but his record was not entirely without blemish and showed traits that would emerge again in his later career. Many of his followers were smugglers or other common criminals, he had a tendency to dispense summary justice, and one report refers to strange weekend truces when his men would emerge to dance and fraternize with the fascists. In 1962 he formed the Movimento d'Azione Rivoluzionaria (Revolutionary Action Movement) or MAR, a latter-day partisan group which operated mainly in the Valtellina area. The group financed its political activities partly through kidnaps and dealing in stolen cars and paintings. Its political objective, like that of Sogno, was a presidential republic with a two-party system to replace the system of proportional representation that produced a proliferation of small political parties and had given Italy thirty-two governments in the preceding twenty-seven years. 'This sort of democracy, which I call parliamentary dictatorship, has led to corruption and to all the forms of moral and material degradation that afflict the nation,' Fumagalli told magistrates in Brescia in 1974. He advocated 'a rapid and bloodless coup' and though unable to achieve it himself he was prepared to give his support to others. 'There are without doubt a number of different groups preparing for a coup . . . I am certain that if one doesn't succeed, sooner or later another will,' he told the magistrates. He also spoke of American contacts who told him in 1970 that their country would never accept a coup directed by the fascists and still less by the left. 'The Americans would only support a Christian Democrat or centre coup,' he said, something that coincided 'with my own political credo and my own programme'.

Fumagalli assured the magistrates that he was opposed to the use of bombings against the civilian population in order to spark off a civil war. Instead, his group specialized in demonstrative actions, in particular the destruction of electricity pylons. Other accounts, however, call into question the sincerity of these scruples about violence. The secret service report published by Pecorelli refers to a coup planned for June 1973, which was to be sparked off by Fumagalli's group creating a situation of tension in the Valtellina area, while other groups extended it into Liguria and further south. 'The state of civil war would have forced the armed forces to intervene to assume power,' the report said. For some reason, however, the Valtellina group failed to move. According to one witness, Mauro Colli, the coup was supported by Interior Minister Paolo Taviani, deputies from the Christian Democrat and Socialist Parties and Sindona, among others. The Mafia was also interested in the change of government but 'would be eliminated once the thing was done'. Colli also maintained that Fumagalli claimed to be a CIA agent. There is considerable evidence to indicate that Fumagalli enjoyed the protection of both the Italian secret service and the police, and in particular of the Interior Ministry's Office of Special Affairs.

In one respect Fumagalli was well ahead of his time. That was in his desire to use the forces of the left to provoke the military coup. According to Alessandro D'Intino, a young right-wing extremist, Fumagalli intended to concentrate his group's attacks on communist targets so as to 'force the communists to bypass the institutions of the state, thus provoking a civil war and finally obliging the special units of the armed forces to intervene, not against the guerrilla groups but against the communists, to prevent them from seizing power'. This plan was based on contacts with army officers who promised to mobilize armoured troops in the Veneto region 'only if Fumagalli's guerrillas succeeded in getting the communists to come out into the open'. D'Intino told Brescia magistrates that Fumagalli 'counted heavily on the actions of extreme left-wing groups such as the Red Brigades' in the early stage of the conflict to get the communists fully involved.[32] The use of left-wing extremism, either to provoke a military coup or simply to discredit the Communist Party, would be the hallmark of a new and more sophisticated phase in the management of Italian terrorism.

Fumagalli appears to have been happy to work with a motley band of supporters. Among those who were to help create an atmosphere of tension in Valtellina prior to the planned 1973 coup were members of the fascist groups Avanguardia Nazionale and Ordine Nuovo, but he was also happy to collaborate with people of left-wing sympathies. According to the testimony of Francesco Piazza,[33] Fumagalli was in contact with Giangiacomo Feltrinelli and even received subsidies from the Marxist millionaire. Feltrinelli was killed in 1972 while trying to blow up an electricity pylon on the outskirts of Milan. The pylon was on land owned by Feltrinelli himself and less than 300 metres from a garage cum breaker's yard owned by Fumagalli. According to Piazza, Feltrinelli had an animated discussion with Fumagalli on the night before his death and was actually in the company of several of Fumagalli's followers and possibly even of Fumagalli himself when the accident happened. 'As I got to know him better Fumagalli spoke to me about his revolutionary programme, about the need to overthrow the system through armed violence . . . and to get all the extremist left-wing groups involved in this type of revolution,' Piazza told a Brescia magistrate. He said Fumagalli considered himself to be firmly anti-communist and anti-fascist but did not attach great importance to the political colouring of the groups involved in bringing about the revolution. This is the kind of ideological flexibility typical of the secret service *agent provocateur*. Another curious link between Fumagalli and left-wing terrorism is the claim that he instigated a Red Brigades arson attack on a Pirelli test track in Milan. The attack, on the night of 25 January 1971, was one of the Red Brigades' earliest actions and destroyed three Pirelli-owned lorries. Brescia Public Prosecutor Francesco Trovato reported that Fumagalli's henchman Gaetano Orlando boasted of being responsible for the Pirelli sabotage.

According to General Gianadelio Maletti, director of the SID counter-espionage office in the early 1970s, five coups were attempted in that period, only two of which posed a serious threat to the security of the state. In 1980 a typewritten document giving a chronology of terrorism between 1968 and 1976 was confiscated by police from Maletti's home.[34] The 1968 entry contained a postscript entitled 'The Guard Dogs'. It began by asking, 'Is Italy the master of its own destiny?' and went on to consider the role of foreign secret services in Italy, with the CIA, DIA (Defence Intelligence Agency) and FBI at the top of the list. 'To what extent do our allies have an interest in maintaining an inefficient, corrupt and therefore weak ruling class in power? . . . the "sabotage" experienced by Italy, an "awkward" industrial rival of its Western partners in the 1960s.' The final entry, for 1976, also contained, in telegraphic style, some interesting reflections on who may have been behind the strategy of tension. It opened: 'Pike Report and Church Report. Maletti [himself] and Labruna in prison. The coup plots originate a long way off (1947–48 . . .) and they go far. The hypotheses of urban guerrilla warfare . . . of the intervention of groups secretly trained by the "Parallel SID": who are the puppetmasters operating in Italy to keep the country tied to "choices" made 30 years ago?' It is unlikely that Maletti kept this document simply as an *aide-mémoire* and, given that he had followed his boss Miceli into prison for protecting right-wing extremists, he probably had a very shrewd idea of the answer to his questions. The document concluded: 'The hypothesis (which in fact is no such thing) of powerful forces operating in Italy, determining its choices and its destiny, comes again to mind. The PCI and "Eurocommunism" are a last-ditch attempt at a "national autonomy" albeit of a Marxist character: but how far can Berlinguer push it?' The answers to these questions would go a long way towards explaining the origins of the strategy of tension and Maletti was as well placed as anyone to provide them. His document is a menacing reminder of the damaging revelations he could make if he were so minded.

As Maletti's document suggested, the Pike report does indeed provide some possible answers to his questions about the strategy of tension. The House of Representatives' Select Committee on Intelligence, under the chairmanship of Otis Pike, carried out an unprecedented review of covert action undertaken by the United States in a ten-year period stretching from 1965 to 1975. What the committee found was that the activities of the American intelligence services were often incompetently managed and sometimes contrary to the United States' real interests. The committee devoted particular attention to a study of US financial assistance to centre and right-wing parties at the time of the 1972 parliamentary elections in Italy. An incomplete version of its report was leaked to the left-wing *Village Voice* newspaper in New York (20 February 1976) and to the Washington correspondent of *La Stampa*. The report found that US foreign policy lacked a long-term direction and that the government had often resorted to covert action by the CIA as a short-term solution to problems that really required long-term remedies. It found that the overall picture did not support the contention 'that covert action has been used in furtherance of any particular principle, form of government or identifiable national interest'. Particularly expensive or politically sensitive projects required review and approval by the Forty Committee, made up of elder statesmen and senior government officials. But Pike and his colleagues found that the executive branch of government 'does not have a clear definition of what constitutes a large or politically sensitive operation' and that the Forty Committee had effectively become little more than a rubber stamp.

Alarmingly for those on the receiving end of US covert operations, the committee discovered that the CIA had often 'been ordered to engage in covert action over the Agency's strong prior objections'. This appears to have been the case in the 1972 election aid to Italy. Far from the CIA running out of control, Pike wrote, it had actually been 'utterly responsive to the instructions of the President', but tended to give weak expression to its misgivings and was 'afflicted with a "can do" attitude'.

The Pike report gives a good idea of the scale of CIA financial assistance to non-communist parties in Italy, revealing that the US had shelled out more than $65 million in the twenty years from 1948 to

1968. The vast bulk of these funds went to a single party, undoubtedly the Christian Democrats. Despite this massive aid, the beneficiaries suffered repeated electoral reverses and American observers concluded that 'another "quick fix" was needed to see our clients through the next vote'. The details of the 1972 electoral assistance, reviewed in some depth by the committee, are highly revealing. Pike found that the 'US, perhaps needlessly, expended some $10 million in contributions to political parties, affiliated organizations, and twenty-one individual candidates'. The assistance began in 1970, coinciding exactly with the period of the Borghese coup, and was initiated by Ambassador Graham Martin, 'who later persuaded the assistant to the President for national security affairs [Henry Kissinger] to authorize him, rather than CIA, to select funding recipients and otherwise control the programme's implementation'. This highly unusual arrangement was, not surprisingly, unpopular with the CIA, which expected to be in control of most covert action undertaken abroad.

Interestingly, it was while the CIA and the ambassador were squabbling over who should control the funds that President Nixon was 'indirectly approached by prominent international businessmen, who were former nationals of the allied country. Their communications to the President were not available to the committee.' It is hard to escape the conclusion that these unidentified 'businessmen' may have had the final say on who ultimately got to control the funds. Ambassador Martin, 'by all accounts a man of unusual force, successfully extracted from the assistant to the President the commitment that he would have total control of the mix and implementation of the project. Thus, the ambassador, who had been in the country less than two years and did not speak the language, would determine which individuals and organizations would receive US funds.' Not surprisingly, 'The results of the aid were mixed and short-lived.' It is equally hard to avoid the suspicion that the unidentified businessmen were people of the calibre of Gelli and Sindona. As we have seen, Gelli fitted the description by a State Department official of an international businessman with 'excellent access to higher echelons' of the government, who had undertaken fund-raising abroad on behalf of the Republican Party. Sindona fits the bill equally well, being a wealthy financier, friend of Nixon's Treasury Secretary David Kennedy and ardent anti-communist. Both might understandably be described as former Italian nationals: Gelli had dual Argentine and Italian nationality and Sindona was spending ever-increasing periods of time in the United States in the run-up to his purchase of the Franklin National Bank. It would also appear that their contacts with the President were of a highly sensitive nature, given that information about them was withheld from the Pike Committee, despite the fact that the committee's report was not intended for publication.

The CIA strongly opposed Martin's running of the project, fearing that exposure would bring down the pro-Western government in Italy, a risk that the ambassador himself acknowledged. The Agency was also unhappy with Martin's choice of recipients. They advised him against giving money to SID director General Vito Miceli and warned of Miceli's links to Pino Rauti, the Ordine Nuovo founder. Miceli's own arrest for subversive conspiracy makes him a singularly unwise choice as a recipient of US funds. 'The ambassador was unmoved by CIA warnings that the man was clearly linked to anti-democratic elements of the right and went ahead with the funding.' Miceli got more than $800,000, supposedly to be used for 'a propaganda effort'. It is difficult not to see the phrase 'propaganda effort' as a euphemism for 'subversive conspiracy'.

The row between the Rome CIA station chief and Martin at times reached comic levels. A cable from the station chief to CIA headquarters at Langley, Virginia, dated 11 February 1970, gives a good idea of the tension between the two. 'Chief of station expressed the view that ambassador [deleted] should first clarify this point in personal exchange with CIA . . . He [ambassador] thereupon accused chief of station of dragging his feet in contacting [foreign intelligence officer (presumably Miceli)] and said if this continued beyond today he would "Instruct Marine guards not to let you in this building and put you on the airplane." Chief of station said he thought this a bit extreme and expressed view that ambassador [deleted] could hardly object to what appeared legitimate Headquarters question. He did object and with vigour.'

The CIA is not an organization noted for its squeamishness but it seems clear that its opposition to Martin's running of the covert action programme in Italy went beyond mere irritation at seeing its own role pre-empted and involved deep-rooted anxieties about the way in which the money was being used. Another cable from the station chief to Langley on 11 February voiced these worries. 'Ambassador [deleted] insists that unless he proceeds quickly "certain people" will push the White House into a disastrous programme. The name of [an international businessman who contacted the White House] finally emerged. If you think the [right-wing foreign intelligence officer's] programme is bad, you should see the kind of stuff [international businessman] is trying to sell. In the ambassador's view "[international businessman] is further to the right than [right-wing politician]."' The cable also noted that the State Department was unhappy about 'these channels to the White House'. Large sectors of the US government were obviously worried at the contact between these unnamed businessmen and the White House. US funds were being channelled directly to individuals involved in subversive conspiracy at a time when Italy was rife with coup plots and right-wing extremists were carrying out bomb attacks on the public in order to provide an excuse for military intervention. The conclusion is inescapable that the 'international businessmen' whose anonymity it was so important for the White House to protect were wholly unpresentable figures from Italy's right-wing terrorist establishment: if not Gelli or Sindona then someone else equally unsavoury.

Another individual who fits the bill and who ties President Nixon into the heart of the Borghese coup conspiracy is Italo-American businessman Pier Talenti. According to French author Frederic Laurent,[35] Talenti had been one of Nixon's press attachés during his 1968 presidential election campaign and as a result enjoyed a permanent right of access to Nixon's office. A letter cabled from Nixon to Talenti on 7 November 1972 expresses fulsome gratitude for Talenti's fund-raising efforts in Italy which had helped to secure Nixon's re-election that year. The letter is now in the Nixon Library at Alexandria, Virginia. The library also contains a letter, dated 19 July 1969, from Talenti to Nixon offering his services in the anti-communist struggle in Italy. Nixon replied four months later (on 14 November 1969) in a letter beginning 'Dear Pier' but thanking Talenti in a non-committal manner for his offer. It has all the hallmarks of having been written merely for the record. If Remo Orlandini is to be believed,[36] the White House did indeed take up Talenti's offer of assistance. According to his account to Captain Labruna, a certain Pierfrancesco Talenti, whose father spent a lot of his time in America and who owned a large factory on the outskirts of Rome, had taken over from Hugh Fenwich as the link-man between the White House and the Borghese conspirators. It was important that no one should be told about this, said Orlandini, because Talenti had agreed to provide transport for a new coup attempt and would also set up a communications link between his factory and Washington when the appropriate time came.

While the Rome CIA station chief was opposing Ambassador Martin's management of covert operations in Italy, another CIA man, James Jesus Angleton, was monitoring developments in the Borghese coup with a probably much more benevolent eye. According to L'Espresso (8 February 1976), Angleton arrived secretly in Italy shortly before the Borghese coup was due to go into effect and left again shortly afterwards. Angleton had been responsible for rescuing Borghese from Milan at the end of the war, saving the fascist warrior from almost certain execution by the partisans, and escorting him to Rome in a US Army jeep, where he was handed over to the US military command. The two remained firm friends thereafter. According to Federico D'Amato, who ought to know, 'Borghese's greatest American friend was Angleton'.[37] Whether or not this clouded Angleton's judgement in regard to Borghese's political project is not clear. It is safe to assume, though, that had the American spymaster thrown his weight behind the coup attempt it would probably have been more successful.

What does emerge clearly is that American government thinking in regard to the strategy of tension in Italy was by no means monolithic and that the CIA took a distinctly doveish attitude towards Ambassador Martin's covert activities. This does not mean that the CIA was taking the moral high ground but merely that they were sufficiently shrewd to realize that a centrist coup or the mere threat of a coup would serve the interests of the United States better than a takeover by the extreme right, with all the difficulties of international condemnation and popular resistance that that might entail. Martin, on the other hand, appears to have become deeply embroiled in the contorted thinking of the 'international businessmen'. The lesson to be drawn from the controversy, perhaps, is that when the United States needed to undertake deep cover operations within the field of European terrorism, it may sometimes have preferred to rely on less formal and more secret organizations than the CIA. These might be irregular offshoots of the CIA or of the less well-known Defence Intelligence Agency (DIA) or even of the FBI which has the advantage that, officially, it 'does not operate outside the United States'.

Notes

1 P2 Commission, *Allegati alla Relazione*, Vol. 7, Tome 16, Rome, 1987, pp. 154–204.
2 Norberto Valentini, *La Notte della Madonna*, Le Monde, Rome, 1978, p. 55.
3 Ibid., p. 135.
4 Quoted in Vittorio Borraccetti (ed.), *Eversione di Destra, Terrorismo, Stragi*, Franco Angeli, Milan, 1986, p. 83.
5 Ibid., p. 84.
6 P2 Commission, *Allegati alla Relazione*, Vol. 3, Tome 4, Part 1, Rome, 1985, pp. 47–55.
7 Paolo Aleandri to the author, 22 June 1989.
8 P2 Commission, *Allegati alla Relazione*, Vol. 3, Tome 4, Part 1, Rome, 1985, p. 121.
9 Licio Gelli to the author, 27 June 1989.
10 Vittorio Borraccetti, op. cit., p. 85.
11 William Colby, *Honourable Men*, Hutchinson, London, 1978, p. 305.
12 *La Repubblica*, 17 August 1986.
13 *Il Giornale*, 21 April 1987.
14 *L'Espresso*, 20 March 1988.
15 Giuseppe De Lutiis, *Storia dei Servizi Segreti in Italia*, Editori Riuniti, Rome, 1984, p. 114.
16 Ibid., p. 119.
17 *L'Unità*, 22 June 1981.
18 P2 Commission, *Allegati alla Relazione*, Vol. 3, Tome 4, Part 1, Rome, 1985, p. 659.
19 Pietro Calderoni (ed.), *Servizi Segreti*, Tullio Pironti, Naples, 1986, p. 70.
20 *L'Unità*, 22 June 1981.
21 Quoted in Pietro Calderoni, op. cit., pp. 71–2.
22 Quoted in Giuliano Turone and Gherardo Colombo, *Sindona, Gli Atti dei Giudici di Milano*, Editori Riuniti, Rome, 1986, p. 207.
23 *Corriere della Sera*, 23 March 1986.
24 Licio Gelli to the author, 13 October 1989.
25 Licio Gelli to the author, 13 October 1989.
26 Paolo Aleandri to the author, 6 June 1989.
27 P2 Commission, *Allegati alla Relazione*, Vol. 3, Tome 4, Part 1, Rome, 1985, p. 435.
28 Norberto Valentini, op. cit., pp. 173–4.
29 P2 Commission, *Allegati alla Relazione*, Vol. 3, Tome 4, Part 2, Rome, 1985, p. 220.
30 Ibid., p. 223.

31 Ibid., pp. 287–8.
32 P. M. Francesco Trovato, Requisitoria, Brescia, 15 March 1976.
33 Achille Lega and Giorgio Santerini, *Strage a Brescia Potere a Roma*, Mazzotta, Milan, 1976, pp. 214–25.
34 P2 Commission, *Allegati alla Relazione*, Vol. 3, Tome 4, Part 2, Rome, 1985, pp. 525–36.
35 Frederic Laurent, *L'Orchestre Noir*, Stock, Paris, 1978, p. 254.
36 Norberto Valentini, op. cit., pp. 55–6.
37 Federico D'Amato to the author, 8 October 1989.

[7]

COVERING UP
FOR THE BOMBERS

HE succession of coup plots which kept the political system under constant pressure in the early 1970s was accompanied and punctuated by a series of indiscriminate bombings against the public. These in turn were part of a wider campaign of bomb attacks on railway lines, electricity pylons, public and private property, which served to maintain political tension at fever pitch. Despite nearly two decades of judicial inquiry, the identity and purpose of the bombers and their relationship with the coup conspirators remain for the most part shrouded in mystery. One explanation for this lies in the tireless efforts of the secret services to undermine the investigations of the judiciary and protect suspects from prosecution.

One of the earliest manifestations of sustained political terrorism in post-war Italy had occurred in the mountainous Alto Adige or South Tyrol region on the north-east border, and events there appear to have provided a model for later terrorist practice. German-speaking residents of the region carried out Fumagalli-style bombings against electricity pylons and other inanimate targets in the early 1960s in support of their call for local autonomy. They naturally attracted the close attention of the Italian secret services and there has been considerable speculation about the extent to which the secret services may have actually incited the violence. Years later, Roberto Cavallaro of the Rosa dei Venti told Judge Tamburino: 'If there hadn't been a [Georg] Klotz [an autonomist leader] in Alto Adige, another Klotz would have to have been invented.'[1] Many of the security officials who played an equivocal role in later events, including Amos Spiazzi, first cut their teeth on terrorism in the South Tyrol. It is perhaps not entirely surprising that north-east Italy, bordering on communist Yugoslavia and with consequently heavy troop concentrations, should have been a breeding ground for terrorism of both right and left.

In 1983 Spiazzi told the P2 Commission of a conversation he had with a superior officer while he was serving in the Alto Adige at the height of the autonomist terrorism, who remarked on the fact that there were no bombings in the area under his control. Spiazzi asked the officer whether he was pleased and was told that 'for reasons of a global character' it was not a good thing. He went on to tell the Commission how he had arrested two *carabinieri* belonging to SIFAR whom he had caught planting a bomb. 'While I was taking them to Bolzano to hand them over to the regional command I was met by *carabinieri* and police who took them from me . . . the next day I was sent back to Verona and that was the end of my work in Alto Adige.'[2] The idea of secret service personnel becoming directly involved in planting bombs is not hard to accept given the industry with which they protected right-wingers involved in terrorism. In 1972 the left-wing newspaper *Lotta Continua* (7 November) published an article claiming that the police had been responsible for placing a bomb outside the Palace of Justice in Trento. The bomb, left on a windowsill on 18 January 1971, had failed to explode. 'We are aware of the existence of a secret SID report on the bomb at the law courts, which states that the inquiry had been pursued to the point where it became apparent that the bombing had been organized "by another police force", so it was decided to discontinue the investigation,'[3] *Lotta Continua* claimed. The paper was prosecuted for 'the publication of false information liable to disturb public order' but finally acquitted. It emerged that the Trento police had blackmailed a convicted criminal into planting the device. It is significant that this sinister police activity should have taken place in this north-eastern city. Several of the officials involved would later turn out to be linked to the P2 lodge and to have played an important role in other murky episodes of the strategy of tension. And it was at Trento University in the late 1960s that some of the future leaders of the Red Brigades first met and began to get actively involved in politics together. It is by no means improbable that this took place under the attentive and benevolent gaze of the secret services.

The first major bombing of the coup season came at 4.30 in the afternoon on 12 December 1969, in the crowded lobby of the Banca

Nazionale dell'Agricoltura in Milan's Piazza Fontana, a stone-throw from the city's famous cathedral. Seventeen people were killed and eighty-eight injured in the blast. Later in the afternoon, three other bombs exploded in Rome, one in a pedestrian underpass which injured fourteen people, and two more on the Victor Emanuel monument which houses the tomb of the unknown soldier, causing damage but no injuries. A fifth device failed to explode and was found by an employee in the Banca Commerciale Italiana in Milan.

Initially, the investigation focused on anarchist and left-wing circles in Milan and Rome. Later, however, it emerged that some of those circles had been infiltrated by members of the extreme right, who were, in their turn, in contact with the secret services. Eventually, the prime suspects became two right-wing publishers and booksellers from Padua, Franco Freda and Giovanni Ventura. The pair were responsible for a series of twenty-two failed or minor bombings carried out between 15 April and 12 December 1969. One of them, at a Milan trade fair on 25 April, injured twenty people. The Piazza Fontana massacre appeared to be the culmination of this bombing campaign. Freda summed up his political philosophy in a book entitled *The Disintegration of the System*. To lay the foundations of the 'true state', he wrote, it was necessary to subvert the current political system. 'The sickness represented by bourgeois society is incurable: no therapy is possible, not even a surgical operation would be effective; we must speed up the haemorrhage and bury the corpse.' Nothing new could be built, he said, as long as 'even the ruins were still standing'. And he called for an alliance with the far left for an all-out assault on the bourgeois state.[4]

Two other suspects in the conspiracy were right-wing journalists Guido Giannettini and Pino Rauti. Rauti was the man whose name was linked to Ambassador Martin's $800,000 payment to General Miceli to finance a 'propaganda effort'. He was born in southern Italy in 1926, fought for the fascist Salò Republic during the war, and in 1956 founded the terrorist Ordine Nuovo organization. In the 1950s he worked for the right-wing Rome newspaper *Il Tempo*, itself a recipient of generous US funding. He was eventually acquitted of involvement in the bombing after an investigation into his activities lasting fifty-one months. In January 1990, his implication in the strategy of tension a faint memory, Rauti was elected secretary of the MSI. Giannettini, a specialist reporter on military affairs and *habitué* of the extreme right over many years, also enjoyed good US contacts. In

1961, he was invited to give a lecture at the US Marines' College in Annapolis on 'Techniques and possibilities of a *coup d'état* in Europe', which was attended by officials from the Pentagon and the CIA.[5] Both were informants of Italian military intelligence and were accused of providing a link between the bombers and the secret services. More specifically, they were accused of having attended an important meeting with Freda in Padua on 18 April 1969, at which the secret services had allegedly given the green light to the Padua group's bombing campaign. It was also at this meeting that the participants had developed what they called 'the second line' strategy: right-wingers were to infiltrate extreme left-wing groups in order to provoke them to violence or falsely implicate them in terrorist activities carried out by the right. This was to be one of the guiding principles of right-wing terrorism.[6]

Seven years after Piazza Fontana, in March 1976, General Gianadelio Maletti and Captain Antonio Labruna were arrested by magistrates investigating the Milan bombing. The director of the SID counter-espionage department and his principal agent were accused of protecting suspects in the first major bombing of the strategy of tension. One of the suspects, Marco Pozzan, a right-wing sympathizer and school janitor from Padua, was hidden in a secret service office in Rome for several days in early 1973 while a false passport was prepared for him and he was subsequently escorted to safety in Spain by a secret service officer. Pozzan's false passport was issued in the name of Mario Zanella, a name which features on the P2 membership list. The real Mario Zanella has never been identified, nor has this strange choice of name on the part of the secret services ever been satisfactorily explained. It was Pozzan who had implicated Rauti in the bombing, claiming that the founder of Ordine Nuovo had attended the crucial meeting in Padua on 18 April. SID presumably feared that he might make other embarrassing revelations. The officers who assisted Pozzan in his escape tried to argue that they had been unaware of his true identity but had been promised that he could help them in locating Stefano Delle Chiaie in Spain. According to their account he simply vanished once they arrived in Spain.

Pozzan/Zanella's account of the affair was slightly different. In a three-page document made available to the investigating magistrate, Pozzan described how he had been questioned several times by the secret services before leaving Rome. They had been particularly interested, he said, in the depositions the magistrates had 'forced' him to make about the role of Pino Rauti, which were 'obviously false' and which he had subsequently retracted. 'Before agreeing to help me get abroad,' Pozzan wrote, 'Tonino [Captain Labruna] said he had to get authorization from his boss, who, in his turn, had to seek it from someone else, Andreotti, I believe.'[7] Far from disappearing in Spain, Pozzan claimed that he had spent the first night in the same Madrid hotel as his SID escort, had been asked to hand back his false passport and was then left on his own.

Maletti and Labruna were also accused of helping Giannettini to escape to Paris after learning that a Milan magistrate had been alerted to his role in the affair. Even after a warrant had been issued for his arrest, Labruna remained in contact with him, meeting him from time to time and supplying him with money.

The two SID officers were also charged with planning the escape from prison in Monza of Giovanni Ventura, one of the suspected bombers. The warrant for the officers' arrest stated that they were instrumental in providing Ventura's family with a key to his cell and two canisters of narcotic gas. Ventura did not actually go through with the escape attempt as he was understandably anxious about what might happen to him once he was free. Concrete proof of the escape plan was provided by Ventura's sister, Mariangela, who in January 1976 handed over to the examining magistrate a copy of the key to her brother's cell and one of the gas canisters. She no longer had the other canister, she said, as she had decided to test its contents on a couple of kittens. The creatures had been wracked by agonizing convulsions and had to be destroyed and in her agitation she had thrown the canister away. The planned break-out was confirmed by Stefano Delle Chiaie in an interview with *Panorama* magazine (4 May 1976). He told the publication that he had been approached by Captain Labruna in November 1972 to see whether he was able to give hospitality to Freda and Ventura in Barcelona and then to assist them in leaving Europe, once Labruna had successfully organized their escape. The arrest warrant stated categorically that the actions of Maletti and Labruna were part of a 'wider criminal plan aimed at preventing the judicial authorities from throwing light on the tragic terrorist events which bloodied Italy in 1969'.[8] Despite the fact that neither of the officers was working in the counter-espionage office at the time of the bombing, and so they could hardly have been covering up a personal responsibility in the affair, they refused to collaborate with the magistrates or provide any convincing explanation for their actions.

[125]

Seventeen years after the bombing the Court of Cassation sentenced General Maletti to one year's imprisonment and Captain Labruna to ten months for their attempts to sabotage the investigation. The same court definitively acquitted the three principal suspects, Guido Giannettini and the fascist publishers Freda and Ventura. Two previous trials had sentenced all three to life imprisonment for carrying out the bombing but they were finally acquitted 'for lack of evidence'. The secret services had done their work well, making it impossible to determine with absolute certainty who was responsible for planting the bomb and who was involved in the Piazza Fontana conspiracy. The court did, however, confirm fifteen-year sentences on Freda and Ventura for subversive conspiracy, a charge relating to the series of non-lethal bombings between April and December 1969. The Piazza Fontana case was the first major example of secret service intervention to undermine a terrorism investigation but it was by no means the last. General Maletti had a reputation as one of Italy's more democratically-inclined secret service officers and yet he did not shrink from participating in the cover-up. The repetition over the years of this secret service role leads one ineluctably to the conclusion that the Italian secret services were active participants, if not protagonists, in the strategy of tension.

The cover-up has continued for two decades, involving secret service officers with no personal connection to the original wrong-doing who were brought in to clean up the intelligence service following the P2 scandal. Catanzaro Prosecutor Domenico Porcelli has described how the appointment in 1984 of Admiral Fulvio Martini as head of SISMI initially introduced a new atmosphere of collaboration between the Piazza Fontana magistrates and the military intelligence service. Martini informed one of the magistrates that the secret service had had seven informers, besides Giannettini, infiltrated into the ranks of the extreme right at the time of the bombing. He said he would have no difficulty in revealing their identities and details of the information they provided at the time. Subsequently, however, the investigators were disappointed to learn that the names had once again been covered by official secrecy. They were simply assured that they had no bearing on their case. Porcelli also revealed that on the day before the bombing a known right-winger, who identified himself as a SID agent, was questioned by police because he was found waiting in his car in a no-parking area near Piazza Fontana. The renamed, supposedly reformed and democratic SISMI was unable to offer any assistance in clarifying his relationship with the secret service or explaining what he might have been doing in central Milan on the eve of the attack.[9] As a result of these difficulties, the associations representing victims of the bombings and their relatives have become convinced that current state secrecy laws are one of the principal impediments to justice and they have been campaigning for their abolition, at least in regard to indiscriminate bomb attacks on the public. The frequency with which judicial investigations have foundered on the rocks of official secrecy is in itself eloquent testimony to the close contacts that existed between the secret services and right-wing terrorism and that can still not be made public today.

In an address to a conference on the judicial response to the right-wing bombings Porcelli highlighted the continuity of the secret service cover-up and the conservative political programme underlying it.[10] He cited numerous examples from the Piazza Fontana investigation of secret service and police intervention to thwart the efforts of the magistrates. These included the suppression of evidence that could have linked the bag that contained the bomb to a shop in Padua, Freda and Ventura's home town, which had sold four of a similar type only two days before the bombing. Police and officials from the Interior Ministry's Office of Special Affairs actually interviewed the owner of the shop and one of his employees four days after the explosion but neglected to inform the magistrates of the result. Fragments of imitation leather from the cases that contained the Rome bombs were sent to Germany for tests which confirmed they were similar to the material used in the manufacture of the four German-made bags sold in the Padua store. Police chiefs in Rome and Milan were told of the results but, again, no one informed the magistrates. Three senior police officers were subsequently charged with suppressing evidence. *Carabinieri* who seized explosives that had once been in the possession of Giovanni Ventura and his brother Angelo had them destroyed before they could be tested to establish whether they were of the same type as those used in the 1969 bombing. The decision was taken on grounds of safety despite the fact that the explosives had been found in open countryside, taken to a *carabinieri* barracks where they were stored for a week and then taken back into the country to be destroyed. And the list could go on.

In a speech marking the twentieth anniversary of Piazza Fontana, the president of a parliamentary committee investigating the right-wing bomb massacres, a cautious Republican Party senator named

Libero Gualtieri, stated that the judiciary had identified at least forty instances of collusion between the secret services and right-wing terrorists (*La Repubblica*, 13 December 1989). It is clear from the frequency and continuity of these secret service interventions that they were not, as is often claimed, occasional aberrations by isolated individuals, but were related to the fundamental nature and purpose of the Italian security services.

Like Carlo Fumagalli and several other leading Italian terrorists, Giovanni Ventura claimed privately to be working for the CIA. He said as much repeatedly to his friend, and later principal accuser, Guido Lorenzon. Publicly he was keen to pose as a man of left-wing sympathies and thus tarnish the left by association with terrorism in accordance with the 'second line' strategy. 'Did he ever put pressure on you to change your story?' Lorenzon, a schoolteacher and member of the Christian Democrat Party, was asked in a newspaper interview (*Paese Sera*, 30 March 1981). 'No. He only wanted me to say he was a left-winger . . . Having a left-wing label was his constant objective.'

In December 1971 magistrates discovered a number of documents in a safety deposit box held in the name of Ventura's mother and aunt in the Banca Popolare in Montebelluna. It contained, among other things, documents on Italian and international politics and on the organization of the United States intelligence services. One typewritten sheet was titled 'Agents of the American secret services in Italy since 1968'. It contained a list of thirteen names, including that of Hugh Montgomery, who was at one time CIA station chief in Rome.[11] Some of the documents were marked with codes that gave the impression that they originated with a regular intelligence service. They included reports drawn up for SID by Guido Giannettini. SID's claim that the documents had nothing to do with the Italian secret service but were based merely on newspaper reports was dismissed by Prosecutor Porcelli as a blatant lie. One of the reports, marked KSD/VI M, stated: 'Italian political and economic circles supported by foreign circles (certainly including the Americans) have decided on the replacement of the centre-left government in Italy by a substantially centrist alternative.' The document, dated 4 May 1969, listed a number of detailed steps to be taken including 'a possible wave of terrorist attacks to convince public opinion of the dangers of maintaining the [government] alliance with the left (industrial groups in northern Italy would finance the planting of a few bombs by isolated neo-fascist groups)'.[12] The Italian secret services understandably did not want to be associated with such prescience.

The Catanzaro assize court devoted considerable attention to an analysis of some of the Montebelluna documents. In particular, it accepted Giannettini's claim that he had supplied Ventura with reports on largely imaginary plans to shift Italian politics to the right, if necessary by resorting to violence, in order to help the latter in his attempts to infiltrate left-wing extra-parliamentary groups. The court added, which Giannettini could obviously not admit, that the probable purpose of the documents, shown by Ventura to his left-wing contacts, was to alarm the extreme left and provoke it in turn to acts of violence. Giannettini's suggestion that the reactionary project had received the assent even of leading moderate figures in Italian politics would have been particularly effective to this end, since it would have driven the leftists to give up all reliance on the democratic process.

Giannettini had been working as a SID informant since 1967, a fact that was steadfastly kept secret from the magistrates, until it was finally revealed by Defence Minister Andreotti in an interview with *Il Mondo* magazine (20 June 1974). In March 1973 Giannettini wrote to General Maletti giving a detailed account of his work for SID and, more to the point, outlining the areas where he would be capable of making embarrassing revelations. The defensive nature of the document was made even more apparent the following year when Giannettini gave a copy to Loreto D'Ambrosio, the Milan magistrate investigating the Piazza Fontana bombing. In it the fascist journalist explained how he was hired by SID after producing a confidential report on 'the background to the CIA response to the rise of the left in Europe'.[13] He went on to enumerate the various reports he had written for SID. These included one in 1968 on American and British control over international protest movements, and a report in 1973 on 'the activities of the Office of Special Affairs in relation to the so-called "black terrorist connection"'. Giannettini also explained how he had made use of Ventura to gather intelligence on left-wing organizations. Especially significant were his veiled calls for military intervention to avert a long and disastrous civil war. After describing the political crisis facing Italy, he wrote: 'All this shows what responsibilities weigh upon each one of us and leads us to consider a limited and routine interpretation of our duties to be no longer valid.' This was the prevailing view among military coup plotters and the suggestion is clear that large sectors of SID, and perhaps even Maletti himself, sympathized with it. Giannettini concluded by warning that 'Every-thing that happens in our country – it's my duty to bring it to your attention – is manipulated from abroad by the German, British, Israeli and American secret services. The only thing missing is an authenti-cally Italian policy and cause.'

Maletti and the Catanzaro assize court considered this letter to be an attempt on Giannettini's part to blackmail the military intelligence service. It is hard to imagine how it could have been effective if there were no substance to his hints. The court clearly believed there was, citing the 'scandalous protection' he received from SID, even after the issue of a warrant for his arrest, as proof that he had not been acting merely on his own account in his 'criminal contacts' with Freda and Ventura. The court ruled that members of the secret service had been prepared to exploit the political consequences of the neo-fascist bombings and that Giannettini represented the point of contact between the political and military level of the conspiracy and the actual bombers.

Hints at the kind of sensitive information he might be prepared to reveal were a constant feature of Giannettini's defence. They alternated, however, with promises of silence, particularly at times when he felt physically threatened. One such moment came on the afternoon of 8 August 1974, when, tired of being on the run, he gave himself up at the Italian embassy in Buenos Aires. He swiftly assured the local SID representative that he did not intend betraying any secrets: 'In particular, to be quite clear, when I am asked if I was a link between a military conspiracy and certain executors I will deny it. Certainly, because it's not true, because above all it would damage the armed forces, and me personally even more.'[14] Giannettini promised he would stick faithfully to what had already been made public by the Minister of Defence. Seventeen years after the Piazza Fontana bombing, this defensive strategy would reap its reward with Giannettini's definitive acquittal. In recent years the former secret agent cum journalist has found work in Rome with Italfin 80, a company with interests in newspaper publishing owned by Giuseppe Ciarrapico. The latter is a wealthy businessman of right-wing sympathies and a close associate of Giulio Andreotti.

Secret service sabotage of the Piazza Fontana judicial investigation is one of the reasons why the magistrates ultimately failed to secure convictions. Another possible explanation, outlined by author Walter Rubini, is that politicians who were opposed to the strategy of tension and were privy to some of the details of the bomb plot preferred to use that information in order to reach a secret political accommodation with the plotters rather than to denounce them publicly. According to Rubini, Defence Minister Luigi Gui, a close supporter of then Foreign Minister Aldo Moro, ordererd a SID inquiry into the bombing. The upshot of this was a report by *carabiniere* Colonel Pio Alferano, delivered to Gui on 22 December, which revealed for the first time the involvement of the extreme right in the atrocity. The following day Moro had a private meeting with President Giuseppe Saragat, a right-wing exponent of the Social Democrat Party (PSDI). Saragat had been tempted by the idea of declaring a state of emergency and wanted to use the tension created by the bombing either to have the Socialist Party (PSI) ejected from the government coalition or to force the socialists to fall in with a hardline anti-communist stance on the part of the government. Moro, on the other hand, advocated a much more moderate solution to Italy's political problems and was keen to widen support for the government to embrace as many parties as possible. He decided to use the contents of the Alferano report to make Saragat back away from his favoured radical, right-wing solutions. In return, according to Rubini,[15] Moro agreed that the report should be kept secret and not passed on to the judiciary.

Rubini's account is by no means implausible. The fact that the Italian justice system has almost invariably failed to obtain convictions against those responsible for the country's right-wing bombings does not necessarily mean that the entire political class had approved the strategy of tension and willingly participated in the cover-up. If Moro did decide to use information on the Piazza Fontana bombing for a covert political deal, his decision may partly have sprung from a sense of responsibility towards the NATO security establishment which he perceived as being in some way involved in the strategy. It was for this reason that Moro, as Prime Minister, frequently imposed state secrecy on sensitive aspects of secret service involvement in terrorism. When, for example, General Miceli appealed to Moro to free him from the constraints of official secrecy so that he could answer magistrates' questions about the so-called 'Parallel SID', Moro refused to do so. When Moro was himself asked by magistrates about the existence of the Parallel SID, he replied: 'I am not aware of the existence among the secret services of the state of an organization with the task of subverting the state.'[16] If such an organization did not exist, it is hard to understand why Miceli could not be freed from state secrecy in order to answer questions about it. If it did exist, Moro's sense of his duty as a statesman would prevent him from ever admitting it. Rubini's account renders all the more significant the remarks made by Moro on the political background to the Piazza Fontana bombing while he was a prisoner of the Red Brigades. As we shall see in a later chapter, a document recording Moro's comments on the subject was captured by the *carabinieri* after his death. Extraordinarily, the Red Brigades had chosen not to publish it.

A small-scale but typical example of the *agent provocateur* tactics of the secret services occurred in November 1972, when an arms cache including explosives and timing devices was found in an abandoned farm near the town of Camerino in central Italy. The following day two newspapers broke the news, attributing the weapons to left-wing extremists on the basis of the documents found with them, and a number of leading left-wingers were subsequently arrested. Right-wing journalist Guido Paglia, a former member of Avanguardia Nazionale, writing in the Bologna newspaper *Il Resto del Carlino* (11 November 1972), was able to reveal that the documents 'clearly indicated the political colour of the owners of the arsenal'. He had, however, jumped the gun, unfortunately for the plausibility of the whole scheme, as the documents were in code and were only officially deciphered three days later. Stefano Delle Chiaie made his contribution to the truth in his interview with *Panorama* magazine (4 May 1976) four years later. 'Those arms, explosives and coded documents were planted by Labruna to unleash an anti-communist crusade,' he told the magazine. 'If Labruna denies this as well, then we will remind him, naming names, who provided the arms and explosives and who prepared the coded documents for him,' he added.

Further subversive activity by Labruna, prior to the 1972 general elections that had caused the US embassy such anxiety, was revealed in a defensive memorandum by his secret service colleague Lieutenant Colonel Antonio Viezzer. Viezzer accused Labruna of being involved in planting explosive devices outside various offices of the neo-fascist MSI 'to help the party and to alienate the electorate from the PCI and from the left-wing parties in general, who would be seen as terrorists responsible for the bombings'.[17] Mino Pecorelli, ever well informed, appears to have been aware of Labruna's terrorist activity from an early stage. An article entitled 'The epic adventures of Admiral Labrunne' (*OP*, 9 November 1973) referred to Labruna's 'specialization in pyrotechnical studies' and his 'innate tendencies towards the pyromaniac and bomber'. The article was one of a series attacking Labruna and Maletti, almost certainly on behalf of SID director General Miceli and as part of a bitter personal feud between two rival secret service factions. A Rome magistrate opened an investigation into these allegations in 1989, some seventeen years after the event. Miceli, Maletti and Labruna were all sent judicial letters notifying them that they were under investigation.

While the secret services were busily engaged in burying the unpalatable truths of terrorism, the political establishment was able to exploit the judicial system to the same effect. Active and independent-minded magistrates, such as those investigating the Rosa dei Venti conspiracy, were relieved of the case. The Court of Cassation ruled that the investigation should be handled in Rome as it spread wider than the narrow jurisdictions of the Padua and Turin magistrates who first brought the case to light. Cases could also be assigned to individual magistrates likely to take a politically sensible view and, unsurprisingly, there was a high concentration of these in the country's political capital. Magistrates with a narrow, local jurisdiction found it difficult to see the full ramifications of nationwide, or even international, conspiracies. And magistrates investigating individual acts of terrorism were often unaware of the political conspiracies underlying them. Institutionally, the appropriate place to draw all the threads together was Rome, where the magistrates tended to be most malleable. The only other people to have a comprehensive, nationwide overview of terrorism were the secret services and the Interior Ministry, and they could be relied on to keep their conclusions to themselves rather than to use them in the furtherance of justice.

Bologna Prosecutor Claudio Nunziata has analysed the way in which the investigation of the Borghese coup and the Rosa dei Venti, which were combined into one major inquiry to be handled in Rome, failed to get to the bottom of either conspiracy and paved the way for the final mass acquittals.[18] 'In substance, the public prosecutor [Claudio Vitalone] admits there is a connection between the bombings and the subversive plots but he avoids investigating to what extent the strategy of bombings and terrorism fits into the coup plot. Nor was this problem considered by those investigating the bombings,' he observed. The only people to attempt to understand the connection, according to Nunziata, were Judges Tamburino of Padua and Violante of Turin, and they had the case taken away from them by the

Court of Cassation.

On 17 May 1973, a self-professed anarchist, Gianfranco Bertoli, hurled a hand-grenade into a crowd outside the Milan police headquarters, killing four people and injuring twelve. The crowd was gathered for the unveiling of a plaque to the memory of Police Chief Luigi Calabresi, who had been assassinated by an unidentified gunman the year before. In 1988 a former member of the left-wing Lotta Continua organization confessed to participating in the attack and accused other members of the group of planning and carrying out the murder. Calabresi was the man held responsible by many for the death of Giuseppe Pinelli, an anarchist railway worker who fell to his death from a window of the central police station while he was being interrogated as a suspect in the Piazza Fontana bombing. The grenade attack could be seen as further revenge for Pinelli's death, so who could doubt the anarchist motives of the attacker? Bertoli claimed that he had intended to murder Interior Minister Mariano Rumor, present at the ceremony, but he had waited until Rumor's car had driven past him before throwing the grenade. That was not the only mysterious thing about Bertoli; it subsequently emerged that he had worked for SIFAR, as well as for Cavallo and Sogno's anti-communist Peace and Freedom Association. He also turned out to have been in contact with several members of the Rosa dei Venti and as a result was accused of subversive conspiracy by Judge Tamburino. In the end, though, Bertoli was sentenced to life imprisonment for his grenade attack and was consigned to judicial history as a 'lone nut'.

The first phase of right-wing terrorism reached a climax in 1974, a year marked by two major bombings against the public and three coup attempts. The first massacre of the year came on 28 May in the main square of the northern industrial city of Brescia, not far from Milan. A bomb exploded in a litter bin in Piazza della Loggia during a demonstration by trade unionist and other anti-fascist organizations to protest against a series of minor bombing incidents in the area, culminating in the death of a right-winger blown up by his own bomb a week earlier. Eight people were killed and ninety-four injured. An hour and a half later the local police chief ordered firemen to clear and hose down the square, causing, in the words of Examining Magistrate Domenico Vino, 'the possible loss of vital evidence and arousing alarming questions as to the haste of the operation'.[19] Brescia was one of the operational zones of Carlo Fumagalli, who had been arrested by magistrates from the city only three weeks earlier, along with more than a dozen of his followers. As with Piazza Fontana, the judicial investigation of the Brescia bombing has been long and tortuous. In May 1987 three right-wingers accused of planting the bomb were acquitted for lack of evidence at the conclusion of the fifth trial to examine the case. 'Repentant' terrorist Sergio Calore had no doubts as to the objective of the bombing. 'All the bombings had a single purpose: to create social tension and prepare the conditions for intervention by the army,'[20] he told the Brescia court.

On 12 May, Italians had voted in a referendum on the proposed abrogation of the country's divorce law. Fifty-nine per cent had voted for the law's retention, a bitter defeat for the Christian Democrat Party, the Vatican and other conservative forces who had campaigned energetically for its abolition. Michele Sindona had contributed generously to the Christian Democrat campaign while Gelli, anticipating the worst, had given money to Augusto Cauchi, the Tuscan terrorist leader and secret service confidant. Gelli's position was somewhat paradoxical, since freemasonry was nominally in favour of a secular state and consequently should have supported the divorce law. He was not alone, however, in seeing wider political implications to a victory of the left in the referendum. Cauchi and his band were ready to take to the hills and become 'partisans in reverse', while others, such as Sogno and Cavallo, were preparing their coup.

A second major bombing in the summer racked up the political tension still further, making 1974 the only year in Italian history to be characterized by two such outrages. On 4 August, at about the same time as Sogno and Cavallo's summer holiday coup was due to go into effect, a bomb exploded on the 'Italicus' Rome–Munich express train as it left a tunnel near the village of San Benedetto Val di Sambro, not far from Bologna. Twelve people were killed and 105 injured by the blast and subsequent fire. In December 1986 two Tuscan neo-fascists, Mario Tuti and Luciano Franci, were given life sentences for the bombing by a Bologna court. The P2 Commission stated emphatically that the secret lodge had provided 'the essential economic, organizational and moral background' to the bombing.[21] There was keen expectation of a coup in masonic circles at this time. One mason, Angelo Sambuco, told Grand Master Lino Salvini of his intention to take his family abroad on holiday. Salvini replied that 'he would not be leaving Florence because he was expecting a coup'.[22]

One of the fortunate side-effects, for those hoping to see a military takeover, of the persistent secret service interference with judicial investigations of the bombings was that the apparent incompetence of the authorities increased the unpopularity of the current government, which inevitably came to be seen as incapable of protecting the public from terrorist violence or securing its perpetrators for justice. The most brutal of all the techniques in the armoury of the saboteurs of justice was the physical elimination of potential witnesses, a technique not infrequently used and with rare efficacy. The implications are particularly grave when this activity takes place in prison, an environment, at least in theory, under the total control of the state. One of the most sinister examples was the murder in Novara prison of Ermanno Buzzi, a right-wing extremist sentenced to life imprisonment by a Brescia assize court for the Piazza della Loggia bombing who had shown signs that he intended to make sensational revelations in the run-up to the appeal hearing. He was strangled with shoe-laces in a corner of the prison exercise yard by two senior right-wingers, Mario Tuti and Pierluigi Concutelli, on the morning of 13 April 1981. Buzzi had been in Novara prison less than forty-eight hours and was killed on the first occasion he stepped into the exercise yard. He had fought hard to avoid being transferred from a prison in Brescia, fearing for his life, and his last words to his lawyer before his departure were along the lines: 'It's all over for me, I am going to fatal Novara.'[23]

The following year Concutelli struck again, strangling Carmine Palladino, a friend of Stefano Delle Chiaie and thought to have had inside information about the Bologna station bombing. Palladino was murdered on 10 August 1982, in the same 'blind' corner of the prison exercise yard. If the prison administration failed to learn from experience Concutelli did not: this time he used nylon cord from a volley-ball net and wrapped it round the metal supports of a ping-pong net so as not to ruin his hands, as he had done with Buzzi. Palladino had been in Novara for ten days. It will probably never be known for sure whether these potential witnesses transferred to their appointment with death were the victims of an incompetent prison administration or of a conscious design. It would certainly not be beyond the wit of the secret services to pilot inconvenient witnesses into oblivion.

Another potentially important witness was eliminated under mysterious circumstances in 1982. According to *La Repubblica* newspaper (21 February 1988), right-wing extremist and Delle Chiaie associate Pierluigi Pagliai had decided to return to Italy from Bolivia, where he worked for the Bolivian security services, and tell magistrates all he knew about the fascist bombing campaigns. At this point a joint CIA/Italian secret service operation was mounted to arrest Pagliai in Bolivia. On 10 October Pagliai was shot in the neck by a Bolivian policeman, ostensibly while resisting arrest. According to *La Repubblica*, however, Pagliai was actually getting out of his vehicle with his arms raised and the shooting was 'a veritable execution'. Only three hours after undergoing surgery for his wound, Pagliai was bundled on to a plane and flown to Italy where he died in Rome on 5 November. The Alitalia aircraft that flew the Italian police contingent out to Bolivia and ferried the captured Pagliai back to Rome gave a lift on the first leg of its return journey, from Santa Cruz to La Paz, to a group of plainclothes Bolivian police commanded by a tall, blond American agent. This was the unit responsible for Pagliai's arrest. During the flight, according to several witnesses, the American began distributing wads of banknotes to his men.[24] The decision to transport Pagliai from Bolivia to Italy despite the severity of his wound has itself given rise to questions: at best it was irresponsible, at worst something closely akin to murder. 'Episodes have been uncovered which call into question the role of the secret services of Bolivia, the United States and Italy,' *La Repubblica* said. It also claimed that suspicions had emerged that 'the Italian government has invoked state secrecy to cover certain circumstances relating to the railway bombings, which had been reported by Pagliai to the American embassy in La Paz'. Both the US and Bolivian authorities refused to co-operate with the Italian judicial investigation into Pagliai's death. Francesco Pazienza also touched on this subject in an interview with a Swiss newspaper (24 *Heures*, 13 April 1986) while he was awaiting extradition to Italy in a New York prison. 'I ask the simple question: why did the American administration collaborate with the Italian secret services in the murder of Pierluigi Pagliai?'

On 31 May 1972, a booby-trapped car exploded near the village of Peteano in north-east Italy, killing three *carabinieri* and seriously injuring a fourth. This incident has produced one of the most bizarre and exemplary police cover-ups in the history of Italian terrorism. Several of its protagonists had previously played an inglorious role in the Trento bombing case, the background to which had been revealed by *Lotta Continua* newspaper. Peteano is also the only bombing for which an individual terrorist has admitted responsibility and in so doing provided a detailed insider's account of the workings of the strategy of tension. The account is all the more convincing because its author has refused the label of 'repentant' terrorist and has not sought any judicial benefit from his collaboration with the authorities, simply taking the opportunity to denounce some of his erstwhile comrades as tools of the secret services. The man's name is Vincenzo Vinciguerra, a virulent fascist of psychopathic ruthlessness, who is currently serving a life sentence for Peteano and other terrorist crimes.

On the evening of 31 May an anonymous caller informed the *carabinieri* in the town of Gorizia that a Fiat 500 with two bullet-holes in the windscreen had been abandoned in a gorge not far from a road near Peteano. Three *carabinieri* patrol cars were sent to investigate and the men were killed when one of them opened the bonnet, triggering a powerful bomb. The call was made from a telephone in a bar in the nearby town of Monfalcone. The caller, it later emerged, was one Carlo Cicuttini, the secretary of a local section of the neo-fascist MSI. Cicuttini escaped to Spain, where he enjoyed the solicitous protection of the Franco-era police and secret services. MSI party leader Giorgio Almirante was subsequently charged with sending Cicuttini money to enable him to have an operation on his throat to prevent his voice being identified with the recording of the mysterious caller to the *carabinieri*. Almirante, who died in 1988, was never brought to trial: the charges against him were waived as the result of an amnesty before they could be tested in court.

The bombing was one of a series of terrorist incidents, including a bomb attack on the home of a local MSI member of Parliament. The series culminated in a failed hijacking at Trieste airport, which had been intended as a fund-raising exercise. All were the work of an active local group of the terrorist Ordine Nuovo organization. Despite the fact that this was clear to some of the investigators from the start, the inquiry was entrusted to the *carabinieri*, who focused their attention instead on left-wing extremists. In order to set the inquiry off in this unlikely direction, the officers running it had no hesitation in inventing information implicating members of the left-wing group Lotta Continua in the attack. The false information was attributed to a police informer, Marco Pisetta. Pisetta had been in contact with the founder members of the Red Brigades and with Feltrinelli's group, Gruppi di Azione Partigiana (Partisan Action Groups) or GAP. He had been arrested in Milan on 2 May 1972, and had subsequently collaborated with police, enabling them to find a number of Red Brigades hideouts. He was released after a few days and was later contacted by Lieutenant Colonel Michele Santoro of the *carabinieri* in Trento, his home town. He was prevailed upon to provide further evidence to Milan magistrates investigating left-wing terrorist activity, who interrogated him in Santoro's home in Trento. It was at this point that Santoro took the opportunity of adding an invented reference to possible involvement of members of the Lotta Continua group in the Peteano bombing to a report on Pisetta's evidence which he sent to SID headquarters in Rome. Santoro had known Pisetta for some time as the latter had previously been in trouble with the police for a number of bomb attacks against public buildings in Trento. According to the testimony of one of Santoro's brother officers, Santoro had been 'working on the embryonic Red Brigades organization and had an informant who, I subsequently learned, was Marco Pisetta'.[25] Pisetta provided the secret services with detailed and accurate information about the Red Brigades which could have been used to nip the terrorist organization in the bud. Instead he was used falsely to implicate other left-wing sympathizers in the Peteano bombing.

The left-wingers accused of the bombing were acquitted at their trial as there was not a shred of genuine evidence against them. The investigators then shifted their attention to a group of local criminals, who were equally unconnected with the bombing. The studious care with which they avoided considering the possibility of right-wing involvement in the bombing originated with instructions received from the officer commanding a division of the *carabinieri* based in Milan, General Giuseppe Palumbo. Santoro and other officers involved in the cover-up formed part of a clique closely associated with the general, who had flirted with right-wing conspiracies since General De Lorenzo's coup attempt in 1964 and became a member of P2 in 1977. Palumbo denied having joined the lodge and an internal Defence Ministry inquiry accepted his word as 'a senior officer with many years' service'. The P2 Commission took a somewhat sterner line. At the end of Palumbo's interrogation by the commission, the president warned him: 'I must tell you, General Palumbo, with considerable disappointment and, I believe, speaking for the whole commission, that you deserve to be arrested for your deposition [as was within the commission's power], not for its obvious reticence but for the innumerable lies it contained: if we have not done so it is out of respect for the *carabinieri* force and not because your attitude did not deserve such a measure.'[26]

The *carabiniere* cover-up over Peteano was not limited to accusing totally innocent people of the crime but also extended to the suppression of evidence and the fabrication of trial documents. Nor did the fact that the victims of the bombing were *carabinieri* deter other *carabinieri* from protecting the bombers. In 1987, three officers accused of perverting the course of justice were given prison sentences ranging up to ten years. Michele Santoro was sentenced to four years' imprisonment.

Even more alarming than this was the strange fate to befall a witness who came forward with valuable information, which could have led to the early identification of the anonymous telephone caller. A man writing under the assumed name of Antonio Minussi sent six letters to the prefect of Gorizia, providing a detailed description of two right-wing extremists who made a call from a bar in Monfalcone on the night of the bombing. The writer suggested a meeting with the Gorizia public prosecutor, which the latter failed to attend. 'Certainly the investigators attach no importance to the testimony of the only person capable of unmasking the criminal and of undermining any possible alibi in the event of his arrest,' Minussi observed bitterly in one of his letters. He also pointed out, prophetically, that 'it is very dangerous to collaborate with the police to combat either common or political delinquency'.[27]

These letters remained buried in a file until 1983 when a new and scrupulous investigation succeeded in tracing their author, an accountant living in Monfalcone and working for a local government office in Trieste. The man's real name was Maurizio Roitero and he had died, in somewhat mysterious circumstances, seven years earlier. Roitero had been found dead in a room next to his office at about 5 p.m. on 11 November 1976. He was slumped in an armchair, with his shoes off and his feet resting on another chair. He was holding a pornographic magazine, his flies were undone and his penis hanging out, but he had not bothered to lock the door. It was assumed he had suffered a heart-attack and he was buried without an autopsy. Seven years later, Examining Magistrate Felice Casson ordered an autopsy, which failed to uncover any traces of poison. Casson's written indictment highlighted the fact that Roitero's 'strange' death occurred at a time when six local underworld figures were on trial for the Peteano bombing and criticism of the investigators was particularly intense. There is no proof that Roitero was murdered but all the indications are that he was fully justified in his cautious approach to the original investigating team.

The most significant thing to emerge from the Peteano investigation is the testimony of the bomber, Vincenzo Vinciguerra. Vinciguerra has consistently refused to provide information to the magistrates that might implicate any of his comrades in crime but he has admitted responsibility for his own terrorist actions and taken it upon himself to denounce those terrorists he suspected of working for the secret services. He attributed responsibility for the strategy of tension to 'a structure parallel to the secret services and dependent on the Atlantic Alliance; Italian political and military leaders were perfectly aware of it. It was a structure trained for sabotage operations in the event of a Soviet invasion. The personnel was recruited in circles where anti-communism was at its strongest, that is to say on the far right.' The members of this secret organization 'had also been used for domestic purposes by national and international forces, and by international forces I mean principally the United States of America'.[28] Vinciguerra claimed that all the indiscriminate bombings against the public, from Piazza Fontana on, were attributable to a single organizational structure. The only exception in the catalogue of murder, he said, was the Peteano bombing, which was intended as a protest against the secret service manipulation of the forces of fascism; but even that bombing 'was covered up by the aforementioned organizational structure'.[29]

He explained that the political purpose of the bombings was to provoke popular rage to justify subsequent repression, leading to the declaration of a state of emergency. The effect would be to shore up the vacillating strength of the government: 'the whole thing obviously in an international context and in the framework of Italian membership of the Western system of alliances.'[30] He was particularly critical of his own organization, Ordine Nuovo, many of whose members, he said, belonged to the secret NATO anti-communist structure and were willingly manipulated by the secret services. He explained that the decision to cover up his own role in the Peteano bombing was prompted by the undesirability of admitting that such an attack on the armed forces in the crucial north-eastern sector of the country could have come from the right: as far as public perceptions were concerned, there should only be one kind of terrorist threat to the state and that was the threat from the left.

In his indictment, Judge Casson expressed some scepticism about Vinciguerra's description of the Peteano bombing as a break with the manipulators of terrorism, pointing out that Vinciguerra subsequently made use of 'untrustworthy' Ordine Nuovo members in order to make good his escape from Italy. What's more, an attack on the *carabinieri* was just the sort of provocative action that the public would assume to be the work of 'red' terrorists.

Vinciguerra has repeatedly denied that Stefano Delle Chiaie's Avanguardia Nazionale organization, to which he migrated in 1974, had the same kind of underhand relationship with the secret services as Ordine Nuovo. In an interview with *Panorama* magazine (29 March 1987), he made his position clear: 'I have no difficulty in admitting that Ordine Nero (an offshoot of ON) was a group invented by the secret services. There is proof of this. But there is no proof against Stefano Delle Chiaie.' It was therefore particularly significant when Vinciguerra informed the Bologna bomb trial that he had decided not to speak to the judicial authorities any more, while confirming his previous statements. He explained that if he continued to assist the magistates he would be 'violating a principle of equity, which prevents me from accusing people from a certain world who have been in the service of agencies of the state in favour of people who have presumably done the same things and to whom I am linked by important human ties'. The reference to Delle Chiaie and Avanguardia Nazionale was clear. Vinciguerra concluded: 'I believe that these people too have been in contact with state agencies without, however, in my opinion, agreeing to participate in a strategy of bomb massacres.'[31] Such an admission, after years of protecting Delle Chiaie from charges of collusion with the secret services and police, carries considerable weight.

Magistrates who have had dealings with Vinciguerra have been struck by a certain prickly integrity about the man and he remains true to his own ferocious personal code as virtually the last 'political soldier' of fascism. He told magistrates how he had discussed the physical elimination of Augusto Cauchi because of his alleged secret service links while the two were in hiding in Spain. 'The proposal remained just that, since Cauchi, having been pressed hard for a clarification, replied by protesting his total good faith and even started to cry. As a result humanitarian reasons prevailed, much against my own personal view.'[32] He was not short of damaging revelations to make about the people he believed to be willing participants in the management of the strategy of tension. He told Venice magistrates of a visit to Padua by Captain Labruna in November 1972, after Peteano and the hijack attempt. Labruna had discussed the two incidents with Ordine Nuovo leader Massimiliano Fachini, warning him to 'stop this mucking about'. According to Vinciguerra, Labruna 'wrongly believed that I was hierarchically dependent on Fachini'.[33] The allegation, if true, is of extraordinary gravity: it shows an amazingly flippant attitude to the murder of three *carabinieri* and indicates that the secret services already knew who was responsible for Peteano only six months after the bombing. Another proponent of the strategy of tension who did not meet with Vinciguerra's approval was Carlo Fumagalli. 'I consider Carlo Fumagalli to be an agent of the American secret services, linked to Italian military and political circles who shared a common past in the anti-communist Resistance and who were working to bring about an authoritarian change in our country, that would have been simultaneously anti-communist and anti-fascist,'[34] he told magistrates.

Perhaps the gravest implications of the Peteano affair stem from the way in which an informant in the Red Brigades was used to lay the blame for the bombing falsely on the left while the genuine information he provided was not used to prevent the rise of left-wing terrorism. The fact that men like Michele Santoro, members of a P2-influenced clique repeatedly implicated in right-wing conspiracies and in the perversion of justice, were the first representatives of the secret services to have contact with the Red Brigades justifies the deepest suspicions about the subsequent course of 'red' terrorism. Vinciguerra himself had something to say on the manipulation of left-wing terrorism. 'What happened in Argentina, where the heads of the Montoneros [left-wing guerrillas] had links with the military junta, has happened in Italy. The logic was the same in Argentina as in Italy, that is to create organizations that are officially against the state but which are, in their turn, led by men linked to the state,' he told Florence magistrates. 'When I say there is a parallel between Italy and Argentina I do not do so only on the basis of logic but because I believe there is a group of people who link the Italian situation to the Argentinian and I say that of this group the person known to the public is Gelli.'[35] From the moment he started making these revelations Vinciguerra was subjected to a campaign of official harassment in prison. This fact, acknowledged by Judge Casson in his indictment, testifies to the official disquiet such revelations are liable to cause.

It is clear then that the secret services spent the early part of the

1970s falsely implicating the left in right-wing atrocities and using rightists to infiltrate the extreme left, to manipulate it and provoke it to violence. It would not be surprising, therefore, if the birth of 'genuine' left-wing terrorism was viewed with considerable satisfaction in the national security establishment. Nor should it be surprising, given the secret services' record, if even 'genuine' left-wing extremism were found to contain a liberal sprinkling of infiltrators and had been piloted into the service of a conservative political project.

Notes

1 Quoted in Gianni Flamini, *Il Partito del Golpe*, Vol. 1, Italo Bovolenta, Ferrara, 1981, p. 33.
2 Quoted in Giuseppe De Lutiis, *Storia dei Servizi Segreti in Italia*, Editori Riuniti, Rome, 1984, p. 119.
3 Ibid., p. 220.
4 P. M. Libero Mancuso and Attilio Dardani, Requisitoria, Bologna, 13 May 1986, pp. 54–5.
5 Frederic Laurent, *L'Orchestre Noir*, Stock, Paris, 1978, p. 193.
6 P. M. Libero Mancuso and Attilio Dardani, op. cit., pp. 99–100.
7 Catanzaro assize court sentence, 23 February 1979, p. 306.
8 G. I. Gianfranco Migliaccio, arrest warrant, Tribunale di Catanzaro, 27 March 1976.
9 Domenico Porcelli, in 'Problematiche sulla Trattativa dei Processi di Strage', Quaderni del Consiglio Superiore della Magistratura, Rome, 1986, pp. 135–6.
10 Ibid., pp. 131–2.
11 Gianni Flamini, *Il Partito del Golpe*, Vol. 3, Tome 1, Italo Bovolenta, Ferrara, 1983, p. 94.
12 Catanzaro assize court sentence, 23 February 1979, p. 158.
13 Quoted in Roberto Pesenti (ed.), *Le Stragi del SID*, Mazzotta, Milan, 1974, pp. 54–66.
14 Catanzaro assize court sentence, 23 February 1979, p. 763.
15 Walter Rubini, *Il Segreto della Repubblica*, Edizioni FLAN, Milan, 1978, pp. 85–6.
16 Norberto Valentini, *La Notte della Madonna*, Le Monde, Rome, 1978, p. 204.
17 Quoted in Giuseppe De Lutiis, op. cit., p. 225.
18 Vittorio Borraccetti (ed.), *Eversione di Destra, Terrorismo, Stragi*, Franco Angeli, Milan, 1986, pp. 79–80.
19 Quoted in Gianni Flamini, *Il Partito del Golpe*, Vol. 3, Tome 2, Italo

Bovolenta, Ferrara, 1983, p. 563.

20 *La Repubblica*, 7 February 1987.

21 Report of the P2 Commission, Rome, 1984, p. 93.

22 Quoted in Gianni Flamini, *Il Partito del Golpe*, Vol. 3, Tome 2, Italo Bovolenta, Ferrara, 1983, p. 616.

23 G. I. Giampaolo Zorzi, Sentenza-ordinanza contro Cesare Ferri ed altri, Brescia, 23 March 1986.

24 Memorandum from Avv. Alberto Seganti (Pagliai family lawyer) to G. I. Luigi Gennaro, Rome, undated.

25 Venice assize court sentence, President Renato Gavardini, 25 July 1987, p. 399.

26 Ibid., p. 507.

27 Ibid., p. 563.

28 Ibid., p. 498.

29 G. I. Felice Casson, Sentenza-ordinanza, Venice, p. 123.

30 Ibid., p. 424.

31 Vincenzo Vinciguerra to G. I. L. Grassi, Prato prison, 18 November 1987.

32 Vincenzo Vinciguerra to G. I. G. Zorzi, Rebibbia prison, 6 May 1985.

33 G. I. Felice Casson, op. cit., p. 426.

34 Vincenzo Vinciguerra to G. I. G. Zorzi, Rebibbia prison, 6 May 1985.

35 Vincenzo Vinciguerra to G. I. Rosario Minna, Viterbo prison, 2 December 1986.

[8]

OPERATION GLADIO

IN August 1990 the veil of official secrecy and lies which had concealed the true nature of Colonel Rocca's civilian 'support units' and the Parallel SID referred to by several of the witnesses in Judge Tamburino's investigation into the Rosa dei Venti was finally drawn aside. What emerged was Operation Gladio, a secret NATO resistance network trained to go into action in the event of an Eastern Bloc invasion of Italy or domestic communist subversion. What made the revelation particularly delicate was the fact that something very like Gladio had been encountered in so many investigations into right-wing terrorism and coup plots. In the past, the judicial inquiries in this direction had always been blocked by the imposition of state secrecy.

On this occasion it was the investigations of two Venice magistrates, Carlo Mastelloni and Felice Casson, that forced the government to admit what the magistrates had already discovered. The first official admission, still not entirely truthful, came on 3 August, when Prime Minister Giulio Andreotti told a parliamentary commission investigating the failure to get to the bottom of Italy's right-wing bomb massacres that a NATO stay-behind network had existed but had ceased operations in 1972. Andreotti promised to send the commission further documentation on the subject. On 18 October the Prime Minister sent the commission a secret service report entitled 'The So-called Parallel SID – Operation Gladio'. It was initially returned to him by the commission president, Libero Gualtieri, who suggested that the document constituted a breach of NATO secrecy. A censored version was then sent back to the commission and later the original document, or something very close to it, was made public.[1]

The document revealed that the resistance network had been set up immediately after the war and later formalized, in 1956, in a secret agreement between SIFAR and the CIA. Its members were trained for information-gathering, sabotage, communications and in helping key personnel to escape from enemy-controlled territory. Senior members of the network attended courses run by the Training Division of the British Intelligence Service. It was clear from the report that the organization had been in large part financed and controlled by the CIA. The report also revealed that 139 arms caches had been buried at secret locations for use by Gladio members in the event of an invasion. That operation began in 1963, just one year before General De Lorenzo's projected coup. The secret services began digging up the dumps in 1972 after one of them had been discovered by accident. Despite all official assurances, public suspicions have focused on the prevalently right-wing membership of Gladio and the fate of the arms and explosives supplied to the organization. Andreotti's report revealed that two cases of weapons had gone missing and that a further ten could not be recovered after the place where they had been buried had been built over. Somewhat grotesquely, two of them had been incorporated into village cemeteries after these had been enlarged.

The sensitivity of the Gladio organization, named after the Italian word for a Roman short-sword, can be gauged by the repeated official denials of its existence. Andreotti had himself denied the existence of such an organization on a number of occasions in the past, and Moro had done the same thing with particular persistence and vigour. On 5 November, after Andreotti had already released details of Operation Gladio, a NATO spokesman in Brussels issued yet another official denial: 'An organization of this kind does not and never has existed within the framework of the NATO military structure,' the spokesman told reporters.[2] The following day a different spokesman issued an embarrassed retraction, saying the previous announcement had been 'a mistake' and that NATO had no comment to make on the subject.[3] In fact, a similar stay-behind network had been set up in most of the countries of Western Europe, including Austria, Yugoslavia and neutral Switzerland.

Andreotti, President Francesco Cossiga and senior members of the secret services have all given repeated assurances as to the legitimacy of Gladio and the democratic credentials of its members. Andreotti's report to the parliamentary commission stressed that Gladio members were recruited from people loyal to the Constitution, with no criminal record, who were not involved in active politics or members of extremist organizations. Another report sent to the commission stresses the importance of the human qualities of the 'gladiators'. 'The human factor remains of paramount importance, both for the qualities that must distinguish the directors of the operation and for the idealistic commitment of operational members who join the stay-behind programme.'[4] P2 boss Licio Gelli revealed a more down-to-earth view of the organization when he was questioned about it by a journalist from the Belgian newspaper *Le Soir*. Gelli said that Gladio had nothing to do with NATO but had been set up by the CIA immediately after the war. The Agency had decided to help the enfeebled Italian Army to face up to the menace of a Soviet invasion by recruiting 'patriots who knew how to fight,' he said. 'They found them among the former soldiers of the Republic of Salò.' So among Gladio's first recruits, according to Gelli, were the fascist veterans of Mussolini's last stand. Gelli was also in no doubt that Gladio had a dual role, to fight the Soviet invader and to prevent the invasion from taking place 'by stopping the Italian Communist Party from achieving power'. (*Le Soir*, 15 November 1990.) This dual role is confirmed in the second report, dating from 1959, received by the parliamentary commission on terrorism, which specifies that Gladio would go into operation in the event of Italian territory being occupied or of internal subversion.[5] Given that many secret service officers considered anyone belonging to the PCI and many members of the Socialist Party to be dangerous subversives, it is quite possible that Gladio's leaders felt counter-measures were necessary throughout the Sixties and Seventies.

The insistence by Andreotti and Cossiga on the absolute legitimacy of Gladio provoked, in the autumn of 1990, one of the gravest political and institutional crises ever seen in Italy. Their statements effectively pre-empted the conclusions of the Venice magistrates, of the parliamentary commission on terrorism, of the parliamentary commission on the secret services and of a commission of five Constitutional Court judges which was appointed by the government to examine the issue on 5 December.

Cossiga set the ball rolling in October by stating that as an under-secretary in the Defence Ministry he had himself been involved in the administration of Gladio. He expressed satisfaction that the secrecy surrounding the organization had been maintained for forty-five years. Subsequently Judge Casson wrote to the President inquiring whether he would be prepared to give evidence relating to his experience of Gladio, a request which Cossiga immediately turned down as incompatible with his office. The President then became embroiled in conflict with the Supreme Council of the Magistrature which had proposed discussing the issues raised by his refusal to testify before Casson. Cossiga wrote to the Council, of which he is officially the head, peremptorily ordering it not to discuss the issue and not to question his decision to ban the debate.

At the beginning of December Cossiga threatened to stand down temporarily from the Presidency unless the Cabinet endorsed his view on the legitimacy of Gladio. This followed a magazine interview in which Socialist Finance Minister Rino Formica had expressed grave reservations on the subject. Andreotti managed to resolve the crisis by getting the Cabinet to pass a resolution affirming the legitimacy of Gladio, on which the Socialists abstained. Cossiga continued to make passionate speeches in defence of the secret organization and passionate attacks on anyone who questioned his judgement, to such an extent that some newspapers began publicly to question his sanity. The President was particularly stung by massive public demonstrations organized by the PCI and calling for the truth about Gladio and the right-wing bombings. These featured a number of colourful attacks on both Andreotti and Cossiga. A popular, if imperfectly rhyming, chant was: 'Cossiga Francesco, you're worse than Ceausescu!' But the President's provocative campaign continued, with public words of praise for coup plotter Edgardo Sogno, a visit to pay his respects after the death of General Vito Miceli, and a friendly public greeting to former secret service officer and Gelli associate General Giovanni Allavena. The upshot of all this was a request by the tiny Proletarian Democracy Party for Cossiga's impeachment on charges of high treason, a request that was immediately rejected by the relevant parliamentary committee.

But the problems are by no means over for Cossiga. He played a leading role in the censorship of reports into secret service abuses in the 1960s, censorship that may have been partly designed to preserve the secrecy surrounding Gladio and which might explain the President's extreme nervousness on the subject today. Captain Antonio Labruna has alleged that he was called on in September 1969 to edit recordings of evidence given to several different government commissions investigating the coup plot hatched in 1964 by General

Giovanni De Lorenzo. Acting on the instructions of SID director Eugenio Henke and, Labruna claims, of Under-secretary of Defence Francesco Cossiga, he eliminated sensitive items of information and edited the tapes so that the censorship would not be noticed. On the basis of Labruna's testimony *L'Espresso* magazine (16 December 1990) has alleged that a profound 'cleaning' of the tapes took place in order to protect particular individuals and political interests. 'Information concerning Gladio and all the mechanisms for the repression of "communist subversion" also disappeared,' the magazine claimed. The role of the CIA in the affair will almost certainly have been discreetly swept under the carpet as well.

General Aldo Beolchini, who presided over one of the inquiries into secret service abuses, has attributed the failure of the government to take firm action at the time to the blackmailing power of SIFAR's archives. As we have seen, he believes that failure paved the way for further illegalities over the following decades. He told *La Repubblica* (21 December 1990) recently that General De Lorenzo had succeeded in getting much of the political class under his thumb. 'He accumulated dossiers of false and true information. He threatened to use both. And all, or almost all, gave in to that aggressive and power-hungry maniac. You should have met him!' He laid the primary responsibility for the cover-up on Aldo Moro, who was Prime Minister at the time. 'De Lorenzo inserted a lie about Moro's private life into his file, but at the same time he had another enormous file on Freato [Moro's secretary], on his wealth, on the payments he could depend on.' According to Beolchini there was even a file on Andreotti, 'but it was a miserable little file. Andreotti is cunning and he must have succeeded in wriggling out somehow.'

Andreotti's response to the Gladio crisis, in contrast to that of Cossiga, has been much more cool and sophisticated. When providing false information he has always taken care to attribute responsibility for it to someone else, usually the secret services, whose job it is to lie in the interests of the state. He outlined the details of the Gladio organization in a masterly speech to the Senate on 8 November, referring to the 'unproven hypothesis' of a connection between 'members of these defensive organizations and the tragic events of terrorism'. 'No one can doubt that any possible wrongful use of such a structure can only have occurred outside the framework of ministerial directives,' he assured the senators. It is ironic that Andreotti, who has presided over Italy's most secret defence arrangements for longer than any other politician, should be the man to oversee the final unveiling and dismantling of Gladio. Consummate politician though he is, it is possible that even his reputation will be tarnished before the last stone is turned. Born in 1919, he has held twenty-eight Cabinet posts and at the beginning of 1991 had been Prime Minister six times. He is a man of great charm, ready wit and subtle intelligence who is admired and detested in almost equal measure by the people he governs. With characteristic sticking-out ears and a hunched back, he is a gift to caricaturists, and his career has itself been a kind of caricature of the Byzantine quality of Italian political life. A regular church-goer and *habitué* of the higher echelons of the Vatican, he has also been suspected of involvement in some of the most nefarious events of Italy's recent, troubled history. If he succeeds in convincing the Italian public that all was well with Gladio and the sinister sister organizations that lurked in its shadow, he will have pulled off his greatest conjuring trick yet.

There are many reasons for suspicion, however. The very title of the document sent by Andreotti to the parliamentary commission, 'The So-called Parallel SID – Operation Gladio', takes the organization to the heart of Judge Tamburino's investigation into the Rosa dei Venti and related coup plots. There are also reasons for suspecting a link with General De Lorenzo's Piano Solo, aside from the coincidence that the Gladio arms deposits were laid down in the year before the coup project went into effect. It has now been acknowledged that the secret training camp at Capo Marrargiu in Sardinia was the official training centre for Operation Gladio. In the event of the Italian mainland being occupied by enemy forces, Gladio sabotage and resistance operations were to be run from the Sardinian base, which could also have become the site for a government in exile. The 1959 secret service report on Gladio sent to the parliamentary commission states that the CIA had specified 'on 7 October 1957, that support for the base "is considered in the war plans of the United States of America"'.[6] It is therefore somewhat embarrassing that several secret service witnesses have testified that left-wing subversives to be rounded up in the course of General De Lorenzo's 1964 coup were to have been sent to Sardinia and interned in that very base. What is more, the base itself was set up in 1963, just one year before the planned coup.

The link between Gladio and the Rosa dei Venti conspiracy has been explicitly made by Roberto Cavallaro, encouraged by Andreotti's decision to lift state secrecy on the subject. 'Operation Gladio? We used to call it Organization X, or, in jargon, Rosa dei Venti. But seeing what the Prime Minister told the commission on terrorism, I think it's all the same thing,' the former coup conspirator told *Panorama* magazine (4 November 1990). He claimed that several of his colleagues had 'Cosmic' level security clearance, which can only be issued at the highest levels of the Atlantic Alliance. He said the organization had been given the task of infiltrating extremist groups in order to create a situation of tension requiring the intervention of the armed forces, in the event of significant electoral advances by the left. His colleagues, he said, had infiltrated both right- and left-wing groups. 'I knew for a fact that a large number of terrorists, both red and black, acted on the orders or under the influence of the secret services,' he told the magazine. These claims are of the greatest importance, since much of what Cavallaro and others like him told Judge Tamburino more than fifteen years ago now appears to have been confirmed by the government.

Despite all official assurances to the contrary, there is a strong suspicion that a complete list of Gladio members, if that should ever be made public, would contain numerous names of right-wing extremists, possibly of people implicated in acts of terrorism. Magistrates in Brescia, for example, have begun examining the possibility that Gladio may have been in some way involved in the 1974 Piazza della Loggia bombing. Judge Casson's investigations have revealed that the gladiators were unusually thick on the ground in that part of the world. One particularly encumbering name discovered by Casson on the cover of an almost empty secret service file pertaining to a Gladio member is that of Gianfranco Bertoli. The secret services insist that it is just a coincidence and that the person involved has nothing to do with the man who attempted to blow up the Interior Minister with a bomb in 1973. It is significant that Vincenzo Vinciguerra, one of the first insiders to lift the veil on secret service manipulation of terrorism, has drawn attention to Bertoli's attack as a particularly good example of secret service-inspired terrorism. He has also claimed that he was himself invited to carry out an assassination attempt on the same minister some two years earlier. The proposal was put to him, he told magistrates, by two members of Ordine Nuovo whom he suspected of being in contact with the secret services.[7] Much of what Vinciguerra had alleged in the past appears to meet with confirmation in Andreotti's revelations about Gladio.

Perhaps where Gladio gets closest to direct involvement in terrorism is with the Peteano bombing, carried out by Vinciguerra himself. It may have been to preserve the secrecy of Gladio that the secret services organized their heavy-handed cover-up over the affair. On 24 February 1972, at Aurisina in north-east Italy, not far from Peteano, some children playing in the woods discovered one of the Gladio arms caches and reported their find to the *carabinieri*. A week later, more arms were found in a cave nearby. In both cases, it appears, the dumps had been interfered with and some of the explosives were missing. The then commander of Gladio, General Gerardo Serravalle, used this incident as a pretext to recommend the dismantling of all the Gladio dumps. As we shall see, he had come to suspect the democratic reliability of many of his own men. The remaining explosives were immediately detonated by the *carabinieri* and the secret services busied themselves in concealing the true nature of the arms caches, encouraging investigators to pursue the theory that the weapons belonged to international arms traffickers rather than to the guardians of Italian democracy. Three months later, on 31 May 1972, Vinciguerra staged the Peteano bombing and there is a strong suspicion that the explosives used in that attack may have originated in one of the Aurisina dumps. When Casson attempted to investigate this hypothesis some eighteen years later, he was told by the *carabinieri* that all the documentation relating to the discovery had been destroyed.[8] It is quite possible that the secret service cover-up over Peteano may have been intended simply to preserve the secret of Gladio. But it is hard to avoid the suspicion that the anti-communist organization may have been more directly involved in the bombing and that someone in the know may have tipped off members of Vinciguerra's group about where they could obtain their explosives.

Some of the most serious doubts about the reliability of the gladiators stem from the testimony of General Serravalle, commander of the organization from 1971 to 1974, who was one of the first secret service officers to lift the veil of secrecy about the organization in evidence to Judge Mastelloni. Serravalle has described how, shortly after his appointment, he made a point of meeting some of the men under his command and was shocked by the extremist views that many of them expressed. Rather than waiting for a Soviet invasion, half of the gladiators were eager to set about eliminating Italian communists without delay. 'I found myself, an officer in the service of the Italian Republic, at the head of an armed band,' the general told

[153]

the parliamentary commission on terrorism.[9] He was even more specific in the course of a television interview: the Gladio arms dumps, he said, were 'an absolute threat to the stability of the country'.[10] The discovery of the Aurisina dump provided him with a convenient excuse to recommend the dismantling of all the arms caches on the grounds that they were no longer secure. But he did not share his suspicions with his secret service superiors because he had so little faith in them. 'Miceli [SID director] was a man of honour, but I was afraid of the other people around him, who had been in SIFAR and were involved in Piano Solo,' he told me.[11]

As a result of Serravalle's recommendation most of the dumps were dug up and the weapons were transported to the base in Sardinia using a secret service plane, Argo 16. This aircraft exploded in flight near Venice on 23 November 1973, and Judge Mastelloni has been conducting an investigation into the hypothesis that it was sabotaged by the Israeli secret service to punish the Italians for their policy of releasing captured Palestinian terrorists. The plane had also been used to provide released Palestinians with free passage out of Italy. Serravalle, however, has publicly speculated that the sabotage may actually have been carried out by aggrieved members of Gladio in revenge for the decision to dismantle their dumps. He was himself due to have flown on the plane on the day of the crash. That the commanding officer could suspect his own men of attempting to murder him speaks volumes about the Gladio membership.

Serravalle's suspicions received apparent confirmation from General Giuseppe Cismondi, who had been his deputy in the Gladio organization. On 30 November 1990, the *Corriere della Sera* published an interview with Cismondi in which the general was harshly critical of the decision to dismantle the dumps and expressed his support for General De Lorenzo, 'a fine man, whose reputation has been unjustly blackened'. The following day, 1 December, the communist newspaper *L'Unità* quoted Cismondi as describing how he nearly lost a case of Tocai wine, as well as his own life, on the Argo 16 plane. After a change of plan Cismondi had had the wine unloaded from the aircraft and he had taken it to Rome where he drank it later that day. 'You drank the wine despite the fact a secret service plane had just gone down?' the journalist asked. 'He gave a slightly crooked smile: "It's always right to drink a toast, especially when the mother-in-law dies."' The *Unità* correspondent commented in astonishment: 'It may have been a slightly unfortunate joke or perhaps a coded message?'

Despite all this, Serravalle finds it hard to believe that his own men were involved in terrorism and, as yet, no concrete proof of this has been found. He has speculated that Gladio may have been made public 'because it was the presentable part of the whole thing. I am afraid that by fixing the searchlights on Gladio the shadows behind it will grow and will serve to conceal the "usual suspects".'[12] The decision to remove the Gladio arms caches was not communicated at the time to the CIA. This may have been a gesture of independence on the part of the Italians, or it may have been because hardliners in the CIA would have disapproved of the decision, but it could also have reflected a suspicion that the Agency supported the use of Gladio members to carry out acts of terrorism.

The view that more dangerous organizations may have operated in the shadow of Gladio is shared by former Socialist Party leader Francesco De Martino, who was leader of the party when it participated in a coalition government with Moro's Christian Democrats in the early Sixties. He believes that one of the purposes of coup plots and right-wing terrorism was to put pressure on the Socialists to become obedient junior partners of the Christian Democrats and to abandon their insistence on a programme of radical reforms. 'My conviction', he told *La Repubblica* newspaper (4 December 1990) 'is that alongside the so-to-speak national organization [Gladio], set up by De Lorenzo, there was another, quite different organization, linked to foreign agencies.' De Martino confirmed that blackmail was a factor in the government's decision to conceal the reality of De Lorenzo's coup plot, a decision he personally had opposed. He told the paper that Moro had warned his Socialist predecessor Pietro Nenni that if he insisted on pursuing the SIFAR scandal 'mountains of mud would have poured out on to individuals and parties, including the Socialist Party, in connection with which photocopies of cheques and other not very edifying stories were beginning to circulate'. He said he believed that certain Christian Democrat leaders may have made use of the subversive activities of right-wing generals to try and bring the recalcitrant Socialist Party into line. And he made it clear that he thought the secret services operating in the shadow of Gladio were linked to the American secret services, 'which don't always follow the line pursued by their government'. 'It may be easy to dismantle Gladio but it will be much harder to get to the bottom of the mechanism that served to torment the political life of our country over the last twenty-five years,' he warned.

There is good reason to suspect, as Roberto Cavallaro has alleged, that members of Gladio or like organizations have succeeded in infiltrating left-wing groups. And it would now appear that the organization may even have played a role in the Red Brigades' kidnap of Aldo Moro, the man who had done so much to protect it during the 1960s. One element to emerge recently concerns the sale by a secret service office, the Special Units Group, known by its Italian acronym RUS, of a cast-off photocopying machine which ended up in the possession of the Rome column of the Red Brigades. The AB DIK photocopier was sold as unserviceable in 1977 and ended up in perfect working order in a Red Brigades printing shop in Via Pio Foà. Neither magistrates nor the parliamentary Moro Commission appear to have shown much interest in this curious coincidence and the head of the secret service office, Colonel Federico Appel, was never questioned about it and is now, conveniently, dead. For one thing, the true nature of the RUS was never apparent to the commission. SISMI director Giuseppe Santovito lied to the parliamentarians, insisting: 'It's nothing special. It's an administrative office for conscript soldiers: drivers and radio operators are known as special units.'[13] It would take the emergence of Gladio and the testimony of General Serravalle for the true nature of the RUS to become clear: it was an administrative office for the Gladio training school in Sardinia, protected by the highest levels of official secrecy. It might be objected that the secret services could hardly have thought of a clumsier way of providing the Red Brigades with a photocopier than to sell them one of their own, almost directly. But stranger things than this have happened.

On 18 March 1978, two days after the kidnap of Aldo Moro, an unnamed secret service officer granted an interview to La Repubblica newspaper. He described the kidnap operation as a technical jewel, 'so perfect as to seem almost artistic'. The kind of people capable of carrying it out were either highly trained soldiers or civilians 'who have undergone lengthy commando training in specialized bases'. The officer went on to say that the organization responsible for the kidnap was very solid, 'both in its genuinely ideologically motivated members and in the sectors that are controlled by other directors, for other purposes, which paradoxically coincide'. What the anonymous officer appears to be suggesting is that the Red Brigades were divided into two sections, the 'genuine' revolutionaries and the secret service infiltrators, and that those responsible for the Moro ambush had received specialist military training. In Sardinia, perhaps?

Once again, Mino Pecorelli is able to offer an illuminating insight into what was going on in the world of secret politics. On 5 September 1972, Christian Democrat deputy Arnaldo Forlani issued an alarming warning, which he subsequently retracted, in the course of a speech in the north-western port of La Spezia. 'The reactionary right has set in motion perhaps the most dangerous operation it has mounted since the Liberation and the plot has also enjoyed international support,' Forlani said. 'This operation is not yet over. We have concrete evidence that the operation is still under way.'[14] Pecorelli returned to discuss this speech in an article published in *OP* in 1974 (17 December 1974). He claimed that then Prime Minister Giulio Andreotti had been using his own personal collaborators within the secret services to manipulate the far right. 'The most likely hypothesis is that the Prime Minister wants to continue to use the lever of right-wing disorder to guarantee for himself, that is for the man who represents a "shift to the right", the possibility of remaining in Palazzo Chigi [the Prime Minister's office],' Pecorelli wrote. 'Forlani and Rumor have discovered this . . . That is why the Christian Democrat secretary spoke out.'

More interesting than this explanation for Forlani's surprising outburst, however, is the evidence that Pecorelli was already aware of the existence of Gladio, sixteen years before it became public knowledge. The *OP* editor claimed that Andreotti's contact with the far right had been established through a secret service colonel, identified only by the first letter of his surname: V. 'This colonel was, until a short time ago, commander of the secret service's sabotage department, which trains in Sardinia and has unlimited availability of explosives. It will be noted, in fact, that in all cases of right-wing bombings the explosives almost never turn out to be stolen.' In the (much rarer) cases of left-wing bombings, Pecorelli said, the explosives used were always stolen. He claimed that Colonel V. had been passing on explosives to right-wing extremists on behalf of Andreotti, who wanted to increase right-wing subversion. The allegation echoes the claim made by Giuseppe De Lutiis, which we have already seen, that Capo Marrargiu graduates were allowed to keep the arms and explosives provided during training.

Pecorelli's apparent familiarity with Gladio takes on a peculiar significance in the light of one of his most enigmatic pieces of coded writing. On 23 May 1978, he published what appears to be an eye-witness account of the scene in Via Caetani, where the body of Aldo Moro was dumped in the boot of a car, parked next to the high wall which runs down one side of the street. A 'blonde woman' is present among the bystanders at the scene and comments that behind the wall lie 'the remains of the Theatre of Balbus, Rome's third amphitheatre'. She continues: 'I read in a book that in those days runaway slaves and prisoners were taken there so that they could fight one another to the death. Who knows what there was in the destiny of Moro that his death should be discovered next to that wall? The blood of yesterday and the blood of today.' Pecorelli is talking about 'gladiators' in the context of Moro's death, but until mid-1990 very few people could have understood what he meant. Few better than the secret service journalist will have known of Moro's role in preserving the secrecy surrounding Gladio by censoring reports into the SIFAR scandal and blocking the investigation of Judge Tamburino into the Rosa dei Venti. But he also appears to be hinting that the gladiators were in some way implicated in Moro's murder.

There are indeed many reasons for viewing the Gladio organization with the deepest of suspicion. For one thing, not all of Italy's elected rulers were informed of its existence by the head of the secret services. President Giovanni Leone is reported to have been furious on learning that he had been kept in the dark about it. 'They tell me that there are 10,000 armed civilians on the loose in Italy,' Leone is quoted as saying. 'As usual I am a president of shit, who is the last person to hear these things.'[15] Nor is it reassuring to learn that the gladiators were in large part armed with Eastern Bloc weapons. Secret service director Admiral Fulvio Martini told the parliamentary commission on terrorism that the Gladio arms dumps contained Kalashnikovs and other Soviet weapons, as well as explosives from Czechoslovakia.[16] It is interesting to remember, in this context, Richard Brenneke's claim to have bought weapons in Czechoslovakia on behalf of the CIA. It is hard to imagine what advantage the gladiators could derive from the use of Eastern Bloc weapons in the event of a Soviet invasion. Their use for acts of terrorism in peacetime, on the other hand, would conveniently point the finger of blame at the communist bloc. It would be interesting to know, for example, how many of Gladio's Soviet-made weapons ended up in the hands of the Red Brigades.

The OP article linking Moro's destiny with the gladiators has received indirect support from Francesco De Martino, who told *La Repubblica* (30 December 1990): 'Today one might even argue that Moro's death may have been facilitated by this practice of letting things slide, of not punishing those who deserve it.' Pecorelli's suggestion that the gladiators were in some way involved in Moro's murder may seem far-fetched but there are other elements that support it, as we shall discover.

Notes

1 *L'Unità* Special Supplement, 14 November 1990, pp. 6–7.
2 ANSA, Brussels, 20.44, 5 November 1990.
3 AGI, Brussels, 6 November 1990.
4 SIFAR Special Forces and Operation Gladio, Report prepared for SIFAR director, Rome, 1 June 1959, p. 7.
5 Ibid., p. 2.
6 Ibid., p. 2.
7 Vincenzo Vinciguerra to G. I. Felice Casson, Venice, 14 August 1984.
8 Leo Sisti, *L'Espresso*, 2 December 1990.
9 Gianni Cipriani, *L'Unità*, 21 November 1990.
10 Telefono Giallo, RAI3, 28 November 1990.
11 General Gerardo Serravalle to the author, 2 December 1990.
12 Ibid.
13 Chiara Valentini, *L'Espresso*, 9 December 1990.
14 Sandra Bonsanti, *La Repubblica*, 17 November 1990.
15 Franco Giustolisi, *L'Espresso*, 18 November 1990.
16 Giovanni Maria Bellu, *La Repubblica*, 16 November 1990.

[9]

STILL
COVERING UP

ONE of the clearest and most plausible rationalizations of the right-wing bombings, which explains the intelligent political purpose that lay behind them, is provided by a secret service report on the background to the 1970 Borghese coup attempt. The report cites a conversation between an unnamed military officer and Prince Prospero Colonna, a member of Prince Valerio Borghese's National Front organization. According to the report, Colonna told the officer that Borghese 'had already prepared a plan of provocation with a series of large bomb attacks to ensure that the military intervention of the right would take place in a climate of general reprobation for the "red" criminals; he also added that in some cases innocent victims are, unfortunately, necessary.' The officer's reaction typified the military's tendency to play down the threat of right-wing terrorism. He considered Colonna's speech to be 'the empty talk of a chatter-box'.[1]

In the light of Colonna's rationalization, the last two major bombings to inflict wanton death and destruction on the Italian public were something of an anomaly. As so often in the past, the target was the railway system: one bomb, in August 1980, destroying the second-class waiting room at Bologna station, the other, in December 1984, blasting a train as it travelled through a tunnel in Tuscany. What was strange about them, though, was that there was no longer any immediately intelligible purpose to the bombings. The coup season was definitively closed. There was no longer any question that such atrocities might provoke a civil war, the declaration of a state of emergency, or military intervention to restore order. And the

Communist Party was no longer a threat; its electoral support was beginning to tail off and any question of its being brought into the government had been shelved with the death of Aldo Moro in 1978. What then was the purpose of these massacres?

It seems clear that some, at least, of those involved in the bombings came from the same right-wing roots as those responsible for the strategy of tension bombings a decade earlier. Once again the secret services were active in their efforts to sabotage the judicial investigations, outdoing themselves over Bologna but somewhat less energetic over the train bombing. By 1984 both their capacity and their desire to cover up for the bombers appear to have diminished as the terrorists' motives moved further away from the original ones of the strategy of tension. The 1980 bombing, however, provoked some of the most blatant, and risky, attempts at judicial sabotage ever seen in Italy.

One of the most striking was a secret service operation codenamed 'Terror on the trains', mounted just six months after the bombing. On 13 January 1981, a suitcase containing explosives and a submachine-gun was found on a train at Bologna station. The discovery followed a tip-off from SISMI, who were able to specify the exact type of suitcase and the carriage in which it would be found. Four days earlier, SISMI had reported that one of their sources had informed them of an imminent campaign of train bombings organized by a group of Italian fascists in conjunction with French and German right-wingers. The whole episode lent weight to the theory that the station bombing was the result of an international conspiracy, an idea put forward by Licio Gelli himself and passed on by the secret services to the Bologna magistrates shortly after the massacre. The argument appeared particularly convincing since the suitcase explosive was similar to the type used in the August bombing.

It later emerged, however, that the suitcase had actually been planted by two secret service officers, General Pietro Musumeci, a member of P2, and Colonel Giuseppe Belmonte. The two were found guilty of conspiring to sabotage the Bologna bomb investigation by a Rome assize court in 1985. That verdict was modified on appeal the following year. The appeal court decided that although the officers were guilty of planting the explosives they had done so merely with the intention of pocketing the 300 million Lire (£150,000) reward that SISMI had paid to its non-existent source and in order to improve the intelligence agency's standing relative to its rival, SISDE, which had recently achieved a number of operational successes. The court decided that the officers could have had no interest in side-tracking the Bologna investigation as it was making no progress at the time. Bologna magistrates tend to disagree. They pointed out that three of their prime suspects were then in prison and one of them, criminologist Aldo Semerari, appeared to be on the verge of a nervous breakdown and had been threatening to make revelations about the political background to the bombing. Semerari was released from prison shortly afterwards. He was kidnapped and murdered by members of the Neapolitan Camorra in March 1982. Examining Magistrate Vito Zincani rejected the notion that the operation was mounted simply as an excuse for theft. He saw it instead as part of 'a determined plan to confuse the evidence in order to prevent the identification of the people responsible for the Bologna bombing'.[2] Zincani's view was also shared by the parliamentary committee responsible for overseeing the activities of the secret services.

One alarming aspect of the secret service hoax was the provenance of the MAB submachine-gun found in the case. It was part of a stock of weapons which had been modified by a right-wing group from north-east Italy and had subsequently been stored in an arms cache in the basement of a Health Ministry building in Rome: the same arms cache from where some of the bullets used to kill Mino Pecorelli are believed to have come. The arms were used by the Magliana band from the Rome underworld, by right-wing extremists and sometimes even by the left. One of those who administered the arms store was Egidio Giuliani, a right-winger whose terrorist career has all the hallmarks of the *agent provocateur*. Giuliani had been in contact with Europa Civiltà (Europe Civilization), a right-wing study group frequented by freemasons and secret service informants. His politics moved apparently to the left over the years and he was happy to supply arms to members of the Red Brigades and to undertake joint operations with left-wing terrorists. But when a fellow right-winger visited his home he found Giuliani's taste in books was still the same as ever: the works of Julius Evola and other rightist gurus still lined his shelves.[3] The Bologna prosecutor stated categorically that the Health Ministry arms cache belonged to Giuliani[4] but in 1989, a Rome prosecutor preparing a case against Magliana members considered responsible for the basement armoury had barely heard of Giuliani and assured me that he was not one of the defendants.[5] It seems the authorities may have turned a benevolently blind eye towards the activities of Giuliani, who was charged with involvement in a bomb attack on the offices of the Milan City Council a mere five days before the Bologna bombing. Strangely, he was acquitted before even being brought to trial, as the examining magistrates decided that although he had supplied the explosives used in the Milan bombing, he did not necessarily know what they were to be used for.[6]

Control over one of Rome's principal arms deposits, from which weapons were loaned on an occasional basis to terrorists of the left and right as well as to common criminals, would have given the secret services an ideal vantage point from which to track criminal activity in the capital. The fact that the secret services should be able so easily to dispose of the Health Ministry weapons for their own secret operations illustrates the close relationship between SISMI and the Magliana/Giuliani group. This is particularly grave given that the Magliana band were in contact with the Mafia, with terrorists of both colours and with members of P2 and were from time to time the source of alarming blackmailing messages based on inside knowledge of some of the most sensitive terrorist operations.

The planting of the hoax suitcase has its own sinister codicil, involving once again the convenient death of a potentially embarrassing witness. Shortly after the discovery of the case, SISMI reported that the two airline tickets it contained, in the name of non-existent French citizens, had been bought in Bari by Giorgio Vale, a right-wing terrorist and member of NAR (Armed Revolutionary Cells). Subsequent investigation would reveal that Vale had not in fact bought the tickets. Vale was killed on 5 May 1982, when police raided his apartment on the outskirts of Rome. According to the official version, Vale opened fire on the police before turning his pistol on himself and shooting himself in the head. Forensic tests, however, showed no traces on the terrorist's hand to indicate that he had indeed fired the pistol. The explanation that someone might have washed Vale's hands during the course of an autopsy was hastily put forward. His parents and friends remain adamant that Vale was not the kind of person to commit suicide. Further complicating the affair are two anonymous phone-calls announcing Vale's arrest, which were made to the Italian news agency ANSA and the *Messaggero* newspaper on 6 and 7 March. In the second call, a spokesman for NAR threatened reprisals against the police if news of Vale's arrest was not made public. It would certainly have been inconvenient if Vale had been arrested and set about demolishing part of SISMI's fantasy background to the suitcase on the train, and this at a time when the Bologna magistrates still had no reason to doubt the secret service version of events.[7]

If the reason for the Bologna blast was not to pave the way for a military takeover, then there must be some alternative explanation. A number of theories have been put forward, some more plausible than others, and some with the obvious intention of creating confusion. Gelli himself has recently suggested that the explosion may have been caused by the accidental detonation of a consignment of explosives while they were being transported through Italy by a group of Arab terrorists.[8] A similar view has been expressed by other figures from the P2/secret service establishment and it should therefore be considered with some suspicion.

Another not entirely reliable account has been offered by Elio Ciolini, a collaborator of the French secret services who had been in contact with Stefano Delle Chiaie in South America. Ciolini was in prison in Switzerland for fraud when he contacted the Italian authorities, offering them information about the Bologna bombing if they paid his bail for him. He initially convinced magistrates that the decision to commission the bombing was taken at a meeting of a secret masonic lodge in Monte Carlo attended by an assortment of Italy's business and political leaders and that its purpose was to distract public attention from the privatization of Montedison, a major state-owned petrochemical company. The takeover was to be financed partly with American funds and the bombing would distract the attention of political forces likely to oppose such a move. Ciolini named several right-wingers from France and Germany whom he accused of having participated in the organization of the bombing. He subsequently went on to embroider his account until he succeeded in totally discrediting it and himself. He could not, though, have embarked on the project without a fund of first-hand knowledge about Stefano Delle Chiaie, who remains one of the suspected participants in the conspiracy behind the bombing. According to one account, the antics of this bizarre 'supergrass' delayed the Bologna inquiry by as much as two years. Ciolini's role followed the pattern of other superwitnesses employed by the secret services to undermine terrorism investigations: they start by telling a story that is true or at least plausible and then go on to add more and more falsehoods until truth and falsehood become indistinguishable and the reliable leads they may have touched on are definitively discredited.

Though Ciolini's word is wholly unreliable, he did offer an

interesting portrait of himself in an interview with *L'Europeo* magazine (30 May 1987). 'I have always considered myself to be a suitable instrument for blocking the rise of communism, both in Italy and abroad,' he said. 'I have worked to this end without ever following my own initiative, but always carrying out orders.' This is a curious autobiography for someone who had been actively involved in blocking the investigation into the Bologna bombing. Ciolini's comment about Delle Chiaie is also revealing: 'He was doing the same work as me, under the mask of a right-wing extremist. But he's a good man, an idealist.' In 1984 and 1985, Ciolini appears to have found refuge in the United States, where he allegedly enjoyed the protection of an FBI agent named Steve Vitale.[9]

The international terrorist connection mentioned by Ciolini was further bolstered by information coming from another unlikely source. Once again, the material was part of a complex SISMI disinformation campaign. What is especially significant about the episode is that two of its protagonists, the SISMI representative in Beirut Colonel Stefano Giovannone and Al Fatah leader Abu Ayad, also played a leading role in another still more delicate aspect of PLO-Italian relations, which we will examine in a later chapter. Abu Ayad, alias Salah Khalaf, was Yasser Arafat's deputy in the leadership of Al Fatah, the largest faction in the Palestine Liberation Organization. He was also responsible for the Fatah intelligence service. Giovannone, a grey-haired, slightly plump man who looked like a well-scrubbed businessman, was SISMI representative in Beirut from 1972 until the mid-1980s, when he became embroiled in a succession of secret service scandals. His death in 1985 extricated him from mounting legal difficulties and doubtless relieved the anxieties of many people in the intelligence world. Throughout his career as a secret service officer, he enjoyed an excellent political and personal relationship with many PLO leaders.

On 19 September 1980, Giovannone's friend Ayad granted an interview to an obscure Italian-language Swiss newspaper, *Il Corriere del Ticino*. The interviewer was an Italian journalist named Rita Porena, one of Giovannone's informants. Ayad told her that the PLO had arrested a number of German right-wingers who had been undergoing training in a military camp run by the Christian Falangist militia near the Lebanese town of Aqura, north-east of Beirut. The Germans belonged to a terrorist group headed by Karl Heinz Hoffman, a name which had been connected to the Bologna bombing

[165]

by Ciolini. Some eleven months before the interview, according to Ayad, a group of Italian fascists had joined the Germans on their guerrilla training course. The Italians said that their principal enemy was the Communist Party and that they were planning a major bombing in Bologna, a city governed by the communists. 'When the massacre occurred, we immediately connected the bombing to what we had learned about the plans of the Italians from the Aqura camp,' Ayad commented.[10]

Ayad's information was later supplemented by a number of SISMI reports. In one, dated 23 January 1981, SISMI stated that it had questioned two of the Germans mentioned in the interview and been told that a group of six to eight Italians had been undergoing training near Aqura in July 1980, only a month before the bombing, and that their leader had spoken of a forthcoming attack on Bologna in his farewell speech. By that time Ayad had already modified his previous account, bringing the timing of the Bologna reference into line with the SISMI version and claiming that he had been mistaken in placing the incident some ten months earlier.[11] On 17 April 1981, SISMI explained that despite having spoken to the two Germans it was unable to provide details of their identity or addresses as the meeting had been arranged by an intermediary. Years later, Giovannone admitted that the secret service had known the identity of the Germans cited by Ayad all along. According to the Bologna prosecutors, this information was kept from the judicial authorities in order to prevent them from discovering that the whole affair was part of a propaganda war being waged between the PLO and the Falangists.[12] The SISMI reports resulted in an examining magistrate from Bologna making two fruitless and confusing visits to Beirut in pursuit of a non-existent international connection to the bombing. The consequences of this disinformation campaign suited both Giovannone and Ayad. For the PLO it represented an opportunity to tarnish the reputation of its Falangist enemies through association with the Bologna bombing, while for Giovannone it was a chance to contribute to the P2-orchestrated sabotage of the judicial investigation. It seems clear that the two men worked hand in glove throughout the whole affair.

Other accounts of the bombing have emerged in the world of the extreme right and offered a motive for it which was endorsed by the Bologna assize court prosecutors. One of these was put forward in the extremist magazine *Quex* (March 1981), which suggested that the bombing was the work of *agents provocateurs* seeking to establish their authority, 'from positions of power, over the whole area of the extreme right and to dismantle those groups devoted to spontaneous action, which were escaping from their control'. Another suggested that the massacre was designed to provoke police repression against the right and thus force unity on the various terrorist groups which had been steadily drifting apart. It was also designed as a warning message 'to those political, military and economic forces, which had been linked in the past to right-wing extremism in the context of coup plans and the strategy of tension'.[13] Interestingly, another account which originated with Pierluigi Pagliai in Bolivia, who was subsequently killed in a joint CIA/Italian police operation, suggested that the bombing had been organized by Stefano Delle Chiaie in order to radicalize and reunify the world of Italian neo-fascism. Another witness claimed that it was Gelli who had ordered the bombing as a kind of re-enactment of the Italicus massacre, in order to 'send a warning to those political and military circles which had supported a military coup in 1974–5 and which were beginning to move away from Gelli and the forces of P2 as the period of the strategy of tension came to an end'. Gelli and his associates, according to this account, represented the link between the political and military circles involved in the coup attempt and the low-level neo-fascists who had carried out their orders.[14] These various interpretations are by no means incompatible with one another.

Yet another explanation for the bombing has emerged since the original assize court trial. It makes a link between the station bombing and the explosion in flight, one week earlier, of an Itavia DC-9 passenger jet flying from Bologna to Palermo. It has now been ascertained that the secret services organized a complex and far-reaching cover-up of the circumstances surrounding both incidents. The two cover-up operations ran in parallel for almost a decade. It has even been suggested that the Bologna bombing may itself have been a part of the Itavia cover-up. At 8.59 p.m. on 27 June 1980, the Itavia jet with eighty-one people on board crashed into the sea near the island of Ustica, 100 kilometres north of the Sicilian coast. Initial accounts spoke of structural failure as the probable cause of the crash but the next day the possibility that it was the result of a terrorist bomb was introduced. An anonymous caller claiming to represent the right-wing terrorist group NAR told the *Corriere della Sera* that one of its members, Marco Affatigato, had been on board the flight 'on a mission'. His body could be identified, the caller said, by the particular type of watch he was wearing. The assumption the public was invited to draw was that Affatigato was carrying a bomb with him which had detonated accidentally.

It would take nine years for a judicial inquiry to establish that the plane was almost certainly brought down by a missile, probably fired by a NATO fighter aircraft. A parliamentary inquiry into the affair found that radar records of the event had been tampered with, withheld from the investigators or destroyed. Air Force officers claimed that the radar at Marsala in Sicily, for example, failed to record the last minutes of the flight because a simulated training exercise happened to coincide with the disaster. Their account would not begin to waver until some nine years after the crash. Licio Gelli has drawn a parallel between the missing radar records and documents belonging to Aldo Moro which disappeared during his kidnap. He clearly intended to suggest that both regarded sensitive secrets of the Italian state.[15]

Radar records that only came to light in 1990 appear to indicate intense military activity in the skies over north and central Italy on the night of the crash. One member of the parliamentary commission has estimated that there were as many as thirty-three military aircraft in the area between 7.30 p.m. and 10 p.m. There are also traces of a plane flying in a curious circular pattern east of the island of Corsica: an airborne radar and communications aircraft directing operations? Despite all this activity neither the Italian Air Force nor any of Italy's NATO allies have been able to assist the investigators in establishing what was going on that night. Members of the parliamentary commission are convinced that they have been lied to. On the night of 27 June the American aircraft carrier the USS *Saratoga* was at anchor in the Bay of Naples. According to the US authorities neither the *Saratoga* nor any of its escort ships were using radar powerful enough to record what was happening only 100 or so kilometres away in the sky above Ustica. The parliamentarians are also convinced that a NATO radar centre in Verona, which collates information from the entire Italian air defence system, must have recorded the last moments of the doomed plane. This information, too, has been denied to them. On 20 June 1990, the director of SISMI, Admiral Fulvio Martini, told the commission that he believed his colleagues in the French, American and British intelligence agencies had all lied by saying that they had no relevant information, in response to his requests. 'If they were in some way involved in this, that is the answer they would have given,' he told the commission.[16]

Rino Formica, a Socialist, who was Transport Minister at the time of the crash, has hinted at the reasons of state that may lie behind the Ustica cover-up. 'I don't want to suggest that the DC-9 was shot down deliberately, but if it was an accident then why didn't they say so immediately?' he said. 'Obviously because the cause was even more important than the accident itself.'[17] Alfredo Galasso, a lawyer representing the victims' families, has suggested that the plane may have been downed by a missile fired in the course of 'an all-out air battle'.[18] The scenario that has begun to emerge is of an aerial dogfight between planes from France, the United States and Libya.

Several witnesses have spoken of the involvement of a number of NATO countries, led by France and the United States, in an operation to overthrow the government of Colonel Moammar Khadafy. The plan involved an attempt to shoot down a plane carrying the Libyan leader from Tripoli to Warsaw on the night of the crash and the simultaneous dispatch from Corsica of a plane carrying arms and mercenaries to support an uprising by anti-Khadafy dissidents. Khadafy was warned of the plot by members of the Italian secret services, who wanted to protect lucrative trade ties with the Libyan regime, and Libyan fighters were sent to intercept the NATO planes. The DC-9 was shot down in the resulting mêlée.

There can be no doubt that relations were strained between Libya and the countries allegedly involved in the plot. France was at loggerheads with Libya over Chad, where, two months earlier, it had sent troops to back Prime Minister Hissene Habré against the Libyan-backed forces of Goukouni Oueddei. On 4 February a mob had burnt down the French consulates in Tripoli and Benghazi and France had responded by expelling the Libyan ambassador from Paris. On 11 May four Libyan diplomats had been accused of involvement in terrorism and expelled from the United States and a further four were expelled from Britain the following day. Italy, too, was at odds with Libya, over relations with Malta and oil exploration rights in the Mediterranean. At the beginning of August troops loyal to Khadafy crushed a revolt by soldiers of the Libyan 9th Brigade based in Tobruk: a delayed start to the insurrection that should have begun on June 27?[19]

A MIG 23 fighter bearing Libyan markings crashed in a mountainous area of Calabria, southern Italy, almost certainly on the same night as the Ustica disaster. The authorities have always insisted that it came down three weeks later, on 18 July, and therefore had no connection with the Ustica affair. The body of the pilot and the aircraft were hastily returned to Libya. It has been reported that Fiat managing director Cesare Romiti intervened to ensure that the operation ran smoothly.[20] At the time, Libya was one of the largest shareholders in the Italian car manufacturing firm and Fiat were not able to buy out the Libyan shareholding until the late 1980s. If someone from the Italian secret services did warn Khadafy of the plot against him, one of the motives may have been to protect Fiat from the consequences of a sudden rupture in relations between the two countries. Investigators now believe that the Italian Air Force may have sent one of its own jets to fly low over the site of the crashed MIG and drop incendiary bombs in order to create the impression among local people that the crash occurred on 18 July, and no earlier.

Bologna magistrates have discovered that the anonymous caller who mentioned Affatigato's name to the *Corriere della Sera* was employed by SISMI.[21] Since Affatigato had not been on the Itavia flight, SISMI were at liberty to use his name again, this time putting it forward in their reports to the Bologna magistrates as a suspect in the station bombing. The detailed information they used to implicate him in the two affairs, including his ownership of a Baume et Mercier wrist-watch, came from one of their informants, Marcello Soffiati, a right-wing extremist who also worked for the CIA and had undergone weapons training at Camp Derby, a US military base near Livorno.[22] Affatigato himself had been in contact not only with the Italian secret services, but also with SDECE, the French secret service, and with the CIA. He was a well-established figure in the world of right-wing terrorism and his name served, in the first instance, to create the impression that the Ustica plane had been brought down by a bomb carried on board and subsequently to link the Ustica incident with a right-wing bombing at Bologna station. The suspicion therefore arises as to whether the secret services may not have organized a 'genuine' right-wing bombing at Bologna station in order to reinforce the idea that the Itavia disaster was caused by a bomb, rather than a missile, and thus strengthen the alibi of whichever NATO air force had been responsible for the disaster. It has been suggested that the intention of the Bologna bombers was to carry out a massacre of traditional strategy of tension proportions, with a dozen or so victims. According to this theory, it was only the unforeseen collapse of the waiting-room roof that caused such unexpectedly high casualties on 2 August.

A compelling reason for concealing the true dynamics of the Ustica incident is the fact that in 1980 NATO was trying to convince European public opinion of the need to deploy a new generation of short-range nuclear missiles to counter the Soviet SS-20s. In a number of countries, governments were encountering considerable difficulties over this issue and the revelation that a NATO fighter had been responsible for the deaths of eighty-one innocent civilians might well have tipped the balance against acceptance. This at least may have been the calculation made by members of the NATO security establishment. The motive for the bombing, then, would have been a weighty one: the security of the entire Western alliance.

Given the Affatigato/secret service link to both Ustica and Bologna and the lengths to which the secret services went to cover up responsibility for both tragedies, this theory is by no means far-fetched. There is yet another element which supports it. On 13 January 1981, SISMI reported that the T4 explosive its agents had planted as part of the 'Terror on the trains' operation was the same as that used at the station. T4 is a military explosive used in missile warheads and it is therefore possible that the choice of explosives at Bologna was designed to replicate the chemical traces left by the missile that destroyed the Itavia jet. What makes this report somewhat sinister is that at the time SISMI identified its own explosive as being T4, and the same as that used at Bologna, the Bologna explosive had not yet been identified and would not be officially confirmed to be T4 until nearly a year later, on 6 December 1981.[23]

A different, but equally sinister, construction was put on these events by Italian police chief Vincenzo Parisi, a former head of the domestic intelligence service, SISDE. In testimony to the parliamentary commission he spoke of the shooting down of the Itavia jet as a deliberate terrorist act, which he also linked to the Bologna bombing. 'A terrorist act serves to send a message. If the message is not understood, it is repeated,' he told the inquiry.[24] The hypothesis that appears to emerge from Parisi's admittedly somewhat unclear testimony is that both Ustica and Bologna may have been organized by the French to punish the Italian secret services for betraying their plot against Khadafy. A possible connection between the French and the Bologna bombing has recently been made by no less a person than Marco Affatigato. In an Italian television interview he claimed that Paul Durand, an officer in the French domestic intelligence service, the

Renseignements Généraux, had been arrested in Bologna on the day of the bombing or the day after. He had later been returned to France on an Italian military aircraft in 'an exchange of spies'. Other of Affatigato's allegations were considered too sensitive, or too far-fetched, to be broadcast and the material was handed over to Rome magistrates.

Durand's name had cropped up in earlier investigations into the Bologna bombing as he had been travelling in Italy in July 1980 and been in contact with members of the Italian far right. It had been thought, however, that he had returned to France well before 2 August. It has been suggested that SISMI's decision to blame Affatigato for the bombing, given that he was in France at the time and was known to work for the French secret services, was a coded way of indicating that they held the French responsible for the atrocity.[25] An Air Force employee who was working in one of the radar stations that did actually follow the sequence of events leading up to the Ustica crash told his family the following day: 'There has been a disaster. We were on the point of war, and we're still on alert now.'[26] At this point it is unclear whether the war that was about to break out was against Libya or against France. The airman was later found hanged and magistrates have recently opened an investigation into his apparent suicide.

Some of these theories may appear contradictory and far-fetched, but they are nevertheless underpinned by a number of concrete facts: the reality of the insurrection against Khadafy and the secret service cover-ups. On 11 September 1980, *Le Monde* reported the sudden resignation of Colonel Alain de Marolles after only a year as director of the Information Division of the French secret service. *Le Monde* was at a loss to explain his unexpected departure but speculated that it might have had something to do with a recent uprising in Libya.

None of the theories put forward to explain the origins of the Bologna bombing enjoyed the kind of convincing corroboration that might come from a full confession by one of the protagonists and they could therefore all be mistaken. They do at least have the virtue of fitting the incontrovertible fact that the secret services were actively involved over an extended period in undermining the judicial investigation, following a pattern of behaviour that had been established with the very first bombing of the strategy of tension. It is quite possible that the atrocity had several distinct purposes, to disguise the reality of the Ustica incident and to draw together the forces which had previously been united by the strategy of tension. Given that the political circumstances which had created that strategy no longer existed, it was reasonable to suppose that many of those who had participated in the security establishment's terrorism conspiracy might plan to return to civilian life and might even be tempted to write their memoirs or collaborate with the judicial authorities. Implicating them in a fresh outrage, and one of such gravity, would effectively put a stop to such ideas. Many right-wingers would be forced to go on the run and few would be tempted to explain how they had become accomplices in such slaughter. Even more telling would be the message the bombing sent to the senior political and military figures who had acquiesced in the P2 strategy of terrorism management: we served you well in the past, so you cannot abandon us now. Whether the bombing was carried out primarily for international or for domestic reasons there are certainly people in authority in Italy who know and it is high time they shared their knowledge with the public.

If the purpose of the Bologna bombing was not immediately apparent, the motive for a train bombing in 1984 was, at first sight, even less clear. But if the Bologna blast was designed to send a message, so too, it appears, was the destruction of a train as it travelled between Florence and Bologna on the night of 23 December 1984. At 7.06 p.m., a remote-controlled bomb exploded in one of the rear carriages of a Naples–Milan express train as it travelled through a 19 kilometre-long tunnel near the village of San Benedetto Val di Sambro, killing fifteen passengers and injuring 267. It was in exactly this same tunnel, some ten years earlier, that a bomb on the Italicus train had killed twelve and injured 105 people. That bomb had come at the height of the coup season and has been explicitly linked to the activities of the P2 lodge. It is hard to escape the conclusion that the Christmas 1984 bombing was a deliberate re-run of the Italicus atrocity, presumably intended as a reminder to all who had supported the 1974 coup plots of a shared complicity.

What was unusual about the 1984 bombing was the composition of the gang held responsible for it and the relative speed with which they were brought to justice. On 25 February 1989, a Florence assize court sentenced five men to life imprisonment for the bombing. Three of them were members of the Neapolitan Camorra and the other two members of the Mafia. The court held that they had staged the bombing in association with a group of right-wing terrorists in order to create the impression that terrorism was still a major problem and so divert police resources away from the battle against organized crime, which had been making notable breakthroughs at that time. Particularly significant was the life sentence for Mafia boss Pippo Calò. Calò was a major figure in Cosa Nostra, a member of its governing body, the Commission or Cupola. He was born the son of a Palermo butcher, rising over the years to become the head of that city's Porta Nuova Mafia family. In the early 1970s he moved to Rome, where he became one of the Mafia's treasurers, investing some of its vast earnings from drug-dealing in legal business ventures. He became, in effect, the Mafia's ambassador to Rome, cultivating political and secret service contacts and encountering such figures as Francesco Pazienza and Flavio Carboni, who gravitated around the P2-controlled Banco Ambrosiano and its president, Roberto Calvi.

Calò's influence within the Rome underworld was further increased when he came into contact with the leaders of the local Magliana band, whom he soon came to dominate. The criminal gang was based on the working-class suburb of Magliana and numbered among its members loan-sharks, kidnappers and drug-dealers. It was originally a loosely-knit association of minor and relatively unferocious Roman criminals, but as the Seventies wore on, its leaders came progressively into contact with Calò and other representatives of the Sicilian Mafia and with envoys of the Neapolitan Camorra and they became increasingly ambitious and ruthless. Members of the gang were in contact with local right-wing terrorists, who used the gang to recycle stolen goods and hot money and also bought drugs from them. As the activities of its leaders moved steadily upmarket, they became increasingly involved in political corruption and came ever more into contact with the secret services, who had always had a particular interest in the weaknesses and foibles of Italy's political class. Magliana member Domenico Balducci, for example, made a number of unexplained flights on the SISMI-owned airline. He naturally travelled under an assumed name, as he was on the run from the police at the time. Joint control over the Health Ministry arms supermarket, with Egidio Giuliani, also gave the gang the chance to keep tabs on who was shooting whom in the capital.

This wide range of contacts and activities made the Magliana band into a purely criminal equivalent of the P2 organization, and it has sometimes been described as the military arm of P2. Contact between P2 and the terrorists and criminals gravitating around the Magliana band was maintained by people such as Aldo Semerari, the criminal psychiatrist and P2 member, who enjoyed ready access to imprisoned gang members because of his work. Another link was provided by Cesare Valsania, a loan-shark who was born in Castiglion Fibocchi, the site of Gelli's Giole mattress factory. Contacts with the secret services were guaranteed by individuals such as Francesco Pazienza and Flavio Carboni. As a result the Magliana band became a criminal extension of the P2 lodge, active in the areas of common crime and terrorism during the course of post-war Italy's most politically turbulent decade. It is not therefore surprising that the gang came into possession of some highly sensitive secrets relating to political violence in the country and equally unsurprising that it chose to make use of that knowledge for purposes of blackmail.

An idea of the extensive influence of the Magliana band can be gathered from the testimony of one of its former members, Fulvio Lucioli, who told a Bologna magistrate that the judiciary in Perugia was investigating a possible connection between the band and justice officials in Rome. 'I have named people linked to the Magliana band including a deputy director of Rebibbia prison and certain Rome magistrates; this is why my statements are currently with the Perugia court.'[27] This impression is strengthened by the account of Angelo Izzo, who told the same magistrate that a leading member of the gang, Danilo Abbruciati, had contrived to send him a knife 'as soon as he heard that I was in prison, in the special wing'. However reassuring it may have been to have a knife, life in the special wing at Rebibbia was not all that arduous for a well-connected member of the criminal fraternity, according to Izzo. 'Since [Francis] Turatello [a major underworld boss] was there and had masses of money, we were constantly having parties with caviar and other sophisticated foods, so solitary confinement was just a phrase from the rule-book.'[28]

The personal influence of Calò was also considerable. While living in Rome he claimed to be an antiques dealer and made use of a number of aliases: Mario Salamandra, Mario Aglialoro, and he even appropriated the name of one of his followers, Luigi Faldetta. According to Mafia boss turned supergrass, Tommaso Buscetta, Calò once had a man killed because he had repeatedly failed to turn up for appointments with him.[29]

The evidence of Calò's involvement in the 1984 bombing is unusually concrete and convincing. Police found Semtex explosive of the same type as that used on the train concealed in a house owned by

Calò in the Umbrian countryside at Poggio San Lorenzo. They also found remote-control devices similar to the one used to detonate the bomb. Calò had noted in his diary the payments he had made for the house and under the rubric 'Radio' the sum of 18,000 Lire, an abbreviated note of the 18 million Lire he had paid to a German electronics engineer, Friedrich Schaudinn, for six such devices.[30] Secret service attempts to throw the investigators off the track were not as extensive or as effective as in the past. One reason may have been that several of SISMI's leading judicial saboteurs were already in prison or under investigation for their role in obstructing the Bologna investigation. It has even been suggested that the bombing may have been intended to ease the position of the arrested SISMI officers at the same time as increasing the workload of the Bologna magistrates, who were initially responsible for investigating the 1984 bombing as well as the station blast. The logic was that if secret service officers were in prison but bombs continued to explode, then any idea that they were in some way linked to the original 1980 bombers must be mistaken; the latter were still at large and still active and could therefore have no possible link with the imprisoned SISMI men.

Anomalous though the Bologna and Christmas bombings may have been in terms of the traditional objectives of the strategy of tension, it is possible to see them both as an appeal for the continuation of the secret service cover-up. Many of those thought to have been responsible for the Christmas bombings have been brought to justice, but the higher levels of political responsibility for the strategy of tension have still to be fathomed.

The extreme ruthlessness of the men who organized the Christmas bombing is illustrated by the thoroughness with which they set about eliminating potential witnesses. The bomb is believed to have been placed on board the train at Florence station by a seventeen-year-old youth, Carmine Lombardo, a junior member of the Camorra. Lombardo was murdered shortly afterwards and the two men responsible for his death were killed in their turn also.[31] Despite these precautions the underworld bombers were sentenced to life imprisonment on the basis of apparently solid evidence. On 15 March 1990, a Florence appeal court confirmed the life sentences on Calò and one of his leading lieutenants but acquitted three members of the Neapolitan Camorra of involvement in the bombing. The verdict thus attributed responsibility for the massacre to the Mafia but eliminated much of the right-wing component to the conspiracy, which had been mediated through the political contacts of the Camorra, according to the assize court verdict. Nevertheless, the verdict marked an important break with the tradition that bomb trials nearly always end with convictions in the assize court but with blanket acquittals on appeal. A Rome assize court had noted ruefully that when Magliana band member Domenico Balducci offered his assistance to film producer Carlo Ponti in resolving differences with the Italian legal authorities over outstanding taxes owed by himself and his wife, Sophia Loren, he warned that there was little he could do at the level of the Rome prosecutor's office or the assize court. 'Good of him to say so,' commented the assize court judge. The opportunities for sweetening the magistrates were greater, Balducci said, at the court of appeal and Court of Cassation (Supreme Court) stage.[32]

Given the Magliana band's contacts with P2 and the secret services, its involvement in the 1984 train bombing and the brokering of the Pecorelli and Mattarella murders, it is clear that the group had participated in some most unsavoury instances of mercenary terrorism. It is for this reason that any message coming from the group that appears to hint at the possession of sensitive insider's knowledge of terrorist events, and the Christmas 1984 bombing seems to constitute just such a message, should be treated with the greatest attention. The Magliana band's messages concerning the kidnapping of Aldo Moro, perhaps the most delicate terrorist act of all, offer considerable food for thought; we will come to them in a later chapter.

Notes

1 P2 Commission, *Allegati alla Relazione*, Vol. 7, Tome 21, Rome, 1987, p. 332.
2 Giuseppe De Lutiis (ed.), *La Strage*, Editori Riuniti, Rome, 1986, p. 273.
3 Paolo Aleandri to the author, 22 June 1989.
4 Pietro Calderoni (ed.), *Servizi Segreti*, Tullio Pironti, Naples, 1986, pp. 193–4.
5 P. M. Andrea De Gasperis to the author, 16 June 1989.
6 P. M. Libero Mancuso and Attilio Dardani, Requisitoria, Bologna, 13 May 1986, p. 522.
7 Adalberto Baldoni and Sandro Provvisionato, *La Notte Più Lunga della Repubblica*, Serarcangeli, Rome, 1989, pp. 401–2.
8 Licio Gelli to the author, 27 June 1989.
9 Letter from Avv. Federico Federici to Francesco Pazienza, deposited at Bologna assize court, 12 November 1986, pp. 15–16.

10 P. M. Libero Mancuso and Attilio Dardani, op. cit., p. 782.
11 Ibid., p. 788.
12 Ibid., pp. 791–2.
13 Ibid., p. 770.
14 Ibid., p. 773.
15 Licio Gelli to the author, 27 June 1989.
16 Andrea Purgatori, *Corriere della Sera*, 21 June 1990.
17 Giovanni Maria Bellu, *La Repubblica*, 2 June 1990.
18 *L'Espresso*, 1 July 1990.
19 Antonio De Marchi and Valerio Gualerzi, *Rinascita*, 10 June 1990.
20 Pierluigi Ficoneri and Mario Scialoja, *L'Espresso*, 18 November 1990.
21 Marcella Andreoli, *Panorama*, 8 October 1989.
22 G. I. Felice Casson, Sentenza-ordinanza a carico di Carlo Maria Maggi ed altri, Venice, 2 September 1984, p. 94.
23 Sandro Provvisionato, *L'Europeo*, 20 October 1989.
24 Samarcanda, RAI3, 29 November 1990.
25 ANSA, Rome, 15.24, 18 October 1990. 'Ustica, On. Staiti su audizione Parisi.'
26 Franco Scottoni, *La Repubblica*, 23 December 1990.
27 Fulvio Lucioli to P. M. Libero Mancuso, Paliano prison, 22 March 1985.
28 Angelo Izzo to P. M. Libero Mancuso, Paliano prison, 22 March 1985.
29 Sentenza contro Giunio Bruto Baccari ed altri, Tribunale Penale di Roma, Presidente Gianvittore Fabbri, 9 May 1988, p. 237.
30 Ibid., pp. 100–1.
31 Giuseppe Peruzzi, *Corriere della Sera*, 20 February 1986.
32 Sentenza contro Filomena Angelini ed altri, Tribunale Penale di Roma, Presidente Giancarlo Millo, 8 February 1986, p. 75.

[10]

MANIPULATING
THE LEFT

Finally, the profound difference that exists – even at a psycholo-gical level – between the two methods of moving the 'wooden actor' should be emphasized: the puppet constitutes a prolonga-tion of the puppetmaster's hand, a direct amplification of his movements; it is given life by the arm and fingers of the person manoeuvring it. The marionette, in contrast, is moved in an indirect manner, which I have heard compared by some marionettists to the act of playing a stringed musical instrument: and it therefore requires attention of a rational type.

Italo Sordi, Introduction to Pëtr Bogatyrëv's *Il Teatro delle Marionette*
(The Marionette Theatre), Brescia, 1980

If many right-wing terrorists were glove puppets, with their manipu-lator's hand inserted up their backs and controlling their every move, left-wing terrorists were more like marionettes, dancing on the end of invisible strings; their manipulation was an altogether subtler art. The ideal for the secret service marionette-masters was, after all, to use left-wing extremists to serve their conservative cause without any direct contact or collusion. This was their greatest theatrical exploit, to have their genuine adversaries unwittingly follow the secret service script. Nevertheless, a number of people involved in left-wing terrorism appear to have been in direct contact with Western secret services, marionettes controlled by real, if barely discernible, strings.

The story of secret service manipulation of left-wing terrorism is highly controversial and will certainly never be told in full. Its implications are, if anything, even graver than the manipulation of right-wing terrorism, with its litany of coup plots and random bombings. Setting aside issues of morality, the manipulation of left-wing extremism turned out to be a brilliantly executed and remarkably successful operation. It made possible a kind of centrist, institutional coup which thrust the PCI firmly back into opposition at a time when the Reds seemed not just to be coming out from under the bed but laying claim to the master bedroom.

Left-wing terrorism in Italy had its roots in the international wave of student protest which began on American campuses during the Vietnam War and reached its peak with the Paris riots in the spring of 1968. Italian students emulated their overseas counterparts with sit-ins and demonstrations, which climaxed in the autumn of 1969, in conjunction with a period of particularly acute industrial unrest. The protest movements of the late 1960s became a breeding ground for the terrorists of the 1970s. Thousands of people joined extremist left-wing organizations such as Potere Operaio (Workers' Power), Autonomia Operaia (Workers' Autonomy), and Lotta Continua (Continuous Struggle) in the hopes of bringing about a Marxist revolution. Their activities ranged from street disturbances to terrorism and murder and many of them subsequently graduated to membership in full-time terrorist groups such as the Red Brigades, Prima Linea (Front Line), or a galaxy of smaller groups. Without a large pool of discontented and rebellious youth to call on for recruits and logistical support, the Red Brigades could never have survived so long or achieved their military successes.

The fear of a military coup, the perceived impossibility of peaceful democratic change, and an idealized recollection of the wartime Resistance all acted as effective recruiting sergeants for the terrorist organizations. It would be absurd to suggest that such a widespread popular upheaval, sparked off in part by genuine social and economic problems, could be deliberately engineered by the secret services. It is possible, however, that the secret services used the extremist political and terrorist groups and guided the course of events to thwart the growing demand for political change and to undermine the rising strength of the Communist Party. After all, they would have been failing in their job if they had not attempted to do so.

Experts on left-wing terrorism tend to fall into two opposing camps: the conspiracy theorists and those who maintain that Italian terrorism was an entirely home-grown and spontaneous phenomenon, wholly immune from the kind of secret service manipulation which is generally acknowledged to have taken place on the right. For understandable reasons, the direct protagonists in the story tend to take the latter view. The police and secret services are not encouraged to talk in public about delicate intelligence operations, while the terrorists cling to the last vestiges of their revolutionary credibility and are not keen to admit that they were outmanoeuvred in the great game of intelligence. This attitude has been succinctly expressed by Alberto Franceschini, a founder of the Red Brigades and considered by some to have been the real leader of the organization in its early years. Franceschini was born in Reggio Emilia in 1947 of working-class parents who were strong Communist Party supporters. Both his father and his grandfather had suffered for their opposition to fascism and he had followed in the family tradition by working for the youth wing of the PCI. He abandoned the party in 1969, disillusioned by its 'revisionist' moderation, and set out on the path of revolutionary struggle. In his autobiography he described his reaction to the news, received in prison, that the Red Brigades had kidnapped Aldo Moro: 'We immediately reject the idea that it could be a "provocation" by some secret service. Not out of political reasoning, but from the feeling of nausea we have built up over the years towards arguments of the type "who benefits?" "who's behind it?"'[1] Since writing the book, Franceschini has himself come to entertain doubts about this episode and about the whole history of his terrorist organization.

It is by no means easy to settle the debate between the conspiracy theorists and their opponents. Sometimes both sides use the same facts, presented in a different light, to support their own contentions. The conspiracy theorists point out the tendency of the Red Brigades to mount their major operations at sensitive moments in Italian political life: kidnapping a magistrate, Mario Sossi, shortly before the important divorce referendum in 1974, seizing Aldo Moro just as the PCI was on the point of giving its support to a government of national unity. The result, they observe, is to discredit the left at crucial junctures in Italian political life. Their opponents simply argue that the Red Brigades, being a political organization, were bound to choose such moments for their armed intervention, in order to have the maximum impact. The way in which terrorism produced government repression and authoritarian laws was viewed by many terrorists as a necessary stage on the path to civil war and ultimate revolution. Some of their critics see this intermediate stage as the real, effective goal of the terrorists, dancing to the tune of the secret services and their conservative political masters. At times, in the turmoil of the 1970s it may actually have seemed that a Marxist revolution was possible in Italy. It is less easy to believe, however, that the intelligent leaders of the extreme left, many of them university professors, can have been sincerely convinced of this: in an important NATO country and with the Army waiting in the wings for an excuse to intervene.

An additional difficulty in deciding whether the leadership of the extreme left were acting in good faith or according to a hidden agenda stems from their fierce hostility towards the PCI, viewed as a revisionist organization that had sold out the dreams and ideals of true communists. Moro's policy of an 'historic compromise' leading to an alliance with the PCI was as fervently opposed by the Red Brigades and the extreme left as it was disliked by the reactionary members of the P2 masonic lodge. This certainly created the potential for the extreme left to be used as unwitting tools of the secret services, even if they were not actually infiltrated and controlled by them. There can be little doubt, however, that the secret services had infiltrators in place in the principal terrorist organizations, who were able to steer the course of the armed struggle on their behalf at crucial moments in its history. For the rest, it was enough that the terrorist organizations existed and acted according to their natural inclinations.

The relationship between terrorist organizations and the extremist political groups that gave them logistical and moral support has also been the subject of considerable controversy. The role of the left-wing intellectuals who rose to prominence in the extremist but legal political organizations, and who were in their turn in contact with groups like the Red Brigades and Prima Linea, is particularly contentious. According to Padua Public Prosecutor Pietro Calogero, some of these intellectuals sought to impose their own strategic direction on the whole area of left-wing extremism and were, at least partially, successful. Some of them have also come to be suspected of having been conduits for secret service influence.

The leaders of Autonomia Operaia, for example, were accused of responsibility for specific Red Brigades crimes, including the Moro kidnap, but were eventually acquitted. It was Calogero who first indicted them, and the expression 'Calogero theorem' has entered the Italian language, unfairly, as a synonym for a mistaken

[182]

prosecution thesis. The main dispute between Autonomia Operaia and the Red Brigades was over tactics. The Autonomia leaders believed that the correct road to civil war and revolution was through 'mass illegality' rather than through the terrorist activity of a small, militaristic élite, which was liable to provoke a police clamp-down damaging to the legal extremist organizations while leaving the Red Brigades virtually unscathed in hiding. Another cause of disagreement was the tendency of Autonomia Operaia to consider the traitorous Communist Party as the principal enemy of the far left, while the Red Brigades preferred to concentrate on their traditional *bête noire*, the Christian Democrats. The relationship was also characterized by strong personal rivalries, as the original Red Brigades leaders resisted attempts by some of the more self-important left-wing intellectuals to establish their authority over all the revolutionary organizations. In many ways the situation closely resembled that prevailing among the right-wing extremist organizations: disputes over tactics, personal rivalries, varying levels of secrecy and military commitment, but all basically marching in the same direction.

This view has been expressed by Milan Examining Magistrate Guido Galli. 'The existence of a dialectic between the Red Brigades and other armed organizations should not create the impression of irreconcilable differences or strict compartmentalization between them: the various organizations exchange men, *matériel*, and information and, despite the diversity of their immediate objectives, often elaborate their short and medium term plans together,' he wrote.[2] Galli was shot dead by gunmen from Prima Linea on 19 March 1980.

One of the sorriest roles in the drama of Italian terrorism was played by the radical university professors, Toni Negri, Franco Piperno and Oreste Scalzone, who preached violence and revolution to their students, were in contact with members of the Red Brigades, but ultimately succeeded in convincing the courts that their own direct involvement in terrorist activity was, at most, marginal. They were happy for others to risk their skins in the struggle while they stayed at home to concoct a programme of political pie-in-the-sky to underpin the improbable revolution. In his book *Dominion and Sabotage*, Negri wrote a panegyric to proletarian violence and described how he felt the warmth of the working-class community enfold him every time he covered his face with a mask to participate in street violence. When the time came to answer for such activity in court those words were a mere fantasy. His political credo was also fairly fantastic. 'Our task is the theoretical restoration of the refusal of work. The refusal of work is, above all, sabotage, strikes, direct action,' he wrote. And he had no difficulty in justifying the violence that was being so widely practised at the time. 'Let us have an end to the hypocritical bourgeois and reformist opposition to violence. Let us speak clearly of it as a necessary, central ingredient of the communist programme.' In the same book, Negri, a middle-class professor of politics from Padua University, extolled the virtues of the working-class struggle. 'Our sabotage organizes the proletarian assault on the sky,' he wrote.[3] In retrospect, it is extraordinary that so many young people could have been swayed by the hysterical rantings of these 'cattivi maestri' or preachers of evil.

After spending eight years in exile in Canada, Piperno, a physics professor from the University of Cosenza, returned to Italy in 1988 and succeeded in getting his sentence for subversive activity reduced to a mere four years. Several former members of the Red Brigades have told magistrates that they believed Piperno tried to impose his political leadership on the Red Brigades and succeeded, to an extent, in influencing the activities of the terrorist organization by the control he exerted over certain of its members. His founding of the political magazine Metropoli was also seen as an attempt to establish domination over all the organizations of the revolutionary left. One of Piperno's colleagues in Potere Operaio has described the Calabrian physics professor as being the leader of the more aggressive wing of the organization and supportive of the Red Brigades' decision to embark on all out armed struggle from the early 1970s. Negri, on the other hand, was the chief proponent of caution, calling for a more gradual approach to revolution so as to ensure full participation by the masses.[4]

Like Negri, Piperno eventually managed to convince his judges that he had no involvement in the Moro kidnap. During the kidnap he was contacted by representatives of the Socialist Party, who were attempting to carve out a political identity for themselves by dissociating themselves from the other intransigent members of the government coalition and negotiating for Moro's release. Piperno insisted that he was not in contact with the Red Brigades at the time but was merely approached by the Socialists for help in interpreting Moro's letters from captivity. It seems surprising that the Socialists should have required such assistance when a direct channel to the Red

Brigades was what they were really after. Suspicions were heightened by the fact that Piperno helped his friends Valerio Morucci and Adriana Faranda to find accommodation in Rome shortly after the kidnap. The couple had participated in the Moro operation and left the Red Brigades shortly afterwards because they disagreed with the decision to kill the Christian Democrat president. Piperno had also been incautious enough publicly to welcome the 'geometric potency' displayed by the Red Brigades in the slaughter of Moro's bodyguard. A handwritten note found in Mino Pecorelli's office after his murder also suggested a closer involvement of Piperno in the kidnap. Titled 'How the Mafia-BR, CIA/KGB-Mafia contact takes place', it read: 'The BR [Red Brigades] heads are living in Calabria. The leader who organized the kidnap and wrote the first BR communiqués is Prof. Franco Piperno, prof. of physics at Cosenza Univ.'[5] The document does not prove Piperno's involvement, but coming from Pecorelli, it should not lightly be dismissed.

One of the most articulate proponents of the idea that left-wing terrorism was actually manipulated by right-wing forces is Angelo Ventura, a professor of history at Padua University, who was shot in the legs by a left-wing group in 1979 for having the temerity to express this view. Ventura has argued that conservative elements within the state decided to use left-wing terrorism as a way of continuing the strategy of tension and gave it free rein in order to discredit the Communist and Socialist Parties and the trade unions. Without official protection, he claimed, 'extremist violence could not have spread with impunity for an incredible decade and red (and black) terrorism could not have developed almost undisturbed until the Moro kidnap. Terrorism could have been strangled at birth, at least from 1972, and reduced to a sporadic phenomenon.'[6] Ventura has highlighted the delusionary quality of Negri's political ideas and the conflict between his followers and the traditional parties and organizations of the left. 'It is natural that the party of armed struggle and civil war should not meet the working class and the masses on its road but encounter instead the protection and the assistance of the secret centres of power in Italy and abroad, which have an interest in destabilizing the country and overthrowing its democratic institutions,'[7] he concluded.

This view is supported by Pietro Calogero. In his indictment of the Autonomia Operaia leadership he pointed out that the hostility of the terrorists towards reformists and trade unionists was 'the aspect that, more than any other, links "red" terrorism to "black" terrorism and may have made it the ideal instrument of an astute and perverse reactionary plan, embedded in the heart of the state and fed, perhaps, by domestic and international political forces.'[8] He described Negri as one of the driving forces of the revolutionary left and an essential reference point for the terrorists.

Many students of left-wing terrorism have been struck by the modest intellectual level of captured terrorist leaders and speculated about the existence of an as yet undiscovered terrorist intelligentsia, who wrote the Red Brigades' political documents for them and planned overall strategy. Calogero has linked this 'superstructure' to what Negri has referred to in his writings as the 'informal party' or the 'invisible party', which Calogero described as a kind of central planning organization for terrorism in Italy. The magistrate also expressed the view that terrorist funds exceeded the sums that could be raised by the terrorists themselves through robberies and kidnaps, giving rise to the suspicion that they were able to rely on additional secret subsidies. Calogero cited documents indicating the existence of an agreement between Potere Operaio, a forerunner of Autonomia Operaia and also headed by Negri, and the Popular Front for the Liberation of Palestine (PFLP) for the provision of military training in Lebanon to members of the Italian revolutionary group. The documents, dating from 1971, illustrated Potere Operaio's international links and the direct involvement of Negri in the procurement of terrorist training for his followers.[9]

·There are a number of reasons for believing that Negri himself may have played an active role in the conservative-inspired manipulation of left-wing terrorism. For a start, there is his own political development, from membership of the Christian Democrat Party in the 1950s, to the Socialist Party in the early 1960s, and to leadership of the radical left by the end of the decade, attacking the PCI from its left. In the course of this evolution in his political thinking one thing did not change: his virulent anti-communism. A biography of Negri published by Il Giorno newspaper (4 November 1979) quotes a friend from his student days: 'Toni has been everything in his life except one thing: communist. On the contrary, he has always been profoundly, viscerally anti-communist.' One reason for this hatred of the PCI could well be the death of his elder brother, killed in 1943 by communist partisans while fighting for Mussolini's last-stand Republic of Salò. According to Il Giorno, the death of his brother had a profound and traumatic effect on the ten-year-old Negri. A blank spot in Negri's life, about which very little is known, is the period of his studies in the United States, financed by a grant from the Rockefeller Foundation. He made a number of return visits to the country and does not appear to have had any difficulty in obtaining a visa. This in itself is strange. At a time when members of the Communist Party were routinely denied visas, the leader of an extremist political organization to the left of the PCI was able to come and go at will.

All this adds up to a somewhat anomalous identikit for a leader of the extreme left. For readers of Pecorelli's magazine, *OP*, the seed of doubt about Negri's real motives was sown by an article published in 1975. In his usual cryptic, elliptical style, Pecorelli hinted that Negri was about to play an important role in a conservative plot devised by the secret services. If true, and given Pecorelli's secret service contacts there is little reason to doubt it, it is an extraordinary revelation. One can only assume that Pecorelli felt justified in making it because of the limited circulation of his magazine and the coded language in which it was couched. Nevertheless, it is the kind of scoop which established his reputation for dangerous unpredictability and which may ultimately have led to his death.

'A film entirely dedicated to the life of the economist J. M. Keynes will shortly be shot by the young film-makers of the Experimental Centre in Rome,' the article (16 September 1975) opened. Practised readers of Pecorelli will have understood the Experimental Centre (Centro Sperimentale in Italian) to be a coded reference to a secret service office (Centro di Controspionaggio, frequently referred to by its initials, CS). The subject matter of the 'film', the life of the economist John Maynard Keynes, whose philosophy combined conservative and socialist strands, indicated the political colouring of the 'story'. Pecorelli went on to reveal that the film had an exceptional cast, 'who will not be professional actors' (not professional secret service personnel). 'It has been decided instead to use people from the worlds of business, culture and politics, where it is considered there is a wide availability of photogenic individuals who are spontaneously drawn to the new style of acting. The protagonists of the film will be Professor Antonio Negri, holder of the chair of political sciences at the University of Padua, and the "independent" trade unionist Vito Scalia, an expert on the world and needs of the workers.' Scalia was a Christian Democrat union leader trying to challenge the traditional

[187]

dominance of the PCI and the Socialist Party over the trade union movement. He has been publicly accused of receiving money from the CIA. The linking of Negri's name with that of a man competing for influence among trade unionists on behalf of the right is remarkable. It also suggests that the reactionary developments in Italian society prompted by left-wing radicalism may well have been the conscious aim of people like Negri.

Pecorelli went on to underline the incongruousness of the Negri/ Scalia pairing: 'Some malicious gossips, having learnt of Professor Negri's "revolutionary" past, have expressed doubt about the completion of the film, even suggesting to the director that he should never shoot scenes where the two characters are called upon to act together. The production's press office, on the other hand, has pointed out that the two actors are on excellent terms with one another. Besides, both Scalia and Negri – it has been said – have long been aware of the requirements of the script and have accepted every nuance and detail of the screenplay.' The message is clear: Negri's role has been written by the secret services and there is every reason for the inverted commas around his 'revolutionary' tag. Pecorelli's intuition has found support, as we shall discover, from an informed and most surprising quarter.

A Rome police report dated 6 March 1979, refers to the possible existence of links between Negri and the Hyperion language school in Paris, suspected of being a co-ordinating centre for terrorism in Italy and elsewhere in Europe. Investigations were continuing, the report said. They were never completed, as an article giving details of the inquiry appeared on the front page of the *Corriere della Sera* newspaper the following month (24 April 1979), prompting the French authorities to withdraw their co-operation. The French showed their pique by destroying all the telephone intercepts carried out till then and informing their Italian colleagues that there was nothing suspicious about the language school so far as they were concerned.[10] The 'indiscretion' of an officer in the domestic secret service, SISDE, had effectively torpedoed the investigation, drawing a protective veil around the Hyperion.

The school was founded in 1976 by Corrado Simioni, Vanni Mulinaris and Duccio Berio, three of the fathers of left-wing terrorism in Italy. They had been together in the Collettivo Politico Metropolitano (Metropolitan Political Collective) in Milan, a forerunner of the Red Brigades organization. When Renato Curcio left the CPM to set

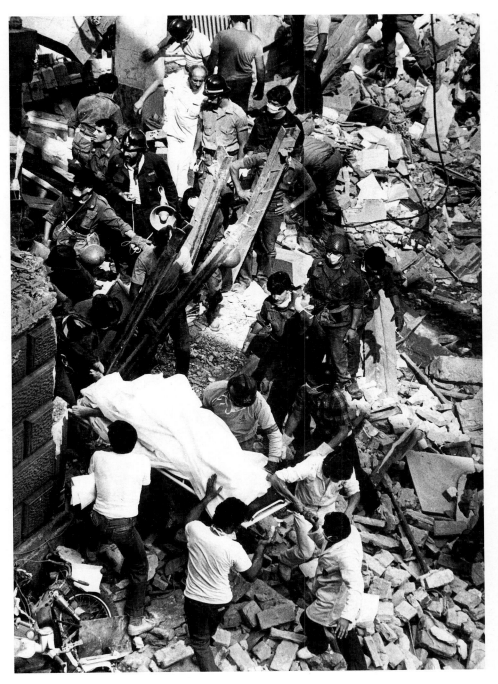

At 10.25 a.m. on Saturday 2 August, a bomb, planted by terrorists, went off in a waiting-room at Bologna Central Railway Station. 85 people were killed, 200 injured

P2 boss Licio Gelli in an expansive mood at a press conference. Since his release from prison Gelli has been campaigning tirelessly for his own rehabilitation

Giulio Andreotti *(left)* with carabiniere General Giovanni De Lorenzo at a military parade in front of the Colosseum. He was Minister of Defence when De Lorenzo mounted his 1964 coup plot

Aldo Moro and General Giovanni De Lorenzo review a detachment of carabinieri

Aldo Moro as a prisoner of the Red Brigades in a photo that may have been taken by underworld forger Toni Chichiarelli

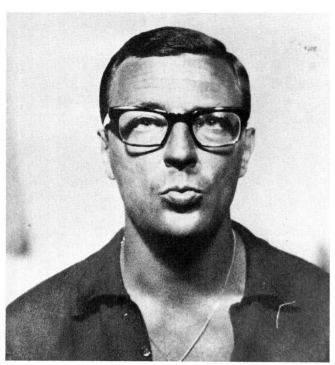

Mino Pecorelli, editor of *Osservatore Politico* magazine, whose indiscretions about the Moro case may have led to his murder in 1979

Imprisoned Red Brigades leader Mario Moretti. His conduct in the Moro kidnap has given rise to suspicions that he was acting on the instructions of Italian or foreign secret services

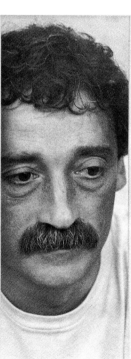

Toni Negri, professor of political science at Padua University. According to a cryptic article published by Mino Pecorelli, Negri was actively engaged in the secret service inspired manipulation of left-wing terrorism

Federico Umberto D'Amato, former head of the Interior Ministry's Office of Special Affairs. His name appears in the P2 membership lists but his and Gelli's recollections diverge as to the level of intimacy that existed between them

The scene in Via Fani shortly after the ambush of Aldo Moro's bodyguard

Former director of military intelligence Vito Miceli during a press conference at the Foreign Press Club in Rome. Miceli was arrested for his alleged complicity with right-wing coup plotters

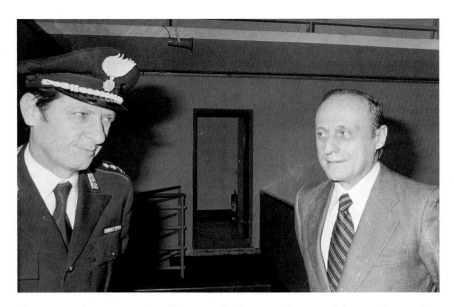

Secret service counter-intelligence chief General Gianadelio Maletti with carabiniere Colonel Antonio Varisco *(left)*. Varisco was murdered by the Red Brigades, possibly to prevent him shedding light on the background to the murder of Mino Pecorelli, of whom he was a friend

A moment of tension for the bodyguard of General Carlo Alberto Dalla Chiesa *(left)*. Dalla Chiesa has been credited with the defeat of the Red Brigades and his knowledge of the background to the Moro kidnap may have led directly to his own murder

up the Red Brigades, Simioni, Mulinaris and Berio founded their own terrorist organization, the Superclan. The name, given them by the Red Brigades, was an abbreviation of Superclandestini (Superclandestine) and referred to their obsession with secrecy. They believed that the masses were not yet ready for revolution but that, to prepare for the day, they should infiltrate their members into all the organizations of the extreme left. According to one former Superclan member, the organization was known to its affiliates as 'the Company' or as 'the Red Aunts' and the 'Superclan' tag was seen as a calumny invented by the Red Brigades. He related that a leading Superclan member had expressed the view that 'the BR were a military organization without a leadership and that the Company was capable of providing the BR with leadership and for that purpose had already infiltrated some of its men into the Red Brigades organization'.[11] During its short history as an active terrorist outfit, the Superclan concentrated most of its energies on fund-raising armed robbers.

Simioni's concern with money and the large quantities he seemed to have at his disposal aroused the suspicion of several of his comrades. Red Brigades founder Alberto Franceschini took a personal dislike to him. 'Elegant and smartly dressed, he was always driving around in Maseratis, arguing that a guerrilla, to conceal himself and spread confusion, should behave like a perfect bourgeois,' Franceschini wrote in his autobiography. After seeing the movie *Queimada*, the Red Brigades dubbed Simioni 'l'ingles'. 'In the film Marlon Brandon plays "l'ingles", the liberal intellectual who first organizes the revolt and then its bloody suppression.' Franceschini distrusted the Superclan so much that he insisted that its members be kept on the fringes of the Red Brigades when some of them asked to be admitted to the organization. After his arrest, the first message he had smuggled out of prison to the BR leaders who were still at large concerned the Superclan and warned them 'to be extremely wary of any comrades coming from Corrado [Simioni's] group'.[12]

Simioni's chequered career amply justifies the suspicion. He was born near Venice in 1934 and began his political career in the Socialist Party, where he was known for his anti-communism. He was expelled from the party for unspecified 'immoral conduct', after which he became involved in cultural activities on behalf of the United States Information Service (USIS). He also spent a couple of years in Munich, where he claimed to be studying theology, but other accounts have him working for the CIA-financed Radio Free Europe, which broadcasts to Eastern Europe from that city. His name appears on a list of CIA agents operating in Italy that came into the possession of the left-wing newspaper *Lotta Continua* in the late 1960s. Whatever he was doing, his experience abroad had turned him into a radical left-winger.[13] Renato Curcio was given a strong personal reason for distrusting Simioni when the Superclan leader tried to persuade Mara Cagol, Curcio's wife, to participate in an expedition to blow up the US consulate in Athens without informing her husband. Cagol told Curcio about the approach and he talked her out of going. Another Italian girl and a Greek Cypriot were sent in her place and the two were killed when their bomb exploded prematurely on 2 September 1970.[14] According to some accounts, the explosives were part of the same stock which cost Giangiacomo Feltrinelli his life as he attempted to blow up an electricity pylon on the outskirts of Milan in 1972.

The role of the Hyperion language school, with an office on the prestigious Quai de la Tournelle close to Notre Dame cathedral in central Paris, tallies with Prosecutor Pietro Calogero's description of a terrorist command structure, dictating the course of political violence in Italy. According to several 'repentant' terrorists, the school handled international relations and weapons procurement for the Red Brigades after the arrest of their original leadership. 'The fact is that the Hyperion was created to provide protection to various fugitives and that function enabled its directors to establish contact with many terrorist organizations,' Red Brigades member Michele Galati told magistrates after his arrest. Galati said the school was in contact with the IRA, ETA and the PLO and was able to purchase arms for the Red Brigades from minority factions within the Palestine Liberation Organization. He described how Moretti had personally forbidden him from using Vanni Mulinaris for terrorist actions in the Venice region, where Galati operated. 'Moretti told me that there was no question of letting Mulinaris run any risks because he was responsible for international contacts and arms procurement.'[15]

The Red Brigades leader who was responsible for weapons procurement, and made regular trips to Paris for that purpose, was Mario Moretti. Before joining the Red Brigades, Moretti had been a member of Superclan. He rose to prominence after the arrest in 1974 of the founding fathers of the Red Brigades and it was he alone who handled the Paris connection. For a while he was even suspected of being a secret service agent by his fellow BR members because of the almost miraculous way in which he avoided arrest when all around

[190]

him were being caught by the police. His early contact with Superclan, his connection with the Hyperion and his refusal to clear up the mysteries surrounding the Moro kidnap, which he personally directed, give further cause for doubt about his revolutionary purity.

In 1980, journalist Guido Passalacqua raised the question of the true identity of the Red Brigades leadership in an article for *La Repubblica* (12 April 1980). 'There is someone higher up, one, two, three people who decide the terrorist campaigns . . . A decidedly impenetrable leadership if one considers that, according to the leaks, Mario Moretti provided the only link with the operational terrorists.' Passalacqua was shot in the legs as a 'class enemy' on 7 May, less than a month later. Shortly after his article, Socialist Party Secretary Bettino Craxi picked up the baton, speculating to parliamentary journalists that the '*grande vecchio*', the grand old man who pulled the strings of terrorism, may have been 'someone who started out in politics at the same time as us' and who 'perhaps today is in Paris, working for the armed party'.[16] Though Craxi subsequently denied he had him in mind, many recognized Corrado Simioni in the portrait.

Aside from the ill-judged secret service interview with the *Corriere della Sera*, there are other elements that confirm the equivocal nature of the Hyperion and the impression that its members enjoyed official protection. With high outgoings and little income, Italian investigators were puzzled that the school could operate at all, let alone support the lavish life-style to which Simioni was accustomed. A further report by the Rome police (1 January 1980) expresses scepticism at statements made to the French police by some of the school's 'employees'. The author is surprised at the 'abnegation' of Duccio Berio, in charge of public relations for the Hyperion, 'who says he receives no salary and adds that he makes an annual contribution of 3,500 francs to the school from his own savings'. The report was also sceptical of Corrado Simioni's claim that he received no payment for his work as cultural adviser to the school, despite having a family to maintain and renting two apartments for a total of 5,400 francs a month. Journalists from *Le Point* magazine gained a similar impression when they investigated the school, noting that the former Hyperion offices in Rue Lesieur had been described as 'very luxurious and almost empty of clients'.[17] The Italian investigators were scarcely reassured when they discovered that an Italian businessman had paid the school 20 million Lire (£13,000), the equivalent of a year's rent of the Hyperion's Paris premises, shortly after his brother had been kidnapped by the Calabrian Mafia. They were also surprised when they found they were unable to approach a weekend villa, said to be owned by the Hyperion, where Simioni was staying, because it was so heavily guarded. Two police officers on a mission to check out the London branch of the school were discouraged to discover that their hotel rooms had been thoroughly searched during their absence.[18] The officers interpreted it as a warning to desist from their inquiries and returned to Italy after consultations with the magistrate who had sent them. By a strange coincidence, the school opened an office in Rome shortly before the kidnap of Aldo Moro and closed it again the following autumn. After Moretti's arrest in 1981 contact with Paris was delegated to Giovanni Senzani, another Red Brigades leader strongly suspected of having secret service contacts.

One of the Hyperion's protectors was, curiously enough, a man called Henri Groues, better known in France as l'Abbé Pierre, a Catholic priest renowned for his work in favour of the poor and homeless. Groues was also a Resistance hero, a former deputy and in 1989 was a candidate for the Nobel Peace Prize. In 1972, however, according to the Italian police, he had been 'in contact with several members of the Red Brigades including Renato Curcio'.[19] L'Abbé Pierre repeatedly activated his high-level contacts in France and Italy in favour of the members of the Hyperion group, who he insisted were the innocent victims of political persecution. One of the people familiar with the group has spoken of l'Abbé Pierre's influential friends in France and of a boast by Simioni that he could 'even contact Giscard d'Estaing for me if I needed it'.[20] Groues had one particularly strong reason for his solicitude on the Hyperion's behalf: his niece Françoise Tuscher was president of the Hyperion Cultural Association. Tuscher, along with her husband Innocente Salvoni, had lived in Milan in 1969, where they had belonged to the Sinistra Proletaria organization, an offshoot of the Collettivo Politico Metropolitano. It was in the framework of Sinistra Proletaria that she had met the three principal animators of the Hyperion project, Berio, Mulinaris and Simioni. According to the Italian police, she and her husband had been leading members of Superclan and Salvoni was at one stage suspected of having participated in the Moro kidnap, although he was later eliminated from that inquiry. A Le Point journalist who interviewed her in 1979 took a less indulgent view of her than did her uncle. 'She says she doesn't know Negri. But she seemed to know much more than she was letting on. She seemed to me to be playing the idiot.'[21]

There is also evidence that the Hyperion had other protectors, more powerful and more sinister than l'Abbé Pierre. One highly significant clue is to be found in the letter, dated 20 October 1978, with which Prosecutor Calogero initiated the whole Hyperion investigation. Clearly acting on detailed information, much of which would later prove to be well founded, the Padua magistrate instructed the Rome police to investigate the relationship between Toni Negri and the French (Workers') Autonomy organization and other groups suspected of terrorist activity, as well as the relationship between Negri and the Hyperion. Most telling of all was his request that the police ascertain whether Hyperion and an affiliated company known as Les Gentils Fantômes, which ostensibly specialized in the discreet cleaning of Parisian apartments, could be construed as 'the centre of political and strategic control over the Red Brigades or other similar terrorist organizations operating in Italy, their logistical and organizational base, or their principal source of finance'. Even more significantly, the letter continued by asking the police to establish whether the two companies were in any way connected with 'politicians or political parties, Italian or foreign intelligence services', and whether these had provided start-up capital for the companies. Calogero's attempt to answer these questions was stymied by the timely secret service leak to the *Corriere della Sera*, but later investigations have established that his original information was alarmingly accurate.

One such investigation was conducted over seven years by an examining magistrate from Venice, Carlo Mastelloni. Mastelloni's inquiry focused on arms deals between the Palestine Liberation Organization and the Red Brigades, mediated by the Hyperion group. It attracted world-wide media attention in 1984 when Mastelloni issued an arrest warrant for Yasser Arafat, claiming that the PLO leader had authorized several arms shipments to the Red Brigades. In his final report, however, Mastelloni recommended that Arafat should be acquitted for lack of evidence. Far more sensitive, though, was Mastelloni's conclusion that the arms traffic between the PLO and the Red Brigades had been protected and perhaps even sponsored by the Italian secret services and the CIA. This view is not openly spelt out in the report but hinted at in a somewhat elliptical manner. The delicacy of the subject was underlined by Mastelloni's apparent conviction that anyone interested in obtaining a more than superficial understanding of his findings could not be a bona fide journalist but must himself be working for a secret service.

One of the most effective ways for a secret service to influence or control a terrorist group is by controlling the supply of arms to it. It is particularly significant then that the supply of arms to the Red Brigades should have passed through the mediation of members of the Hyperion, a group strongly suspected of having secret service links.

A key figure in the arms traffic between Palestinian groups in Lebanon and Italian terrorist organizations, Mastelloni's investigation reveals, was Colonel Stefano Giovannone, the SISMI officer in Beirut who collaborated with Abu Ayad in a disinformation operation over the Bologna bombing. One curious episode, described by Mastelloni, shows how Giovannone reacted to the arrest of two members of Autonomia Operaia who were caught in possession of a consignment of missiles at Ortona in east central Italy in October 1979. Giovannone immediately persuaded George Habbash, leader of the hardline Marxist Popular Front for the Liberation of Palestine (PFLP) to issue a statement saying that the weapons belonged to the PFLP and were merely in transit in Italy in an operation that had the approval of the Italian embassy in Beirut. The operation certainly appears to have had Giovannone's approval, though not the approval of the Italian ambassador in Beirut: a Jordanian student arrested in connection with the missiles a few days after the Autonomia members was described by Mastelloni as being an 'infiltrator of Giovannone's or "of interest" to him.'[22] Given the evidence that the PFLP was providing guerrilla training in Lebanon to Autonomia Operaia, it is not unlikely that they were also providing them with arms, with the tacit assent of the Italian secret service. It would certainly have been much less embarrassing all round for the PFLP to claim that the arms were in transit rather than to admit to this state of affairs.

Still more sensitive was Giovannone's role in regard to arms deals between the PLO and the Red Brigades. In the summer of 1979 Mario Moretti sailed to Lebanon in a yacht with three Red Brigades companions to collect a consignment of arms from the PLO. The yacht was the *Papago* and belonged to a psychiatrist from Ancona, Massimo Gidoni, who was also a member of the Red Brigades and acted as skipper on the journey, which included a stop-over in Cyprus. According to several former BR members, the deal had been organized through the good offices of the Hyperion and involved the immediate redistribution of some of the weapons to the Basque terrorist group ETA, to the Irish Republican Army and to the German Red Army

Faction. The arms were provided free but some of them were to be kept available for use by the PLO and the Red Brigades undertook to use their own weapons in operations against NATO and Israeli targets. The weapons not for use by the Red Brigades were marked with pale blue labels and the name 'Francis' was written on the crate. They did, however, receive twenty-five Sterling submachine-guns, Energa grenades, munitions and explosives for their own use.[23] Mastelloni's inquiries established that an RPG7 rocket-propelled grenade launcher provided for BR use came from a Fatah workshop in Lebanon and that the Sterling submachine-guns were part of a stock of weapons ceded to Fatah by the Tunisian government in 1968.[24] Though Mastelloni eventually decided to acquit Arafat of responsibility for the *Papago* arms consignment, he recommended that his deputy, Abu Ayad, should be sent for trial.

In February 1981, Turin magistrates sent two police officers to Beirut on a secret mission to gather information from the Lebanese police and from Christian sources about the relationship between the PLO and the Red Brigades. Giovannone learnt of the mission by intercepting cable traffic between the Beirut embassy, for whose security he was responsible, and the Italian Foreign Ministry. He immediately tipped off his contacts in the PLO, who promptly called a press conference to denounce the visit as being part of a plot to murder senior PLO officials. As a result of this publicity, the police fact-finding mission proved utterly fruitless.[25] Giovannone justified his decision to torpedo the police visit, and earlier attempts to cover up the fact that the PLO had been supplying the Red Brigades with arms, by saying that Arafat had previously denied the existence of any such relationship and a political decision was taken to spare him embarrassment. A more plausible and more sinister explanation can be found by careful reading of Mastelloni's report.

In the course of his investigation, the Venice magistrate discovered that SISMI director Giuseppe Santovito, a member of the P2 masonic lodge who earlier in his military career had been suspected of participating in a 1974 coup plot, had set up a special and highly unusual unit within military intelligence, which he placed under his own direct supervision. The unit, which included Giovannone, was active between April and October 1979, exactly the period during which Moretti was organizing his Lebanese arms shipment. Another member of the unit, Lieutenant Colonel Silvio Di Napoli, was charged with assisting the arms traffic between the PLO and the Red Brigades.

Di Napoli refused to clarify the nature of the special operations in which he had been involved, stating merely that he had undertaken three foreign missions and that the resulting intelligence had been passed on to allied security services. He said the missions were covered by state secrecy, a view that was upheld by the Italian Prime Minister in 1985, prompting Mastelloni to acquit him of the charge.[26]

Giovannone too ran into legal difficulties for his role in the special SISMI unit and he too was forced to invoke state secrecy. As Mastelloni continued his inquiry into the PLO-BR arms deals, he discovered evidence of what he called a 'paradoxical', secret, tripartite traffic in weapons between the Italian government and the PLO and between the PLO and the Red Brigades.[27] The secret service explanation for this paradox is that the Italian government had struck a deal with the PLO following a number of Palestinian terrorist atrocities in Italy in the early 1970s, which gave the PLO a virtually free rein to pursue its activities in Italy provided it undertook to prevent future attacks on Italian targets. Nevertheless, it is hard to believe that the Italian secret services could have considered that arming the Red Brigades, who were busily engaged in a violent attempt to subvert the Italian state, fell under the terms of this agreement.

Another, more plausible explanation emerges from the pages of Mastelloni's report. In it he outlines the thesis that Giovannone had been entrusted by the Italian government with the role of mediator in secret contacts between the CIA and the PLO leadership and that this had resulted, in 1976, in a secret agreement between the CIA and Fatah secret services.[28] Numerous diplomatic and secret service witnesses whom Mastelloni interrogated invoked state secrecy on this subject. It is not difficult to understand why, when one considers, as Mastelloni points out, that the Americans had signed an agreement with Israel in 1975 in which they undertook to avoid any political contact with the PLO.[29] What is particularly sinister is the fact that the secret CIA-PLO agreement, mediated by Giovannone, should emerge in the context of an investigation into arms trafficking between the PLO and the Red Brigades. Mastelloni states clearly that testimony about 'the de facto secret service level accord between the USA and the PLO was considered relevant to the present investigation into the historic, political and logistical relationship between the Red Brigades organization and the PLO . . .'[30] The unstated but inescapable conclusion is that the arms deals between the PLO and the Red

Brigades formed part of the secret accord between the PLO and the CIA. Mastelloni's discoveries cast a curious light on a handwritten note confiscated from General Maletti in 1980. The document was one of more than 100 giving a brief agenda for the regular meetings Maletti held with the director of the military intelligence service, which he kept at his home. On 25 March 1975, one of the topics for discussion was: 'BR-PLO co-ordination, our brilliant action, report on it.'[31] It would appear that the brilliant secret service action was likely to have involved the promotion of BR-PLO co-ordination rather than its prevention.

In December 1990 a Venice assize court acquitted all fourteen defendants accused of complicity in the PLO-BR arms trafficking. The public prosecutor had already watered down Mastelloni's case, calling at the end of the trial for guilty verdicts for only four of the accused. The court may not have been convinced by the prosecution evidence, but it is hard to escape the conclusion that a discreet veil has been drawn over a particularly sensitive chapter of Italy's terrorist history. For virtually the first time, secret service officers and left-wing terrorists had been placed in the dock together.

It comes as little surprise then to discover that Duccio Berio, one of the Hyperion triumvirate, had taken the precaution of writing to his father-in-law in 1972 about an attempt by the secret services to recruit him as an informer. The recipient of the letter was Alberto Malagugini, a lawyer, who acted for Berio, and was a prominent member of the PCI. In it Berio described how he had been approached by a man claiming to be an agent of military intelligence, then known as SID, who had asked for information about the CPM and Sinistra Proletaria political organizations to which he had belonged and which later gave birth to the Red Brigades and Superclan. Berio wrote that he had agreed to tell the man what he knew about the two organizations 'but that my opinion is that the terrorist activities that he attributed to offshoots of these groups are in fact part of a plan of provocation, the proof of which can be seen in the move to the right which is currently under way in our country'.[32] This looks remarkably like an attempt by Berio to get on record the fact that he had collaborated with the secret services and, if that was not enough to resolve any legal problems he might encounter, he had also hinted at his knowledge of the right-wing design behind apparently left-wing terrorism. As a member of Hyperion in later years, he would be ideally placed to observe the process in action. Who knows, the agent, who gave his name as

Ballini, may even have been the person who recruited Berio to the cause? Corrado Simioni suggested much the same thing in a 1985 interview with *L'Espresso* magazine. Most of the interview was devoted to Simioni's insistence that he had never been remotely involved in terrorism. At the end he was asked whether he believed the armed struggle was over in Italy. 'In my opinion it ended years ago, when they arrested Curcio and the other [BR] founders. The rest, including the Moro case, was something else: the triumph of military technocracy.'[33] This is not quite the same thing as saying that the Moretti Red Brigades were manipulated by conservative forces, but it is not far from it.

The Moro Commission tried repeatedly to persuade the Italian police and secret services to resume their investigation into the activities of the Hyperion and was unconvinced by the reply that this was not possible given the refusal of the French secret service to co-operate. SISMI director General Santovito reacted in a surprisingly limp manner when questioned about the school. One of the commission members drew attention to the failure to mount an independent secret service investigation of Simioni after the initial setback caused by the *Corriere della Sera* revelations: 'I must tell you that the thing is becoming so strange that I am beginning to suspect that, in fact, you never investigated him because he is your own man,' the commissioner observed. Instead of protesting that this was arrant nonsense, or even denying it was true, Santovito replied mildly: 'I will try to give greater satisfaction. Obviously my information is insufficient . . .'[34] A police report from the end of 1979 offers a more credible explanation for SISMI's inactivity: 'It is suspected that the Hyperion language school is the most important CIA office in Europe.'[35]

The foundation stone of the Red Brigades organization was laid at a meeting in Pecorile, a town at the foot of the Apennines, in August 1970. From then on, the group's history would be a parabola, with arrests and setbacks only spurring its members on to ever increasing levels of violence. The first activities were low-key: sabotage in factories, burning directors' cars and culminating in the first kidnaps. A company director would be seized on the street, bundled into a van and then photographed with a pistol pointed at his head and a placard round his neck bearing slogans such as 'Bite and run' and 'Strike at one to educate 100'. He would be released shortly afterwards, bruised and very frightened but otherwise none the worse for his experience.

The first major Red Brigades operation was the kidnap on 18 April 1974 of Mario Sossi, a right-wing magistrate from Genoa. He was held for five weeks and then released without the Red Brigades obtaining any concessions from the authorities. The bizarre activities of the secret services during this period came to light two years later when *Tempo* magazine (20 June 1976) published a detailed account of the affair. According to the magazine, secret service chief Vito Miceli had planned to kidnap Giovanni Battista Lazagna, a left-wing lawyer in contact with the Red Brigades, and force him to reveal the location of Sossi's prison. However, according to an unnamed SID official this ostensible plan concealed a somewhat different reality. 'Lazagna, who did not know the prison where Sossi was being held, could never have told us where it was. The hiding place would in fact have been "discovered" by someone who already knew it. It would have been surrounded and there would have been shooting. And inside they would have found the corpses of the Red Brigades, of Sossi and of Lazagna.' The plan was never put into effect, partly because of opposition to it from within the secret service. This account later received authoritative confirmation from several secret service officers. If true, it is a significant precedent that the secret service should have known the whereabouts of Sossi's prison but done nothing to secure his release, while planning instead, in the best traditions of the strategy of tension, to engineer a massacre.

The article was accompanied by an interview with former counter-espionage chief Gianadelio Maletti, who described how he had received reports in 1975 of a reorganization of the Red Brigades under more aggressive leadership. 'They were recruiting terrorists from all sides and the leaders remained in the shadows, but I wouldn't say you could describe them as leftists,' Maletti said. The interviewer asked him whether he would agree with a description of the Red Brigades provided by an anonymous secret service officer, which divided the organization into three levels: the young fanatics, the Eastern Bloc agents and 'further in, in the most secret compartment, the infiltrators of the Interior Ministry and Western secret services'. 'I would say yes, broadly,' Maletti replied. Maletti had reported this analysis to the Interior Minister in 1975 and been promptly fired for his pains. Whatever the level of secret service involvement with the Red Brigades at the time of Sossi's kidnap, the magistrate was clearly shaken by his experience. He no longer had any faith in either the police or the *carabinieri* and sought instead the protection of the finance police, who provided him with a round-the-clock guard on his return to Genoa.

The Red Brigades committed their first murders on 17 June 1974, during a raid on the Padua office of the neo-fascist MSI. According to their own account, the killings were an accident. Two Red Brigades members, Fabrizio Pelli and Roberto Ognibene, entered the office early in the morning in order to steal documents. They encountered two neo-fascist sympathizers, whom they were forced to shoot when they attempted to put up a fight. Pelli has since died in prison, but Ognibene has described how one of the two victims actually grabbed the barrel of the pistol he was pointing at him and started to struggle. However, according to Prosecutor Lorenzo Zen, there was no sign of a fight in the office. 'Everything was in order, even piles of cyclostyled paper which would have been spread around if there had been a bit of movement.'[36] Sixteen years later, the dynamics of the event had still not been fully clarified.

Many people initially imagined that the killings were part of an internal struggle within the extreme right. They were unconvinced by the Red Brigades communiqué claiming responsibility for the murders. It accurately stated: 'The Padua MSI, which has produced groups and individuals involved in anti-proletarian terrorism, has controlled the black conspiracies since the Piazza Fontana bombing.'[37] The fact that one of the victims, a travelling salesman named Graziano Giralucci, had acted as a go-between linking secret agent Guido Giannettini to the Padua terrorist group led by right-wingers Franco Freda and Giovanni Ventura only added to the suspicions. The second victim was Giuseppe Mazzola, a sixty-year-old security guard employed by the office. His son told magistrates: 'When I bent over my father, I touched the back of his neck. It was soaking wet. It was not blood but sweat. He was soaking, as though he had sweated for a long time, terrorized, waiting for his execution.'[38] The Red Brigades' involvement with homicide had got off to an inauspicious start, under circumstances which would make it virtually impossible to know whether the killings were an accident, the result of a secret service plot or of an internecine neo-fascist feud.

In June of the following year the Red Brigades were given their first 'martyr'. Mara Cagol, a founder of the original terrorist nucleus and wife of Renato Curcio, was killed on 5 June, in a shoot-out with *carabinieri* at a remote farmhouse in north-east Italy. The accounts of her death which circulated among the Red Brigades afterwards had it that she had been wounded while trying to escape and had then been finished off in cold blood by one of the *carabinieri*. The Red Brigades were holding a wealthy businessman, Vallarino Gancia, kidnapped the previous day. One *carabiniere* died in the shooting and Gancia was rescued unhurt. Only two months earlier, on 18 February, Cagol had led a bold raid on Casale prison and succeeded in freeing her husband. Despite the patently inadequate security arrangements surrounding the imprisoned Red Brigades leader – the prison director described the jail as being 'as secure as a hen-house' – that enterprise and her death 'in battle' turned Mara Cagol into a romantic heroine and an inspiration for future generations of terrorists. From the moment of her death onwards, however, there would be less romance and more violence in the Red Brigades' struggle.

On 8 June 1976, the group carried out its first deliberately planned murder, shooting dead Public Prosecutor Francesco Coco and his two bodyguards in the centre of Genoa. Coco had distinguished himself by taking an uncompromising line during the Sossi kidnapping but, given his wide judicial experience, the Mafia might have been just as interested in his elimination as the revolutionary left. From then on, the story of the Red Brigades would be littered with an ever-increasing number of corpses. Moro's five bodyguards in 1978 and Moro himself, killed in cold blood after fifty-five days; four terrorists killed by the *carabinieri* in a Genoa apartment on the night of 28 March 1980. By the end, the Red Brigades had embarked on an indiscriminate killing spree, simply to prove they still existed, and virtually anyone was a valid target. Before their almost total dismantling in 1982, the line between revolutionary and *agent provocateur* had become so fine as to be non-existent. Since then, the bedraggled leftovers of the revolutionary movement have continued to kill sporadically but without the remotest prospect of achieving political change, justifying their new murders with the claim that they have embarked on 'a civil war of long duration'.

By the late 1970s, the Red Brigades had unleashed an authentic reign of terror. The Milan column of the organization selected their targets on the basis of the most superficial research and trivial considerations. They included doctors, hospital workers and company directors. Some of the potential victims became so worried about their chances of being shot in the legs that they adopted the habit of carrying a tourniquet with them at all times, just in case. On one occasion the BR shot and wounded a Fiat director whom they had mistaken for a

Siemens director living in the same block of flats. On learning of their mistake, they simply rewrote the communiqué claiming responsibility for the attack, to give the impression that the victim was indeed their intended target. On another occasion, the terrorists asked an employee of the Ercole Marelli company to carry out research on one of the firm's directors whom they had already murdered, so that they could explain the motive for the assassination in their propaganda. 'I did the research in the factory and I realized that almost everyone said [the victim] was a fine person, even though he was personnel director, so I began to think that the BR had caught a crab in hitting this target,' the man later told Milan magistrates. In 1980 the Red Brigades shot dead Falck company director Manfredo Mazzanti. According to the examining magistrate's indictment: 'Mazzanti was chosen from a long list of Falck directors published by the magazine *Panorama*, principally because his photo had been published in the in-house factory newspaper . . . making him easier to identify than the others.' The magistrate expressed his dismay at the 'ease and superficiality with which the terrorists decide to cut short human lives'.[39]

One of the most extreme examples of this utter disregard for the value of human life was seen in Turin. On 21 October 1982, a Red Brigades commando raided a bank, disarming the two security guards and forcing them to lie on the floor before shooting them dead in cold blood. On the scene, the Red Brigades left leaflets claiming that one of their recently arrested members, Natalia Ligas, was a police spy. The whole operation, and in particular the murder of the guards, was designed to attract maximum publicity for their communiqué. Without the double murder, the robbery and the communiqué would have had less impact. This was terrorism in its purest form: armed propaganda that is intended to hasten the onset of civil war and revolution but which is equally likely to turn a society in on itself and block political change.

This steady process of degradation in the terrorist experience has been described by former BR member Enzo Fontana. 'We were like Theseus, we entered a labyrinth of mirrors to carry our assault to the heart of the Minotaur, of the capitalist, imperialist state. The subversive Theseus fed himself, as he advanced through the labyrinth, on abstract ideas, words, weapons, human flesh, the same food as that of the Minotaur. And finally he found it, it was not at the centre of anything, but it was there, there in a mirror that reflected a changed Theseus, more heavily armed and ferocious than the one who had begun the adventure. Theseus had entered the Minotaur and the Minotaur had entered Theseus, where, in reality, he had always been.'[40]

The choice of targets by the Red Brigades and their Prima Linea cousins has been the subject of considerable discussion. Often their victims were chosen from the most honest, efficient and progressive representatives of the state. Often too, conservative forces such as those embodied in the P2 masonic lodge shared a direct interest in the victim's elimination. It has been suggested this may have been the case in the murder of Examining Magistrate Emilio Alessandrini, shot dead by Prima Linea gunmen in Milan on 29 January 1979. Alessandrini was a strange target for a left-wing terrorist group. He was best known for the dogged and courageous way in which he had handled the investigation into secret service involvement in the Piazza Fontana bombing. Shortly before his death he had been given responsibility for an investigation into the financial affairs of the Banco Ambrosiano, the Milan bank headed by P2 member Roberto Calvi. He had also voiced suspicions about the involvement of Toni Negri in the Moro kidnap. His murderers have stated that he was chosen simply because he was well known and a relatively easy target. This explanation for the assassination of a man renowned for his investigations of right-wing terrorism shows a staggering political obtuseness. Any organization capable of it was liable to alienate its own potential supporters and to play the role of *agents provocateurs* even without being manipulated from outside. Marco Donat Cattin, the son of a powerful Christian Democrat politician and leader of the assassination squad, later admitted that Prima Linea knew so little about Alessandrini that they had to wait for the newspapers on the day after his death in order to draw up a document justifying his murder. Alessandrini's widow has publicly expressed her doubts about the motives of her husband's killers and subscribed to the view of terrorism as a phenomenon manipulated from on high.

Another terrorism widow, Carol Beebe Tarantelli, an American who has been elected to Parliament in Italy as a member of the Independent Left political grouping, takes a similar view. Her husband, the left-wing economist Ezio Tarantelli, was murdered in Rome by the Red Brigades in 1985. She underlined the right-wing consequences of left-wing terrorism in an interview with *Il Messaggero* newspaper (30 June 1988). 'I think they are "objectively" on the right. Objectively is a word they love. Objectively means that acting in the way they did they served the interests of someone who is against the left. I have always thought so, even before people started to talk about it openly. I don't know who this someone is but he certainly exists.'

Another Red Brigades murder with potentially crossed motives is cited by journalist Luca Villoresi in an article about the Hyperion language school (*Repubblica*, 1 February 1983). Girolamo Tartaglione, a magistrate and director general of penal affairs in the Justice Ministry was shot dead by the Red Brigades in Rome on 10 October 1978. He had requested an urgent meeting with Justice Minister Francesco Bonifacio in order to communicate with him on a serious matter. He had also confided to friends that he had understood many things about the Red Brigades and that he could no longer think of them as 'a fruit of the season'. Tartaglione was murdered before he got a chance to speak to the minister. After gunning him down on his doorstep, his assassins made off with his briefcase. When they abandoned their getaway car, however, they forgot the bag. In breach of the most elementary security precautions they were sent back to retrieve it and, as luck would have it, the car had not yet been found by the police. 'Did some well-informed insider alert Moretti to the danger? What was there in the briefcase that could be so important?' Villoresi asked.

If the Red Brigades were in contact with the secret services and the upper echelons of the state it would not be surprising if some of their victims were chosen for reasons quite independent of the Red Brigades' own concerns, nor would it have been unduly difficult to ensure that the 'contact's' candidate for elimination drew the short straw. At the very least, the terrorists' selection criteria show a remarkable similarity to the canons set out by secret agent Guido Giannettini in his book *Techniques of Revolutionary War*. 'Selective terrorism is carried out by eliminating particular men carefully chosen for a series of motives: either because they can be used by the enemy, or because their disappearance paralyses (or slows down) the enemy's organizational machine; or because, being moderate and moderators, they prevent the accentuation of the struggle by the other side; or even, finally, because their removal will provoke harsh reprisals which increase the tension, creating an irreversible process leading to civil war.'[41] This passage from Giannettini's manual, written in 1965, could easily have guided the Red Brigades in their later years. Giannettini himself hinted at the manipulation of left-wing terrorism

[204]

in a memorandum written while flying back to custody in Italy from a period of exile abroad, in August 1974. He divided Italy's terrorist history into three phases stretching from 1967 to the year of writing. 'Third phase (1973–1974): both right- and left-wing groups have operated . . . among the left-wing groups, the Red Brigades. A parallel manipulation of secret right- and left-wing groups by a single command centre cannot be ruled out. The techniques used are designed to provoke chaos and civil war.'[42] These observations were a preface to Giannettini's defence against charges of involvement in the Piazza Fontana bombing and were presumably designed to remind his erstwhile secret service masters of his ability to make damaging revelations, should the need arise.

The watershed between the relatively mild and relatively idealistic Red Brigades of the early years and the blind terror of the later years came in 1974 with the arrest of Renato Curcio and Alberto Franceschini, two of the movement's founding fathers. Their removal from the scene gave the ambitious Mario Moretti control over the organization and paved the way for his policy of constant military escalation, culminating in the Moro kidnap. The arrests were the fruit of a successful infiltration of the organization by the *carabinieri*. It is worth bearing in mind the observation of author Gianfranco Sanguinetti that nothing is easier for the secret services than to infiltrate a terrorist group and supplant the original leadership 'either through certain timely arrests or through the killing of the original leaders, which generally occurs in a shoot-out with the police, prepared for the operation by their infiltrators'.[43]

The successor to Marco Pisetta, the first known infiltrator of the Red Brigades, was an ex-Franciscan friar named Silvano Girotto. Girotto had acquired the nickname 'Brother Machine-gun' for his exploits as a left-wing guerrilla in South America. It is fairly clear that from the very start his revolutionary persona was a fraud, created for him by a secret service, probably the CIA. On his return to Italy he set about gaining admission to the Red Brigades. He was assisted in this aim by a profile of him as a left-wing revolutionary published in *Candido* (14 May 1974), a right-wing magazine linked to the Italian secret services. It appeared during the Sossi kidnap under the title: 'This is the man who could save Sossi.' After a couple of exploratory meetings with Red Brigades leaders, Girotto was admitted to the organization, which decided to make him responsible for terrorist training. Both meetings had been watched and photographed by plainclothes *carabinieri* and after a third, on 8 September, Curcio and Franceschini were arrested at Pinerolo near Turin. Their capture changed the Red Brigades profoundly; from then on the tactics of the organization were increasingly violent and its principal enemy was no longer the Christian Democrat Party and the right, but the revisionist traitors of the PCI and the policy of the historic compromise. The new BR policy would bring it increasingly into line with the thinking of Toni Negri.

There were a number of anomalies about the Pinerolo incident. Most glaring was the question why Curcio and Franceschini were arrested at all, thus blowing Girotto's cover. Had the ex-friar been allowed to continue his infiltration, the entire organization could very probably have been rounded up. When questioned about this by the Moro commission, General Dalla Chiesa, who commanded the operation, offered the lame explanation that he was obliged by law to arrest suspected criminals as soon as they were identified. Dalla Chiesa was not a man noted for his attention to legal niceties and it is hard to believe that he really gave higher priority to such scruples than to the defeat of the Red Brigades.

In 1988 *Panorama* magazine (12 June 1988) published some of the photos taken by the *carabinieri* at the meetings between Girotto and the Red Brigades leaders. They were dug up by the magazine from the documents presented at the trial of the original nucleus of the Red Brigades, which began in Turin in 1976. Though Mario Moretti had attended one of the meetings, there was no photo of him in the file. It is possible that it had simply been mislaid; or that some friendly hand had removed it. While Moretti was still at large the fewer photos of him there were in circulation the easier it was for him to avoid capture. A photo had certainly existed. It was shown to Franceschini after his arrest by Turin Magistrate Giancarlo Caselli, with the words: 'Try asking yourself why they decided to make the arrests when it was you and Curcio [who attended the meeting]. You're not the only one to have met Girotto, the man in the photo met him too.' Franceschini's reaction was, 'I could not understand what Caselli was trying to tell me: perhaps he was insinuating that Mario was protected by the *carabinieri*?'[44]

Stranger still was the phone call to a Red Brigades supporter on 5 September, warning that Curcio would be arrested in two days' time. The source of the call has never been established. Some Red Brigades members have assumed it came from the Israeli intelligence service, which had recently approached the Red Brigades with an offer of arms and assistance. Mossad had an obvious interest in the destabilization of Italy as it helped to ensure that Israel would not be supplanted as the United States' most dependable ally in the Mediterranean region. Others have suggested that it may have been Girotto himself, out of fear. Another alternative has the call coming from P2 members in the Milan *carabinieri* with an interest in protecting the Red Brigades and putting a spanner in the spokes of their rival, Dalla Chiesa. Whoever called the Red Brigades, the message was passed on to Mario Moretti, who assumed responsibility for relaying it to Curcio and Franceschini. He was unable to contact them and arrived an hour late at the meeting-place, after the two had already been arrested. In his book, Franceschini remarked that Moretti did exactly the opposite of what he should have done on that occasion. 'Instead of dashing backwards and forwards through half of Italy, as he said he did, he could simply have waited for us on the road to the meeting-place (he knew which route we would take and even the car we would use) to warn us of the danger.'[45]

Moretti, of course, was the principal beneficiary from the arrests and the whole episode has a distinctly fishy odour. In evidence given to magistrates in October, Girotto implicitly confirmed the later *Tempo* account of the secret service plan to end the Sossi kidnap with a massacre. 'Curcio told me that they had intended to execute Sossi but then the BR . . . had learnt from a reliable source in the Interior Ministry that the *carabinieri* had been ordered to kill everyone, including Sossi.' All in all, the reflection of Turin Public Prosecutor Luigi Moschetta seems amply justified: 'There was someone at a high level who was concerned that the Red Brigades' activities should continue . . . We can believe that the BR had an informant in the Interior Ministry's Office of Special Affairs.'[46]

If the Red Brigades had their informants within the institutions of the state, the state too had its own infiltrators in the terrorists' ranks. Marco Pisetta told the Moro Commission that he was surprised that the Red Brigades were not wound up on the basis of his information in 1972 and Girotto, if he had been allowed to continue his penetration, could have dismantled the whole organization two years later. After this date, little is known about the identity of the Red Brigades infiltrators. This is partly because it would be extremely embarrassing for the authorities to admit their existence, given that the Red Brigades continued to commit actions of the utmost gravity, yet nothing was done to avert them. There can be little doubt, though, that there were infiltrators in place. 'Infiltrating the Red Brigades was relatively easy at the ideological level,' according to one of Dalla Chiesa's collaborators. 'We had *carabinieri* who spoke and thought in "brigadese" after studying the leaflets and documents . . . and frequenting the subversive milieu for years. But then came the insurmountable barrier, the test of armed violence. We couldn't ask our *carabinieri* to shoot someone in order to enter the BR. The only place where the infiltrators were exempt from the weapons test was in prison.'[47] This at least is the official version. It is nevertheless significant that *carabinieri* had been frequenting the world of subversion for years, giving the lie to the official claim, trotted out after every major Red Brigades outrage, that the secret services were in disarray and had no channels to the terrorists. The extremist group Potere Operaio was so leaky it prompted journalist Giorgio Bocca to remark, 'Of every four Potere Operaio activists, two are policemen.'[48] A colonel in the Rome *carabinieri* and secret service agent even admitted to the Moro Commission that he had an informant in contact with the Red Brigades in the capital throughout the Moro kidnap. He claimed the contact produced no useful information whatsoever during that traumatic period.[49]

Moretti himself is a candidate for the role of infiltrator in the Red Brigades. Like Negri, his upbringing and youthful political convictions were a far cry from those he professed in later life. After the death of his father, he was educated at boarding-school, the fees being paid by a wealthy Milanese aristocrat, the Marchesa Anna Casati-Stampa. While at school he was a member of a right-wing Catholic youth group and after studying at the Catholic University in Milan he got a job with the Sit-Siemens electronics company. His local parish priest helped him with a reference stating that 'he professed sound religious and political ideas'. He was remembered at Siemens for delivering a strong speech condemning the trade unions at a workers' meeting, and this just a year before becoming a full-time revolutionary.[50] His luck in avoiding arrest, which lasted him until April 1981, his secret international travel, his contacts with the Hyperion and his evasiveness over the true dynamics of the Moro operation would all add to the suspicions in later years. In the autumn of 1990 repentant terrorist Michele Galati revealed to magistrates that Moretti had actually been put on trial by fellow BR members in prison immediately after his arrest. He was accused of being a spy and faced death if found guilty.

In the event, Galati said, he was neither acquitted nor convicted but set to one side and isolated by his companions.

Licio Gelli, the P2 boss, made his own eloquent contribution to the debate over the manipulation of Italian terrorism in 1981. In March of that year the P2 membership lists had been found and Gelli had been forced to flee the country. On 4 July, his daughter was stopped as she arrived at Rome airport and a wide range of documents found in the false bottom of her suitcase. The most interesting was the photocopy of a document entitled 'Stability Operations, Intelligence – Special Fields', marked Top Secret, and published under the authority of General W. C. Westmoreland, chief of staff of the US Army. It was General William Westmoreland who commanded US military forces, with conspicuous lack of success, during the early stages of the Vietnam War. Dated 18 March 1970, and described as Supplement B to Field Manual 30–31, the twelve-page booklet described how US Army intelligence operatives should respond to communist insurgencies in Allied countries. The Field Manual itself, clearly intended for application in South-east Asia, was also concealed in Maria Grazia Gelli's case. Parts of the supplement had been published in a Turkish newspaper in 1976 and subsequently in other European publications. Excerpts from it had been published in Italy by *L'Europeo* magazine (27 October and 3 November 1978) in the context of a discussion of the Moro affair and the possibility that an international plot lay behind it. US authorities denied the authenticity of the document. Given its contents this is hardly surprising.

'This Top Secret classified supplement FM 30-31B, owing to its specially sensitive nature, is not a standard issue in the FM series,' the document stated in its introduction. 'Operations in this special field are to be regarded as strictly clandestine, since the acknowledged involvement of the US Army in HC [Host Country] affairs is restricted to the area of co-operation against insurgency. The fact that US Army involvement goes deeper can in no circumstances be acknowledged.' In a section on 'Penetration of the Insurgent Movement', the document stated that US Army intelligence should 'endeavor to identify agents infiltrated into the insurgency by HC agencies responsible for internal security with a view to establishing clandestine control by US Army intelligence over the work of such agents.' Furthermore, 'It should endeavor to infiltrate reliable agents into the insurgent leadership, with special emphasis on the insurgent intelligence system directed against HC agencies.' Supplement B also recommended that 'Where the existence of separate HC archives not officially accessible to US personnel is known or suspected, careful consideration should be given to the possibility of operations designed to gain the desired access.'

The most sensitive remarks came in a section titled 'Agents on Special Operations'. This section warned that Host Country governments may sometimes be lulled into a false sense of security by a temporary halt in insurgent violence or be prone to passivity and indecision in the face of communist subversion. 'In such cases, US Army intelligence must have the means of launching special operations which will convince HC governments and public opinion of the reality of the insurgent danger and of the necessity of counteraction. To this end, US Army intelligence should seek to penetrate the insurgency by means of agents on special assignment, with the task of forming special action groups among the more radical elements of the insurgency. When the kind of situation envisaged above arises, these groups, acting under US Army intelligence control, should be used to launch violent or non-violent actions according to the nature of the case.' The section concluded: 'In cases where the infiltration of such agents into the insurgent leadership has not been effectively implemented, it may help towards the achievement of the above ends to utilize ultra-leftist organizations.'[51]

All the indications are that the document is authentic and it is highly significant that Gelli should be in possession of it. What is particularly significant is that he chose to send it into Italy at a time when his organization was being publicly disgraced and he needed all his powerful friends to rally round to his assistance. It is unclear whether he intended the document to be seized by the police or whether he meant to have copies of it sent to a few selected recipients. P2 member Federico D'Amato was head of the Italian border police at the time, so he may have imagined that his daughter would be able to slip unmolested into the country. Gelli's response when questioned about the document was somewhat evasive but, nevertheless, extremely revealing. 'Well, I don't know. I can't even remember it. It was a plan to destabilize certain communist countries, I think, well done, but it was already old, out of date. Perhaps it was posted to me anonymously and I attached no importance to it. But it was stuff I was sending to myself. It was to test whether my correspondence was being confiscated.' He had not, then, meant to suggest that the Americans had been responsible for destabilizing Italy, as well as countries in

South-east Asia? 'No, good heavens, no. I think that the Americans' interest in Italy has always been very great and that many Italians have not understood the gratitude they owe the Americans. I say it, and I am someone who fought against them. The Italians don't know how much they should thank the Americans for what they did after the war, from the Marshall Plan onwards.' What about the theory of the strategy of tension, that the country was destabilized in order to stabilize it to the right? Gelli coughed, then replied: 'I wouldn't rule anything out, because there were plenty of dirty tricks at that time. . . There have been dirty tricks in the past, there are today and there will be tomorrow, because we haven't reached an equilibrium. You see, dictatorship and democracy always march side by side, because democracy is being undermined by dictatorship and dictatorship is always being undermined by democracy.'[52] Despite his curiously worded denial, the message Gelli intended to convey, when he entrusted Supplement B to his daughter, seems startlingly clear: this is what has happened in Italy. The document fits the story of Italian terrorism to a 't'. And Gelli, as head of the anti-communist security agency P2, knew it.

Notes

1 Alberto Franceschini, *Mara, Renato e Io*, Mondadori, Milan, 1988, p. 150.
2 Guido Galli, quoted in Gianni Flamini, *Il Partito del Golpe*, Vol. 4, Tome 2, Bovolenta, Ferrara, 1985, p. 503.
3 Quoted in *Il Messaggero*, 10 April 1979.
4 Gianni Canova to G.I. Luigi Nunziante and P.M. Pietro Calogero, Padua, 19 May 1979.
5 P2 Commission, *Allegati alla Relazione*, Vol. 7, Tome 17, Rome 1987, p. 86.
6 Quoted in Giorgio Galli, *Storia del Partito Armato*, Rizzoli, Milan, 1986, p. 143.
7 Quoted in Giovanni Palombarini, *7 Aprile: Il Processo e la Storia*, Arsenale Cooperativa, Venice, 1982, p. 176.
8 P.M. Pietro Calogero, Requisitoria, Padua, 1981, p. 114.
9 Ibid., pp. 820–22.
10 Luca Villoresi, *La Repubblica*, 1 February 1983.
11 Antonio Carlucci, *Panorama*, 25 May 1986.
12 Alberto Franceschini, op. cit., pp. 43–4.
13 Luca Villoresi, *La Repubblica*, 29 January 1983.

14 Marcella Andreoli, *L'Europeo*, 10 September 1983.
15 Ibid.
16 Quoted in Giuseppe Zupo and Vincenzo Marini, *Operazione Moro*, Franco Angeli, Milan, 1984, p. 271.
17 *Le Point*, unpublished notes on Hyperion.
18 Marcella Andreoli, *L'Europeo*, 29 March 1982.
19 Rome police report, 3 January 1980.
20 G.I. Carlo Mastelloni, Sentenza-ordinanza, Venice, 1989, p. 40.
21 *Le Point*, unpublished notes on Negri affair.
22 Carlo Mastelloni, op. cit., pp. 257–60.
23 Ibid., pp. 9–11.
24 Ibid., pp. 23–7.
25 Ibid., p. 108.
26 Ibid., pp. 277–83.
27 Ibid., p. 412.
28 Ibid., p. 489.
29 Ibid., p. 495.
30 Ibid., p. 508.
31 P2 Commission, *Allegati alla Relazione*, Vol. 7, Tome 21, Rome, 1987, p. 182.
32 Antonio Carlucci, *Panorama*, 25 May 1986.
33 Sandro Acciari, *L'Espresso*, 13 January 1985.
34 Marcella Andreoli, *L'Europeo*, 10 September 1983.
35 Luca Villoresi, *La Repubblica*, 29 January 1983.
36 Franco Giustolisi, *L'Espresso*, 27 May 1979.
37 Giorgio Galli, op. cit., p. 81.
38 Marco Sassano, *SID e Partito Americano*, Marsilio, Padua, 1975, p. 126.
39 G.I. Antonio Lombardi, Sentenza-ordinanza a carico di Roberto Adamoli pp. 96, Milan, 19 May 1983, p. 392.
40 Giorgio Bocca, *Noi Terroristi*, Garzanti, Milan, 1985, pp. 9–10.
41 Quoted in Giuseppe De Lutiis, *Storia dei Servizi Segreti in Italia*, Editori Riuniti, Rome, 1984, p. 168.
42 Quoted in Gianni Flamini, *Il Partito del Golpe*, Vol. 3, Tome 2, Bovolenta, Ferrara, 1983, p. 636.
43 Gianfranco Sanguinetti, *Del Terrorismo e dello Stato*, Milan, 1980, p. 28.
44 Alberto Franceschini, op. cit., p. 121.
45 Ibid., p. 118.
46 Quoted in Giuseppe De Lutiis, op. cit., pp. 247–8.
47 Giorgio Bocca, op. cit., p. 197.
48 Quoted in Giorgio Galli, op. cit., p. 49.
49 Mimmo Scarano and Maurizio De Luca, *Il Mandarino è Marcio*, Editori Riuniti, Rome, 1985, p. 174.

50 Giuseppe Zupo and Vincenzo Marini, op. cit., p. 22.
51 P2 Commission, *Allegati alla Relazione*, Vol. 7, Tome 1, Rome, 1987, pp. 287–98.
52 Licio Gelli to the author, 27 June 1989.

[11]

THE MORO KIDNAP

The Ghost of Hamlet's father:
                              Now, Hamlet, hear:
'Tis given out that, sleeping in mine orchard,
A serpent stung me; so the whole ear of Denmark
Is by a forged process of my death
Rankly abus'd.

William Shakespeare, *Hamlet*, Act 1, Scene 5.

The kidnap and murder of Christian Democrat Party leader Aldo
Moro has given rise to more suspicions about the true nature and
objectives of the Red Brigades than any other single incident. Moro's
removal from the political scene took place at a time when he was
pursuing a policy of alliance with the Communist Party. That policy
was opposed by the US government, the P2 masonic lodge and Italy's
left-wing extremists, and it died with him. Four trials and the
testimony of a number of 'repentant' terrorists have failed to clarify
crucial aspects of the affair. The account of the kidnap that has
emerged from the trials has in the past been dismissed by Mario
Moretti, the Red Brigades leader who commanded the operation, as
an official cover-up. More recently, Moretti has joined the chorus of
voices insisting that there is nothing more to be learned about the
affair. His conversion is in itself grounds for the deepest suspicion.
    Moro was kidnapped on the morning of 16 March 1978, as he drove
to Parliament for the opening of a confidence debate on a newly

formed government of national unity, which would enjoy the support of the PCI for the first time since 1947. Moro's car was approaching a crossroads, where Via Mario Fani meets Via Stresa, in the residential suburb where he lived, when a white Fiat 128 with diplomatic number plates reversed around the corner into its path. The sudden manoeuvre forced his driver to brake abruptly and the escort car, following close behind, rammed into the back of them. Two men from the white car and a further four who had been waiting in the street, wearing the uniforms of Alitalia airline pilots, opened fire on Moro's bodyguards, killing all five of them. Only one guard succeeded in returning the fire, loosing off two shots. Three of the bodyguards were not killed outright but were finished off at close range.

Of the ninety-one shots fired by the terrorists, the majority were fired by just two people, one of them responsible for forty-nine and the other for twenty-two shots. One of the witnesses to the scene described the principal gunman as calm and determined, showing 'complete mastery of his weapon',[1] a submachine-gun. A ballistics report on the attack described it as a textbook operation, perfectly planned 'both to leave Moro unharmed and to prevent the accidental wounding of accomplices'. It also noted that the professional skill of the principal gunman did not correspond to that of any known Red Brigades member.[2] A strong candidate for the role of expert marksman at the Via Fani shooting is Giustino De Vuono, a member of the Calabrian Mafia and former soldier in the French Foreign Legion, from which he was expelled for being excessively violent. He escaped from prison, where he was being held for involvement in a 1975 kidnapping organized by Autonomia Operaia, shortly before the Moro operation. De Vuono was among the twenty suspects whose photos were issued to the media by the police on the day of the kidnap. One witness also identified him as 'strongly resembling' a man dressed as a street-sweeper seen leaving one of the Red Brigades' Rome bases.[3] He was subsequently eliminated from the inquiry but there are grounds for suspecting the security services' report which placed him conveniently out of the country at the time of the ambush.

The first Moro trial convicted ten BR members of involvement in the Via Fani attack. In June 1988 Rome magistrates issued arrest warrants for two more terrorists, Alessio Casimirri and Alvaro Loiacono, to account for the last outstanding members of the Via Fani commando. Loiacono, who was living in Switzerland, was suspected of being the principal Via Fani gunman, according to press reports.[4]

And, just in case he failed to fit the bill, Casimirri, who was also in hiding abroad, was described as a crack marksman too. Many of the Rome magistrates responsible for the case in recent years have held tenaciously to the view that there is nothing of any moment left to be discovered. Public Prosecutor Domenico Sica told *Il Messaggero* newspaper on the tenth anniversary of the kidnap (16 March 1988), 'There are no hidden truths in the Moro affair. Everything that could have been discovered has been discovered . . . I am convinced that what remains to be learned is absolutely insignificant as regards the substance of the whole terrorist affair.' And this only three months before two new names were added to the official tally of Via Fani participants.

On 9 May, after fifty-five days in captivity, Moro's bullet-riddled body was found in the boot of a red Renault 4 car abandoned in Via Caetani, a central Rome street half-way between the headquarters of the Christian Democrat and Communist Parties. He had been shot eleven times, ten times with a Browning 7.65 mm 'Skorpion' submachine-gun and once with a 9 mm pistol.[5] Ballistics experts found that two of Moro's entry wounds were not aligned with the bullet holes in his clothes, while the other nine were. This led them to deduce that the first two shots were fired while Moro was alive and able to move and the others on a separate occasion, after he was unconscious or dead. Surprisingly, although the evidence pointed to Moro having been shot while he lay in the back of the car, there were hardly any traces of blood, leading to the assumption that he may have initially been laid on a plastic covering, which was subsequently removed. His wounds had been staunched with paper handkerchiefs to prevent the outflow of blood or body fluids.[6] No Red Brigades member with direct knowledge of the circumstances of his death has contributed any information about it to the authorities. Prospero Gallinari has been named by 'repentant' terrorists as the man who actually carried out the murder, a charge he has neither confirmed nor denied. Gallinari was arrested in September 1979, suffering a bullet-wound to the head in the process, but recovered and is currently serving a life sentence in prison.

Moro's captivity proved a drawn-out national agony for the Italian people. He was not a particularly popular politician, being closely associated in the public mind with the thirty years of corrupt and incompetent government over which his party had presided. He was also remembered for his censorship, as Prime Minister, of reports into secret service abuses, for his determined defence of party colleagues implicated in the Lockheed affair and for the dubious characters who handled the financial affairs of the small Christian Democrat faction loyal to him. Despite all this, many people still had a high regard for Moro. The questionable financial practices some of his assistants were involved in were not considered to be for his personal enrichment but merely to provide the money without which it was not possible to operate in Italian politics. His personal following in the party was small because he was more interested in public service than in power for power's sake. Yet, as a result of his shrewd intelligence and a talent for compromise allied to strongly held political and religious convictions, he had, by 1978, become the key figure in Italian political life.

Aldo Moro was born in the south eastern province of Puglia in 1916. He studied law at Bari University, where he was president of the Federation of Catholic Students (FUCI), becoming president of the national organization in 1939. His first important ministerial post was as Justice Minister in 1955. In 1959 he was elected to the powerful position of Christian Democrat Party secretary and in 1963 became Prime Minister for the first time. By the time of his kidnap, Moro would have held that office in five different administrations. The foundation-stone of his political creed was a belief in dialogue and the conviction that all sectors of opinion should be represented in Parliament and find expression in the political life of the nation. It was this conviction that conferred on him the crucial role of mediator between his own party and the PCI at a time of acute political tension. His solution to the problems posed by the growing electoral strength of the communists, against a background of industrial unrest and terrorism, was a government of national unity, the only one capable, in his opinion, of coping with the mounting crisis. Moro's plan for a 'historic compromise' with the PCI was to be implemented in three distinct stages: the communists were to pass from a period of non-opposition, or benevolent neutrality, to one of active external support for the government and finally to power-sharing, with communist ministers representing their party in the Cabinet. It was only the close personal relationship that Moro enjoyed with PCI secretary Enrico Berlinguer that made this project possible and Moro's removal effectively brought the experiment to an end.

It was this cynical, world-weary idealist, with his shock of white hair brushed back from his forehead, his features a melancholic, introspective mask familiar from countless television news reports, who was seized from a Rome street on 16 March 1978. Whatever the public thought of him, the mental anguish imposed upon him and his family over the next fifty-five days would be played out as a macabre and gruelling drama beneath its fascinated and horrified gaze. The traumatic effect of the tragedy was heightened by the periodic release to the press of letters from Moro to his family and colleagues and of the Red Brigades' own communiqués, on two occasions accompanied by photos of their captive in front of a BR flag. The Red Brigades agreed to deliver more than twenty of Moro's letters to their recipients and produced a total of nine communiqués, which were generally distributed in a number of different cities. Officially, there is no indication that the police succeeded in intercepting or following any of the numerous couriers who must have been involved in this activity on the Red Brigades' behalf.

In his letters, Moro sought to persuade his party colleagues to negotiate the release of terrorist prisoners in exchange for his own freedom and he reacted angrily on learning that many in the outside world thought that he was writing under coercion or the influence of drugs. The Christian Democrat leader summed up his argument in a letter to his party: 'How can you deduce that the state will fall into ruin if, once in a while, an innocent person survives and, in return, another person goes into exile rather than to prison?'[7] The Red Brigades obviously had an interest that this message should get through, and the blackmailing pressure was reinforced by their own announcements that Moro was undergoing a 'people's trial' and, in communiqué no. 6 published on 16 April, that he had been condemned to death. Moro too stepped up the pressure, telling party secretary Benigno Zaccagnini that he held him personally responsible for his predicament for having persuaded him to accept the presidency of the party. 'So here I am on the point of dying for having said yes to you and to the DC. You have a very personal responsibility for it. Your saying yes or no now is crucial. But you should know that if you take me away from my family, you will have done so twice. You will never free yourself from the weight of this burden.'[8] This last prediction proved prophetically true, since Zaccagnini emerged a broken man from the Moro tragedy. The full human dimension of the drama emerges in Moro's moving, final letter to his wife. 'Kiss and caress everyone for me, face by face, eye by eye, hair by hair. To each I send an immense tenderness through your hands. Be strong, my sweet, in this absurd and incomprehensible trial. These are the ways of the Lord. Remember me to all our relatives and friends with immense affection, and to you and all of them I send the warmest embrace as the pledge of my eternal love. I would like to know, with my small, mortal eyes, how we will appear to one another afterwards.'[9]

In late April the Red Brigades proposed an exchange of prisoners, demanding the release of thirteen left-wing terrorists, including Renato Curcio and Alberto Franceschini, in return for Moro's life. The list, made public in communiqué no. 8, was almost certainly intended to be unacceptable. It contained the name of Cristoforo Piancone, a Red Brigades member who had been wounded and captured only a week earlier, as he participated in the murder of a prison officer in Turin. The government remained firm in its refusal to negotiate with the terrorists until the end, supported in this by the PCI. It did however explore the possibility of a unilateral gesture of clemency in the hope that the Red Brigades would reciprocate. Senate leader Amintore Fanfani had decided to broach the subject formally at a meeting of the Christian Democrat Party leadership on 9 May, the day of Moro's murder. There has been speculation that this apparent softening of the Christian Democrat position may have actually hastened Moro's demise. Though much ink has been spilt on the subject, it will never be known whether the possibility of negotiating Moro's release ever really existed. Throughout the kidnap the Socialist Party stood out as the champions of a negotiated solution. There can be little doubt that Moro's family and friends succeeded in opening secret channels of communication with the Red Brigades and that the Socialists were also able to communicate with the kidnappers through the Autonomia Operaia leaders Franco Piperno and Lanfranco Pace. Examining Magistrate Ferdinando Imposimato believes that many aspects of the negotiations have remained obscure. In an interview with *La Stampa* newspaper (11 March, 1988), he cited the account of a Genoese terrorist, Carlo Bozzo, according to which 'Moretti met the Socialist (Claudio) Signorile. It strikes me as absurd, but I went to the Transport Ministry and left Signorile a series of written questions. He has never replied.'

Moro's policy of seeking an accommodation with the PCI had encountered powerful and long-standing opposition. This was made particularly explicit during a visit he made to the United States as Foreign Minister in September 1974. One of his collaborators, Corrado Guerzoni, has described a traumatic meeting with Henry

Kissinger during which the US Secretary of State attempted to dissuade Moro from pursuing a political course which he considered profoundly dangerous and mistaken. Moro's pro-Arab foreign policy also added to the suspicion with which he was viewed in US government circles. 'The next day he was taken ill in St Patrick's Cathedral and when he returned he told me repeatedly that he did not intend to resume political life for a long time, without telling me the reason,' Guerzoni told the Rome assize court.[10] Moro also insisted that Guerzoni should inform the press of his intention to withdraw from politics. According to another account, Moro held a secret evening meeting with an unnamed US intelligence official, who warned him of the determination within the security services to block the implementation of his policies. In the course of this meeting, which took place during the same US visit, he was advised that groups on the fringes of the official secret services might be brought into operation if he did not abandon his policy of negotiating with the communists.[11]

Moro's wife, Eleonora, confirmed these threats to her husband in testimony to the Moro Commission. 'It's one of the few occasions when my husband told me exactly what had been said to him, without telling me the name of the person concerned. I will try and repeat it now: "You must abandon your policy of bringing all the political forces in your country into direct collaboration. Either you give this up or you will pay dearly for it."'[12] After his collapse in St Patrick's, Moro decided to cut short his visit by four days and returned to Italy on 29 September. His personal doctor has testified to the state of anxiety Moro was in at this time: 'He was actually afraid that he might not be able to embrace his family again, this was his worry.'[13] Less than a week before the Italian delegation arrived in America, Kissinger had given public expression to the US position in a meeting with Congressional leaders intended to head off criticism of CIA activities in Chile. His views were reported in the *New York Times* (27 September 1974), only two days before Moro decided to curtail his US visit. 'At that meeting, he reportedly defended the need for covert activity by asserting that despite criticism of the CIA, if Italy went communist, there would be criticism that the United States had not done enough to save her,' the paper wrote. Other, Italian accounts of the briefing quoted the Secretary of State as saying: 'You blame us for the CIA's activities in Chile. But wouldn't you blame us even more if we allowed Italy to fall to the communists without doing anything to prevent it?' (*L'Unità*, 28 September 1974.) The message can hardly have been lost on the visiting Italian delegation.

The Christian Democrat leader replied to his American critics in an article he wrote for *Il Giorno* newspaper in early 1978 but decided not to have published. It was printed after his death by the communist newspaper *L'Unità* (29 May 1978). In it he pointed out that American criticisms of his policy had produced controversy and tension but that this was acceptable from an ally, provided they were expressed through the appropriate channels. He took exception, however, to indiscreet government pressure which 'might disturb and embarrass the sincere friends of America'. Moro explained that an alliance with the communists was essential to save Italy from political paralysis and ended his article with an appeal to 'the prudence, intelligence, open-mindedness of those on whom the highest responsibilities fall'. The article is written in the cautious and roundabout style characteristic of Moro but it is significant that he withheld it from publication, considering the subject too delicate for public discussion, only a few months before his kidnap by the Red Brigades. During this period Moro was acutely aware of the need to explain his policy to the US government and to overcome its objections. 'Shortly before 16 March I spoke to him at length: we discussed the possibility of his travelling to America to enable him to explain the realities of the Italian situation at the highest level,' his party colleague Luigi Granelli told *La Repubblica* (17 August 1978). 'He was well aware of the need for our link with the United States and knew that their objections had to be taken seriously, not underestimated. But he also had an extraordinary sense of national dignity.' Clearly, one of Moro's major preoccupations in the run-up to his kidnap was US opposition to the 'historic compromise'.

Warnings against the dangers of admitting the PCI to the government had been repeated periodically in the years leading up to 1978. In 1976 the right-wing magazine *Il Settimanale*, two of whose editors were members of P2 and whose 'lively formula' was singled out for praise by Gelli in his Democratic Revival Plan, published an interview on the subject with Democratic presidential candidate Henry Jackson (3 March 1976). The hardline anti-communist senator warned of the dire consequences if the PCI were to achieve power in Italy. 'I have studied the problem in detail and I can say that the United States would not stand idly by,' he told the magazine's New York correspondent. Jackson warned that any European country that admitted the communists to government would be immediately expelled from

NATO. 'Let it be quite clear that, if disastrous consequences are to be avoided, the Italian communists must not enter the government,' the presidential hopeful told Italian readers three months before they themselves were due to vote in their own general elections.

Threats directed personally at Moro came from another P2-influenced publication, Mino Pecorelli's *OP*. The magazine (2 July 1975) referred to the Christian Democrat leader as '*Moro . . . bondo*' (Mori . . . bund) and asked 'Is Moro the only minister who must die at 1 p.m.?' borrowing the title of a historical novel by Giulio Andreotti, *1 p.m.: The minister must die*. The following year Pecorelli returned to his theme (9 January 1976) with a cartoon of Moro wearing a Christian Democrat badge with a hammer and sickle superimposed on it and captioned: 'The saint of compromise. Virgin, martyr and . . . sacked.' He added, in a comment on the collapse of Moro's government: 'Today the last possible centre-left government that could painlessly have buried Berlinguer's strategy has been assassinated with Moro.' Moro is the only victim of Pecorelli's literary attentions whose name is so frequently associated with the idea of death. Pecorelli's allusions have a prophetic ring to them, which is all the more striking in the light of what he wrote after the politician's kidnap. One of the most remarkable of Pecorelli's prophetic writings was a brief note which appeared on 13 September 1975, a year after Moro's traumatic visit to the United States. Under the title 'Expert America jokes and predicts', *OP* reported: 'An official visiting Rome with [President] Ford told us: "I see darkness. There's a Jacqueline in the future of your peninsula."' The implication is clear; someone in Italy was going to meet the same fate as President John F. Kennedy.

A precedent to the Moro operation had been planned by the Red Brigades in the summer of 1974. In June, shortly after the conclusion of the Sossi kidnap, Alberto Franceschini travelled down to Rome to investigate the possibility of seizing Giulio Andreotti, then Defence Minister. He found Andreotti an easy target, walking the city streets without an escort. He returned to northern Italy to report the good news to the BR leadership, Moretti, Curcio and Cagol, and on 8 September he and Curcio were arrested. As far as possible, Franceschini tried to avoid contact with the Rome column of the Red Brigades as he had already learned that they were not entirely reliable. Rules of compartmentalization were rarely observed and their favourite fund-raising activity was stealing pieces of ancient statuary. When Franceschini tried to convince them that the members of a revolutionary force should not be living like grave robbers, they would merely reply: 'You're right, comrade, but in the meantime see if you can place this head for me.'[14]

By the time of his kidnap in 1978 Moro and the head of his bodyguard, Oreste Leonardi, had become increasingly worried by indications that they were being watched and followed and by a sense of impending threat. Their attempts to draw the attention of the authorities to the danger elicited no response and do not even appear to have been put on record. Moro was particularly alarmed by the kidnap in April 1977 of the son of a former secretary of the Socialist Party. Francesco De Martino was, like Moro, in the running for the State Presidency at the time. The kidnap of his son and the payment of a ransom for his release effectively ended his hopes of achieving that office. Moro was struck by the political background to the kidnap and subsequently became extremely anxious for the safety of his own children, insisting that they should be given a police bodyguard. With his access to sensitive government information and given the connections between P2 and underworld figures involved in the kidnap business, it is significant that the De Martino kidnap should have made such a strong impact on Moro.

His sense of foreboding increased in the run-up to March 1978. A number of incidents had given rise to the suspicion that Moro was being kept under surveillance. Mrs Moro told the assize court that the head of her husband's bodyguard had noted the number of a car he had frequently seen following them. He had asked the police to investigate the matter, but to no avail. She also claimed that her husband had requested a bullet-proof car but the request had been turned down because of the cost. A telephone tap produced in evidence at the trial showed that Francesco Cossiga, Interior Minister during the kidnap, had discussed this subject with one of Moro's assistants, Nicola Rana, four days after the discovery of Moro's body. 'Cossiga: "Sorry if I'm disturbing you. Late yesterday evening I had to issue a denial . . . because *La Nazione* [newspaper], a certain Paglia, whom I don't know . . . said that Moro had asked me for a bullet-proof car in his presence and that I had refused." Rana: "Eh!" [A whistling noise obliterates the rest of the conversation.][15]

According to the widow of bodyguard Leonardi, her husband had been noticeably agitated in the period leading up to 16 March. One possible reason for his anxiety emerges from Mrs Moro's account to the court. She described how Leonardi told her, about a fortnight before the kidnap, that 'he had heard that one of the police departments responsible for these matters had noticed that suspected Red Brigades members from other Italian towns had arrived in Rome. Worried about this discovery and anxious to do their duty, they had asked their superiors what to do, whether they should arrest them or follow them, and they had been told that they should leave them be and not concern themselves with the matter'.[16] The official underestimating of the threat continued right up to the eve of the 16th, when police chief Giuseppe Parlato visited Moro's offices and reassured his collaborators that recent incidents that had aroused their alarm were nothing to worry about and that the suspects involved were common criminals.

In contrast, senior police officers were convinced that the kidnap was the work of the Red Brigades from the moment they arrived at Via Fani, thus arousing the suspicion of Eleonora Moro. 'When I asked them what had happened, they told me without hesitation: "It was the Red Brigades." So much so that I ventured to say: "But sir, how can you be so sure that it was the Red Brigades? It could have been a hundred thousand things!" . . . I still ask myself how these people could be sure and had decided without hesitation,'[17] she told the parliamentary commission. "How is it possible? The day before the police chief says they were only muggers spotted in Via Savoia [where her husband's office was situated] and the next day in Via Fani he tells me without a shadow of doubt: "It was the Red Brigades."'[18]

The inadequacy of the official response to the kidnap exactly mirrors that of the preventive measures taken beforehand. In the first few days the Red Brigades were able to return to the Via Fani area and dump three of the cars used in the operation under the noses of the police. A massive mobilization of the security services, with 72,000 road-blocks, 37,000 dwellings searched and almost 6.5 million people questioned in less than two months, brought no progress in the search for Moro's prison. 'One had the impression then . . . that they wanted to impress public opinion with the quantity and visibility of the operations, totally regardless of the quality,' novelist and Radical Party deputy Leonardo Sciascia wrote in his minority report for the parliamentary commission.[19] He observed that the commission was told by the then head of the Rome police that he did not have enough men to allocate to following suspects, at a time when more than 4,000 police were bustling about in spectacular but fruitless operations. Sciascia summarized the gist of his report in the words, 'How did they manage not to find Moro?'[20]

In a normal criminal inquiry the activities of the police are directed and co-ordinated by a public prosecutor. The magistrate initially in charge of the Moro case was wholly unsuccessful in injecting intelligence and vigour into the search. Luciano Infelisi received little help, however: no colleague was assigned to assist him and he was not relieved of his normal workload. 'I was unable to check the newspapers because I did not have the time,' he told the Moro Commission. 'In the period in which I was directing the inquiries, my office did not have a police officer at its disposal. I ran the investigation with a single typist, without even a telephone in the room.'[21] Infelisi complained to the commission that he received no useful intelligence from the secret services throughout the fifty-five days of the kidnap.

In practice, the search for Moro's prison was co-ordinated by the Interior Ministry and a special crisis committee, many of whose members belonged to or later joined P2, the right-wing masonic lodge which opposed Moro's policy towards the PCI. Among the eight P2 members appointed to the committee were the heads of the domestic and military intelligence services, the head of the finance police and the regional commander of the *carabinieri*. Given their political orientation it would not be entirely surprising if they did less than their utmost to secure Moro's release. The minutes of the committee's meeting on 17 March give an idea of the quality of their contribution to the task in hand. SISMI Director Giuseppe Santovito informed the group that he believed two Japanese and a West German had participated in the Via Fani attack. He also drew the committee's attention to the imminent arrival of a ship from Cyprus at the port of Marina di Grosseto.[22] There is no evidence whatever that his contribution had any grounding in fact. Santovito continued to provide the committee with misleading information, reporting the next day on the need for increased patrols on the Yugoslav border.[23]

On 24 October 1977, Parliament had passed a bill reforming the secret services, replacing the Defence Information Service (SID) with the Military Security Information Service (SISMI) and the domestic Democratic Security Information Service (SISDE). This reorganization would be used as an excuse to argue that the security services were 'without eyes and without ears' at the time of the Moro kidnap. The reform effectively led to the demolition of the most reliable anti-terrorism organization and to the appointment of P2 members at the top of the new agencies. The Interior Ministry's Anti-terrorism

Inspectorate, which had been founded in 1974 and had worked effectively to combat both right- and left-wing terrorism, was disbanded, while the entire staff of SID was taken on by its successor agency. This discrepancy was not a response to any lack of reliability on the part of the Anti-terrorism Inspectorate's staff. The Inspectorate had achieved notable successes and had been engaged, since May 1977, on a comprehensive investigation of the Red Brigades and other terrorist groups, which was left unfinished. Many of the SID officials, however, were suspected of active involvement in the strategy of tension. The result was to punish the honest servants of the state and to leave the least honest as its only guardians against the terrorists. 'The commission has not been able to ascertain whether this happened as the result of a pre-ordained plan to paralyse the domestic security service in the run-up to Via Fani,' the Socialists commented in their minority report to the Moro Commission.[24]

Given the keen interest Gelli showed in military and secret service appointments it is not unreasonable to suppose that he may himself have played a role in the shake-up which placed his own supporters in key security service posts. The director of the Anti-terrorism Inspectorate, Emilio Santillo, was a strong candidate to head the new domestic intelligence service. He had been responsible in the past for investigating Gelli's links with right-wing terrorism, producing three reports on the activities of the P2 lodge. During the Moro kidnap he asked the Arezzo police chief for information on Gelli, giving him to understand that he suspected Gelli was in some way involved. He did not get the job. In contrast, the man who was appointed, Giulio Grassini, was a member of P2 and actually turned to Gelli for information on the Moro case. 'When I joined SISDE at the end of September 1978, I was immediately informed by Grassini that Gelli was a highly valued informant of the service because of his knowledge of terrorism,' a former SISDE officer told the Moro Commission.[25]

The argument that the security services were in total disarray at the time of the Moro kidnap is, in any case, not wholly convincing. As we have already seen, the authorities had succeeded in infiltrating the Red Brigades in 1972 and again in 1974. In 1978, their knowledge of the terrorist group was by no means negligible. The day after Via Fani, newspapers published photographs of twenty-two suspects being sought by police. Two of the suspects were already in prison and the photos contained other errors, but eighteen showed genuine members of the Red Brigades, some of whom had taken part in the Via Fani attack. The Moro Commission has pointed out that police reports on political extremists active in Rome prior to 1978 contained the names of many people subsequently arrested for terrorist offences. 'These reports were the fruit of complex and time-consuming work which has clearly involved dozens and dozens of police personnel,' it commented.[26] It would seem, then, that the authorities were not quite as ill prepared as they subsequently tried to make out.

Another arm of the state to perform distinctly below par during the kidnap was the state-controlled telephone company SIP. The various Moro trials reveal a litany of blunders and omissions on the part of people responsible for carrying out telephone taps during the fifty-five days of Moro's captivity. This, after all, was one of the most promising methods for identifying Moro's captors and locating his prison. But the technique appears to have produced virtually no useful intelligence whatever despite a wide range of contacts between the kidnappers and the outside world. Instead, numerous recorded conversations have been obliterated, tapes have gone missing, surveillance has lapsed for 'technical reasons' just when the Red Brigades needed to make important calls, and on one occasion a policeman actually intervened in a conversation he was listening to, repeating some of the words he had just heard, and so warning the people under surveillance that their phone was tapped. 'During the fifty-five days of the Moro kidnap I observed a complete lack of collaboration with the police as regards telephone tapping and the blocking of calls on the part of SIP,' Domenico Spinella, the head of Rome's political police told the parliamentary Moro Commission. Greater co-operation, Spinella said, might have completely changed the outcome of the affair. 'In my opinion the attitude of SIP was one of absolute non-collaboration and even today the judicial authorities ought to prefer charges.'[27]

Once again these failures have been explained away as being the result of confusion and inefficiency, but there are reasons for suspecting that the real reasons may be somewhat more sinister. The secret services have always been strongly represented within a crucial public service such as the telephone network. During the 1960s SIP officials collaborated actively in large-scale illegal telephone tapping carried out by SIFAR in order to fill up its archives with potential blackmail material. In 1974 the ever well-informed Mino Pecorelli published an article about the government's emergency communications network operated by SIP and controlled by the secret services.

This parallel network enabled ministers, senior state administrators and the military to remain in contact in the event of a breakdown of the public telephone system. Pecorelli referred to two recent mysterious power failures which he suggested may have been intended to test the emergency system, and this at a time when right-wing coup plotters were particularly active. 'The suspicion grows that these black-outs . . . are really exercises, the finalization of programmes which for now remain obscure,' he wrote. Pecorelli referred explicitly to SIP as one of a number of 'obscure organizations, laden with shadows and in collusion with events and activities on the borderline of legality' (*OP*, 19 September 1974). It is therefore interesting to learn, from a usually reliable source, that the SIP emergency network was put on alert on 15 March 1978, the day before Aldo Moro's kidnap. Perhaps the state was not so unprepared after all?

There are a number of testimonies that appear to implicate Gelli in the Moro affair. One of them was found among notes confiscated from the home of Gelli's secretary, Nara Lazzerini, who worked for the P2 boss in Rome between 1976 and 1981. The document describes a meeting with Gelli on the day of Moro's kidnapping, news of which comes over the radio as Lazzerini is driven by taxi from the station to Gelli's headquarters in the Hotel Excelsior, on the prestigious Via Veneto. Lazzerini wants to 'freshen up' and is accompanied by Gelli to his bedroom. 'While I am in the bedroom to tidy myself up, Licio receives two people in the sitting room whom I am unable to see, but I hear them say: "The major part is over. Now we'll see the reactions."' Questioned by a magistrate from Bologna, Lazzerini was confident that she had not misheard. 'The phrase struck me and I noted it down that same morning in the hotel, taking advantage of the fact that Gelli had left,' she said, adding that she had received frequent death threats in the year following Gelli's flight from Italy.[28] The P2 Commission found her evidence altogether too embarrassing and turned down a proposal that she should be called as a witness. Christian Democrat commissioner Bernardo D'Arezzo, in particular, opposed the suggestion 'on the grounds of the witness's morality': Lazzerini had been Gelli's mistress.[29] This high moral stand contrasts with the remarkable patience shown by the commission in the face of the lies and evasions of the secret service chiefs who had belonged to Gelli's lodge.

A memorandum sent in 1982 to the office of the Florence public prosecutor by Federico Federici, a Florentine lawyer and P2 member, makes a similar claim. In it Federici said he had been told that Gelli reacted to news of the kidnap with the words: 'We have finally resolved the Moro problem.'[30] Federici, who died of a heart attack in 1988 while he was defence lawyer for a number of suspects in the Bologna bomb trial, is by no means a reliable witness. He was, however, close enough to Gelli to have access to sensitive information and it is interesting that both he and Lazzerini should have drawn attention to a possible link between the Master of P2 and the Moro affair. As we shall see later, Gelli himself found it expedient to do likewise, making it clear to the journalist Marcello Coppetti that he was privy to inside knowledge about the kidnap.

Gelli may have been dropping a hint to this effect when he granted an interview to the *Corriere della Sera* newspaper in 1980 (5 October). The interviewer was a fellow lodge member, Maurizio Costanzo, and the article appeared as part of a series on 'The Discreet Charm of Secret Power'. 'What is democracy for you?' Costanzo asked half-way through the interview. 'I'll tell you about a meeting I had with Moro when he was Minister of Foreign Affairs,' Gelli replied. 'He said to me: "You mustn't hurry things. Democracy is like a saucepan of beans: to be good they must cook very, very slowly." I interrupted him, saying: "Be careful that the beans don't boil dry, Minister, because then you might burn them."' Reading between the lines, one may perhaps discern the message: I warned Moro and we all know what happened to him.

There has been much speculation about what may have prompted Gelli to break with his longstanding practice of discretion by granting the interview. Some analysts have seen it as a blunder, the result of pride and overweening vanity, that hastened the collapse of Gelli's power. It is hard to square this with the image of the cunning schemer so frequently evoked elsewhere. By 1980 Gelli was under pressure from a number of judicial investigations and newspaper allegations linking P2 to terrorism and other crimes. Seven months earlier, Ronald Reagan had been elected President of the United States. According to some accounts, he had decided to dispense with P2 as a US intelligence tool in Italy since the lodge was becoming dangerously discredited and in any case was too closely identified with the secret services of the Carter era. If Gelli felt he was being dumped by his erstwhile friends, the *Corriere* interview gave him a convenient opportunity to remind them of the services he had previously performed. Gelli himself had no regrets about the interview when I asked him about it. 'It wasn't a mistake and I would do it again today.

The aim was to defend ourselves against the defamatory accusations which the press were already levelling at us. They tended to demonize us, but we had nothing to be ashamed of.'[31]

Costanzo asked him if he was aware of an Interior Ministry report alleging he was at the head of the most powerful organization in the country. 'I have many friends, both in Italy and abroad. But there's a wide gap between having friends and having power. However, there is a basis of truth in these rumours: having always acted in accordance with certain basic ethical principles, I have succeeded in gaining the respect and friendship of many people, even if, at the same time and inevitably, I have aroused hostility.' Gelli's mention of his foreign friends and his ethical principles may well have been a subtle reminder of his steadfast anti-communism. A later question cited allegations that he was a fascist coup plotter who subsequently 'did not disdain the company of people of the opposite tendency' and invited Gelli to clarify his political orientation. 'I have often been unable to remember my own name, so do not ask me to remember my political orientation. Ask me another time. Perhaps then I will be able to give you a less vague reply . . .' This sibylline response seems to combine an offer of silence with the threat of possible future revelations. Lest these interpretations appear too fanciful, it is worth bearing in mind that Gelli himself invited his intended audience to read between the lines. Costanzo's last question, which must surely have been included at Gelli's own request, was: 'How used you to reply to the question: "What do you want to be when you grow up?"' 'A puppetmaster . . .' came Gelli's sphinx-like reply.

The Moro Commission raised the issue of P2's role during the Moro kidnap in its majority report. It highlighted the presence of lodge members at the head of the security services and the fact that the organization represented political and material interests that would have been severely threatened if Moro's policy of accommodation with the PCI had been implemented. The commission said there was no proof that the failures and omissions of the security apparatus during the fifty-five days of Moro's imprisonment were deliberate. But it added that very grave examples of negligence had been recorded, 'which appear to be inexplicable unless they were motivated by a desire not to see a positive conclusion to the drama or by a substantial lack of interest in what was happening'.[32] The commission also declared that it did not exclude the possibility of direct P2 involvement in the activities of the Red Brigades, given the shared objectives of 'those who seek an authoritarian change and those who prepare the ground for it with blind and irresponsible violence'.[33] The commission concluded that it should not rush to grave conclusions in the absence of a serious investigation of this subject. The P2 Commission failed to carry the investigation forward, giving the distinct impression that many of the commissioners considered the matter was simply too delicate to tackle. Their view was almost certainly well founded, as the writings of Mino Pecorelli show. The P2 journalist with an unhealthy appetite for journalistic scoops is an ideal guide to what was happening behind the scenes during what was arguably the greatest political convulsion in post-war Italian history.

Notes

1 In Quaderni della Giustizia, Ministry of Justice, Rome, October 1983, p. 72.
2 Quoted in Giuseppe Zupo and Vincenzo Marini, *Operazione Moro*, Franco Angeli, Milan, 1984, pp. 70–74.
3 Ibid., p. 81.
4 *Corriere della Sera*, 10 June 1988.
5 In Quaderni della Giustizia, Ministry of Justice, Rome, October 1983, p. 53.
6 Giuseppe Zupo and Vincenzo Marini, op. cit., p. 113.
7 Moro Commission, Relazioni di Minoranza, Rome, 1983, p. 110.
8 Ibid., p. 102.
9 Ibid., p. 122.
10 Giuseppe Zupo and Vincenzo Marini, op. cit., p. 279.
11 Mimmo Scarano and Maurizio De Luca, *Il Mandarino è Marcio*, Editori Riuniti, Rome, 1985, p. 26.
12 Giuseppe Zupo and Vincenzo Marini, op. cit. p. 280.
13 Mimmo Scarano and Maurizio De Luca, op. cit., p. 27.
14 Alberto Franceschini, *Mara, Renato e Io*, Mondadori, Milan, 1988, p. 106.
15 Giuseppe Zupo and Vincenzo Marini, op. cit., p. 356.
16 Ibid., p. 39.
17 Mimmo Scarano and Maurizio De Luca, op. cit., p. 72.
18 Ibid., p. 88.
19 Moro Commission, Relazioni di Minoranza, Rome, 1983, p. 403.
20 Leonardo Sciascia to the author, 1986.
21 Report of the Moro Commission, Rome, 1983, pp. 68–9.
22 Sergio Flamigni, *La Tela del Ragno*, Edizioni Associate, Rome, 1988, p. 50.

23 Ibid., p. 57.
24 Quoted in Mimmo Scarano and Maurizio De Luca, op. cit., p. 176.
25 Marco Nese, *Corriere della Sera*, 9 June 1988.
26 Report of the Moro Commission, op. cit., p. 53.
27 Moro Commission, Allegato alla Relazione, Vol. 5, No. 5, Rome, 1984, p. 440.
28 Quoted in Giuseppe Ferrara, *Il Caso Moro*, Tullio Pironti, Naples, 1987, p. 222.
29 Giuseppe De Lutiis (ed.), *La Strage*, Editori Riuniti, Rome, 1986, pp. 345–6.
30 Quoted in Giuseppe Ferrara, op. cit., p. 223.
31 Licio Gelli to the author, 27 June 1989.
32 Report of the Moro Commission, op. cit., p. 87.
33 Ibid., p. 181.

[12]

THE PECORELLI
VERSION

As we have seen, Pecorelli was responsible for publishing a series of menacing articles in which Moro's name was associated with the notion of death. This may well have been part of a concerted P2 effort to pressure Moro into abandoning his political programme. At the end of 1977 (7 December), he published another prophetic story, this time not aimed personally at Moro but with a grim message of foreboding for Italian society as a whole. Under the title 'Fireworks mark the end of the festival', Pecorelli opened the short piece with a list of seven of Italy's principal political and financial scandals and an observation: 'We're seriously afraid that Italian democracy will not be able to bear the weight of such filth.' He compared the situation to a fireworks display at a village festival. 'Every minute there's a new Catherine-wheel, a new explosion of sound and colour. But the party is nearly over. There will be a minute of oppressive silence and then the last dull bangs. They are dark explosions, without light.' It is a gloomy forecast, only three months before Moro's kidnap.

We have also seen how the *OP* editor was privy to sensitive information and prone to be dangerously free with it, as in his revealing article about the 'cinematic' career of Toni Negri. He was particularly active at the time of the Moro affair and a change in the nature of the publication, from daily newsletter to weekly magazine, coincided with the kidnap. What Pecorelli wrote, both during Moro's imprisonment and after his death, offers a remarkable insight into events at the time. His account has had relatively little impact on public perceptions of the affair because the magazine had a limited

[233]

circulation and was distrusted by many: startling revelations jostle for space with incomprehensible messages and sheer disinformation. But careful sifting pays surprising dividends.

Pecorelli was nothing if not well informed. During the kidnap he published extracts from some of Moro's letters to friends and political colleagues, which were officially covered by judicial secrecy and which no other publication had succeeded in obtaining. He also revealed, on 2 May, that 'a second letter should have reached a holy personage at the head of the religious hierarchy'. The existence of a second letter from Moro to the Pope was not publicly acknowledged until 1980, when Giulio Andreotti, who became Prime Minister on the day of Moro's kidnap, confirmed as much to the Moro Commission. In another brief note, dated 4 April 1978, Pecorelli wrote: 'We are informed by authoritative sources that the Vatican has begun concrete negotiations.' This claim was also confirmed by Andreotti, but not until some ten years after the event. Following Pecorelli's death, internal documents on the structure and organization of the Red Brigades were found in his possession, testimony to the closeness of his relationship with the security services, if not to the existence of a direct channel to the terrorists.

Pecorelli's diary for the period reveals the identity of some of the potential sources of his information. It shows he was in contact with Gelli before, during – he had a meeting with him on 2 May – and after the kidnap. During the fifty-five days he had at least three meetings with Prosecutor Luciano Infelisi, who was supposed to be directing the investigations, and three meetings with his boss, Giovanni De Matteo, head of the Rome prosecutor's office. Other well-connected individuals were deputy police chief Emilio Santillo, whom he met five times, former secret service boss Vito Miceli, and ex-counter-espionage director Gianadelio Maletti, whom he saw four times. Particularly useful must have been the days when he met clusters of security service personnel, either at the same time or in quick succession. One such was 10 May, the day after Moro's body had been delivered to the centre of Rome. The names of five security service personnel are listed for an appointment in the late morning. Next to their names Pecorelli had noted: 'Major Boero SID officer from Trento (300 mil)', a possible indication that the officer expected payment for his expertise. If he felt so inclined, he could discuss what he had learned with Gelli the following day; 'Dinner/Licio' was pencilled in for 10 p.m.[1]

These contacts led Pecorelli to some surprising conclusions, which were spelled out in a remarkable series of articles, beginning while Moro was still in the hands of his captors and continuing for a year after his death. In an article dated 2 May, but which following the tradition of Italian magazines would have been distributed a week earlier, Pecorelli analysed the political significance of Moro's kidnap under the title 'Yalta in Via Mario Fani'. He started by highlighting the country's confused response to the event. 'Life is a dream wrote Calderon de la Barca, but nothing that is happening around us today has anything to do with poetry. On the contrary, the ambush in Via Fani bears the hallmark of a lucid superpower.' Pecorelli described the seizing of Aldo Moro as 'one of the biggest political operations carried out in recent decades in an industrialized country integrated into the Western system. The primary objective is without doubt that of removing the Communist Party from the area of power, just when it is preparing to take the final step into a direct participation in the government of the country. *It is a fact that there are people who do not want that to happen.*' He said the superpowers had a common interest in 'mortifying the rise of the PCI, that is of the leader of Eurocommunism, of communism that aspires to become democratic and democratically lead an industrialized country.' He observed that such a development was unwelcome to the Americans because it would upset the balance of economic power within Italy and, even more so, because of its repercussions on international relations. The article went on to make some surprisingly sympathetic comments about the PCI. It acknowledged the party's commitment to democracy and its nationalistic desire to stand out against 'the servile obedience/ observance of the directives of the only great power in the West: the United States of America'. The PCI was described as a moderately pro-American party 'rejecting the hegemony of the dominant power in the name of a rediscovered right to national sovereignty'.

Such comments are astonishing, considering Pecorelli's political outlook and the privileged sources of his information. He went on to state that the PCI's participation in government would be 'still less welcome to the Soviets'. According to *OP* 'The historic demonstration that democratic communism can achieve power through popular consensus would represent not only the collapse of the Soviet Communist Party's ideological primacy over the Third International but the end of Moscow's imperial system.' Pecorelli concluded: 'Once again the logic of Yalta has prevailed over the heads of the minor powers. It is Yalta that caused Via Mario Fani.' There is no denying that Pecorelli's analysis of Soviet motives for opposing the westernization of the PCI is grounded on common sense. It is worth noting, however, that he deals with US motives first and in three paragraphs, compared to a single paragraph on why a communist Prime Minister in Italy would constitute 'an even greater threat' to the Soviet Union. After all, the logic of Yalta had decreed that Italy lay within the US sphere of influence.

Pecorelli spelled out the practical consequences of his analysis in another, shorter article published in the same issue. Under the title 'Renato Curcio does his duty too', he observed: 'The kidnappers of Aldo Moro had nothing to do with the Red Brigades as they are commonly known. Curcio and his companions have no connection with the great politico-technical fact of the Moro kidnap.' He said the request for an exchange of prisoners put forward by Moro's captors was merely a ploy to prevent the BR leaders then on trial in Turin from denouncing 'the web being woven above their heads'. 'In this phase, Curcio and Franceschini must supply a credible cover before the eyes of the Italian masses for people whom they believe to be their occasional allies.' In exchange, Pecorelli wrote, they would receive favourable treatment 'when national pacification has been completed and a great amnesty will cleanse all and consign all to oblivion'. Once again Pecorelli had shown a remarkable prescience. Ten years later, the question of an amnesty for terrorist offences was just beginning to come up for debate. The truth about the Moro case is one of the more valuable chips in a poker game being played by its protagonists as the latter generation of Red Brigades leaders try to barter their silence in exchange for their liberty.

Pecorelli continued his analysis of the political background to the Moro affair in an article published four months after Moro's death (12 September 1978). He explained that an attempt to identify Moro's kidnappers should be based on their probable motives in relation to the political programme that Moro represented. After reiterating the interest of Washington and Moscow in halting the rise of Eurocommunism, he observed that there was enough evidence 'to be certain that the BR acted on behalf of others, Italians or foreigners, Italians and foreigners'. He said the Red Brigades' activities were not 'revolutionary' in the traditional sense of the word and that it was highly unlikely that their leaders aimed to become ministers after overthrowing the existing government. 'The BR do not represent the missile's principal rocket; they act as small steering rockets to correct the course of spaceship Italy.' He emphasized Italy's role in an international political system 'in an epoch of limited sovereignty in the West as much as in the East' and commented: 'Moro has always been one of the principal navigating officers on spaceship Italy, having, what's more, ideas of his own on the course to be followed.' The article ended by predicting that General Carlo Alberto Dalla Chiesa of the *carabinieri*, who had been given responsibility for co-ordinating the nationwide fight against terrorism in August, would concentrate on arresting the lowly Red Brigades foot-soldiers, 'leaving the important politicians in our country and abroad to their untroubled slumbers'.

Carlo Alberto Dalla Chiesa was born the son of a *carabiniere* general in Piedmont, north-west Italy, in 1920. One of his earliest missions, when he became a *carabiniere* himself, was to command the paramilitary police force in Corleone, a heartland of the Sicilian Mafia. His experience in combating the Mafia would teach him much about the realities of crime and power in his own country and he would return to his unfinished business with the Mafia at the end of his life. Dalla Chiesa's career was characterized by a strong devotion to his military calling and an equal determination to obtain results. A heavily built, pugnacious-looking man, he had achieved notable successes against the Red Brigades as the head of the *carabinieri* anti-terrorism unit in 1974 and 1975. It was he who had been responsible for the Girotto infiltration and the consequent arrest of Franceschini and Curcio in 1974. The unit was disbanded after these early successes, for no apparent reason. Only a month after his appointment in 1978 the *carabinieri* discovered several important Red Brigades bases in Milan and made a number of arrests. Commenting on this rapid success in an article titled 'Why only now?' (17 October 1978), Pecorelli highlighted the 'inexplicable' removal of Dalla Chiesa from his anti-terrorism role in 1975 and pointed out that 'it was known by many that Dalla Chiesa had maintained the privileged channels, sources of information, and contacts that he had set up in the past'. Why, Pecorelli asked, had the general not been appointed earlier, since he would almost certainly have been in a position to take effective action against the BR? 'Why was Dalla Chiesa not called immediately after the Via Fani massacre, when Moro was still alive in the hands of the Red Brigades?' *OP* supplied its own blunt answer: 'Before turning to the *carabinieri*, before unifying the command of anti-terrorism activity in the hands of a real expert, they wanted to wait for the grape to ripen and for the worst to be accomplished.' Dalla Chiesa played his own delicate role in the political mine-field of the Moro affair and that role, as we shall see later, may even have cost him his life.

Pecorelli's writings on the Moro affair went beyond theoretical analysis of who may have been behind the elimination of the Christian Democrat statesman. Some show an insider's knowledge of the circumstances of the kidnap, revealing facts that have subsequently been confirmed by official investigations or making sensational allegations. One of the most extraordinary items, presented as a letter to the editor but almost certainly written by Pecorelli himself, was published in the issue dated 17 October 1978. The letter is set out as though the reader was talking to himself, asking a number of questions and then supplying his own answers. It opens: 'Sir, Allow a short note from one of your devoted readers, who, following this summer, asked himself the question, "Cossiga knows everything about Moro but doesn't speak." And answered himself, "He will never speak, otherwise . . ." [sic].' The letter continues: 'He says: but the minister knew nothing about it, DIGOS [the police] discovered nothing, and the secret services . . . He replies: the police minister knew everything, he even knew where he was held prisoner: in the area of the (Jewish) . . . ghetto . . . [sic].'

According to one practised interpreter of Pecorelli, mention of 'the (Jewish) . . . ghetto' was a coded reference to a Red Brigades base in Via Camillo Montalcini. The street is in the working-class suburb of Magliana, colloquially referred to by the Romans as 'the ghetto', and Montalcini is the name of a well-known Jewish family. The base in Flat 1, Via Montalcini 8, was officially identified in 1985 as the prison where Moro was held during the fifty-five days of his captivity. Some experts, however, believe it may have been only one of several prisons and others doubt that it was his prison at all. Whatever the truth, Pecorelli appears to have anticipated the official account by seven years.

One of the major mysteries of the Moro case gravitates around Via Montalcini and its discovery. In 1988 it emerged that the police had been informed by two residents of the Via Montalcini apartment block of the presence of a red Renault 4, similar to the one in which Moro's body had been dumped, parked outside the building at some time prior to his death. The exact date of the tip-off, thought to have been shortly after Moro's murder, has never been established. The fact that its existence only emerged some ten years after the event appears to indicate considerable official embarrassment about the circumstances under which the authorities received it and the poor use they made of it. The Red Brigades' flat was occupied by a young couple, the terrorist Anna Laura Braghetti and a man using the name Maurizio Altobelli, who has never been satisfactorily identified. An initial investigation in July cleared the couple of suspicion, partly because Braghetti had not hesitated to break the lock of her own garage in a dispute with the previous occupant. He had promptly called the police, and the investigators concluded that a terrorist would not have risked behaving in this high-handed manner. Given that Braghetti was a member of the Red Brigades, it would appear that she was either somewhat foolhardy or for some reason not afraid of the police. In October, the police informed the residents that they would be raiding the suspect flat. A few days later Braghetti and her companion moved out. A resident who called the police to inform them that the couple were leaving was told by the original officers that they were no longer on the case.[2]

The tip-off had originally been passed to Virginio Rognoni, who succeeded Francesco Cossiga as Interior Minister following Moro's murder, by one of his Christian Democrat colleagues. Attempts by Examining Magistrate Ferdinando Imposimato to obtain the full details of the original investigation met with a partial and reticent response from the Interior Ministry in 1982. The extreme secrecy surrounding the genesis of the Via Montalcini investigation has led some people to suspect, as the *OP* letter suggested, that the authorities knew the location of the prison even before Moro's death. On the very day of Moro's seizure, the Rome *carabinieri* were ordered to keep a look-out for a red Renault. The tip came from Lieutenant Colonel Antonio Varisco, a close friend of Pecorelli's who met the journalist at least six times during the fifty-five days of Moro's imprisonment. Varisco was murdered by the Red Brigades on 13 July 1979, a few days after resigning from the *carabinieri*.[3]

Judge Imposimato has drawn attention to the mystery surrounding the Via Montalcini base in numerous interviews with the press. He was understandably perplexed at the Interior Ministry's refusal to supply him, the examining magistrate, with full details of the July 1978 police investigation. In 1987 he told the author that Braghetti and Altobelli had been seen making their departure from Via Montalcini in a vehicle with American number plates, then modified this to 'foreign' plates. He may have had this in mind when he discussed the mysteries of the Moro case in an interview with the *Corriere della Sera* (28 April 1987). On that occasion he emphasized the importance of understanding 'the role of various secret services in the history of terrorism'. Asked which countries he was thinking of, he replied: 'On this most delicate subject I can say nothing more.' In another interview, with the Catholic magazine (*Il Sabato* 4–10 June 1988), he expressed his surprise at the location of the Via Montalcini base. 'When I discovered that Moro's prison was there, in Via Montalcini, I asked myself: how could the BR have chosen a place like this, which is under the total control of the Magliana band?' This powerful Rome underworld organization, with links to the Mafia and the Neapolitan Camorra, appears to have played a disquieting role in the Moro affair; a subject that Imposimato was not prepared to discuss. The man with probably the most profound knowledge of the Moro case gave up his work as a magistrate after his brother was murdered by the Mafia on 11 October 1983. He has since been elected to the Senate on the Communist Party ticket.

Pecorelli's 'letter to the editor' provided its own sinister explanation as to why the authorities should be so reticent about the investigation into the Via Montalcini base. It said Cossiga had been secretly informed of the location of Moro's prison by a *carabiniere* general while 'the body was still warm'. Continuing the interior dialogue, the letter ran: 'He says: why did he do nothing? He answers: the minister could not decide anything on the spur of the moment [literally: on two feet], he had to consult a higher authority and here is the puzzle: how much higher, perhaps even up to the lodge of Christ in Paradise?' The mention of the 'lodge' and the use of the idiomatic expression '*su due piedi*' (on two feet) appears to be a cryptic reference to P2. Given Gelli's response to the kidnap and the activities of his followers within the security services at this time, such an interpretation hardly seems over-imaginative. After all, the author had made it clear he was presenting us with 'a puzzle'. The next day, according to the letter, the reply from the higher authority was relayed to the *carabinieri*: there would be no attempt at an armed rescue, lest Moro be killed by an accidental shot from his rescuers or be executed by the terrorists. The letter stressed the potentially devastating consequences if the truth of the matter should ever come out. 'Nothing was done and Moro was eliminated, because if the story had come out it would have made a noise like a bomb!' This implies that Moro's elimination was essential to prevent the truth about the kidnap from emerging and that, if that truth did emerge, it would have highly destabilizing consequences. It was the second time that the letter mentioned bombs. The first was as a figure of speech, but it gave the author the opportunity to observe: 'with bombs, at least for the moment, nothing can be resolved.' The hinted message seems to be that the Moro kidnap is a continuation of the strategy of tension by other means. Perhaps most remarkable of all, the letter went on to predict, in coded language, the assassination of General Dalla Chiesa because of his role in this affair. We will consider this in a later chapter.

Another of the Moro mysteries of which Pecorelli had detailed knowledge was the discovery of a Red Brigades base in Via Gradoli. The Rome street had been under surveillance in connection with left-wing extremism even before the kidnap. Two days after Moro's seizure police visited Via Gradoli 96 and knocked on the door of Flat 11, a Red Brigades apartment occupied by Mario Moretti. Receiving no reply and after being reassured by the neighbours that the occupant was a respectable gentleman, the police abandoned their search. This official account of the visit contrasts with the testimony of one of the neighbours, a woman, who told the police that she had heard the sound of Morse code being transmitted during the night. She even drew up a written statement to this effect, which she asked the police to deliver to a senior officer of her acquaintance. The officer said he never received it and the police who were allegedly entrusted with it denied in court that such a document had ever been produced.[4]

The story became still more complex when a tip-off mentioning the word Gradoli reached the police in early April. The information came from a group of Bologna University professors, who claimed the name had been thrown up during a session at a Ouija board, used to consult the spirit world on the whereabouts of Moro's prison. A police search in the central Italian town of Gradoli drew a blank. When Eleonora Moro heard about this she suggested that the tip could refer to the name of a Rome street but was told by Interior Minister Cossiga that no such street was listed in the Yellow Pages map of the city. The street exists and was listed. Mrs Moro and other members of her family testified in court about this conversation with Cossiga but the Interior Minister 'firmly denied this circumstance' when questioned about it in his turn.[5] He told the Moro Commission that he did not feel he could blame the police for lacking the imagination to connect the town of

Gradoli with the Rome street of the same name.[6]

On 18 April the fire brigade were called to break into the Red Brigades flat in Via Gradoli because water was leaking from its bathroom into the flat underneath. The source of the leak was a shower attachment which had been left full on and propped up on a broom handle with the jet of water pointed at some cracked tiles above the bath.[7] Contrary to all the rules of the good terrorist, the flat was in considerable disorder and contained a spectacular display of Red Brigades memorabilia. The documents in the flat were bundled up and were not examined for a matter of months, fingerprints were never taken and the police did not attempt to keep the building under discreet surveillance in order to try and catch its occupants. Moretti himself reportedly arrived outside the building and was able to make his escape undisturbed after seeing television cameras and a crowd of curious bystanders gathered outside the police's providential 'find.'

It was Pecorelli who first revealed (*OP*, 25 April 1978) that the police had already been to Via Gradoli 'in the first ten days of the Moro kidnap, following a valuable tip-off'. Pecorelli mistakenly gives the number of the building as 92, rather than 96; either a simple error on his part or a reference to a second terrorist base in the street which was never officially discovered. Pecorelli had no doubt that the flooding of the bathroom was deliberate. 'The flooding is only a pretext dreamed up by the police to distract the attention of the press from the person who twice, from Rome and from Turin, provided information on the base. Information which might have been decisive if it had been better used.' He was even more specific in another brief article in the same issue, claiming the discovery of the base was 'the result of a tip-off from the Rome underworld, despite the fact Infelisi and the police maintain it was caused by a fortuitous flooding'. It is quite possible that the tip-off, if it existed, came from a member of the Magliana band, given the suspicions about the band being involved in the kidnap in some way and the links between some of its members and the secret services. Elsewhere in the magazine, Pecorelli, self-contradictory as ever, suggested that the Red Brigades may have decided to attract attention to the base by flooding it themselves. This would not have been as odd as it might seem; if the BR thought the base was under police observation, arranging for it to be publicly discovered would be one way of warning other militants to steer clear. Had this been the case, though, one might have expected the BR to admit it and so put an end to the damaging suspicion and speculation aroused by the whole bizarre episode.

The Red Brigades leaders have consistently and vehemently denied that the discovery of the Via Gradoli base was the fruit of anything but chance. 'The discovery of Via Gradoli was normal: I knew there was a leaking water tank in a flat near ours and the administrator had been informed. So it wasn't P2 [behind it] but the dishonesty of Roman property speculators,' Moretti told journalist Giorgio Bocca. He gave full vent to his frustration at his inability to dispel the suspicions about the true role of the Red Brigades. 'I can never convince the Italian bourgeoisie that the Moro kidnap was something exclusively ours, organized by twenty or so mere workers. You don't want to admit this truth. You are always looking for the person who commissioned it or the foreign brain behind it, which don't exist.'[8] Another Red Brigades leader, Antonio Savasta, was equally eager to provide a natural explanation for the base's discovery. Unfortunately it differs from Moretti's. 'The fall of Via Gradoli was due to two concomitant factors,' he told *L'Espresso* magazine (26 June 1988). 'On the one hand the large number of shirts owned by Moretti, for which reason his bath was always full of rinsing shirts. On the other the virtual blindness and natural carelessness of Barbara Balzerani [the woman living with Moretti at the time]. Probably after having a shower and being late as usual for some appointment, Balzerani put the shower attachment down hurriedly and clumsily to rinse the same old shirts.' Neither account squares with that of the firemen who broke into the flat and found the shower attachment propped up on a broom handle and switched full on.

Pecorelli poured scorn on the discovery in yet another article from the 25 April issue, describing how firemen and police were confronted by 'an unequivocal demonstration of the Red Brigades' role in the Moro kidnap'. He commented: 'There's no doubt, it's them. Only the typewriter, at first proudly presented as an IBM golf-ball [the type used for the BR communiqués], is later reduced to a less incriminating model, perhaps so as not to overdo the elements confirming the prime role played by the base in question.' He pointed out that even the man in the street knew the Red Brigades' rule about keeping compromising material packed in a suitcase and ready for instant departure.

Mentioning the presence of airline pilots' uniforms in the base, Pecorelli made the curious parenthetical observation '(didn't they actually go in a helicopter to deliver Moro?)'. This seems to imply state involvement in the kidnap as the Red Brigades, as commonly known, were not thought to have had access to helicopters. It also ties in with the testimony of a doctor who saw two of the Red Brigades' get-away cars not far from Via Fani between 9.10 and 9.20 on the morning of 16 March and who heard the sound of a helicopter overhead at about the same time. Police helicopters did not take off in response to the kidnap until after 9.30.[9] Pecorelli had voiced this suspicion in an earlier article (28 March 1978) in which he discussed events immediately following Moro's capture. 'On to what means of transport was the Christian Democrat president transferred? Ruling out a helicopter, on to any other vehicle.' The idea of government involvement in the kidnap was suggested even more clearly in an article entitled 'Diary of the absolutely unreal' (25 April 1978). In it Pecorelli cited 'a strange Freudian slip' by a television announcer: 'The people responsible for the Moro kidnap met in Palazzo Chigi [the Prime Minister's office] . . . sorry, sorry!'

Other of Pecorelli's writings were potentially embarrassing for the government. On 4 April 1978, he wrote an article which indirectly supports Mrs Moro's contention that her husband had been denied his request for a bullet-proof car. 'Twenty-eight bullet-proof cars ordered by the Interior Ministry for political and financial figures, potential targets of communist terrorism, had been parked at the ministry for four months. But Minister Cossiga chose to postpone the distribution of the vehicles.' OP also kept a close watch on the international ramifications of the affair, recording (25 April 1978) a visit to the United States by former secret service chief Vito Miceli, where the P2 member gained the firm impression that the Italian case was receiving the undivided attention of 'certain American circles'. Two months later (13 June 1978) the magazine reported that 'the CIA, asked for its assistance during the Moro kidnap, courteously declined the invitation'. This last claim was confirmed by the director of SISDE, General Giulio Grassini, in testimony to the P2 Commission in 1983. Grassini said he had contacted the CIA Rome station chief to seek his assistance, but to no avail. 'I can only imagine that they had nothing useful to give us. Whatever the reason, we got no collaboration. The contribution of the CIA was nil,' he told the commission.[10]

In Pecorelli's penultimate article dedicated to the Moro case (16 January 1979), titled 'Shame on you, you clowns!', he threatened to deal in the future with a number of the unresolved mysteries of the affair. 'We will talk about Steve R. Pieczenik,' he wrote, 'the Deputy Secretary of State in the US government, who participated for three weeks in the Interior Ministry's expert meetings, then returned to America before Moro was killed, and reported to Congress that the measures taken by Cossiga on the Moro affair were the best possible in the circumstances.' The presence in Rome of the thirty-four-year-old Deputy Assistant Secretary of State from the State Department had been kept secret from the press, from most US embassy officials and from Italian officials outside Cossiga's office.[11] Pieczenik's role appears to have consisted in strengthening the Italian government's resolve not to negotiate for Moro's release by demonstrating that 'no man is indispensable to the viability of the nation state'.[12]

Some of the things Pecorelli chose not to publish are as illuminating as what he did. In his diary under 3 April 1978 (during Moro's captivity), he had noted, 'Cartoon: Zamberletti talking about the CIA.'[13] No picture of Christian Democrat politician Giuseppe Zamberletti being so indiscreet ever graced the pages of the magazine. Pecorelli also had second thoughts about an article titled 'Moro: the head of the Italian government accuses the United States'.[14] A typewritten copy of the piece was found in the journalist's office after his death but it was never published. In it Pecorelli related that a neo-fascist deputy, Ernesto De Marzio, had told parliamentary colleagues and journalists that Prime Minister Giulio Andreotti had expressed to him his worry at 'the glacial coldness shown by the United States over the kidnap of Moro'. But according to the article, Andreotti had gone further, 'stating unequivocally that it was "the Americans who commissioned the kidnapping of Moro"'. Pecorelli goes on to scoff at the idea: 'The motive for this presumed and original transatlantic initiative was not revealed. Probably Andreotti will find an appropriate opportunity to provide further details on his grave accusations.' This apparent mirth gives a less accurate indication of Pecorelli's true judgement on the story than the fact that he decided to withhold it from publication. De Marzio, who was head of Destra Nazionale, a pro-Atlantic offshoot of the MSI, has denied that any such episode took place. 'Andreotti would never have said anything of the sort and least of all to me,' he told me. 'I don't think Andreotti could ever have thought such a crude thing.'[15] Pecorelli's motive for writing and then withholding this sensitive article remains unclear.

In his truculent article 'Shame on you, you clowns!', the OP editor outlined a hypothetical scenario according to which Cossiga and others in the Christian Democrat leadership were awaiting the imminent release of Moro following successful negotiations. 'But someone didn't keep the bargain . . . the "*carabinieri*" (?) were to have checked that Moro was alive and let the red car go. Then someone raised the price to an unacceptable level because they wanted the *anti-communist* Moro dead anyway and the BR killed the president of the Christian Democrat Party in the car, in the centre of Rome . . . But we won't speak of this because it's a lunatic theory, without substance. We won't say that the legionnaire's name was "De" and the butcher Maurizio.' Whether secret negotiations were embarked upon and what point they may have reached remain an open question. As usual Pecorelli provides a detailed and confident version of his own, which finds echoes in other unorthodox accounts of the kidnap, as we shall see. His legionnaire sounds remarkably like Giustino De Vuono, at one time candidate for the role of expert marksman in Via Fani but subsequently eliminated from the inquiries. Maurizio could be Moretti, who used that name with some of his contacts, or the as yet unidentified Maurizio Altobelli. Whether or not Pecorelli had succeeded in identifying the latter will never be known, as he was unable to fulfil his promise to return to the topics touched on in this article. He was shot dead as he sat in his car in a Rome street below his office on the evening of 20 March 1979. He had been shot in the mouth, the Mafia's way of punishing those who break its code of silence.

As we have seen, there were many people who could have had an interest in the elimination of Pecorelli but there is also considerable evidence linking his death to the information he possessed about the Moro affair. Former SID agent Captain Antonio Labruna told the P2 Commission that he had received a phone call from Pecorelli on the day before his murder. The journalist had told him that he was about to collect some highly sensitive documents, which could put his life in danger but which he did not intend to publish. According to another account, Pecorelli had promised Prosecutor Luciano Infelisi new documents on the Moro case shortly before his death. And then there was his published promise to expound on the unsolved mysteries of the affair. Pecorelli's sister Rosita visited her brother's apartment four days after his murder and found it in a state of utter chaos, with papers strewn all over the place. 'It looked as though it had been visited by burglars,' she said.[16]

The parliamentary Moro Commission wrote to the head of the Rome public prosecutor's office in 1980 asking him to supply them with copies of all Pecorelli's papers with a bearing on the Moro affair. The prosecutor replied that none of the documents had any relevance to the commission's inquiries.[17] The P2 Commission subsequently acquired the documentation, enabling parliamentarians who served on both commissions to realize just how inaccurate the prosecutor's original response had been. Two days after Pecorelli's murder, an anonymous informant telephoned a senior Rome magistrate to inform him that the man behind the shooting was 'a certain Lucio Gelli, currently staying at the Hotel Excelsior in Rome, room 127'. The caller went on to provide a series of accurate biographical details about Gelli. 'The motive for the crime was revelations made or about to be made on the basis of exclusive documents concerning senior personalities.' The magistrate passed on the lead to *carabiniere* colonel Antonio Cornacchia, the man whose infiltrator in the Rome Red Brigades provided no useful intelligence during the period of the Moro kidnap and who himself joined P2 in 1980. Cornacchia's investigations produced a thirty-line report correcting the spelling of Gelli's first name and concluding that 'nothing negative has emerged regarding the aforementioned, at least for the moment'.[18] And there the matter rested for another three years, until a number of 'repentant' right-wing terrorists began to give evidence implicating Valerio Fioravanti in Pecorelli's murder. Fioravanti, they said, had carried out the shooting on Gelli's behalf.[19] He has still not been charged with the crime, however.

Pecorelli's relationship with Gelli was a complex one. We have seen how he discussed the P2 boss's fascist past and his relationship with Romania in *OP* articles which Gelli would presumably have preferred unpublished. These appeared in January and February 1979 not long before Pecorelli's murder. Tension between the two had come to a head on 18 May 1977, when the *OP* editor had written to Gelli to inform him of his intention to resign from P2. 'Dear Licio,' he wrote, '... the brotherly assistance among members of the Family has ceased, or perhaps it never existed ... Are there, by chance, grade A and grade B brothers? Recognizing such disparity, I notify you of my irrevocable decision to leave the Organization.' The letter sounds rather as though Pecorelli had been disappointed in a request for financial assistance. It is not clear whether he actually posted it and in any case he expressed the hope that personal relations between the two would remain unchanged.[20] Judging by the frequency of their meetings in subsequent years this appears to have been the case.

Given Gelli's predilection for operating in the shadows he would not have been unduly pleased with the coverage *OP* devoted to his activities. One of the first references to Gelli (18 January 1972) speaks of 'a very efficient organization, brilliantly camouflaged, which is run by a Personage whose identity we cannot reveal, since he is unknown to almost all the enrolled members. This personage is the decisive factor in the most delicate and complex affairs of Italian political life.' Another of Pecorelli's barbed references to the lodge appeared on 25 June 1977, apparently sycophantic but perhaps not entirely reassuring for P2 readers: 'It's no good saying that it's a den of coup plotters and subversives . . . Politicians of all colours belong to it, but all of the first rank . . . One could say that Gelli represents what remains of the state.' Another article was more forthright. Published a week before Pecorelli's death but dated 20 March 1979, it read: 'Assassinations, bombings, coup attempts, the shadow of freemasonry has hovered over them all: from Piazza Fontana to the Occorsio murder, from the Borghese coup to kidnappings, to the flight of Sindona from Italy.' Pecorelli rashly promised to return soon to the Sindona affair, another threat he was unable to deliver on.

It is perhaps surprising that Pecorelli lived as long as he did, considering his access to inside information and the apparently ill-disciplined way in which he used it. He may actually have been seeking a financial accommodation with Gelli at the time of his death. Several of his articles hinted at the damaging revelations he was capable of making but he had a dinner appointment with 'Licio' at 8.30 on the day after his murder and another pencilled in for 23 March. Curiously, his appointments for 22 March are not known, as that page has been removed from his diary.[21] It has even been suggested that Pecorelli was under pressure from two opposite quarters in the last weeks of his life. He was being threatened with death if he published certain documents in his possession, while another group had threatened to kill him if he did not.[22]

Notes

1 P2 Commission, Allegati alla Relazione, Vol. 7, Tome 15, Rome, 1987, pp. 769–92.
2 Sergio Flamigni, *La Tela del Ragno*, Edizioni Associate, Rome, 1988, pp. 155–60.
3 Ibid., p. 23.
4 Ibid., p. 53.
5 Report of the Moro Commission, Rome, 1983, p. 40.

6 Quoted in Giuseppe Ferrara, *Il Caso Moro*, Tullio Pironti, Naples, 1987, p. 349.
7 Sergio Flamigni, op. cit., p. 185.
8 Giorgio Bocca, *Noi Terroristi*, Garzanti, Milan, 1985, p. 217.
9 Sergio Flamigni, op. cit., p. 32.
10 P2 Commission, Allegati alla Relazione, Vol. 3, Tome 4, Part 3, Rome, 1985, p. 528.
11 Robert Katz, *Days of Wrath*, Doubleday, New York, 1980, p. 54.
12 Corriere della Sera, 24 April 1978.
13 P2 Commission, Allegati alla Relazione, Vol. 7, Tome 15, Rome, 1987, p. 777.
14 P2 Commission, Allegati alla Relazione, Vol. 7, Tome 17, Rome, 1987, p. 432.
15 Ernesto De Marzio to the author, 30 June 1989.
16 Sergio Flamigni, op. cit., p. 258.
17 P2 Commission, Allegati alla Relazione, Vol. 7, Tome 18, Rome, 1987, pp. 116–17.
18 Ibid., pp. 113–14.
19 Ibid., p. 81.
20 P2 Commission, Allegati alla Relazione, Vol. 7, Tome 15, Rome, 1987, pp. 899–900.
21 Ibid., pp. 954–5.
22 Giuseppe Rosselli, *Paese Sera*, 26 May 1981.

[13]

THE MAGLIANA
MESSAGES

Pecorelli's murder has been explicitly linked to the Moro affair in a series of detailed and disquieting messages originating within the Rome underworld. Three weeks after the journalist's death a case was found abandoned in a Rome taxi and was handed in to Colonel Cornacchia of the *carabinieri*. It contained a Beretta 9 mm pistol, documents and other items relating, by analogy, to the Moro kidnap. Together the contents appeared to constitute a coded message to the security services and revealed an insider's knowledge of the circumstances of Moro's captivity and murder. The bag contained eleven bullets of 7.65 calibre and one larger-calibre round: Moro was shot a total of eleven times, one of which was with a large-calibre weapon. It also held an IBM golf-ball revolving head marked Light Italic 12, similar to the lettering used by the Red Brigades for their communiqués written during Moro's imprisonment. There was also a key-ring with nine keys attached (possible reference to the nine terrorists who participated in the Via Fani operation); two Silvania flash cubes (two Polaroid photos of Moro were sent to the newspapers while he was a prisoner); a packet of Paloma paper handkerchiefs (these were the type used to staunch Moro's wounds); and three small white pills, a possible reference to the medication Moro was taking.[1] There were a couple of other items, of which the meaning is somewhat more complex and which we will come to later.

The documents in the bag included ten pages torn out of the Rome phone book and listing a number of government ministries. The pages contained several handwritten messages using the same military code as had been adopted by the Red Brigades for a communiqué delivered in Rome on 20 May 1978. There were also four one-page documents, each outlining plans for attacks on establishment figures. One states as its objective the elimination of the bodyguards of the communist president of the Chamber of Deputies, Pietro Ingrao, suggesting a possible plan to kidnap him. Another proposes the kidnap of the son of a senior Rome magistrate, Achille Gallucci. Yet another outlines a plan to kidnap a prominent Milan lawyer, Giuseppe Prisco. Alarmingly for Prisco, it had been rubber-stamped with an address stamp taken from his office and contained details of his plans to participate at a reunion of Alpine soldiers the following week, the accuracy of which Prisco confirmed to the author. It also contains faintly ironic references to the involvement of 'the comrades from Padua'. The document speaks of holding an 'analytical debate' on the Padua comrades' participation, at a planned meeting. The reference to the Autonomia Operaia organization led by the intellectual Toni Negri, whose revolutionary commitment Pecorelli had cryptically questioned, is clear. None of these projects was ever put into operation. Nevertheless, the documents cannot lightly be dismissed. They are written in the kind of bureaucratic jargon associated more usually with the secret services than with the Red Brigades. What's more, the note on Gallucci gives his unlisted home telephone number, dating from the late 1960s, a time when the Red Brigades organization had yet to be established.[2]

Most striking though, only three weeks after his murder, was the page headed 'Pecorelli Mino (to be eliminated)'. The document gives Pecorelli's home and office address and a description of his Citroën GxL car, together with its number plate. 'Action to be taken before 24 March, allowing him more time would be problematic. Under no circumstances should responsibility be claimed. Lay a false trail instead.' The document ended by acknowledging responsibility for the murder and adding a menacing comment: 'Tuesday 20, 21.40, news arrived that the Operation had been satisfactorily concluded: material recovered but unfortunately it is incomplete, paragraphs 162, 168, 174, 177 are missing.' The gist of the message was to link Pecorelli's murder to the Red Brigades and to the Moro affair, at the same time as suggesting that the killing had been intended to prevent Pecorelli from publishing particular documents, of which the writer had detailed knowledge.

Another paragraph suggested that the journalist's movements had been kept under close surveillance for an extended period and launched another coded message for those capable of deciphering it. 'Tuesday 6 March 1979, the operation has been postponed because of a long conversation with a senior *carabiniere* officer in the Piazza delle Cinque Lune area.' The officer was Pecorelli's friend Colonel Antonio Varisco who, the intended recipients of the message would be aware, lived in that central Rome square. Varisco was the man who gave orders for the security services to keep a look-out for a red Renault 4 on the day of Moro's kidnap. His murder, on 13 July 1979, has been attributed to the Red Brigades, though the killers' choice of weapon, a sawn-off shotgun, was more typical of the Mafia than of the left-wing terrorist group. The financial magazine *Il Mondo* (11 April 1980) has tentatively linked Varisco's murder to his investigation of Pecorelli's death, citing the opinion of an unnamed Christian Democrat deputy, who was a friend of the slain magazine editor: 'The feeling is that Colonel Antonio Varisco had a lead to follow. But then they killed him too. Since then there has been utter darkness.' One of Varisco's colleagues, Captain Antonio Straullu, met a similar fate at the hands of right-wing terrorists of the Nuclei Armati Rivoluzionari (NAR). His signature appears on almost all the reports on the investigation which followed the discovery of the bag and he is said to have confided to a friend that he knew enough 'to bring the palace [Italian metonymy for the political establishment] down'.[3]

The bag had been deliberately left in the taxi by a Rome underworld figure, Antonio Chichiarelli, a skilled forger who specialized in faking the work of modern Italian painters such as Giorgio De Chirico. Chichiarelli had had a colourful and hectic career and the wide range of his criminal contacts helps to explain the inside knowledge on which he was able to draw in drafting his menacing messages. He had been in contact with members of the Magliana band, with the *'ndrangheta* (Calabrian Mafia) and with neo-fascist terrorists. He was a close associate of a chubby Rome criminal named Luciano Dal Bello, who was also an informant of the *carabinieri* and domestic secret service, SISDE. What's more, there is evidence that Chichiarelli was directly involved in the Moro kidnap and had inside information on both the Pecorelli and Varisco murders. Years later Dal Bello told Rome magistrates: 'On the subject of the Pecorelli murder, Toni, although he never went into detail, claimed to know a great deal about the affair . . . Toni told me that he needed money for a lad who had been involved in the Pecorelli case and he asked if I could cash some cheques for him.'[4] Another of Chichiarelli's associates linked him to the assassination of Varisco. 'On the subject of that murder, the only comment Toni made to me was to say that he had buried the shotgun used to kill Varisco in his garden,' Chichiarelli's accountant told the magistrates.[5]

Numerous witnesses have linked the enterprising forger with a particularly important and obscure episode in the Moro kidnap. On 18 April 1978, the same day as the 'fortuitous' discovery of the Red Brigades' Via Gradoli base, what appeared to be a seventh communiqué since the seizure of Aldo Moro was delivered to the authorities in Rome. It informed them of the 'execution . . . by "suicide"' of the Christian Democrat president and told them that they would find his body in Lake Duchessa in the mountainous Abruzzi region of central Italy. The document revealed a macabre sense of humour, declaring that this would be the first of a long series of 'suicides', which would 'no longer be a prerogative of the Baader-Meinhof Group'.[6] From the outset it gave rise to scepticism. Some police officers were convinced from the start that it was not a genuine Red Brigades message, but scientific examination seemed to show that it had been written on the same typewriter as the previous communiqués. A letter from the head of the scientific department of the Rome police, dated 18 April 1978, states that the lettering of the communiqué was 'exactly analogous to that found in previous Red Brigades communiqués'. It says the handwritten title, 'BRIGATE ROSSE', was different from that in previous communiqués but suggests that this may have been because it was done in a hurry. In actual fact, the lettering is not exactly the same as in other BR communiqués: the length of tail in the letter 'f', for example, is not the same, a difference immediately visible to the naked eye. Magistrates investigating the case have since come to believe that the police deliberately accredited a document which they knew to be false.

Despite the fact that the lake was covered in a thick layer of ice and surrounded by undisturbed snow, a massive search was launched, with fire brigade frogmen being lowered into the freezing water through holes broken in the ice. Not surprisingly, nothing was found. A couple of days later the Red Brigades delivered their 'genuine' communiqué no. 7, denouncing the previous document as a fraud and a provocation. According to the new message, the fake was 'a lugubrious manoeuvre by the specialists in psychological warfare' and had been drawn up by 'Andreotti and his accomplices'. Given the impact on public opinion of the announcement of Moro's murder and of the mountain search, it is somewhat surprising that the Red

Brigades only got round to denouncing the false communiqué after devoting the first eighty-six lines of their new missive to other matters.[7]

It is vital to understand who was responsible for the false communiqué as in effect it constituted a trial run, testing public reaction to the news of Moro's death. Red Brigades leaders have appreciated its significance and provided varying accounts of its genesis. 'Repentant' terrorist Patrizio Peci told the Moro Commission that a member of a minor left-wing group, Azione Rivoluzionaria (Revolutionary Action), had admitted responsibility for the communiqué while they were sharing a prison cell.[8] The man involved was Enrico Paghera, and he in turn confirmed Peci's account to the Moro Commission, explaining that the communiqué was a stratagem to relieve police pressure on Rome so that members of his group could leave the city. Much later, however, Paghera admitted in an interview with *Panorama* magazine (26 June 1988) that he had lied about this at the request of an unnamed *carabiniere* captain, who had approached him while he was in prison. Paghera added that the same officer had tried, unsuccessfully, to persuade his group to claim responsibility for the murder of Mino Pecorelli. He also claimed that he had become an informant of the Interior Ministry through the good offices of an American citizen whom he had met in prison. The American was Ronald Stark, who had been arrested for drug trafficking in 1975 and who spent his time in prison, where he remained until April 1979, cultivating the friendship of left-wing terrorists. We will hear more of him later.

The idea that the false communiqué was a diversionary tactic to relieve police pressure on the Red Brigades has been given credence by Mario Moretti, who as organizer of the Moro operation should have been in a position to know.[9] But his account is not always very convincing. Discussing the subject in an interview with Giorgio Bocca (*L'Espresso*, 2 December 1984), he showed an evasiveness and susceptibility that clearly illustrate his grasp of its significance. 'I have read many interpretations of that false communiqué. According to some, it was the secret services on behalf of . . . Andreotti who wanted to tell Moro: we consider you a corpse already. Or P2 that wanted to throw the investigators off the track, prolong the kidnap and thus the destabilization.' Moretti then launched into a spirited attack on a leading political commentator who had had the temerity to adopt the latter view. Without saying who actually *was* behind the communiqué, he moved on to answer a question that had not been asked: 'There was no premeditated permissiveness [on the part of the police]. We were in the middle of a battle. We were killing one another. The war was becoming ever more ferocious and no one took prisoners.' The question of the authorship of the false communiqué seems to have led Moretti spontaneously and inevitably to the subject of secret service manipulation of the Red Brigades.

The authorities had in fact discussed the possibility of writing and distributing false Red Brigades messages. One of the people who proposed this tactic was Public Prosecutor Claudio Vitalone, a close political ally of then Prime Minister Andreotti. One of the reasons for Vitalone's suggestion was that it would remove the guarantee of authenticity from the Red Brigades' communiqués (communiqué no. 1 had concluded: 'The communiqués will all be typed on the same machine: this one.') and so make management of the whole operation more difficult for them. 'Cossiga approved the proposal and I was startled when the Lake Duchessa communiqué came out, because it seemed like a belated application of my suggestion but badly implemented in that the judicial authorities had not been informed in advance,' Vitalone told author Sergio Flamigni.[10] According to Prosecutor Infelisi, however, the idea was rejected when the secret services said that they were technically not up to the task. Mino Pecorelli made his own confident assessment of the communiqué, which he described as 'anomalous' and 'rickety' (*OP* 25 April 1978). 'The seventh message and the second seventh were both written by the BR. Our secret services and the Interior Ministry's brains trust would never have had the imagination and the courage to attempt the "Duchessa bluff". That means that within the BR there are two factions pursuing different strategies (and perhaps different aims) . . .' It is curious that he should attribute both the false communiqué and its denunciation to the same authors. It is possible that Pecorelli was deliberately helping to cover up the fact that the secret services were responsible for the communiqué. Equally, he may genuinely have believed that the Red Brigades themselves had drawn it up. He was not necessarily wrong in suggesting this. There is one possible interpretation that combines the apparently contradictory belief of Rome magistrates that the police knowingly accredited a false document with Pecorelli's analysis: that the false communiqué was the work of a 'secret service faction' within the Red Brigades.

It was actually Toni Chichiarelli, the underworld forger, who had drawn up the false communiqué which started the authorities on their wild-goose chase to an ice-bound lake in the Abruzzi mountains. Right-wing terrorist Massimo Sparti told magistrates: 'Toni told me that he prepared Red Brigades communiqué no. 7 as a joke, to send the police running to Lake Duchessa.' His account was confirmed by Chichiarelli's wife, Chiara Zossolo: 'I know for a fact that the false lead to Lake Duchessa was the work of my husband, who told me so while the story was unfolding, that is while the television was broadcasting a report about it . . . I immediately believed his statement, partly because it related to an area very close to the town where Toni was born.' Another of Chichiarelli's friends testified that the forger had told him that he wrote the communiqué on behalf of the organization to which he belonged. 'Toni told me that he had been a member of the BR and that he had played an important role in that organization,' the witness said.[11] A discreet reference to Chichiarelli's role in the Duchessa affair was contained in the bag he had left in the Rome taxi: it contained a map of the Abruzzi region including the site of the lake. On the evidence so far, it would appear that Chichiarelli wrote the false communiqué, was privy to secret information about both the Pecorelli and Varisco murders, and had even been in contact with the Red Brigades. 'Toni showed definite extreme left-wing tendencies and claimed to be an admirer of the Moretti line,' his accountant later told the authorities. By abandoning his case in the back of a taxi he sent a message to the security services that linked Pecorelli's death with the Moro affair and implicated, but in a crude and unconvincing way, the Red Brigades in the journalist's murder.

Giannino Guiso, a lawyer acting for Renato Curcio at the time of the kidnap, has even suggested that Licio Gelli may have been involved in the Lake Duchessa episode. 'That was the dress rehearsal for Moro's death . . . The fact that this false document was considered credible, when in fact it was an obvious fake, must signify something. Chichiarelli certainly didn't prepare it on his own initiative.'[12] The fact that the police decided that an 'obvious fake' was a genuine BR document is indeed of the utmost significance. It implies that Chichiarelli was acting on behalf of the secret services in an operation that had the knowledge, approval and participation of the police. What is even more grave is the evidence that Chichiarelli was at the same time in contact with the Red Brigades and possibly even a member of that organization. As we shall see, there is convincing evidence that he actually came into contact with Moro during the kidnap.

Five years later Chichiarelli took the opportunity to drive home his message still further in a spectacular and profitable manner, but one which would ultimately prove fatal. On the evening of 23 March 1984, security guard Franco Parsi finished his shift at the Brink's security deposit on the outskirts of Rome and returned to his home. He was approached in the underground garage by four men who identified themselves as plainclothes policemen and told him they had come to search his flat for drugs. Once inside the apartment they said they were members of the Red Brigades and that they intended to rob the Brink's vault. Parsi was forced to accompany three of the gunmen to the Brink's premises the following morning, while the fourth remained behind, holding his wife and daughter hostage. The raiders were escorted into the Brink's building by Parsi, where they disarmed two more guards and made off with a record-breaking 35 billion Lire (£17 million) haul of cash and securities. Before tying up the three guards, the gunmen emphasized the political aspect to the robbery by putting one of them up against a wall and photographing him in front of a red flag bearing the words 'Red Brigades' and an encircled five-pointed star, symbol of the terrorist organization.

Before leaving, the 'terrorists' deliberately abandoned a number of items, which were clearly intended to convey a symbolic message to the investigators. These included an Energa rocket-propelled smoke grenade, seven NATO 7.62 calibre bullets, seven short lengths of metal chain and seven keys. The keys and chain appear to be references to the Moro kidnapping and the repetition of the number seven a possible reference to the false Red Brigades communiqué.[13] The Energa smoke bomb seems to have been a reference to the Varisco murder, during which two similar grenades were set off by the officer's attackers. It came from a stock of ten American-made smoke bombs, which had once been stored in Egidio Giuliani's Health Ministry weapons cache. And it was Giuliani who had supplied SISMI with the weapons and explosives for their 'Terror on the trains' operation, intended to lead astray the Bologna bomb investigators. The Energa smoke bomb appears to have been intended to convey the following message: we know who killed Varisco and why. Also left behind was a photocopy of a political document drawn up by the Red Brigades leadership. It was unlikely to convince investigators that the heist was the work of left-wing terrorists: it had obviously been copied from a reproduction of the document in a book on the Red Brigades by journalist Giorgio Bocca.[14]

The organizer of the robbery was Antonio Chichiarelli and he continued to elaborate on his messages even after it had been successfully completed. Two days later an anonymous caller told a journalist from the Rome newspaper, *Il Messaggero*, that he would find some interesting material in a litter bin in Piazza Gioacchino Belli. The journalist found an envelope containing three more 7.62 calibre bullets and Brink's payment slips, proving beyond doubt that it came from the robbers. There were also a number of documents conveying a complex and menacing series of messages. According to the examining magistrate, the documents create an association between apparently unconnected events and the messages were based on 'such a detailed knowledge of people and situations that they can only be alarming'.[15] Continuing the unconvincing theme of Red Brigades involvement in the robbery was a typewritten document claiming responsibility for it on their behalf. Attached with sellotape to the top of the page was another piece of paper bearing the words 'Red Brigades', the organization's symbol and a series of political slogans. On examination, this fragment turned out to be an original, rather than a copy, and to be identical to the heading of a document known as Red Brigades 'coded communiqué no. 1'. The communiqué referred to police operations in Via Gradoli and at Lake Duchessa and had been distributed in Rome on 20 May 1978. What's more, it had been found in the same Piazza Belli bin after a phone call, again to the *Messaggero* newspaper. The evidence is therefore overwhelming that the person who claimed responsibility for the Brink's raid on behalf of the Red Brigades in 1984 was the author of the 1978 coded communiqué, or had at the very least been in contact with him. In the 1984 document, the author claimed responsibility for the 'proletarian expropriation' of a 'Sindona multinational'. The involvement of Sicilian financier Michele Sindona in the Brink's concern was not generally known at the time and its mention again illustrates Chichiarelli's access to confidential information. The fact that massive robberies occurred at Brink's premises in London and Paris the following year gives rise to the suspicion that the co-operation from insiders may have gone beyond the corruption of a few lowly guards.

Also included in the package for the *Messaggero* were the originals of the reports on Pecorelli, Gallucci and Ingrao which had been left by Chichiarelli in the abandoned bag in 1979. The Pecorelli document had a number of words added by hand at the bottom of the page: 'To the archive of the Central Military Command' and 'Sereno Freato'. The archive reference smacks more of the secret services than it does of the Red Brigades, while the reference to Sereno Freato evokes the Moro case once again. Freato was Moro's secretary and he provided the link between the personally uncorrupt Christian Democrat leader and the disreputable sources of finance without which it is virtually impossible for a major political leader to operate. There can be no doubt that Chichiarelli was responsible for sending these documents to the *Messaggero* as one of his accomplices was present when he telephoned the paper and others said they saw him working with papers relating to the Red Brigades a few days prior to the Brink's raid.

Probably the most alarming items received by the *Messaggero* were two fragments of Polaroid photographs showing the Red Brigades' symbol and the words 'BRIGATE ROSSE'. According to journalist Marcella Andreoli (*Panorama*, 12 June 1988), the fragments correspond exactly to the photos taken of Moro against the background of a Red Brigades flag during his captivity. 'There are even the same folds in the cloth and a shadow over the bottom half of the second "s" in the word ROSSE, just where Moro's head was in the so-to-speak official Red Brigades photos. So it is plausible that Chichiarelli may really have entered Moro's prison with his Polaroid camera in his hand.' This extraordinary claim is supported by the evidence of Chichiarelli's accomplice Gaetano Miceli (to Rome magistrates, 14 November 1984): 'I remember seeing a Polaroid-type camera in Toni's possession . . . with which, according to Toni, he had not only photographed the Brink's employees during the robbery but he had also photographed Moro while he was being held by the Red Brigades . . . Toni told me that he had been a member of the Red Brigades and played an important role in that organization . . . Toni had promised to show me the photos of Moro; he told me later that he had destroyed the photos and the Polaroid.' Miceli (no relation of the secret service chief) repeated his allegations during a later interrogation (30 March 1985): 'On the subject of the Moro kidnap, Toni told me he had photographed the parliamentarian with his Polaroid and that he had kept a couple of the photos he had taken then.' Sending the fragments of the photos was a subtle reminder to the authorities of their existence. The implications are enormous: that a member of the Rome underworld in contact with the secret services was able to enter Moro's prison while he was still alive, that the secret services must therefore have known the location of the prison (as Pecorelli had claimed), but that despite this, nothing was done to secure his release.

This interpretation is reinforced by two of the more cryptic items abandoned in the Rome taxi in 1979. One was a driving licence, with no photo attached, in the name of Luciano Grossetti. This was a possible reference to Chichiarelli's associate Luciano Dal Bello, who acted as an informant for both the domestic intelligence service and the *carabinieri*. Dal Bello is a man of heavy build and the root of the word Grossetti means large. The other was a ferry ticket for the transportation of a car from the southern port of Villa San Giovanni to Messina in Sicily. The ticket immediately conjures up the idea of the Mafia but it also contains a cryptic reference to the *carabinieri*. When questioned about it by magistrates (22 February 1985), Chichiarelli's wife explained that the only time her husband had been to Sicily was to attend the wedding of a *carabiniere* officer, Major Raffaele Imondi, not long before the discovery of the bag. Naturally, she insisted, the major had nothing whatever to do with the affair 'and I can't therefore understand why my husband left the ticket in the bag with the clear and unconcealed intention of giving it a precise significance, which obviously escapes me.' The significance could well have something to do with what Pecorelli had alleged in his 'letter to the editor' about the *carabinieri*'s role in the discovery of Moro's prison and the failure to free him.

Chichiarelli's documents appear to show a profound knowledge of a number of complex and violent episodes. Aside from the detail of his messages, there is a recurrent theme in them: that of false Red Brigades. Chichiarelli himself had drawn up the false communiqué no. 7, to which he repeatedly alluded; the bag left in the taxi implied, but in a crude and unconvincing manner, that the Red Brigades were responsible for Pecorelli's murder; the BR 'strategic resolution' photocopied from Bocca's book and the original BR heading attached with sellotape to the leaflet claiming responsibility for the Brink's robbery were also unlikely to convince the police that they were dealing with genuine Red Brigades terrorists. With so many false terrorists about, the underlying suggestion seems to be that even Moro's kidnappers were not the genuine article. This was just what Pecorelli had written (2 May 1978): 'The kidnappers of Aldo Moro have nothing whatever to do with the Red Brigades as commonly known.' And Chichiarelli's allusive messages had insistently linked the journalist's death to the Moro case, implying, perhaps, that he had been killed because of his coverage of it in *OP*.

Someone, at least, took Chichiarelli's messages very seriously. He was shot dead outside his home on 26 September 1984. His mistress, who was with him at the time, was also seriously injured in the attack. A search of his home subsequently revealed a large quantity of cash and financial documents coming from the Brink's robbery. With them in Chichiarelli's safe was a video of a television documentary about the robbery, which had been labelled 'B-OK', suggesting that the organizer of the raid had not been unduly alarmed by its content. Immediately after Chichiarelli's death, his friend Luciano Dal Bello arranged for the removal of a considerable quantity of documents that had been hidden in the forger's attic. One of those who helped in the clear-up operation told magistrates that Dal Bello had asked 'if we could help him remove from Chichiarelli's house some very sensitive material that belonged to Toni and which concerned, from what he [Dal Bello] told me, his previous activity as a member of the Red Brigades'.[16] After Chichiarelli's death, most of his accomplices were arrested and much of the stolen money recovered. The surviving Brink's raiders have been tried and convicted for their role in the robbery at a trial that studiously steered clear of the political aspects of the crime. The defendants, in any case, knew little about Chichiarelli's messages, an aspect of the robbery that they had left entirely up to him.

From the testimony of Chichiarelli's wife, Chiara Zossolo, it emerges that she suspected Dal Bello of involvement in her husband's murder. Speaking of the bag full of messages left in the Rome taxi, she told magistrates (21 February 1985): 'My husband would certainly not have been capable of conceiving and organizing an operation like that on his own.' She suggested that Dal Bello, 'because of his considerable intellectual abilities, was the only person capable of setting up an operation of that type'. Dal Bello had informed his *carabinieri* contacts of Chichiarelli's role in drawing up the false Red Brigades communiqué no. 7 and this while Moro was still alive, lending strength to the theory that if Chichiarelli knew the location of Moro's prison the authorities would have known it too. A junior *carabiniere* officer has admitted receiving the information but claimed that he did not pass it on up the military hierarchy because Dal Bello had told him that Chichiarelli was a 'right-wing lunatic'.[17] Certainly, no investigation was made of this important lead. Another *carabiniere* officer testified that Dal Bello had told him 'that Chichiarelli deserved to be punished because he was half-mad and a danger to society'.[18]

One reason for not dismissing the surprising implications of Chichiarelli's messages is the range and nature of his contacts. According to his accountant, Chichiarelli and Pecorelli had actually met one another.[19] They may also have had a friend in common, a shady businessman named Ezio Radaelli. Pecorelli's diary for 1977 shows frequent meetings with Radaelli and occasionally a third person adds an extra interest to the gathering. On 10 June, for example, Pecorelli had a morning appointment with Radaelli and a certain Romagnoli. Given the OP editor's excellent relations with the secret services, it is likely that the man in question was Sandro Romagnoli, a colonel in military intelligence.[20] On 26 October, there is an appointment for 'Gelli/Radaelli', while the day's proceedings on 17 November open with 'Licio/Ezio'. The meetings continued in 1978. On 15 June, Pecorelli had a 10 a.m. appointment: 'Excelsior (Radaelli/Licio)'. Most interesting, though, in the context of the Brink's story, was a cutting from the left-wing newspaper Lotta Continua found in Pecorelli's office. Dated 22 August 1978, it reported the arrest of Radaelli for trafficking in fake paintings, notably De Chiricos and Guttusos.[21] It is not unlikely that this business activity of Radaelli's would have brought him into contact with the Rome underworld's most proficient forger of De Chiricos.

Another document found in the OP offices was a copy of an interrogation of Radaelli in the course of an investigation into his handling of the forged paintings. In it Radaelli revealed his twenty-year friendship with Sardinian businessman Flavio Carboni.[22] Radaelli was still handling Carboni's relations with the press in the mid-1980s. This too has a certain bearing on the Moro case. Carboni was the man who accompanied P2 banker Roberto Calvi on his ill-fated trip to London in 1982, which ended with the president of the Banco Ambrosiano swinging by the neck from scaffolding under Blackfriars Bridge. Carboni enjoyed a close relationship with members of the Rome underworld gang based on the Magliana quarter and also with the secret services. He even boasted of his attempts to intercede on behalf of SISMI director Giuseppe Santovito when the latter's career was threatened by the discovery of his name on the P2 membership lists. What makes this connection relevant to our story is the effort made by the Sardinian businessman to enlist the help of the Mafia in identifying Moro's prison. Carboni had been activated by a Christian Democrat Member of Parliament, Benito

Cazora, on whose behalf he contacted leaders of the Sicilian-American Mafia. Initially he was told that the Mafia would be glad to help secure Moro's freedom as its business activities had been damaged by the massive mobilization of police throughout the country. Later, Carboni reported that the criminal organization had changed its mind and he offered his own interpretation: 'The Mafia is very anti-communist and Moro is known as someone who supports communist participation in the government.'[23]

Aside from his work as a forger, Chichiarelli used to boost his income by hiring out weapons to the Rome underworld. According to Dal Bello, he acquired some of the arms at a NATO air base near Naples and others came from contacts in the Calabrian Mafia. Calabria, home to a particularly ruthless brand of the Mafia known as the 'ndrangheta, is a name that recurs frequently in the Moro story. Giustino De Vuono, the crack gunman at one time suspected of having done most of the shooting at Via Fani, hailed from Calabria. The brother of one of the 'ndrangheta's kidnap victims had made a payment to the Hyperion language school. More importantly, Mario Moretti signed the lease for the Via Gradoli apartment and set up the Rome column of the Red Brigades in between two visits to southern Italy. Under the name of Mario Borghi and accompanied by a woman named Giovanna Curro, thought to be the terrorist Barbara Balzerani, he arrived in the Sicilian port of Catania on 12 December 1975, where he stayed for several days in two different hotels. On 31 December, Mr Borghi put his name to the lease of the Via Gradoli flat, and on 6 February, he was back in the south again, staying for a single night in the Grand Hotel Excelsior in Reggio Calabria. Authors Giuseppe Zupo and Vincenzo Marini have highlighted this strange southern interlude, about which Moretti's Red Brigades colleagues were not informed. 'It's not the season for bathing, nor are there Red Brigades columns to be founded or assisted in the extreme south and in Catania in particular. There has never been any talk of "revolutionary" projects in that city. It is however the period in which the new Mafia ... beginning from Catania, is laying the economic foundations of its bloody rule.'[24] The authors suggest a possible alternative motive for Moretti's winter break in the south: both Catania and Reggio Calabria are close to American military bases housing sophisticated communications terminals.[25] Completing the Calabrian coincidences, Luciano Infelisi, the magistrate effectively in sole charge of the Moro investigation, chose to disappear for several days to the southern province on 25 March 1978, without informing his superior. When he reappeared he told the astounded press that he had been looking for a holiday home.[26]

A still more substantial Calabrian lead emerges from the interception of a telephone conversation between Benito Cazora and Moro's secretary Sereno Freato on 1 May 1978.[27]

Cazora: I need the photos of March 16.

Freato: The ones from the place, there . . .

Cazora: Yes, because they . . . [tape partially cancelled] it seems that one of them is there, I was told from down south.

Freato: There aren't any. Ah, the photos of them, of the nine?

Cazora: No, no. They telephoned me from Calabria to tell me that you can make out an individual known to them in a photo taken on the spot that morning.

Freato: That's a problem.

Cazora: That's why I called you yesterday evening.

Freato: What can we do? We'll have to think a moment, consult, tell the minister. There'll be lots of them.

Cazora: A copy, you understand, maybe it's in the papers of March 16 or 17.

A number of photos of the scene in Via Fani were taken by an amateur photographer shortly after the shooting, from his flat overlooking the street. His wife handed the film in to Infelisi, the pictures were examined by senior police officers who decided they were of no value to the investigation, and the film was subsequently lost. Another account, published in the Communist Party newspaper *L'Unità*, however, describes the photos being hugely enlarged in order to identify the first bystanders. 'As well as passers-by and the emergency services, a number of faces corresponding to known Red Brigades suspects from the north have been spotted.'[28] If the police had succeeded in identifying suspicious individuals at the scene of the shooting this might explain Cazora's eagerness to get hold of the photos. From the tenor of his conversation, though, one has the impression that the suspects he had in mind hailed from the south rather than the north and were of a rather different ilk to the Red Brigades. 'It would seem that the Calabrians wanted the photos for reasons that put them more on the side of the kidnappers than of their victim,' commented Sergio Flamigni, a communist member of the

Moro Commission and author of a book on the affair.[29]

As we have seen, it was Cazora who encouraged Carboni in his efforts to secure Mafia help in the search for Moro. Cazora himself was in contact with members of the Calabrian 'ndrangheta and in particular with one of its leading exponents, Rocco Scrivà. At a meeting with Scrivà on 7 May, Cazora was told that nothing more could be done to obtain Moro's release. Two days later Moro's body was found in Via Caetani. Curiously, Pecorelli had written the name 'Rocco Zingaro' (Rocco the Gypsy) in his diary on the day of Cazora's appointment, suggesting that he too may have been a party to the negotiations.[30] He also appears to have been aware of the background to the disappearance of the Via Fani photographs. 'The roll of film' was one of the subjects he threatened to return to in his OP article of 16 January 1979, along with 'the negotiations that were undertaken' and 'the jackals who raised the stakes'.

Hints that these Calabrian links may conceal a more sinister truth than a mere good-faith attempt to secure Moro's release have been dropped by Camorra boss Raffaele Cutolo, the Neapolitan gangster who mediated between the secret services and the Red Brigades for the release of kidnapped local politician Ciro Cirillo in 1982. During a break in one of his trials in 1987, Cutolo told journalists that his help had also been sought during the Moro kidnap. 'I could have done something but I realized that they perhaps didn't want to save him. He was an honest man. They had a lead that took them to Calabria . . . don't make me say any more.'[31] His statement has all the hallmarks of a classic Mafia-style message to the authorities: help me or I will talk. Adding substance to his threats, Cutolo has hinted that one of his senior lieutenants, Vincenzo Casillo, who was murdered in 1984, was already working for the secret services when Moro was kidnapped. 'I have been wearing chains for all these years, and some of them belong to other people. Now I'm getting tired of it,' Cutolo complained.[32] Another prominent underworld figure has also suggested that the authorities may not have done all in their power to facilitate Moro's release. Tommaso Buscetta, a Mafia boss turned supergrass, told Palermo magistrates: 'I was asked to intervene. I was in prison in Turin in 1978 and the Mafia was interested in intervening to save the life of the statesman. An order for my transfer arrived suddenly and unexpectedly while I was seeking information. I was sent to Cuneo prison where I didn't know anyone.'[33] The implication is clear: that Buscetta's transfer was designed to thwart his efforts on Moro's behalf.

It seems then that there were a number of attempts to use contacts with criminal organizations to find and free Moro but that these failed for political reasons. There is also evidence, however, of direct criminal involvement in the kidnap. We have seen how the forger Chichiarelli may have had access to Moro's prison but, as yet, it is unclear for whom exactly he was working. Several witnesses have offered suggestions as to who was pulling the strings. Chichiarelli's wife, who insisted that her husband was not capable of organizing his complex political operations off his own bat, has spoken of meeting 'a strange individual who spoke several languages' and whom her husband brought home in 1978. 'I tried to forbid him from meeting the aforementioned person but I know that Toni continued to see him on his own account,' Zossolo told the magistrates.[34] His friend Dal Bello has spoken of Chichiarelli holding several secret meetings at Fiumicino airport with a man whose identity Dal Bello did not know.[35] Chichiarelli's accountant went further, claiming that the Brink's robbery had been commissioned by 'a member of P2, linked to Michele Sindona'. He also said that Chichiarelli had worked for Pippo Calò, the Sicilian Mafia's ambassador to Rome, who controlled the Magliana band and was in contact with the secret services.[36] A contact between Chichiarelli and Calò is highly plausible. Chichiarelli's mistress had a sister who had been the lover of Nunzio La Mattina, one of Calò's principal lieutenants who had fallen from favour and been murdered on his boss's orders.[37] Given the close links between the Camorra and the Magliana band it is also perfectly credible that Cutolo might have had inside information on underworld involvement in Moro's kidnap.

If Calò had been in some way involved in the Moro kidnapping, and the fact that the Via Montalcini prison was in an area controlled by the Magliana band makes this all the more likely, he might well have decided to use Chichiarelli as the conduit for a series of menacing messages based on his knowledge of the background to the kidnap. The messages had a political dimension that went beyond a simple request for immunity after the Brink's robbery. After all, the taxi episode using some of the same information came five years before the robbery and at a time when the authorities had made no real progress in their investigation of Pecorelli's murder. It is not inconceivable that the Christmas 1984 bombing, for which Calò was sentenced to life imprisonment, was a continuation by different means of the political blackmail implicit in Chichiarelli's messages. As we have seen, the bombing took place in the same railway tunnel as the 1974 Italicus bombing, in which the P2 masonic lodge was almost certainly involved. Once again, Calò may have been reminding powerful former accomplices of a shared guilt.

Yet another element pointing to underworld involvement in the Moro kidnap can be found in a finance police report dated 28 April 1978. 'A reliable confidential source has reported that the Red Brigades terrorist Prospero Gallinari met a convicted criminal who is being sought in connection with a number of kidnaps, in Rome on 15 November 1977, in a bar on the Via Appia Nuova,' the report said. 'Gallinari asked him to participate in a sensational, political kidnap. The convict did not agree to the proposal, as he considered it not worth his while financially.'[38] If the report is well founded it would certainly dent the myth of the Red Brigades' revolutionary purity. There is no saying whether the professional criminal subsequently changed his mind or whether other underworld figures agreed to take his place.

In 1982, Rome magistrates Domenico Sica and Ferdinando Imposimato questioned the Christian Democrat deputy, Benito Cazora, about Carboni's attempt to contact the Mafia for information on the kidnap. Cazora began his reply by saying that Carboni had never spoken to him about Domenico Balducci and Ernesto Diotallevi, two leading members of the Magliana band. He went on to say that Carboni had told him that he would contact the Mafia to try and discover if there was any connection between organized crime and the kidnap. Subsequently, according to Cazora, Carboni told him that he had been unable to gather any information on the matter. 'I have never heard of Lorenzo Di Gesù, Mario Agliorolo [sic] and Luigi Faldetta, whose names I hear for the first time today,' Cazora said.[39] This interrogation is important, not so much for Cazora's replies but for the questions he was asked and the context. Mario Aglioloro is one of the pseudonyms used by Pippo Calò and the other two names mentioned refer to Mafia associates of Calò. All three had close links with the Magliana band and they had been involved in property deals with Carboni in Sicily and Sardinia. They were therefore the kind of people that Carboni might well have turned to for information on Moro's whereabouts. Given the suspicions about criminal involvement in the kidnap, it is significant that Cazora should be questioned, first about two members of the Magliana band and then about Calò, the man who controlled the band and who may also have controlled Chichiarelli. As we have seen, Judge Imposimato was not prepared to discuss the delicate subject of the possible involvement of the Magliana underworld gang in Moro's kidnap and other informed people tend to become nervous when questioned about the subject.

The link between Pecorelli's death and the Moro case, so insistently made in Chichiarelli's messages, emerged in 1980 during the hearings of the Moro Commission. Appropriately enough, it was Sereno Freato who raised the issue. His testimony to the commission may well explain why Chichiarelli added his name to the document on Pecorelli's assassination when he sent it to the *Messaggero* after the Brink's raid. In the face of hostile questioning from a neo-fascist deputy about his involvement in financial malpractice, Freato blurted out: 'It wasn't us who killed Pecorelli. It wasn't us who handled relations with Libya, Iran and Saudi Arabia.' Clearly Freato had a culprit in mind, both for the murder of Pecorelli and for the political scandals prompted by illegal kickbacks on Italian oil imports. It has been reported that he went further in his allegations: 'Find the people behind the Pecorelli murder and you will find those behind that of Aldo Moro.'[40] This last statement is nowhere to be found in the commission's transcript of the hearing but it could well have been said, as the official account of Freato's heated exchanges with his interrogators is patently incomplete. Freato subsequently received death threats while he was in prison awaiting trial for his role in a massive tax fraud involving the evasion of government duty on petrol. His claims lend further weight to Chichiarelli's messages.

The comments on the Brink's affair of Giuseppe De Gori, a Calabrian lawyer who represented the interests of the Christian Democrat Party at the various Moro trials, are also illuminating. 'Chichiarelli wrote the Lake Duchessa communiqué for the Israeli secret service, Mossad,' he told the author. 'In return they let him carry out the Brink's robbery and then murdered him.' Considering the institutional importance of De Gori's role, this is an extremely serious allegation. He was fully aware of its gravity and highlighted the consequences of the false communiqué: 'After that communiqué Moro could no longer be saved.' He explained that Mossad had been prompted to play this key role in Moro's elimination from the political scene because of the Christian Democrat leader's avowedly pro-Arab foreign policy.[41]

Otherwise, De Gori is confident that there are no mysteries left to be cleared up in the Moro affair. 'I have studied all the documents and I am convinced that the truth established at the trials coincides with the historical truth, or 99 per cent of it,' he told *Panorama* (19 June 1988) in an interview. 'Behind the Red Brigades there were only the Red Brigades.' This view chimes exactly with the one expressed with such tenacity, and flying in the face of the evidence, by Mario Moretti. De Gori reacted strongly when I suggested that the United States had, in its opposition to Moro's policy towards the communists, as strong a reason as Israel for wanting him out of the way. 'Get the notion that the Americans were involved out of your head,' he said and dubbed as 'nonsense' the idea of Calò having a role in the kidnap. It is hardly surprising that such ideas should cause alarm in a legal representative of the party that has been the United States' most dependable political ally in Italy for more than forty years.

Technical experts called in the course of the Moro investigation to compare the IBM revolving head left in a bag by Chichiarelli with the documents found with it reported that they had been unable to find any typewriter capable of fitting that particular part. If the part would not fit IBM models available in Italy, one can only assume that it might have worked on typewriters domestically available within the United States. Perhaps Chichiarelli was intending to point a finger at the country of origin of IBM when he dropped that particular 'golf-ball' into his bag of messages? He is not the only person to suggest that America was in some way involved in the Moro kidnap. The claim has been made on a number of occasions and under circumstances that justify giving it the most serious consideration.

Notes

1 Maurizio De Luca and Mimmo Scarano, *Il Mandarino è Marcio*, Editori Riuniti, Rome, 1985, pp. 264–5.
2 Sandro Acciari and Mario Scialoja, *L'Espresso*, 8 April 1984.
3 Giuseppe Zupo and Vincenzo Marini, *L'Operazione Moro*, Franco Angeli, Milan, 1984, p. 259.
4 Marcella Andreoli, *Panorama*, 12 June 1988.
5 Ibid.
6 Sergio Flamigni, *La Tela del Ragno*, Edizioni Associate, Rome, 1988, p. 297.
7 Giuseppe Ferrara, *Il Caso Moro*, Tullio Pironti, Naples, 1987, pp. 358–65.

8 Sergio Flamigni, op. cit., p. 193.
9 Giorgio Galli, *Storia del Partito Armato*, Rizzoli, Milan, 1986, p. 304.
10 Sergio Flamigni, op. cit., p. 192.
11 Marcella Andreoli, *Panorama*, 12 June 1988.
12 Sandra Bonsanti and Silvana Mazzocchi, *La Repubblica*, 10 June 1988.
13 Sergio Flamigni, op. cit., p. 195.
14 Sandro Acciari and Mario Scialoja, *L'Espresso*, 8 April 1984.
15 G.I. Francesco Monastero, Sentenza-ordinanza contro Germano La Chioma ed altri, Rome, 12 July 1986, p. 5.
16 Marcella Andreoli, *Panorama*, 12 June 1988.
17 Maresciallo Antonio Solinas to Rome magistrates, 22 November 1984.
18 Maresciallo Alessandro Giombetti to Rome magistrates, 22 November 1984.
19 Osvaldo Lai to Rome magistrates, 30 May 1985.
20 P2 Commission, Allegati alla Relazione, Vol. 7, Tome 15, Rome, 1987, p. 561.
21 P2 Commission, Allegati alla Relazione, Vol. 7, Tome 17, Rome, 1987, p. 322.
22 Ibid., p. 797.
23 P2 Commission, Allegati alla Relazione, Vol. 3, Tome 22, Rome, 1984, pp. 298–300.
24 Giuseppe Zupo and Vincenzo Marini, op. cit., p. 24.
25 Ibid., p. 175.
26 Sergio Flamigni, op. cit., pp. 92–4.
27 Ibid., p. 76.
28 Quoted in Giuseppe Zupo and Vincenzo Marini, op. cit., p. 80.
29 Sergio Flamigni, op. cit., p. 268.
30 Ibid., pp. 267–8.
31 ANSA dispatch, 18.59, 6 October 1987.
32 Renato Caprile, *La Repubblica*, 14 March 1989.
33 *La Stampa*, 12 March 1988.
34 Chiara Zossolo to Rome magistrates, 26 January 1985.
35 Luciano Dal Bello to Rome magistrates, 24 May 1985.
36 Giuseppe Ferrara, op. cit., p. 368.
37 Ferdinando Imposimato to the author, 22 October 1987.
38 Marcella Andreoli, *Panorama*, 12 June 1988.
39 Benito Cazora to G.I. Ferdinando Imposimato and P.M. Domenico Sica, Rome, 8 October 1982.
40 Maria Antonietta Calabrò, Il Sabato, Rome, 29 November–5 December 1980.
41 Giuseppe De Gori to the author, 25 July 1988.

[14]

THE MORO
DOCUMENTS

ONE of the greatest mysteries in the whole Moro affair is what the imprisoned Christian Democrat leader told his Red Brigades captors during the course of his 'people's trial' and what subsequently became of that information. It was in the Red Brigades' interests to extort from their prisoner as many damaging revelations about himself and his political party as they could. As someone who had been five times Prime Minister, Moro was certainly privy to the sensitive secrets of both the Christian Democrats and the Italian state. From their very first communiqué, the Red Brigades promised that the results of Moro's trial would be made public. 'Everything regarding the political line followed by our Organization and its military activities has always been dealt with publicly; this will also be the case in everything concerning the trial of ALDO MORO,' the communiqué stated.[1] But the Red Brigades were not to live up to their promise. In their second communiqué they explained that his interrogation was aimed at 'clarifying the imperialist and anti-proletarian policies promoted by the Christian Democrat Party; identifying the international structures and national affiliates of the imperialist counter-revolution; ... determining the personal responsibilities of Aldo Moro for which he will be judged according to the canons of PROLETARIAN JUSTICE.'[2] In communiqué no. 3 they made great play of their policy of openness, saying that the information provided by Moro would be made public as soon as it had been checked. They also reported that Moro had asked to send a secret letter to Interior Minister Cossiga, observing in parentheses that 'secret manoeuvres are normal for the Christian Democrat Mafia'.

The Red Brigades said that the request had been granted 'but since nothing must be hidden from the people, and this is our custom, we are making it public'.[3] Later they announced, in communiqué no. 6, that they had changed their minds, and that information from the trial would only be published in their own clandestine newspapers 'because the regime's press is entirely at the service of the class enemy'. They told the public that Moro had supplied information about corruption and state-sponsored murder, but paradoxically declared: 'There are no secrets regarding the Christian Democrat Party' and 'There are no sensational revelations to be made.'[4] In reality, the BR leadership changed its mind yet again and Moro's revelations were not divulged even to the terrorist organization's own supporters. Responsibility for this decision has been attributed to Mario Moretti.[5]

It was an extraordinary choice, for which there are a number of possible explanations. One is that Moro's interrogation showed up the naïvety of the Red Brigades' own political analysis and the organization decided to suppress it in order to avoid embarrassment. The terrorists' obsession with the implausible notion of the 'Imperialist State of the Multinationals' (SIM), an international capitalist conspiracy that made puppets of leading politicians throughout the Western world, was one plank of their ideology that may not have stood the test of a lengthy conversation with Moro. Another explanation, offered by Mario Moretti in an interview with Giorgio Bocca (*L'Espresso*, 2 December 1984), was that Moro's revelations were of no real political significance. 'Do you think we would have organized an operation of that type, in which we risked our entire organization, just to discover the scandals of the Christian Democrats? Those didn't need to be discovered. The whole of Italy knows them. They are so-to-speak routine, normal.' If this was genuinely the reason, it represents a serious underestimation of the destabilizing effect of the repeated political and financial scandals that have rocked successive governments and contributed so much to popular disenchantment with the Christian Democrat Party. There is, however, a more sinister explanation, which casts doubt on the genuineness of the Red Brigades and of the political objectives they were ostensibly pursuing.

Moro himself made it clear that he was in a position to make damaging revelations in his letter to Cossiga. He pointed out that he was under the total control of his captors and undergoing a 'people's trial' whilst 'having all the knowledge and sensibilities that derive from long experience, with the risk that I may be asked or forced to speak in a manner that could be unpleasant and dangerous in certain circumstances'.[6] Obviously, it was Moro's intention in writing, and that of the Red Brigades in allowing him to send the letter, to pressure the government into negotiating for his release. The effort would have been futile, though, if there were no substance to the threat.

The mystery surrounding Moro's revelations centres on the fate of a number of crucial documents. One is the typewritten transcript of a handwritten document in which Moro elaborated on the verbal answers he had given during the course of his interrogation. As we have seen, the Red Brigades decided not to release this but an incomplete copy of it was found by *carabinieri* commanded by General Dalla Chiesa in a Milan terrorist base in Via Montenevoso on 1 October 1978. The document consists of fifty typewritten pages in which Moro passes trenchant judgement on his political colleagues and makes some illuminating comments on the strategy of tension. It is obviously incomplete as some pages contain large blank spaces and the discourse makes abrupt thematic leaps but it was clear from the first that it genuinely represented Moro's thoughts and utterances. There has been much controversy over what happened to the taped recording of Moro's voice and to the missing parts of the typescript.

The other documents, the disappearance of which has given rise to suspicion, were in two briefcases snatched from Moro's car during the Via Fani ambush. Moro's widow has given considerable emphasis to this matter, pointing out to the parliamentary inquiry the ease with which the terrorists had identified the two cases containing important documents, while leaving behind another three that Moro had with him. Asked about the bags by a member of the commission, she replied: 'This is another of the problems which, if solved, would lead one to the truth. They must have known which ones they were and where they were in the car, because there was a great constellation of bags . . .'[7] She told the commission that she believed that one bag in particular was likely to contain confidential documents. 'He came up and down with this bag; he took it with him in the car and when he came home he would have it. He wouldn't even entrust it to the police bodyguard who kindly offered to carry it.'[8]

Moro himself attached particular importance to the cases as he made a point of inquiring what had happened to them in a letter from prison to one of his assistants. 'Have the bags from the car been recovered? Have they been sequestered as evidence and can you arrange their release?'[9] It sounds almost as though Moro was hoping to recover some of his documents in order to use them as bargaining counters in his own negotiations with the Red Brigades. Clearly he was unaware that the terrorists already had the cases in their possession. This is probably why his kidnappers decided not to deliver the letter, which was later found with the Moro typescript in Via Montenevoso. Delivering the letter would have been tantamount to letting the authorities know that Moro was being kept in the dark about the fate of his documents and could have raised suspicions about what had really become of them and the way in which the whole kidnap was being run.

Aside from the documents with him in the car, Moro may have been tempted to offer the Red Brigades other sensitive papers in his possession in exchange for his life. This hypothesis was outlined by Pecorelli (*OP*, 18 April 1978), who pointed out that many politicians had established their own personal archives, held in secret locations in Italy or abroad. 'Often they contain documents that are compromising for their political opponents. But equally often those documents concern the vital interests of the state. It is not difficult to imagine that in the event of a kidnap this delicate material might become the subject of very private negotiations between the victim and his captors.' In a later issue, (23 May 1978), Pecorelli suggested that this had actually happened, and that compromising documents belonging to Moro had been handed over to the BR by his collaborators. 'In any case, even without them, the Red Brigades now possess documents that could make members of the Italian establishment tremble and reduce them, from Andreotti down, to the obedient slaves of anyone who decided to make use of them [the papers].' The magazine suggested that the documents were finding their way into the possession of the PCI, a somewhat implausible hypothesis. It also claimed that following the kidnap, NATO had decided to change its operational plans for the entire European theatre.

Moro's assistant Corrado Guerzoni confirmed to the Rome assize court that one of Moro's briefcases contained sensitive documents regarding the Lockheed affair. At the time, investigators were attempting to establish which Italian politicians had received kickbacks from the US aircraft manufacturer to secure their support for the purchase of Hercules military transport planes. Attention was focused in particular on identifying the politician, known by the Lockheed codename 'Antelope Cobbler', who had pocketed a substantial bribe. Moro himself had come under suspicion. His secretary, Freato, hotly rejected suggestions that Moro was Antelope Cobbler when questioned by the parliamentary inquiry. In the same breath, he denied that Moro had been behind the murder of Pecorelli, showing that the two issues were linked in his mind.[10] According to Guerzoni, Moro had documents in his briefcase which he could use to rebut the allegations linking him to the Lockheed scandal. He said he had urged Moro to publish them: 'Let us say how things really are. The documents say that this information stems from the office of the [US] Secretary of State. Let us reveal that it is a politically motivated thing.' And he added his own interpretation: 'Besides, it's obvious that [Moro] was following a particular policy and that those who opposed that policy had an interest in showing him in a certain light.'[11]

On the morning of Moro's kidnap (16 March 1978) *La Repubblica* newspaper published an article identifying him as Antelope Cobbler. The paper reported the testimony of a former Italian diplomat, Luca Dainelli, to the magistrate investigating the Lockheed affair. Dainelli's information originated with the US State Department and had been relayed to him via sources close to the American embassy in Rome and by a former CIA operative, Howard Stone. From the American point of view, the timing may have been somewhat unfortunate: the public emergence of their efforts to discredit and undermine Moro coincided with the very day of his kidnap.

Moro touched on the friction between himself and Kissinger in his written reply to his Red Brigades interrogators. He explained that one of the causes of the rift had been the Italian refusal to allow the Americans to use airbases in Italy for their resupply of Israel during the Six Day War, 'above all because of a lack of advance notification and adequate explanation of the reasons'.[12] The Italians, Moro said, were not prepared to accept that the war constituted a crisis for NATO. He went on to describe Kissinger's 'animosity for the Italian side and for my person' based on the mistaken notion that Moro was seeking 'an indiscriminate accord with the PCI'. In this context, Moro referred to 'unpleasant episodes' as American views on the subject were made plain to him. He may perhaps have been thinking of the threats he had received during his visit to the United States. These observations, expressed in the elliptical style typical of Moro and obviously based on direct personal experience, are ample testimony to the genuineness of the Via Montenevoso document. Some twelve years later an extraordinary new development would confirm the authenticity of the text.

Moro also spoke implicitly of American involvement in the strategy of tension. He said the strategy was aimed at returning Italy to 'normality' after the disruption of 1968. 'One can assume that countries variously associated with our politics and therefore with an interest in our taking a certain direction were in some way involved through their intelligence services,' he said.[13] Of the indiscriminate right-wing bombings, he commented: 'One can neither state there was foreign involvement nor exclude it, in my opinion there was.' He added: 'It's my conviction, even though I have no proof, that the interest and the intervention were more foreign than national.'[14] This did not mean that he acquitted his own political colleagues of all responsibility. 'The Christian Democrat Party of that time . . . did not distance itself from an attitude of complicity and acquiescence enough to place the party above all suspicion.' Of the Piazza Fontana bombing, he noted that the judicial inquiries had not yet fully clarified 'the pre-eminent role of SID and the more minor one of the police. But there is no doubt that they were implicated in it.'[15]

Moro delivered a number of unflattering judgements on his political colleagues, reserving particular venom for then Prime Minister Andreotti. After acquitting a series of Christian Democrat leaders of involvement in the strategy of tension, he concluded: 'Andreotti has always been in power, his origins are somewhat to the right . . . Now he is following a hard line in relation to the Red Brigades, with the intention of sacrificing without scruple the person who was patron and organizer of the present government accords.'[16] He described the Prime Minister as 'a cold, inscrutable manipulator, without doubts, without hesitations, without ever a moment of human pity. This is Andreotti, whose orders all the others have obediently followed.'[17] He ended a series of vitriolic pen-pictures of Christian Democrat politicians by highlighting his incompatibility with the party and announcing his resignation from it, with the comment: 'I have an immense pleasure in having lost you and I hope that everyone loses you with the same joy. With or without you, the Christian Democrat Party will not go far.'[18] All this should have been grist to the Red Brigades' mill. It is therefore quite extraordinary that they chose to keep it to themselves.

Several P2 members have offered an illuminating commentary on this strange episode. As usual, one of the best informed and quickest off the mark was Mino Pecorelli. Writing in OP on 24 October 1978,

Pecorelli warned: 'Via Gradoli should have taught us that the Red Brigades scatter poisoned bait amidst the cyclostyled documents in their bases.' He reported that Dalla Chiesa had found 'a bomb without a safety catch' waiting for him in the Via Montenevoso flat. Among the items Pecorelli listed as being present in the apartment were the transcript of Moro's interrogation and *several sound tapes with original recordings of Moro's voice* (in italics in the original). The latter claim has surfaced on a number of occasions subsequently. Pecorelli's opinion about the importance of Moro's revelations was quite categoric: 'If the detonator is the interrogation transcript, the bomb consists of the scandals and the revelations.' The Red Brigades, he commented, had handed the magistrates 'a time-bomb that would undermine the already crumbling structures of the Republic'. Changing metaphors, he described Moro as taking on the role of public prosecutor on behalf of the Red Brigades in an anomalous trial of the Christian Democrat Party. A week later Pecorelli was expounding exactly the opposite view (*OP* 31 October 1978). He now claimed that the transcript contained nothing that was not already known to even the lowliest parliamentary doorman. 'Are Moro's personal judgements on Andreotti sensational, or his revelations about the "state bombings" or the battles between ministers for the control of the secret services? It's stuff we've been reading and writing for years in all the weekly magazines . . .' It is interesting that this latter view, adopted presumably on secret service instructions, coincides exactly with the argument put forward by Moretti for withholding the document from publication. Even while playing down the content of the document, Pecorelli did not omit to draw attention to its incompleteness. He quoted a newspaper article (*La Repubblica*, 8 October 1978) referring to a seventy-page document, while the one distributed to the press by the Interior Ministry, Pecorelli said, was only forty-nine pages long.

The most interesting commentary on the affair comes from the horse's mouth, from Licio Gelli himself. It is contained in a two-page document drawn up by Florentine journalist Marcello Coppetti, which provides a telegraphic account of a meeting between Gelli, Coppetti and Major Umberto Nobili of the Air Force Intelligence Service. Gelli denied that any such meeting had taken place when I questioned him about it.[19] 'I knew Coppetti very well, because he often came to visit me but he never came to see me with this Nobili,' Gelli said. According to Nobili, this was his first meeting with the P2 boss and he intended to gather intelligence on him while ostensibly seeking his assistance on professional matters. The document appears as a monologue by Gelli and summarizes a conversation that took place over two hours in Gelli's Tuscan villa on 1 December 1978. It therefore came two months after the discovery of the Via Montene-voso base and after much press speculation over what may or may not have been found in the Red Brigades hideout. The part relevant to the Moro affair is preceded, curiously enough, by a comment on the Lockheed scandal. 'After the Lockheed sentence two things will happen: we'll understand why Leone has been [politically] eliminated and why he hasn't been sent for trial by the high court of justice if he is guilty. We will know who the antelope is.'[20] Giovanni Leone, who was State President from 1971 to 1978, was in fact one of the candidates for the role of Antelope Cobbler. According to one theory, Antelope Cobbler was a garbled version of Antelope Gobbler, a cryptic reference to Leone, the lion.

Coppetti's note continued: 'The Moro case is not over. Dalla Chiesa had infiltrated a very young *carabiniere* into the BR. The latter knew that the BR holding Moro also had compromising material from Moro. Dalla Chiesa went to Andreotti and told him that the material could be recovered if he gave him *carte blanche*. As Andreotti feared Moro's documents (the two missing cases?) he appointed Dalla Chiesa. The latter recovered what was necessary. So the Moro transcript is incomplete. Even the one the magistrates have. Because it is a state secret.' Gelli's account contains a number of undisputable historical facts: Dalla Chiesa was appointed anti-terrorism co-ordinator by Andreotti in August, he commanded the Via Montene-voso operation in October, the Moro transcript is incomplete and Moro's briefcases have still not been officially recovered. Like Moro and Leone, Andreotti had also been implicated in the Lockheed bribery scandal. On 5 September 1976, *L'Espresso* magazine had published three documents that appeared to indicate that Lockheed had paid or had intended to pay Andreotti two substantial commis-sions, one of $28,000 and the other of $15,000, for mediation efforts on behalf of the company at a time when it was attempting to sell military aircraft to the Italian Navy and, later, to Turkey. An Italian parliamentary inquiry subsequently decided that the letters were forgeries.

Coppetti had underlined various sentences, including the reference to the antelope, and written a number one beside them in the margin.

At the bottom of the page he had written another one and a handwritten note: 'The material had been taken by the BR. It was recovered by the infiltrator (the *carabiniere*!) or the *carabiniere* is an excuse? In this case, Moro was an affair of state and Gelli knows it:' The note ends abruptly with a colon. In it Coppetti appears to be offering the reader a choice of two interpretations of the Moro affair. If the sensitive documents were recovered by the infiltrator then the official account of the Moro kidnap can still stand. If, however, the documents were recovered but not by the infiltrator, then the *carabiniere* story is an invention to distract attention from the truth: that Moro was not kidnapped by the Red Brigades at all but by agents of the state acting under the guise of Red Brigades. 'In this case, Moro was an affair of state and Gelli knows it.'

While denying that this meeting ever took place, Gelli was not averse to dropping some gentle hints about his knowledge of the affair. Asked about the fate of Moro's briefcases, he replied: 'It's still a mystery. They have caught the guilty people, they have been sentenced, they have had the first, the second, the third and even the fourth trial and they haven't recovered the documents. So do we really want to find the documents? Do we want to find the interrogation of Moro? It's obvious that either they haven't succeeded in recovering this material or they aren't interested in recovering it. But I believe that one day, I don't know whether it will be tomorrow or in fifty years' time, this material will come out.' Gelli also mentioned the existence of a film of Moro, an item mentioned by other informed sources, as we shall see. 'The Red Brigades, who were in the habit of filming everything, will have filmed him even when they killed him, I believe . . . I don't think he was expecting his death, at least that is how it has been explained [to me].' This account is supported by the text of Moro's written answers, where at one point he thanks his captors for their generosity in sparing his life.[21] But in case his comments gave the impression that he was excessively well informed, Gelli went on to say that his knowledge of the affair was based entirely on a reading of the newspapers. 'We were like the devil and holy water, because I have always been against these extremisms, these acts of violence . . . I have had no knowledge of Red or Black Brigades, because if there was anyone who was combating them it was me. I never had even a distant connection with either.'[22]

Coppetti and Nobili were questioned by the Moro Commission in 1982. Both confirmed the authenticity of the document but otherwise

Coppetti put in a supremely slippery performance. The transcript of his interrogation covers 107 pages but sheds almost no light on the genesis and significance of his document and he was equally unforthcoming when I interviewed him in person. Nobili, who refused to discuss the episode with me, was more communicative before the commission but the grave implications of what he had to say led to his being cut short after a mere thirty-nine pages. He began by expressing his suspicions about P2 involvement in the Lockheed affair. He described how Gelli spoke of the *carabiniere* force as though he owned it and how he claimed to have been responsible for the appointment of General Enrico Mino as head of the paramilitary police force. He also told how he called on Gelli at the Excelsior Hotel in Rome to drop off his curriculum vitae only to be informed that Gelli was closeted with Arnaldo Forlani. It was Forlani who was forced to resign as Prime Minister in 1981 following the discovery of the P2 membership lists. He was elected to the powerful post of Christian Democrat Party secretary in 1989. Nobili described Coppetti as a *trait d'union* between Gelli and sectors of the armed forces and said that the journalist had shown distinct signs of fear during their joint researches into Gelli's activities. Commenting on the traumatic effects of the Moro kidnap, Nobili suggested that Gelli and the Red Brigades shared a common interest in destabilizing the country: 'It is for this reason that Gelli and the Red Brigades are probably closely related; but that's only my opinion.'[23]

Nobili also commented on the surprising freedom with which Gelli chatted about highly sensitive matters. Gelli's garrulousness has also been remarked upon by P2 police chief Federico Umberto D'Amato, who described his meetings with Gelli in a report to the Interior Minister explaining the presence of his name on the P2 membership lists. Like so many others, D'Amato was merely gathering information on the P2 boss. 'The contact, even though limited to a few casual meetings, enabled me to gain a better knowledge of the subject thanks in part to Gelli's exceptional loquacity.'[24] These observations may cast light on a rather cryptic passage in the Moro transcript. After running through a series of political and financial scandals, several involving Sindona, with which Andreotti's name had been associated in the press, Moro commented: 'You, Mr Andreotti, have a man not of the second level but of the first level with you; a loquacious person, but a man who understands and who knows how to act. Perhaps if you had listened to him, you would have avoided making so many mistakes in your life.'[25] Gelli would certainly be a candidate for this role. He was undoubtedly a great talker, he enjoyed a close association with both Andreotti and Sindona and was suspected of involvement in many of the scandals which Moro had enumerated. The strange wording when Moro spoke of a man 'not of the second but of the first level' (*non di secondo ma di primo piano*) suggests a possible hint at the P2 lodge. It is not inconceivable that the Christian Democrat Party president should have tried to send coded messages to the outside world and it is possible that he may even have come to suspect a P2 role in his kidnap.

A number of Red Brigades members have denounced the disappearance of documents from the Via Montenevoso base. *Il Messaggero* (6 June 1982) has reported on the testimony to the Rome assize court of a terrorist, Anna Brioschi, which appears to confirm part of the Coppetti document's allegations. 'From the evidence sequestrated in Via Montenevoso a cardboard folder containing photocopies of everything that Moro wrote has allegedly disappeared. Brioschi intended to give this disappearance a political significance. She made a connection between the name of General Dalla Chiesa and that of then Prime Minister Andreotti. What Brioschi implied was this: someone made these papers disappear because some of Moro's statements were objectionable to Andreotti. A grave charge, if it is proved.'

The Coppetti document's allegations about a *carabiniere* infiltrated into the ranks of the Red Brigades is also corroborated by other evidence, although the controversy is far from being resolved. It is worth bearing in mind that infiltration was one of General Dalla Chiesa's most effective techniques and one can safely assume that he had continued to employ it from the time of his successful handling of the Brother Girotto operation in 1974 onwards. One of Dalla Chiesa's collaborators told *Panorama* magazine (28 April 1980) that at the time of the interview the *carabinieri* had a dozen infiltrators within left-wing terrorist organizations, three of them in prison. He may have simply been attempting to spread suspicion and dissension among the terrorists but the ploy could not have been successful if his claims were not plausible. Asked which of Dalla Chiesa's major operations were made possible by the work of spies, the unnamed officer replied: 'All of them.'

This makes the Coppetti account all the more believable and also lends weight to some remarkable claims made by journalist Massimo

Caprara in an article in the left-wing magazine *Pagina* (25 February 1982). Caprara, who had been secretary to Communist Party leader Palmiro Togliatti and as a journalist obtained a number of important interviews with Andreotti on the role of the secret services in the strategy of tension, identified Dalla Chiesa's infiltrator in the Red Brigades as Patrizio Peci. Peci was arrested in Turin on 19 February 1980, and became, at least officially, the first 'repentant' terrorist of the Red Brigades, collaborating with the authorities in exchange for a light sentence. Not long after his arrest, however, there was speculation in the press that he had been kept under surveillance for many months and that he may even have agreed to collaborate before his capture. *La Repubblica* (15 April 1980) quoted Red Brigades defence lawyer Sergio Spazzali: 'I don't know his name but I have a strong suspicion that whoever has talked talked a long time ago, before his arrest. And that for a long time he continued his political and military work within the BR and that he therefore may have been involved in some kind of provocation.'

Caprara claimed that Peci had been arrested by Dalla Chiesa's men not once but twice and that the first time he had been released in order to act as a *carabiniere* informant. He also identified him with Maurizio Altobelli, the occupant of the Via Montalcini apartment thought to have been Moro's prison in Rome. A number of the local residents similarly identified Peci with Altobelli, but it has never been officially confirmed. According to Caprara, it is precisely because of this identification that the authorities were forced to deny that either of the two Rome bases frequented by Peci could have been Moro's prison. 'Dalla Chiesa has Peci's confession, he has worked out the consequences, there can be no mistake. One of the greatest secrets of the Republic has to be preserved. It was neither of them. The prison was elsewhere.'

Two months after Peci's arrest, as Caprara points out, newspapers were suggesting that he had participated in the Via Fani ambush. The *Corriere della Sera* (12 April 1980) attributed to Peci the words: 'I participated at Via Fani but did not shoot.' Four days later, *La Repubblica* (16 April 1980) reported: 'Via Fani. Someone who has read the seventy pages says: Peci says: "I was there and Moretti too, who directed operations on the ground."' Later, it would emerge that Peci's account was somewhat different. The text of his statements to the magistrates was leaked to the *Messaggero*, perhaps to put an end to this kind of dangerous speculation. Reassuringly, the public read (4

May 1980), Peci had not been to Rome since 1976 and his account of the Via Fani operation, which is the cornerstone of the official reconstruction, was drawn from that of other Red Brigades members. The extreme left newspaper *Lotta Continua* (29 November 1980) commented scornfully on the decision of the Rome magistrates to remove Peci's name from the Via Fani indictment under the headline: 'Peci wasn't there. And if he was he was sleeping.'

Peci told the Moro Commission that his account of the Via Fani operation derived from snippets of information given him by Raffaele Fiore, the leader of the Turin column of the Red Brigades. But his own description of the events is so detailed and vivid as to call this seriously into question: 'When they started firing, Moro immediately threw himself down between the seats . . . his newspapers even fell on his head. Then he was taken away. He was probably in a state of shock because he didn't know whether or not he was wounded. They asked him: "Are you hurt?" and he answered "Yes." But in fact he wasn't wounded, he was really in shock.' It is hard to believe that this graphic account of the ambush could have come from Fiore, who, according to Peci, didn't tell him much as he, Peci, was anyway only interested in how the operation had gone in military terms.[26]

Caprara's account reinforces suspicions about the circumstances surrounding the discovery of the Via Montalcini base. He describes the building being visited by police, who even had a plan showing the interior of the base with the extra dividing wall put up by the Red Brigades. Nevertheless, the terrorists living there were allowed to depart unhindered. He draws attention to the change found in Moro's pockets, 'enough to pay for a taxi from the outer suburbs, from Ostiense, Magliana, the Cassia or slightly further out'. The money could have been a ploy to make Moro believe he was about to be released, as Gelli has suggested he did, but Caprara offers an alternative explanation. 'The Moro family has continued to emphasize this worrying detail, which leads to an equally alarming conclusion. Was Moro freed by one group and murdered by another?' This is a thesis we shall have reason to examine again. But more relevant to Coppetti/Gelli's claims is Caprara's categoric assertion that the Rome column of the Red Brigades contained 'two infiltrators, one of each sex,' at the time that Dalla Chiesa was given responsibility for the war on terrorism. Following on from this, he wrote: 'The bags that Aldo Moro was forced to abandon in the bloody street of Via Fani were delivered to Palazzo Chigi [the Prime Minister's office] by Dalla

Chiesa. What did they contain?'

Dalla Chiesa was himself questioned about these matters by the Moro Commission, though most of its members appear to have been overcome by embarrassment at having to raise so unsavoury a subject. He went to considerable pains to refute the kind of allegations put forward in the Coppetti document and in Caprara's article but without, it must be said, being entirely convincing. The Via Montenevoso operation, Dalla Chiesa told the commission, began with the identification of Lauro Azzolini, a BR member, after he forgot a bag containing a pistol on a tram in Florence in July 1978. It was surveillance of Azzolini, not Peci, that led to the discovery of the Via Montenevoso base. As for documents being purloined from the base, this was out of the question. A Milan magistrate went to Via Montenevoso as soon as the apartment was discovered, he was there all day and nothing could have been smuggled past him. The general concluded his account: 'These are stories that have been denied by the people concerned, by [the magistrate Ferdinando] Pomarici . . . Andreotti issued a denial for his part, the Interior Ministry issued a denial. I don't see why, years later, people should be believed who are somewhat less credible, I would hope, than I am.' The commission's president hastened to reassure him: 'The commission, when it asked you for clarification, did not want to give credence to . . .'[27]

A little later on, however, Dalla Chiesa was himself giving credence to the kind of suspicion he had just been rejecting, and emphasizing the significance of Moro's missing briefcases. He was asked by Leonardo Sciascia whether he remained satisfied that Moretti was the real brains behind the Red Brigades. 'A doubt has come into my mind just recently,' the general replied. After a parenthetical couple of paragraphs discussing Moretti, he returned to his doubt. 'I ask myself now – because I have been out of the thick of things for a while and I can play the role of the observer with a bit of experience behind him – where are the briefcases, where are the originals (because we only found reproductions), the only copy found of the Moro document was not an original . . .' Sciascia: 'Do you think they may be in some terrorist base?' Dalla Chiesa: 'I think there is someone who may have taken possession of all of this.' Sciascia: 'I am glad this doubt has occurred to you.' Dalla Chiesa: 'We also have to think of the foreign trips these people made. Moretti came and went.'[28] It is significant that this entire exchange originated with a question about the identity of the real head of the Red Brigades. It is extraordinary that Dalla

Chiesa should put such a sinister construction on the disappearance of Moro's documents and on Moretti's travels when a moment before he had been hotly contesting similar conspiracy theories. It may be that he too wanted to issue a message of warning.

It is also significant that Peci's terrorist career should have taken place under the patronage of Mario Moretti. Friends from his home town of San Benedetto del Tronto expressed surprise at Peci's rapid progress in the Red Brigades organization. 'Someone like Peci could be a corporal at most. It makes one think that one can get on in the Red Brigades Italian-style, just through friendship, loyalty and coming from the same home town as the leaders,' one of them told *Panorama* magazine (28 April 1980). There is insufficient evidence to say for sure whether Peci had been an infiltrator even before his arrest. The gravity of the situation if he had been an infiltrator and also participated in the Moro kidnap needs no underlining. Equally, if that had been the case, neither Peci nor his manipulators could ever admit it. The authorities would certainly not welcome a re-evaluation of his role, given that so much of the official account of the Moro kidnap rests on his testimony. The fact remains, and it emerges clearly from Dalla Chiesa's testimony to the commission, that Peci was responsible for some eighty-five arrests within the Red Brigades organization. It is hard to understand how he could have achieved this in a tightly compartmentalized and security-conscious organization unless he had been actively involved in intelligence-gathering while he was a member.

Dalla Chiesa's role in the battle against terrorism is by no means simple. His methods were undoubtedly ruthless and effective and ultimately led to the virtual elimination of left-wing terrorism from Italy. Very little detail has emerged as to who his agents were and how they were used. A curious glimpse of the general at work is offered by the text of a conversation between Dalla Chiesa and an imprisoned terrorist, Michele Galati, who was proving less co-operative than the general had hoped. 'I don't want to arrive at the level of blackmail, at the level of saying, I'll throw the name of Galati into the storm and see how he gets on. I won't ever do that, but at a certain point . . .' Dalla Chiesa told his recalcitrant informant. And later he suggested that the Red Brigades were perhaps being used by foreign organizations. 'For example, there can be times when people want to destabilize a government or a country and that's decided at an economic and financial level and you can be used.' 'No,' replied Galati.[29] It is unclear whether Dalla Chiesa was merely trying to shake the terrorist's faith in his own organization or expressing a genuine belief. It is interesting that he should be holding this type of discussion with Galati, one of the better-informed witnesses on the activities of the Hyperion language school.

Dalla Chiesa had applied to join P2 in 1976 although he had never completed the formalities to become a member. He told Milan magistrates in 1981 that he had agreed to put his name forward after coming under intense pressure to do so and at a time when his career was in the doldrums. He also claimed, as did many other military officers, that he considered joining the lodge in order to gather intelligence about Gelli. Curiously, his would-be recruiter told him not to worry about any religious qualms that he might have as a practising Catholic since 'many cardinals and other prelates were also freemasons'. He described a single meeting with Gelli in Rome in 1979, during which he discussed his hopes of being appointed head of the Milan Division of the *carabinieri*, a clear acknowledgement of Gelli's influence in the sphere of military appointments.[30]

Dalla Chiesa's testimony to the Moro Commission was in February 1982. Four months later he was appointed anti-Mafia prefect of Palermo and on 3 September, after 100 days in the Sicilian capital, he and his young wife were shot dead by Mafia gunmen as they drove home in the evening. Dalla Chiesa was well aware of the dangers of his new job and had requested a number of specific powers from the government before agreeing to accept. The government's promises had not been kept. Writing in his private diary, he drew a connection between the sensitive secrets about the war against terrorism of which he was custodian and the dangers of his new assignment. 'I, who know more than anyone about all the affairs of the recent past, find myself called to a difficult and, why not, dangerous task.'[31]

The head of the P2 lodge has suggested, in typical allusive style, that there may be more to the murder of General Dalla Chiesa than immediately meets the eye. In his memoirs, Gelli describes the shooting of the general and his wife and comments: 'The massacre was carried out by the Mafia. But it was not only the Mafia. Others were responsible for the assassination of the man who had undertaken to restore Sicily to order and democracy.'[32] He was still more explicit in an earlier, unpublished version of the book, referring to the general's death 'in an ambush, the sinister background to which suggests grave responsibilities at the very highest level'.[33] But he had no intention of clarifying what he meant when I asked him about it in person, merely observing: 'I think that to send a general down south, having promised him the necessary powers and then not to have delivered them, is like sending a general to the front, promising him munitions and then not sending them or sending the wrong ones. He was an inconvenient general because he was very able, an honest man and a leader of men.'[34] Gelli's published remarks seem to hint at something more sinister than this rather bland analysis of murder by neglect. 'One day we will know whether it was a Mafia crime or a political crime,'[35] he commented, surprisingly explicitly, in his book.

The connection between Dalla Chiesa's knowledge and his death was made in one of Mino Pecorelli's most remarkable pieces of writing. Incredibly, it was published four years before his assassination. What appears to be an uncanny prediction of Dalla Chiesa's murder is contained in the anonymous 'Letter to the editor' published in *OP* on 17 October 1978. In it, as we have seen, the writer claimed that Interior Minister Cossiga knew the location of Moro's prison 'because a *carabiniere* general had been to apprise him of it in the utmost secrecy'. Cossiga, according to the letter, had sought instructions from the P2 lodge and the decision had been taken to do nothing. The letter ended with a cryptic and uncannily accurate prediction: 'One can only ask oneself, dear Editor, who will be the Anzà of the situation: in other words, which *carabiniere* general will be found to have committed suicide with the classic pistol shot that does everything itself . . .' The death in 1977 of General Antonino Anzà, officially registered as suicide, gave rise to considerable scepticism. He was found shot to death in his home. His pistol was neither in his hand nor next to his body but resting on his desk. It had been fired twice, once into the wall as a 'test shot', according to the investigators. Speculation in the press suggested that he might have been murdered because of his knowledge of corruption in military procurement contracts and the use he intended to make of it. At the time of his death, Anzà was a candidate for the job of commander of the *carabinieri*.[36] But the really remarkable part of Pecorelli's 'letter' is where he identifies the future victim. 'Unfortunately the *carabiniere* general's name is known: amen.' According to those skilled at deciphering Pecorelli's messages, this was a reference, by analogy, to Dalla Chiesa. Where do people say amen, the interpretation runs, if not in church? The Italian for church is *chiesa*.

It is worth bearing in mind that this letter was published within a matter of weeks of the Via Montenevoso operation and the concomitant discovery and alleged disappearance of various of Moro's documents. Pecorelli's articles had consistently challenged official accounts of the Moro kidnap and he had repeatedly alluded to the sensational nature of Moro's revelations to the Red Brigades, before making a sudden volte-face on the subject. A handwritten note found in the *OP* office after his death refers to several of the elements mentioned in the Coppetti document. 'The secret papers in Dalla Chiesa's hands . . . Grave things are going on in the world of the Brigades.' On the same page he also mentioned Dalla Chiesa's appointment as anti-terrorism chief, 'signed only on 31 August'.[37]

The disappearance of documents also crops up in connection with Dalla Chiesa's death. His son Nando is convinced that something was taken from his father's Palermo residence immediately after his death. 'The key to the safe was missing and his servant, a former *carabiniere* faithful to my father, was absolutely terrified,' he told the author. 'They could have killed my father alone but they killed his wife as well, to ensure there was no one in the house. When my uncle arrived at 2 a.m. they [the authorities] wouldn't let him in.'[38] The key to the safe was found a week later, in a drawer that had previously been searched. The top half of the safe turned out to be empty and an empty green box was found on the third shelf. It is somewhat unusual to keep empty boxes in a safe. One of Dalla Chiesa's maids told a Palermo court that she overheard the general tell his wife: 'If anything should happen to me you know where to go to find what I have put down in black on white.'[39]

As anti-terrorism chief, Dalla Chiesa enjoyed a close and harmonious relationship with Andreotti but the privileged relationship that had lasted over many years broke down not long before the general accepted his appointment in Palermo. According to his son Nando, Dalla Chiesa had come to the conclusion that Andreotti was 'too compromised' as a politician. 'Once in particular he said that [Andreotti] was "treacherous", an expression that took on a typically military significance in my father's speech.'[40] An indication of the potential for friction between the two former allies emerges from the entry in Dalla Chiesa's private diary for 6 April, after his nomination as anti-Mafia prefect. 'Then yesterday, Andreotti asked me to call and naturally, given his electoral strength in Sicily, he showed himself indirectly concerned by the problem. I was very clear and I gave him to understand that I will have no regard for that part of the electorate which supports his grand electors.' In effect Dalla Chiesa seems to have been putting Andreotti on notice that their previous collaboration was no reason for the general to hold back from pursuing those of Andreotti's Sicilian supporters whom he considered to be most entangled with the Mafia. The entry continued: 'I am convinced that a lack of knowledge of the phenomenon . . . has led him and continues to lead him to errors of judgement and of fact. The fact of his telling me that in connection with the Sindona affair a certain Inzerillo, who died in America, arrived in Italy in a coffin and with a $10 note in his mouth, illustrates the point: the folklore still dominates and the messages are not understood.' Putting money in the mouth of a corpse is the Mafia's way of indicating that the person, who has normally been murdered, had broken its code of silence. 'My father made a brief mention of that meeting to the family: "I went to see Andreotti and when I told him everything I know about his people in Sicily he went white in the face,"' Nando Dalla Chiesa has written. 'This reference and the notes in his diary together constitute, in my opinion, an absolutely central passage in the last months of my father's life.'[41]

Andreotti was questioned about this incident in 1987, when the Palermo assize court visited Rome to hear the testimony of a number of ministers on the government's failure to honour its pledges and to give Dalla Chiesa adequate powers to take on the Mafia. Andreotti told the court that he probably had met Dalla Chiesa on 6 April, but that it had been at the general's request and not his. He said he did not mention the Inzerillo episode as he knew nothing about it until reading newspaper accounts of Dalla Chiesa's diary entry. 'Perhaps [Dalla Chiesa] saw several people that day and got a bit confused in his summarizing, that's the only explanation I can give,' Andreotti said. Nando Dalla Chiesa's lawyer, Giuseppe Galasso, asked the prosecutor to charge the minister with lying under oath because the implication of his statement was 'that General Dalla Chiesa had lied to himself'. The prosecutor eventually decided that Andreotti had not lied, and that even if he had, it had no bearing on the trial. Andreotti took the opportunity to issue his own allusive message at the Rome hearing. Asked why General Dalla Chiesa should have told his son that Salvo Lima, a Sicilian ally of Andreotti's, was one of the politicians most deeply embroiled with the Mafia, the minister replied: 'I don't know. Out of respect for General Dalla Chiesa and because it cannot be the case . . . for example I never talk about what General Dalla Chiesa told me about some members of his family.' The reference was clearly to Nando Dalla Chiesa's youthful involvement in extreme left politics but Andreotti refused to elaborate on it, saying he preferred not to talk about the subject. The court president accepted his preference, rejecting Galasso's insistent demands that Andreotti explain himself, and ruling that the matter was irrelevant to the case.

On 9 October 1990, a builder redecorating the Red Brigades apartment in Via Montenevoso removed a plaster panel under a window in one of the rooms and discovered a secret cache of arms and documents. The hideaway contained 60 million Lire, the ransom from a 1977 Red Brigades kidnap, weapons including a Soviet-made Tokarev submachine-gun wrapped in a newspaper dated 9 September 1978, and 416 photocopied pages in the handwriting of Aldo Moro, much of it identical to the typescript found in the flat by the *carabinieri* twelve years earlier. The find caused widespread consternation and suspicion. The flat had been empty since the *carabinieri*'s 1978 raid, sealed up for eleven years by the court authorities. It seemed incredible that Dalla Chiesa's men should have missed such a relatively obvious hiding place. The magistrate in charge of the search had assured doubters in 1988 that the flat had been 'taken apart, wall by wall, brick by brick'. (*L'Espresso*, 7 August 1988). After the find, a former *carabiniere* told newspapers he remembered visiting the flat a couple of days after its discovery in 1978 and seeing that the panel had been removed and was propped against the wall (*L'Europeo*, 2 November 1990). Leading politicians voiced the suspicion that some secret service faction or other had planted the documents in recent times. Socialist Party leader Bettino Craxi said he thought 'a little hand' must have put them there, widely interpreted as a reference to the Prime Minister, Giulio Andreotti. Andreotti replied that it might have been 'a large hand' that did the deed, seen as a reference to the robustly built Craxi. The entire episode gave a vivid insight into the climate of intense suspicion that surrounds the Moro case. Rome magistrates investigating the affair came to the conclusion that the panel had almost certainly been left intact and undisturbed since the flat's discovery in 1978.

The discovery of Moro's handwritten replies to his captors confirmed once and for all the authenticity of the previously known typescript and raised again the issue of why the Red Brigades had decided not to make it public. The handwritten documents are longer than the typescript, though in some cases they too are incomplete.

What is not clear, however, is who was responsible for eliminating sensitive parts of the manuscript from the typewritten version, whether the Red Brigades practised self-censorship or whether the material was removed by the secret services or *carabinieri* when it was first discovered by General Dalla Chiesa. The allegation that the security services were responsible for the disappearance of some of the documents was repeated in an anonymous letter to Senator Flamigni in 1988 signed 'Union of *carabinieri* junior officers'. The letter said a *carabiniere* officer had carried off some of the most sensitive documents before the magistrate could examine them and added: 'The evening of that 1 October [Public Prosecutor] Vitalone came up from Rome by plane and took away material . . .' (*Avvenimenti*, 24 October 1990). The implication is that those documents too went missing, rather than ending up in court files.

Some of the additions are of considerable note and should have supplied ideal ammunition for the Red Brigades' political campaign. In one document, for example, Moro talks of the CIA's financing of the Christian Democrat Party. This subject is in fact briefly alluded to in the 1978 typescript but the reference is so truncated as to be virtually meaningless. In the manuscript, however, Moro discusses the subject at length. He confirmed that CIA funds had flowed into the DC for a number of years. 'Frankly it must be said that this is not a good way, a dignified way of harmonizing our policies. Because when this happens it should happen out of authentic conviction and free of all conditioning. But here you have a brutal "do ut des" [tit for tat].' Elsewhere, Moro refers to Andreotti's close relations 'with his colleagues in the CIA' and to the fact that he had directed the secret services both as Defence Minister and as Prime Minister 'for longer than anyone else'. This in reply to a question about Christian Democrat responsibility for the strategy of tension. These comments, too, are nowhere to be found in the Red Brigades' typescript. Another significant addition to the typescript appears to contain a cautiously worded reference to the Gladio organization. Moro said that when he was Foreign Minister 'no particular emphasis had been attached to anti-guerrilla activities that NATO could, under certain circumstances, deploy'. He referred to training for guerrilla activities 'to be carried out against occupying enemy forces or counter-guerrilla activities to be undertaken against enemy forces operating as such on our territory'. (*L'Unità*, special supplement, undated). Given that it was Moro who had imposed state secrecy to prevent magistrates from understanding the true nature of the Parallel SID it is quite possible that he may have further elaborated on this theme in order to try and persuade the Red Brigades to spare his life in return for his revealing important NATO secrets. Again it is extraordinary that the Red Brigades found nothing in his answers that might further their cause.

Imprisoned Red Brigades leader Alberto Franceschini was also amazed at his companions' decision not to publish the Moro transcript after reading the text in *La Repubblica* newspaper at the end of 1978. 'Even though it was incomplete it seemed very important to me,' he told the same paper recently (*La Repubblica*, 14 December 1990). 'Lauro Azzolini and Franco Bonisoli [who ran the Moro kidnap along with Moretti] were with me in Asinara prison. I asked them straight out why they had told us that that stuff wasn't important and why it hadn't been published. They were unable to answer.'

Whatever became of Moro's missing documents, they have continued to cast a shadow over Italian politics. One has the sinister impression that the secrets of the Moro case have become bargaining chips in furtive negotiations between Italian political leaders and the Red Brigades. The kind of deal that seems to be taking shape would involve BR leaders maintaining the veil of secrecy over the Moro mysteries and endorsing official accounts of the affair in return for some form of amnesty, as predicted by *OP*, which would bring Italy's terrorist season to an official close. Other politicians who were not directly involved in the affair at the time have an interest in the secrets because they could provide them with material with which to blackmail or damage their rivals.

One of the politicians spearheading the drive for an amnesty is former Christian Democrat Party president Flaminio Piccoli, whose northern constituency of Trento contains the university which played a crucial role in the gestation of the Red Brigades organization. 'Men like Curcio and Moretti are in a position to reveal all the secrets, to cast a ray of light over our history,' Piccoli told the *Corriere della Sera* on 25 April 1987. 'Why was Moro kidnapped on the very day that the government of national unity was being presented to Parliament? Who really took the decision to kill him and why?' As Piccoli explained, his statements were based on contacts in prison between BR leaders and emissaries of his party. 'I have never met either Curcio or Moretti. But there are friends of ours who have had the proper permits to see them, to talk to them, to pursue a discussion.' On 10 May he outlined to the Catholic magazine *Famiglia Cristiana* what he considered to be the gaps in the available information about the Moro affair. 'It's not true that we know everything about the Moro kidnap. Many important facts are not known and, above all, we don't have the film from the closed circuit television which recorded every moment of the kidnap victim's day. This material is in the hands of not more than two or three people who will make it public, one presumes, when they consider it to be most politically convenient for themselves.'

Piccoli's references to meetings in prison, to the television film and its possible possessors, give the impression that he had detailed first-hand knowledge of the subject he was discussing. But when he was interrogated by the Rome assize court it turned out that his statements were merely the fruit of personal deductions based on close reading of the newspapers. A lawyer representing the families of Moro's bodyguard summarized Piccoli's account to the court: 'In short, the journalists had misunderstood or added to his interviews.' The lawyer commented: 'But that is not at all the tenor of the interviews; what today have become deductions were previously the certain knowledge of the Christian Democrat deputy.'[42]

A possible channel of communication between Piccoli and the terrorists was Remigio Cavedon, deputy editor of the party news-paper *Il Popolo*, who held numerous meetings with Moretti in prison in 1987. Cavedon spoke about his meetings with the BR leader in an interview published by *Corriere della Sera* on 28 April 1987. He denied that he was one of the emissaries mentioned by Piccoli in his interview three days earlier, but Cavedon's statements seem implicitly to contradict this. 'As was my duty, I reported what I learned to the leaders of my party. They were very important things about the Moro case. We will reveal them at the appropriate moment.' It is hard to imagine what these revelations could be if, as so many in authority still maintain, almost everything about the Moro case is already known. Lest anyone fail to grasp what Cavedon was saying, he reiterated it: 'They were problems of enormous political significance and I certainly couldn't keep them to myself. But I can't talk about them now either.' Subsequently Cavedon attempted to backtrack on the interview, claiming that he had been misreported. The journalist who inter-viewed him, however, was adamant that this was not the case. Cavedon had telephoned him asking to make a statement and had been perfectly well aware that the conversation was being recorded.[43] Given that Italian politicians are not noted for their naïvety, one can only assume that Cavedon was using the front page of the *Corriere della Sera* to broadcast a message. The gist of the message, it would appear, was that he and his political friends had come into possession of important information about the Moro affair. Clearly they did not intend to share their secret with either the public or the judicial authorities, but it was important that their political rivals should know that they knew.

A similar but even more blatantly Mafia-like message was published in the pages of *Il Borghese*, a magazine akin to *OP* and edited by Mario Tedeschi, a former neo-fascist senator and member of P2. The magazine claimed (17 February 1985) that videocassettes of Aldo Moro's interrogation by the Red Brigades had been found in a trunk at the time of the arrest of terrorist leader Giovanni Senzani. *Il Borghese* helpfully offered its readers a number of conjectures as to the possible fate of the recordings. 'Presumably the secret services had the first complete viewing and perhaps they made a number of copies. For whom?' The magazine put forward three hypotheses. '1. The secret services decide to keep the video recording in their own archives, without informing the government. A copy is given to representatives of an allied secret service [the CIA?]. 2. The secret services hand over a copy of the film to an important personality who shows it to a few close friends from his own power group. And then hides it. 3. The secret services inform the Prime Minister's office of the discovery and the video is covered by state secrecy.' The 'hypotheses' are put forward in a truculent and self-confident style reminiscent of *OP*. Like *OP*, *Il Borghese* enjoyed excellent secret service contacts. It is curious to note how closely its allegations correspond to those made by Piccoli two years later about the existence of a closed circuit television film of Moro.

The magazine went on to speculate about the reasons for such secrecy surrounding the discovery. It suggested that Moro's replies to his captors might reveal 'truths and states of mind hitherto unknown, which could force a reappraisal of the tragic case'. The questions, it said, might show 'the main theme of the interrogation, probably focused on a political objective quite separate from that of the guerrillas who carried out the kidnap operation'. It also pointed out that the transcripts of Moro's statements found in various Red Brigades bases were incomplete, reiterating the claim made in the Coppetti document. The article concluded by commenting on the 'understandable' silence with which the major political parties had reacted to questions in Parliament on the subject by a member of the neo-fascist MSI Party. 'The fact is that those fifty-five days of the Moro kidnap still weigh heavily and everyone has, at the very least, sins of omission to atone for.' The piece appears to be based on a detailed knowledge of the facts and is distinctly menacing in tone.

The custom of publicly disseminating threatening political messages through the media is by no means rare in Italian politics and can sometimes give the impression that political dialectic has become a cat's cradle of criss-crossing blackmail notices. Political commentator Giovanni Ferrara published a damning analysis of the role of corruption and blackmail in Italian political life under the title 'I blackmail, therefore I am' (*La Repubblica*, 13 December 1987). 'The dark side of politics, the world of bribery, is often where the real game is played out,' he wrote. 'But who can really know it? Only those who are part of it. In this way we have reached the point where not only does the person who is unable to blackmail count for little in politics but also the person who cannot be blackmailed: he has nothing to sell and nothing to buy in the disreputable market of power, he is honest and therefore outside the game.' Ferrara is by no means a maverick, alarming though his view may be.

Even Mario Moretti, who in recent years has steadfastly maintained that the facts of the Moro case are as clear as the day, once admitted to communist Senator Sergio Flamigni that 'some of Moro's writings were subsequently made to disappear by the secret services'.[44] It is hard to imagine why they should have bothered to do this if their content was not of some gravity. On 21 March 1988, Moretti, Curcio and Barbara Balzerani gave a joint interview to the main state-run television network, RAI 1. While Curcio and Balzerani were unsure whether or not to participate, Moretti had made up his mind to give the interview with or without the other two. Before it was broadcast, the programme was viewed by no doubt anxious representatives of the Christian Democrat Party, who evidently found nothing to object to. In it, a distinctly nervous-looking Moretti forcefully insisted that there were no mysteries to be solved in the Moro case. 'I know exactly what happened inside the Red Brigades and this has all been written, it is all known, there is no secret background to it, there is nothing that hasn't been published, there are no interrogation transcripts, no tapes, there is nothing that is not substantially known . . .' he told the interviewer. 'I challenge anyone to find a single episode in which you could suspect a link between the Red Brigades and anything else.' This drew a sharp riposte in an open letter from BR founder Alberto Franceschini. 'Are you really sure, Mario, that everything there is to know about the Moro kidnap has been said and written?' he wrote. 'Or in the three years since the trial has something happened to make you change your mind and confirm what you yourself used to call the state's truth?'[45]

Notes

1 Giorgio Bocca (ed.), *Moro: Una Tragedia Italiana*, Valentino Bompiani, Milan, 1978, p. 36.
2 Ibid., p. 39.
3 Ibid., pp. 42–3.
4 Ibid., pp. 120–2.
5 Rocco Tolfa, Il Sabato, Rome, 11–17 June 1988.
6 Moro Commission, Relazioni di Minoranza, Rome, 1983, p. 92.
7 Moro Commission, Allegato alla Relazione, No. 5, Vol. 5, Rome, 1983, p. 15.
8 Ibid., p. 38.
9 Moro Commission, Relazioni di Minoranza, Rome, 1983, p. 121.
10 Moro Commission, Allegato alla Relazione, No. 5, Vol. 5, Rome, 1983, p. 184.
11 Giuseppe Zupo and Vincenzo Marini, *L'Operazione Moro*, Franco Angeli, Milan, 1984, p. 73.
12 Moro Commission, Relazioni di Minoranza, Rome, 1983, p. 168.
13 Ibid., p. 126.
14 Ibid., p. 160.
15 Ibid., p. 126.
16 Ibid., p. 162.
17 Ibid., p. 153.
18 Ibid., p. 154.
19 Licio Gelli to the author, 27 June 1989.
20 P2 Commission, Allegati alla Relazione, Vol. 3, Tome 4, Part 3, Rome, 1985, pp. 545–6.
21 Moro Commission, Relazioni di Minoranza, Rome, 1983, p. 154.
22 Licio Gelli to the author, 27 June 1989.
23 P2 Commission, Allegati alla Relazione, Vol. 3, Tome 4, Part 3, Rome, 1985, p. 590.
24 P2 Commission, Allegati alla Relazione, Vol. 7, Tome 22, Rome, 1987, p. 439.
25 Moro Commission, Relazioni di Minoranza, Rome, 1983, p. 154.
26 Quoted in Giuseppe Ferrara, *Il Caso Moro*, Tullio Pironti, Naples, 1987, pp. 386–7.

27 Moro Commission, Allegato alla Relazione, No. 5, Vol. 5, Rome, 1983, p. 228.

28 Ibid., p. 233.

29 *Panorama*, 17 November 1985.

30 General Carlo Alberto Dalla Chiesa to G.I. Giuliano Turone, Milan, 12 May 1981.

31 Giuseppe Zupo and Vincenzo Marini, op. cit., p. 231.

32 Licio Gelli, *La Verità*, Demetra, Lugano, 1989, p. 261.

33 Licio Gelli, unpublished version of *La Verità*, p. 18.

34 Licio Gelli to the author, 27 June 1989.

35 Licio Gelli, op. cit., (1989), p. 267.

36 *La Repubblica*, 24 May 1978.

37 P2 Commission, Allegati alla Relazione, Vol. 7, Tome 17, Rome, 1987, p. 313.

38 Nando Dalla Chiesa to the author, 1988.

39 Franco Coppola, *La Repubblica*, 1 August 1986.

40 Nando Dalla Chiesa, *Delitto Imperfetto*, Mondadori, Milan, 1984, p. 35.

41 Ibid., p. 34.

42 Franco Scottoni, *La Repubblica*, 9 October 1987.

43 Paolo Graldi to the author, 1987.

44 Sergio Flamigni, *La Tela del Ragno*, Edizioni Associate, Rome, 1988, p. 173.

45 Marcella Andreoli, *Panorama*, 8 May 1988.

[15]

MR BROWN'S
STORY

THE notion that the CIA was involved in the Moro kidnap has been put forward persistently and in some detail by a strange Scotsman named Martin Woodrow Brown. Brown has been officially dismissed as a crank and it does appear that he was somewhat unbalanced, at least in the last years of his life. Nevertheless, his claims deserve serious consideration because they are surprisingly precise and because there is other evidence that corroborates them. Most persuasive of all, though, is the reaction of people who met Brown when questioned about him. This ranged from outright alarm, through lies and evasiveness, to curiosity and an open assumption that the questioner must be working for his country's intelligence services. Brown was born in Brookfield near Glasgow on 20 May 1919. He served in the British Army in Italy during and immediately after the war, where he acted as a cryptographer and also had dealings with Italian prisoners of war. In the 1950s and 1960s he worked as a civil engineer in New York and in Canada and returned to Britain in 1968. His work in North America appears to have been fairly lucrative, as he was able to buy himself an Aston Martin car in the early 1960s. On his return to Europe he began to work as an antique dealer, travelling extensively in Germany, Spain and Italy. For the last few years until his death from a heart attack in Pisa on 12 June 1986, he lived as a tramp, despite the fact that he owned a house in Scotland and sizeable shareholdings.[1] It appears he may have spent some time in a mental asylum in Spain.[2]

Brown began disseminating his views not long after Moro's death, writing to, among others, Christian Democrat Senator Giuseppe

Giovanniello. The latter was a personal friend of Moro's, hailing from the southern port of Bari, the Christian Democrat leader's home town. The Moro trial documents include an envelope addressed to Giovanniello by Brown and postmarked 4 August 1978. Curiously, the letter it contained is missing. Its drift can be surmised from the contents of another letter, sent from Spain and dated 2 April 1979. It is written in capital letters and rather stilted, telegraphic English:

Senator CIA plot – Signor Aldo Moro.
With reference to the plot CIA USA against Signor Aldo Moro. I have proof of this. Please advise if you wish confirmation with Xerox copies. Research period June 1977 to date with in Rome Oct. 1978. Regarding this case contacted Prof. Semerari, criminology, Rome University. Please confirm receipt by return. Its name noted on linked pages assassination list in a published book.

The letter was signed by Brown. Rather than immediately throwing it away as the work of a nutcase, Giovanniello sent it on to Examining Magistrate Achille Gallucci with a covering note expressing the hope that 'it does not take up too much of your precious time and that it may be at least a grain of contribution towards the truth'.

A month earlier Brown had sent an even stranger and more complex letter to the headquarters of the finance police in Rome.

Dear Sir,
I apologize for my poor written Italian. I am writing to you in connection with the murder of Aldo Moro. In the course of a year's research carried out in a British library, in a book whose subject and title is *The Gang That Couldn't Shoot Straight*, published by J. Breslim, Bantam Books. . . I found a list of anarchist assassinations, partially concealed by resorting to a system suggested by me in Manhattan in 1956–58, at the time of the book's publication. Others provided the ideas for the book, adding the list of the assassinations, which included the name of Aldo Moro. The use of the encoding anagrams provides the names, forty of which, I repeat, I have discovered, including that of a certain Jacques Chaime, president of the Crédit Lyonnais who was killed in May 1976 in Paris, Blvd des Italiens.
Write to me if you would like to know more details about the code used.

The list of murders also includes racing drivers, among whom Mario Andretti is cited. In all, six of the drivers named have already died in car or plane crashes.

Brown concluded by saying that he had been put in touch with the press officer of the Italian embassy in London by the Italian naval attaché.

Once again, the letter bears all the hallmarks of being the work of a crank. It does, however, appear to have been treated with some seriousness by the Italian authorities. A report on the letter, probably drawn up by SISMI, and marked 'Most Confidential' (*Riservatissimo*), is included in the Moro trial documents. According to those who participated in the trial, it is most unusual for documents relating to any of the numerous cranks' letters regarding the Moro case to be marked in this way. The report noted that Brown had put forward the name of Enrico Triaca as Moro's murderer. Triaca was the owner of a Red Brigades printing press who had been arrested on 17 May 1978, and the author of the report speculated that newspaper accounts of the event may have prompted Brown's identification of him, given that his letter was written some three weeks after the arrest. The report observes that the identification was made in a note written at the foot of a photocopy from Brown's book, but the photocopy itself is missing from the trial documents. The report states that in a letter dated 8 August 1978, 'the collateral British agency' informed the Italians that there was no reference to a list of murders or to Aldo Moro in the book cited by Brown. It identified an M.W. Brown living in Scotland and offered to contact him if required. The Italians decided to take up the offer but 'after repeated reminders' they were told in the following January that their British colleagues had been unable to trace Brown and that 'he was anyway mentally unbalanced so any information received from him would be unreliable'.

The remarkable thing about this report is that it shows that the investigation was handled by the Italian secret services rather than the police or magistrates, that they reacted very quickly and that they repeatedly requested their British counterparts to question Brown about his letter. What's more, the report's conclusion that Brown was unbalanced seems to clash with its 'Most Confidential' heading. It is extremely unlikely that Brown was claiming that the name of Moro's murderer had been published in a book, in coded form, several decades before his kidnap and long before he embarked on the policy of compromise with the PCI that led to his death. What is rather more plausible is that Brown could identify his killers using a published book and a code system he himself devised. As we have seen, he was actually in New York at the time he claimed to be and he had been a cryptographer during the war.

There are other elements of corroborating evidence that justify taking Brown's claims seriously. For a start, there is a curious echo of Brown's reference to the murder of the president of the Crédit Lyonnais in the evidence to Rome magistrates of 'repentant' right-wing terrorist Walter Sordi. 'I remember that one evening, travelling on the Turin–Rome train with Pasquale Belsito and Stefano Procopio, who were also members of NAR [Armed Revolutionary Cells], I heard references for the first time to the Pecorelli murder as being a matter connected with our world,' Sordi told the magistrates. 'In particular, Belsito said that Valerio Fioravanti was not the clean person we all believed him to be, but someone involved in complex and sinister manoeuvres, including the Pecorelli murder. Belsito added that Fioravanti was in contact with Gelli, whom he had met in France. Valerio Fioravanti had also murdered a number of bankers in France. Belsito was very vague about this but he said he was certain of Giusva [a nickname] Fioravanti's participation in the Pecorelli murder.' Angelo Izzo, as we have already seen, offered magistrates a similar account. It is unlikely that Fioravanti was involved in the Jacques Chaine (the banker's name is actually spelt with an 'n'; Brown seems to have had some difficulty with his spelling, mistakenly giving Triaca's name as Triaco and author Jimmy Breslin as Breslim) murder as the banker was actually shot by a young French anarchist, Jean Bilski, who committed suicide immediately afterwards, and Fioravanti would only have been in his mid-teens at the time. Brown was obviously aware of the circumstances of Chaine's murder, probably from newspaper reports, as he cited Bilski's name and the fact that he had used a 9 mm pistol, at the foot of the photocopied page where he named Triaca as the murderer of Aldo Moro. What is interesting is that Belsito should have spoken of the murder of French bankers in connection with Gelli and his links with right-wing terrorists.

An even stranger coincidence relates to Brown's reference to the accidental death of famous racing drivers. Given that the driver he mentioned, Andretti, was not dead, one can only assume that their names were a coded reference to other people who had actually died. Among a series of documents confiscated from Marcello Coppetti in

1981 was a single page containing a handwritten list of seven racing driver's names. Coppetti had entrusted copies of the documents for safe keeping to a lawyer and to his brother, who kept them for him in a bank security box. One of the documents, relating to the journalist's research on Gelli, contains the statement: 'I am giving several copies of this note to people in my confidence, in a sealed envelope to be opened in the event of something happening to me or my dying of other than natural causes.'[3] It is hard to understand why Coppetti should have kept a list of racing drivers alongside other documents which he clearly considered to be highly sensitive. The names listed are: Villeneuve, Sheckter, Jarier (which appears to have been crossed out), Andretti (mentioned by Brown), Reutemann, Lauda and Piquet.[4] All the drivers were alive when the document was handed over to the judicial authorities by Coppetti. The only one to die subsequently was Gilles Villeneuve, killed in a racing accident in 1982. More curious still, a document detailing Gelli's personal financial affairs was confiscated from the P2 boss when he was arrested in Switzerland in 1982. A payment of 31,000 in an unspecified currency (pesos or dollars?) was listed against the entry 'Risarcimento incidente Piquet' (Compensation Piquet accident). When I asked him about this, Gelli at first looked absolutely blank. After a while he suddenly appeared to understand the question but pronounced the name Piquet like the word 'cricket' rather than in the French manner: ostensibly the reason why he had initially failed to understand my question. He said Piquet was the name of his Uruguayan chauffeur, who had had a car accident in Montevideo, and the entry was to remind him of his insurance claim. 'It was just a note to remind me of all the questions I had to deal with. Piquet is still alive and well.' If this is the case, it is somewhat surprising that Gelli should have added the handwritten note about the 'incidente Piquet' at the foot of a typewritten document mainly devoted to substantial financial operations carried out in conjunction with Banco Ambrosiano President Roberto Calvi. The matter was clearly open to misinterpretation, as Gelli quickly commented: 'That's another thing where, who knows what you may have thought?'[5] Indeed, one might have been tempted to think that the racing drivers' names had been used as a coded reference to a linked series of political assassinations, about which both Brown and Coppetti had information.

Along with the list of racing drivers and much documentation on Gelli, Coppetti also kept several documents relating to the Moro affair, in addition to the notes of his conversation with Gelli and Nobili about Moro's missing papers. In one of these he refers to contacts between Gelli and Army Commander-in-Chief General Giuseppe Aloia that took place in the mid-1960s. 'This is a period worth focusing on because the infiltration of someone into SIFAR begins, which will lead to the rapid decline of the Italian secret service, with consequences which will affect SID then SISMI and SISDE, with the result that when the Moro operation comes to fruition the service no longer exists.'[6] Coppetti expanded on this idea in another document entitled, appropriately enough, 'CIA – NATO'. The document is in two parts. The first part reads: 'Directive: when the NATO survival plan goes into operation (either for total war or "non-orthodox war" or "war of ideological aggression") the plan is for all the secret services of NATO countries, although remaining independent, to give a co-ordinating role for so-called "camouflaged operations" to the CIA. The latter obviously throws the country that is undergoing the ideological attack into confusion.' The second part of the document describes a plan known by Coppetti as A-2, which outlines how an agreement between the United States and the Soviet Union stipulates that whatever happens in Poland, the same must occur in Italy. 'See what happens in Poland and Italy in 1976 and why A-2 takes more initiative in Italy and it ends up with SID being blinded and Moro eliminated.'[7] Whether or not one accepts Coppetti's thesis of some sort of reciprocal agreement between the CIA and the KGB, it is interesting to note that he places the elimination of Moro fairly and squarely within the context of NATO security arrangements. Moro's policy of a historic compromise with the communists may well have been construed as 'ideological aggression' by NATO security chiefs.

There are other elements that lend support to some of Brown's claims. In his letter to Giovanniello, he said that he had contacted Professor Aldo Semerari, a criminologist at Rome University, about the Moro affair. This was confirmed by Semerari in an interview with *Paese Sera* (21 June 1981). Semerari told the newspaper that he had received a letter from Brown, addressed to the director of the Rome University Criminology Department, shortly after Moro's death. In it, the writer stated that 'on the basis of an interpretation of passages from an already published book he had succeeded in predicting a series of crimes, including the murders of Kennedy, an actress and Moro, and for the future, that of the racer Andretti (who's fortunately still alive), as well as other people whom I don't remember. The letter appeared to be clearly the work of a psychopath.' Despite holding this opinion of the letter, Semerari decided to send it on to General Giuseppe Ferrara, a friend of his at *carabiniere* headquarters, and was thanked for it a couple of days later by the general. 'A little while later, someone calling himself Brown came to my private office, saying that he was the author of the letter. He was a middle-aged man, neglectful of his clothes and personal cleanliness and incapable of speaking Italian.' Semerari passed him on to his colleague Professor Franco Ferracuti, who he knew had an interest in the Moro case as he had been one of Cossiga's panel of advisers during the kidnap. Since then, Semerari said, he had had no more contact with Brown. Evidently keen to distance himself from the affair, he added: 'It is in these terms and only in these terms that my name can be linked to the Moro case.'

As someone claiming that the CIA was behind Moro's kidnap, Brown could not have stumbled upon a more unsuitable audience. Both Semerari and Ferracuti were members of P2 and had close links to the Italian secret services. Ferracuti also worked for the CIA and had done so since before the Moro kidnapping. 'Ferracuti often boasted of his contacts with the American secret services for whom he is continuously travelling to the United States,' Semerari's widow told Bologna magistrates in 1985.[8] Semerari, who had been a communist in his youth but became an extreme right-winger in later life, was one of Italy's most influential criminologists. His work brought him into contact with Mafia bosses and terrorists and he was a regular frequenter of the social gatherings of the extreme right. This enabled him to act as a bridge between the P2 lodge and its occasional allies in the worlds of terrorism and organized crime. He was able to provide prisoners with favours of information and assistance with their legal problems as well as certifying some of them as insane so that they could be transferred from prison to a less rigorous life in a mental institution. Semerari was arrested in connection with the Bologna station bombing and sent ripples of unease through the secret services by threatening to write a memorandum on the affair while he was in prison in the autumn of 1980.[9] He was released shortly afterwards but was terrified that people would assume this was because he had talked and named those responsible for the bombing.[10] Ferracuti has also been suspected of having inside knowledge about the Bologna bombing. Semerari's brother told magistrates in 1984: 'I think it is important to report the following: when my brother was arrested, Ferracuti assumed an aggressive attitude towards my sister-in-law, whom he even went so far as to threaten with reprisals: he told her that if Aldo had been arrested "because of Bologna", he [Ferracuti] had nothing to do with it and he did not intend to be implicated in such events and if he was implicated in them, he would know how to react.'[11]

Semerari took his secrets, on Bologna and many other matters, with him to the grave. He was kidnapped by the Camorra on 27 March 1982 and his decapitated body was found in the boot of a car near Naples on 1 April. His head was found separately, in a plastic bag resting on the back seat of the car. That same day his secretary committed suicide in Rome, ensuring that his secrets remained such. It has not been established whether Semerari was murdered because he had offended a powerful Camorra boss or because the secret services were worried about his reliability over the Bologna case. It is not always easy to distinguish between the Camorra and the secret services in some of the murkier chapters of recent Italian history. Semerari may not have been as sceptical of Brown as he would have had people think. Among the Scotsman's belongings discovered after his death was a letter of introduction from Semerari addressed to a police officer. His true opinion about Brown's claims also went with him to the grave.

Despite Semerari's assertion that he had referred Brown to Ferracuti, the latter insisted he had never actually met the Scotsman, when I spoke to him in 1989.[12] 'Semerari said Brown was unbalanced but said I should meet him. If I recall correctly, he was unavailable to meet me,' Ferracuti told me. But he was given a copy of Brown's letter from Spain, which he passed on for analysis to colleagues in SISDE. Ferracuti is a tall, balding, distinguished-looking man and speaks fluent English. He was a professor of criminological medicine and forensic psychiatry at Rome University when he was invited to join the team of five experts advising Interior Minister Cossiga on the Moro kidnap. Ferracuti gave advice on Moro's mental state on the basis of his letters from captivity and attempted to glean information on the Red Brigades' intentions by analysing their communiqués. 'I believed at the time and I still do, that Moro was suffering from the Stockholm Syndrome,' he said. The consequence of this conclusion that Moro was emotionally in thrall to his captors was inevitably to reduce the statesman's prestige and diminish the significance of his letters. This is significant, given that there was fierce debate over the genuineness of his letters, in which Moro appeared to be giving perfectly lucid advice on how best to resolve the kidnap. Mino Pecorelli had taken exactly the opposite view: 'The truth is hard to say, very hard for the Christian Democrats to accept: Moro wrote what he has written in the full possession of his mental faculties. The words, the forms of expression, the logical connections, all bear his unique imprint.' (OP, 18 April 1978.)

Following the Moro affair, Ferracuti became a consultant to the domestic secret service, SISDE, and in 1980 he joined P2. He told me that he joined the lodge for protection because of the dangers involved in his secret service work and claimed, somewhat implausibly, that he was unaware of the negative publicity about P2 which had been gathering pace in the media at that time. He added the revealing comment: 'If I had not been invited to join P2 it would have been an insult. When you reach a certain level in the secret services you are invited to join, invited is an understatement.' Again, this confirms the nature of the lodge as a club for the top ranks of the security services.

Despite his membership of P2 and his work for the CIA, Ferracuti retains a sophisticated view of Italian politics. 'I'm not a communist or I couldn't have worked for the CIA but I am not a rabid anti-communist. To me, the defeat of the Red Brigades and the co-operation in this of the PCI were more important than keeping the communists out of government. I tried to tell the Americans this was the only way to defeat the BR but the Americans are very childish in foreign policy. Without communist assistance we could not have defeated the Red Brigades.' Ferracuti said he never believed that Moro would be killed, especially since the longer a kidnap lasts, the less chance there is of the hostage being killed. 'It was not in the Red Brigades' interests to kill him. Moro would have been much more destabilizing alive than dead.' He also confirmed, from his privileged vantage point, Pecorelli and Grassini's account of the CIA's contribution to resolving the crisis. 'The CIA's contribution was zero. I exchanged information with CIA colleagues but got no help. They would not even provide us with secure radios, so we had to buy them from the Japanese,' he said. 'Moro was not popular with them.' These are surprisingly candid admissions by someone who has made no secret of his collaboration with American intelligence.

Brown's claims are lent extra weight by the reaction of Senator Giovanniello to questions on the subject. He was considerably alarmed when I telephoned him in 1987 to ask whether we could meet to discuss the matter. He told me he had carried out no investigations of his own and had immediately passed on the letter to Judge Gallucci. He was not prepared to discuss the matter any further. This alarmed reaction was also registered by *Paese Sera* in the article reporting Semerari's account of his dealings with Brown (21 June 1981). 'He [Giovanniello] cut short a phone conversation with a journalist with the words: "I can't say any more. I don't want to. . ."' the paper reported. It is understandable that Brown's allegations should be regarded as somewhat sensitive but incomprehensible that they should provoke fear, unless there were some truth in them. One possible reason for Giovanniello's anxiety can be gathered from an interview he gave to *La Repubblica* newspaper on 14 September 1978, and which he subsequently disowned. The interview contains grave and detailed allegations which echo the claims made by both Brown and journalist Massimo Caprara. At the time of the interview, Giovanniello would almost certainly have received Brown's first (now missing) letter, sent from Madrid on 4 August. Unless a lot of people's imaginations were working overtime, one can only assume that the claims made by normally sober senators and journalists were based on what they considered to be reliable information.

Giovanniello began by saying that the proposal, put forward by *La Stampa* newspaper, that the captive Moro should be elected State President was 'the culmination of a series of contacts, the choice taken when certain things were understood'. Interviewer: 'That Moro was the victim of an international plot?' 'There's no doubt about that. I am not interested in pointing out which foreign power was likely to benefit from Moro's disappearance. I only say that Moro being State President, with all that that implied, would certainly not have impressed the few desperadoes who took possession of the [Christian Democrat] president in the last stage in order to eliminate him. The message went much further than that.' Giovanniello said he realized that it would be very difficult to get Moro back alive 'when we understood the level of the people behind the kidnap'. He and his friends, he said, did everything possible. 'In particular, when we learned that Moro was about to be handed over to common criminals for the terrible final act, we did the most unheard of things to try and get to him before the others, but without success.'

The senator's account tallies with Caprara's claim that Moro had been released by one group only to be murdered by another. His reference to the foreign power with most to gain from Moro's removal seems to be a discreet reference to the United States, echoing Brown's claim. The claim that the kidnapped statesman had been handed over to common criminals might also explain how underworld figures like Toni Chichiarelli could have come into possession of inside information about the kidnap. Giovanniello's account finds faint echoes in Pecorelli's article 'Shame on you, you clowns' (*OP*, 16 January 1979), where he referred to negotiations with the Red Brigades and to 'someone breaking the pact'. According to Pecorelli, Moro was to have been released, 'the "*carabinieri*" (?) were to have checked that Moro was alive and let the red car go. Then someone raised the stakes to an unacceptable figure because they wanted the *anti-communist* Moro dead anyway. . .' Giovanniello's description of secret negotiations and a race to get to Moro first plausibly ties in with this version. It is, in any case, far too detailed and specific to be easily explained away. Giovanniello concluded the interview with a reference to the false BR communiqué no.7. When he and his friends heard news of it they rushed to the nearest *carabiniere* station and contacted the force's commander-in-chief, General Mario De Sena. 'As we know, it was all a hoax, but why did De Sena immediately reply that it was all over for Moro? How could he be so sure?' Given the tenor of the rest of the interview, this last question seems to be prompted by more than an idle curiosity.

Another document, almost certainly from Brown, adds further detail to the catalogue of conspiracy allegations. A police report dated 16 May 1979 explains: the previous day, copies of a typewritten document were found in two telephone booths in Florence following anonymous phone calls to the local newpaper and to the ANSA news agency. The opening is in the familiar Brown style:

Please forgive my Italian, furthermore, I don't know how to type. Don't ask me either why a stranger should write such things only now; whether they are true or false. It's up to you to judge. This is not a confession but simply a true account of the facts. The man who really organized the Via Fani massacre and the kidnap of Aldo Moro is an Italo-American and a close friend of Ronald Stark (whom the police have been protecting so much). His name is David, born 18.3.1954 in San Diego, California, blue eyes, 1.77 metres tall, chestnut hair, average build, he sometimes wears a moustache, former marine in Vietnam with the rank of captain, then entered the Green Beret special forces. Most recently he was a military counsellor with Central Intelligence Defence in West

Germany. David is the only one of the top directors who personally organized the Via Fani massacre and the kidnap of Aldo Moro together with his other companions who are already known to the police. David, however, did not participate in the elimination of Aldo Moro. Most recently he has been living in Rome, but he generally lives in Milan (he frequents the USIS library in Via Bigli 1/A).

The document was found about a fortnight before Brown wrote to Giovanniello from Madrid. One wonders whether his first letter, posted on 4 August 1978, which has gone missing from the Moro trial documents, was equally specific. An attempt to discuss these allegations with Judge Domenico Sica in 1988 elicited the reply that the magistrate had important things to do and that anyway almost everything about the Moro case was already known.

The mention of Ronald Stark in the context of the Moro kidnap is interesting. Stark was the American arrested in Bologna for drug trafficking in February 1975. It was he who had been in contact with Enrico Paghera, the man who falsely claimed responsibility for the Lake Duchessa communiqué on behalf of Azione Rivoluzionaria. While they were both in prison, Stark had given Paghera instructions on how to reach a guerrilla training camp at Baalbeck in Lebanon and, according to Paghera, the American had set him up as an Interior Ministry informant. Stark was a balding, overweight man in his middle thirties with a drooping Mexican-style moustache who dabbled in drug dealing and revolutionary politics to such an extent that it is impossible to be sure whether his main aim was self-enrichment or intelligence-gathering on behalf of the US government. His involvement with drugs began in the late 1960s as a member of a hippy drug-dealing association known as the Brotherhood of Eternal Love. This transformed his personal finances, enabling him to set up a drug laboratory in Belgium in 1971 with an investment of $300,000.[13] His involvement with intelligence work began even earlier, with a stint of secret work for the Defense Department between 1960 and 1962.[14] It is worth remembering that some of the earliest research into hallucinogenic drugs was carried out by the CIA, prompted by a desire to find a response to the brain-washing of captured US troops during the Korean War and by an interest in the mind-control potential of drugs such as LSD. The work was carried out as part of an operation codenamed MK-ULTRA, authorized by Allen Dulles in 1953, and designed to investigate covert means of modifying human behaviour. More recently, the international drug market has offered plentiful supplies of untraceable funds and information, both of which have a powerful attraction for the world's security services.

Stark's arrest in Italy was prompted by a mysterious phone call to the police and he seems to have been quite happy to go to prison, where his time was gainfully employed in winning the confidence of captured Red Brigades leaders, given that he turned down the opportunity of bail in August 1978.[15] One of his ploys to convince them of his bona fides was to emphasize his links with the left-wing Palestinian faction led by George Habbash, the Popular Front for the Liberation of Palestine. It was this group that had been training and arming Toni Negri's Autonomia Operaia organization. He was well equipped for this role as he had travelled frequently to Lebanon, doubtless convenient for his arms and drug deals, and one of his many identities was that of Ali Khoury, a stateless Palestinian. According to Paghera, Stark spoke of forming an international terrorist organization free of Marxist-Leninist ideology,[16] an ideal vehicle for acts of controlled political provocation.

When the time came that he was ready to leave prison, Stark had no difficulty in persuading the authorities that he had been working for American intelligence all along. Examining Magistrate Giorgio Floridia ordered his release on 11 April 1979, saying that a number of circumstances justified the hypothesis 'that Stark, a member of the American secret services from 1960 onwards, entered the Middle East drug world probably in order to infiltrate armed organizations operating in that area and to gain contacts and information about European terrorist groups'. Floridia based this judgement on Stark's close links with the US consul in Rome, Philip Taylor, with officials from the Florence consulate and with Charles Adams, an economic counsellor at the US embassy in London. The magistrate cited the US authorities' failure to seek Stark's extradition, despite the fact he was wanted in the United States on charges of drug dealing and tax evasion. He also referred to 'periodic payments to him from Fort Lee, known to be the site of a CIA office'.[17]

While in prison, Stark cultivated the friendship of BR leaders Renato Curcio and Pietro Bertolazzi. As well as offering to put them in contact with the PFLP, he provided them with a cryptographic system for coded radio communications. Having gained their confidence he was then able to pass on information to officers from the *carabinieri* and from the Interior Ministry's anti-terrorism unit, who came to visit him in prison. In 1976 he told the Pisa public prosecutor about a Red Brigades plan to assassinate the Genoa magistrate Francesco Coco, four months before the murder actually took place. He also told the prosecutor about the existence of a plan to kidnap Andreotti, but he was not believed on either score.[18] Stark told a Bologna prosecutor that he had provided certain people with names and addresses which would make possible the arrest of the real Red Brigades leadership. He said the recipients should have no difficulty in making the information available as it did not concern their own country, again a hint that he was working for US intelligence. He also told the magistrate that he was surprised that information he had provided to a *carabiniere* officer had not led to any arrests.

The American provided a somewhat anomalous account of the structure of the Red Brigades organization during a meeting with officials from the Interior Ministry's anti-terrorism unit in July 1977. Their report says Stark described the terrorist organization as being divided into three levels. The lowest level was that of the factories, the second was the 'operational group', with more than 300 members, and the most secret level was that of the 'Military and Industrial Information Centre', whose members operated mainly in Rome and about whom 'everything is known'. The officers drew a small sketch to illustrate Stark's description. When I showed it to BR founder Alberto Franceschini in 1988 he said he knew nothing of such a structure. One can only assume that by 1977 the Red Brigades were no longer divided into columns (by city) and fronts (by activity), under the control of the Strategic Directorate, but that the organization had a secret structure, unknown even to one of its founder members. Alternatively, if Stark was neither lying nor mistaken, he may have wanted to convey some kind of message to his interlocutors by challenging official accounts of the Red Brigades organization. His challenge went further, claiming that Curcio was not the real head of the organization but made to appear so in order to mislead the police.[19] His account is somehow reminiscent of magistrate Guido Calogero's conclusions, which question whether the known Red Brigades members were the ones that really counted and highlighted the manipulative role of the Hyperion language school in Paris. The suggestion that Stark was about to make revelations along these lines would certainly have given a jolt to the custodians of these secrets.

Stark's activities offer other surprises. As well as cultivating imprisoned left-wing terrorists, he appears to have been in contact with leading exponents of the right. Documents confiscated at the time of his arrest show that he had been in touch with Salvo Lima, Andreotti's political ally allegedly linked to the Mafia, and with Prince Gianfranco Alliata di Montereale, linked to freemasonry and the Mafia and implicated in the Borghese coup attempt. There was also evidence of contact with Graziano Verzotto, an associate of Sindona's and president of the Sicilian state mining corporation, Ente Minerario Siciliano, who fled to Lebanon in 1975 after being caught up in a financial scandal. He was equally at home with the rightists as he was when masquerading as a left-wing sympathizer. A confiscated letter to Wendy Hansen, American vice-consul in Florence, expressed the view that circumstances were not yet ripe for a military coup in Italy.[20] Most interesting of all, though, was evidence that he had been in touch with Vito Miceli, former director of Italian military intelligence. A complex and never fully resolved tale involving Miceli leads back, by a roundabout route, to the Moro affair.[21]

One of Stark's co-defendants at the drug trial was an architect from Rome, Count Roberto Fiorenzi, known to his friends as Bubi. Fiorenzi had come under suspicion of involvement in the Italicus train bombing after it was discovered that he was staying at the Hotel Locarno in Rome at the same time as other suspects in the bombing were meeting there.[22] According to another of the drug defendants, a car thief named Franco Buda, Stark had told him that Fiorenzi had given shelter in his house in Siracusa, Sicily, to at least one of the men involved in the 1973 Fiumicino airport massacre at the request of a senior officer in the Italian armed forces. From Buda's account the examining magistrate in Rome deduced that the officer in question could have been Miceli, but the matter was never fully clarified.[23] On 17 December 1973, seven Arab gunmen attacked a Pan American Boeing 707 at Rome airport. They threw incendiary bombs into the aircraft, causing the death of thirty-two people, before five of them escaped to Kuwait aboard a hijacked Lufthansa jet. According to *Lotta Continua* (24 October 1978), the other two were allowed to escape to Rome, where they were taken into the protective custody of the Italian secret services, before being smuggled out of the country. These two could well have been concealed in Fiorenzi's Sicilian house, as Buda had claimed. *La Repubblica* (13 June 1976) also voiced the suspicion that the airport attack could have been planned 'with the agreement of important sectors of SID'. The paper cited the account of an eyewitness who claimed to have seen the seven gunmen being escorted through airport security checks by policemen three hours before the attack. The suggestion was that right-wing police and secret service agents assisted the hijackers as part of their contribution to the strategy of tension. The attack sparked off energetic efforts on the part of the Italian secret services to persuade Palestinian terrorist groups to refrain from further attacks on Italian territory. One of the methods adopted was the supply of large amounts of humanitarian aid to Palestinian refugees. The man chiefly responsible for Italy's placatory policy towards the PLO was Aldo Moro and the go-between he chose for political contacts with the PLO leadership was Colonel Stefano Giovannone of military intelligence.

Just over a month before the Fiumicino attack, the Italian government had made one of its most generous gestures in its continuing attempt to shield the country from Middle Eastern terrorism. Five Arab terrorists had been arrested a couple of months earlier as they prepared to shoot down an El Al airliner with a ground-to-air missile from the balcony of a house in Ostia, a coastal town directly under the flight path of planes landing and taking off at Fiumicino.[24] Rome judges granted them provisional liberty and on 11 November they were flown to freedom on board an Italian military aircraft. Twelve days later, the plane that had ferried the terrorists to freedom blew up in the sky near Venice. The crash is widely regarded as having been the result of sabotage carried out by the Israeli secret service as a reprisal for Italy's weak-kneed approach to Palestinian terrorism.[25]

Curiously enough, Moro referred to both these incidents in a letter from captivity to Flaminio Piccoli in which he argued the case for a flexible attitude towards negotiations with the BR. Moro would certainly have known of the secret service involvement in both episodes and it is not inconceivable that he may again have been trying to send some kind of a message to his friends in the outside world. He began by saying that negotiations were a regular occurrence. 'And you who knew everything will certainly be informed about it. . . you can call [Erminio] Pennacchini who knows all about it (in more detail than I do) and is a sensitive and reliable person. Then there's Miceli and if he's in Italy (and from all points of view it would be good to have him come) Colonel [Stefano] Giovannoni, whom Cossiga admires. So, not just once but several times, detained and convicted Palestinians were freed by various mechanisms, in order to avoid serious reprisals.'

It is ironic that Moro's mention of these incidents should introduce us to the world of Miceli, Fiorenzi and Stark, and this could well have been his intention. It is strange that the letter misspells Giovannone's name as the secret service officer had at one time been Moro's personal bodyguard. For many years he represented the Italian secret service in Beirut and his name immediately conjures associations with Lebanese terrorism and with corruption scandals linked to Italian oil purchases, precisely the associations made by Sereno Freato when he linked the Pecorelli murder to that of Moro. But, most significantly of all, as Judge Mastelloni's investigation has shown, Giovannone's name takes us to the heart of the secret agreement between the CIA and the PLO and the concomitant arms supplies from the PLO to the Red Brigades. It is possible that Moro, who had long experience as Foreign Minister and a close personal relationship with Giovannone, may have been hinting in his letter at this murky international background to his kidnapping. Mino Pecorelli suggested as much in an article dated 17 October 1978. 'Just as the *Corriere* proclaims the baselessness of the hypothesis of an international plot, in Lisbon Craxi maintains the exact opposite, leaving aside the fact that it is no accident that Moro himself in his letter called to his aid Colonel Giovannone, on station at Beirut.' The OP article was titled 'The Red Thread' and was devoted mainly to emphasizing the Eastern Bloc connections of the Red Brigades, but Pecorelli may have had Giovannone's CIA contacts more in mind when he referred to Moro's appeal for the SISMI officer's assistance and linked this to speculation about an international plot behind the kidnapping.

It is not in the least unlikely that Ronald Stark, with his contacts in Lebanon and with the Red Brigades, straddled the same arms route that Giovannone had so skilfully mediated and protected. What links Stark most closely to the Moro case, though, is clearly Brown's document, in which the Scotsman refers to Stark's close friend by the name of David. At first sight, the claims are unconvincing. Brown stated that David, who was born in 1954, was a captain in the Marines in Vietnam only a decade later. Either the date of birth was wrong or the Marine captain was someone else. What is true, though, is that Stark had a close friend called David. Witnesses have spoken of seeing Stark with an American named David in Lebanon. They described him as blond, aged twenty-three to twenty-four, and having a passport in the name of Emilio Messaggio. This could well be Brown's Italo-American, as it would not have been easy for David to assume the identity of an Italian unless he either had Italian blood or spoke the language perfectly. David also appears to have used the identity of David Mears, born in Bradford, UK, on 8 November 1952.[26] An Englishman named John Mears, born on 23 September 1949, was authorized to have access to Stark's security deposit at the Union de Banques Suisses in Lugano in 1975. The man in question may also have used the name David Linker. Stark's Parisian lawyer, John Crawford, who was also on the board of directors of his Belgian drug laboratory, told two US Inland Revenue Service agents in 1972 that a number of things had led him to become suspicious about the nature of the Le Clocheton laboratory. One of them was the character of the laboratory director, David Linker, which seemed inappropriate for someone supposedly running a research laboratory. Crawford described Linker as being more a 'man of action' than a research scientist.[27] There is no evidence that this lead on the Moro case has ever been seriously investigated and Prosecutor Domenico Sica was unwilling even to discuss it. For all the strangeness and inaccuracies in Brown's claims, it is difficult to imagine that he could have known about the existence of Stark's friend David without being privy to first-hand information. It is interesting to note that he described David as working for 'Central Intelligence Defence' in West Germany. It sounds rather as though he meant to indicate the Defence Intelligence Agency, the organization implicated in Italian terrorism by the documents found on Gelli's daughter and probably the agency for which Stark was working.

Among the many aliases used by Stark was the name Maurizio Borghetti. This sounds almost like a jocular reference to Mario Moretti, who himself used the alias Mario Borghi and sometimes the name Maurizio. Given Stark's access to inside information about the Red Brigades, his choice could well be more than a mere coincidence.[28] Stark was released from prison in April 1979 and ordered to report to the *carabinieri* twice a week. Within a matter of days he had left the country. A telex to the Interior Ministry from the Bologna police chief indicated the probable route he had taken. 'A reliable confidential source has reported that Ronald Stark, according to what he himself said at the beginning of the month, was in a position to leave the country secretly with the assistance of American personnel. The localities indicated for his probable departure are Pisa or Vicenza.'[29] Both are the sites of US air bases. Stark's charmed life continued after his departure from Italy. Drug-dealing charges against him in Holland were dropped in 1983 and he was merely expelled from the country, and the FBI found they were unable to gather sufficient evidence to prosecute him in connection with his drug trafficking with the Brotherhood of Eternal Love. This made him virtually the only member of the Brotherhood to escape imprisonment. When a Bologna prosecutor sought Stark's extradition from the United States to face the charges against him in Italy he received a copy of Stark's death certificate, dated 8 May 1984, from the US authorities; a document he viewed with some scepticism but which effectively places Stark beyond the reach of Italian justice.

Returning to Mr Brown: the eccentric Scotsman collapsed and died of a heart attack in Pisa on 13 June 1986. In his bags, found at the left luggage office at Pisa station, police discovered a mass of documents concerning terrorism and organized crime, many of them simply newspaper cuttings. There were documents indicating that Brown had been arrested in 1963 as a suspect in the assassination of President John F. Kennedy. A cutting from a Belgian journal reported that Brown had been staying in the same hotel in Dallas as the gunman Lee Harvey Oswald. Other documents gave the impression that he had been suspected of belonging to an anti-communist organization linked to the Mafia and financed by a New Orleans millionaire.[30] Over the years it has been alleged that right-wing CIA men, anti-Castro Cubans and members of the Mafia conspired together to assassinate Kennedy. New Orleans millionaire Clay Shaw was at one time investigated as a suspect in the murder. These elements seem to square remarkably well with the contents of Brown's documents. Furthermore, Brown claimed to know the identity of the men behind the Kennedy assassination and claimed that the same group had been responsible for Moro's murder. His papers also claimed that there was a common denominator to the Red Brigades, right-wing terrorism and the Mafia, a concept we have already discussed and which is by no means implausible.

Following his death and newspaper reports on the unusual contents of his cases, complete with much speculation as to whether or not he worked for British intelligence, the authorities embarked on a course of mendacity and evasiveness which only goes to bolster the view that Brown was in possession of information that was both accurate and grave in its implications. When I interviewed Mattia La Rana, the head of the political office of the Pisa police in 1987, he told me that he had at first considered Brown's documents to be of considerable importance but had been forced to modify this view when he found that Brown's assertions contrasted with the judicially verified facts. When I asked him on what subject Brown had got it wrong he answered, 'The Moro case,' implying, like Sica, that everything on the subject was already known. When I showed him the anonymous leaflet Brown had left in Florence, the officer said he would have taken the matter more seriously if he had been aware of the connection at the time. He did not, however, propose doing anything further on the matter. La Rana confirmed to me that one of the documents in Brown's bags was a letter of introduction for Brown addressed to an Italian police officer and signed by the criminologist Aldo Semerari. This had been reported in the press at the time of Brown's death but the existence of the letter had been officially denied by the police a few days later.

La Rana told me that he had returned the bags and their contents to Brown's nephew, also Martin, when he visited Pisa for his uncle's funeral. In fact, Mr Brown Junior had already told me that he had made a selection from his uncle's papers, most of which had no meaning for him as a non-Italian speaker, and then passed on the rest to the British consulate in Florence. The consulate held on to two of Brown's bags for three or four months before deciding to throw them away. The consulate staff showed admirable self-restraint: despite holding newspaper cuttings describing the sensational contents of the cases, nobody, according to Consul Ivor Rawlinson, thought to examine them.

Presumably, copies of the documents have ended up in the archives of both the British and Italian intelligence services, the Italian set being, one imagines, somewhat more complete. A SISMI report obtained through parliamentary channels in 1988 only compounds the misgivings. Side-stepping my request for access to Mr Brown's papers, the secret service sent me a one-and-a-half-page report into the circumstances of his demise. According to the report, Brown had been found in possession of 'numerous newspaper cuttings concerning terrorism and organized crime'. An initial examination led the Pisa police to the perceptive conclusion that Brown 'might be a collector of cuttings or a student of terrorism and crime'. Other statements in the report are somewhat more illuminating. 'This office learnt from the corresponding British service, immediately contacted on the subject, that Brown was well known for his manias about "intelligence". In fact, in 1982, he drew attention to himself in Holland through his statements about a supposed threat of an attack on a Concorde airliner. On that occasion it was discovered that his information was based on an interpretation of a novel described by Brown as being "encoded".'

What is interesting is that Brown's documents appeared to be sufficiently important to justify the Italian secret service 'immediately' contacting its British equivalent. But there is no mention of the fact that they had already contacted their British counterparts in 1978 in connection with one of Brown's letters about the Moro case, receiving substantially the same reply, that Brown was a nut. Even more interesting is the fact that there is no mention whatsoever of the Moro case, a subject which obsessed Brown and which, according to La Rana, his documents discussed. The secret service report concluded by pointing out that the British police had supplied information through Interpol indicating that Brown had made numerous false statements 'about murders, drug trafficking, the poisoning of elephants, as well as the fact that he knew the true identity of the murderer of President John F. Kennedy. Although he has no criminal record in England, Brown has been registered as being mentally unstable.' The fact that SISMI preferred not to discuss Brown's alarming claims about the Moro case is not, of course, proof that the claims are true and that the secret service was intent on a cover-up. An open and frank discussion, or even a mention of them, might on the other hand have provided convincing evidence that there was no substance to the Scotsman's allegations.

Another reason for giving Brown's claims serious attention is the quality of his informants. Besides his contact with Semerari, Brown appears to have met the Camorra boss Raffaele Cutolo on a number of occasions. It was Cutolo who acted as a mediator to obtain the release of kidnapped Neapolitan politician Ciro Cirillo from the Red Brigades and who has dropped menacing hints about the existence of a 'Calabrian connection' in the Moro kidnap, as we have seen. Cutolo told a Naples magistrate in 1986 that during a pause in one of his trials he had been approached by a man aged between forty-five and fifty (a good ten years younger than Brown would have been at the time) who said he was 'aware of matters concerning the Cirillo kidnap and the Moro kidnap'.[31] He said the man claimed to have been in contact with his own lieutenant, Vincenzo Casillo, both during and after the Cirillo kidnap. Casillo, who was a wanted man at the time, played an active role in negotiations for Cirillo's release. 'He added that he had met

Casillo just a few days before his death [Casillo was blown up in his car in Rome in 1984], about which he was also informed.' Cutolo said the man gave his name as Martin Brown and that they had met subsequently on several occasions. 'In June of this year, I read in the papers that a certain Martin Brown had died of a heart attack in the street in Pisa (the same city and the same illness as in the death of Luigi Bosso).' Bosso was a criminal who had joined the Red Brigades while in prison and had also played a part in the complex negotiations for Cirillo's release. Cutolo's suggestion appears to be that there was something suspicious about both deaths. In reality, there is no evidence that Brown died of anything but natural causes. However, Cutolo's hint that Brown may have been a victim of foul play could be an indication of the sensitivity of the matters that he had discussed with him and a reminder that the Camorra boss was privy to some of Brown's secrets. There can be little doubt that Cutolo intended his references to Brown to be seen in a threatening light, since he prefaced them with complaints about his treatment in prison and remarked: 'I realize once again that I am being subjected to this special treatment in order to prevent me from speaking about delicate and compromising matters.' The Scotsman's allegations certainly merit some kind of an answer and a first step in the right direction would be to make available his papers.

Not long after Moro's murder, another baffling and alarming account of his ordeal came to light. It too challenged the official versions of the affair and saw the involvement of a number of personalities whose names crop up in other 'alternative' accounts. Once again, it has never been fully fathomed. The episode began while Moro was still alive. Ernesto Viglione, an Italian journalist working for Radio Montecarlo, told senior Christian Democrat Party figures that he had been contacted by the Red Brigades and offered the opportunity to interview the captive Moro. The interview never materialized, but after Moro's death Viglione's contacts, claiming they felt betrayed by the decision to kill the statesman, offered the authorities the opportunity to arrest the Red Brigades leadership with their help. This too failed to materialize and eventually it was discovered that Viglione's Red Brigades contact was a simple-minded man named Pasquale Frezza, who had a history of mental illness. Both were found guilty of concocting their story in order to prise money out of Christian Democrat politicians, though Viglione was acquitted of this on appeal.

What is of interest in this bizarre affair is the account of the kidnap that Viglione relayed to the authorities, the character of the people involved and their reactions as the story unfolded. It is hard to believe that Viglione, and through him some of Italy's most senior political and military figures, could have been taken in by a mediocre person like Frezza. Viglione was by no means naïve. He had been a parliamentary reporter before working for Radio Montecarlo and had also written for the P2-influenced magazine *Il Settimanale*. In 1976 he succeeded in interviewing the fugitive Stefano Delle Chiaie in Madrid for the magazine (26 May 1976). Another of his scoops, clearly laid on by the secret services, was entitled 'The strategy of tension has its headquarters in Prague' (9 June 1976) and claimed that the KGB used the Cuban and Czech secret services as proxies in the manipulation of European terrorism. This is hardly the kind of man one would expect to mistake a mental patient for a member of the Red Brigades. Among the normally perceptive people who appear to have taken Viglione's claims seriously were *carabiniere* generals Ferrara and Dalla Chiesa, the Defence and Interior Ministers and Christian Democrat leaders Flaminio Piccoli, Oscar Luigi Scalfaro and Amintore Fanfani.[32]

Still more remarkable was the content of Viglione's tale. One of his principal contacts was Moro's friend, Senator Vittorio Cervone, who was a leading campaigner for the establishment of a parliamentary inquiry into the Moro affair. The journalist played Cervone a recorded message from his Red Brigades contact: 'I am a member of the Red Brigades, I was at Via Fani but did not shoot; Moro should not have been treated as he was, he should not have died; we in the first group of the Red Brigades did not shoot, others fired because they were afraid of being recognized by Moro's escort. . . the whole operation was led by two Members of Parliament and a figure linked to the Vatican.'[33] Subsequently Viglione testified that, according to his contact, Moro's murder had not been carried out by the Red Brigades but by people working for men of power. He added that members of the *carabinieri* and the police were among those who did the shooting at Via Fani.[34] This last claim would go some way to explain the suspicion, voiced by the Moro family's lawyer during the trial, that the head of Moro's bodyguard had not immediately responded to his attackers because at least one of them was someone he recognized. Among other elements to emerge were Viglione's claim to have been offered access to Red Brigades documents and to the text of Moro's interrogation, and indications that Toni Negri, whom Viglione referred to as the leader of the Red Brigades group opposed to Moro's murder, may have been in some way involved in the affair. Furthermore, it emerges that at one time Viglione referred to the person who later turned out to be Frezza as Francesco, a Calabrian, whom he believed to be Giustino De Vuono.[35] Viglione spent a considerable amount of time during the relevant period in Calabria, where he may well have been following up the Calabrian lead knowingly referred to by Raffaele Cutolo. He also claimed to be in possession of a number of sensitive documents which he had stored in a Swiss bank.

All this gives the impression that the street-wise Viglione, a friend of Mino Pecorelli's, may well have had a genuine channel of communication with the Red Brigades. It is simply not credible that he and all the others involved could have been duped by Frezza or that he could himself have dreamed the whole thing up; if so, what was his motive? The amounts of money he was given for his research efforts were in any case modest. Some light may be cast on this by Frezza's own account. He claimed that Viglione asked him to play the role of a terrorist in a meeting with Senator Cervone because the people he was in touch with did not want to come out into the open. Frezza agreed and learnt by heart the story he was to tell Cervone and which Viglione had written down for him.[36] What seems likely is that Viglione did have a genuine contact with people involved in the Moro affair, possibly with Giustino De Vuono, but that when the full gravity of it emerged it was decided to put an end to the matter by passing it all off as the invention of a lunatic. Alternatively, the whole affair may have been concocted in order to convey a message to particular politicians, making it clear that Viglione and his friends had inside information on the affair, regardless of whether or not all the ingredients of his own account were true. At his trial, five leading Christian Democrat politicians testified on Viglione's behalf, as did three influential members of the P2 lodge.[37]

Franco Ferracuti was the expert called in to do a psychiatric analysis of Frezza for the Rome assize court. 'He was a mythomaniac but I said he was telling the truth on that occasion,' he told me. 'The court didn't believe me, which didn't surprise me.' Even more significant than Ferracuti's analysis of Frezza is his response to the ingredients of Viglione's tale, 'I have heard that story from people in SISDE.' Both parts of the story? About the *carabinieri* participating in the Via Fani ambush as well as the two Christian Democrat politicians and the man from the Vatican having organized the operation? 'Yes, there was something about people from the Vatican being involved.' It is indeed extraordinary that what at first sight would appear to be ludicrous rumours should have been discussed by members of the domestic secret service without immediately being rejected as such. Again, one gets the impression that the truth may be a far cry from the official versions of the kidnap.

A number of other statements may cast further light on what was at issue in the Viglione episode. In an article for *L'Espresso* (25 February 1979), journalist Gianluigi Melega, who had first broken the story in the magazine, asked a series of detailed questions that were all clearly based on the results of his own research. 'Is Viglione aware of links between common criminals, who are fascist sympathizers and specialize in kidnaps, and political terrorism?' he asked, reviving the suspicions about underworld involvement in the affair. Cervone's own utterances are also illuminating. In a book published shortly after the Moro affair, he wrote: 'Freeing one's own party from suspicion is a duty. And don't say that there are no suspicions, that it's pure fantasy, that people are not saying whatever they like in public and in private about this or that Christian Democrat leader, that they are not talking about the possibility of saving Moro, of his prison being known, of a team ready to go into action, of a veto and countermanding order.'[38] Some of the questions he proposed for the parliamentary commission to consider, but which were subsequently dropped from its brief, were based, at least in part, on his involvement in the Viglione affair. 'Whether ex-members of the disbanded Italian secret services had a role in the affair and what that role was; whether it is true that the Red Brigades, when they wanted to use a secret code, adopted an old military cipher that could only be known by members of the secret services; whether it is true that there are recordings, made at the time, of statements by Red Brigades members; what is their content and how reliable are they. . .?'[39]

The suggestion that the authorities had identified Moro's prison, made by Pecorelli in October 1978 and repeated by Cervone, was also advanced by a small Milanese news agency, ANIPE, similar in style to Pecorelli's *OP*. 'It would appear that the *carabinieri* had found Moro's prison. Furthermore it seems that they had discovered the food store where the BR members bought their supplies. It was a place selling roast meats in the centre of Rome near Piazza Nicosia. According to our confidential sources, the *carabinieri* intended to intervene in a military operation to free the prisoner. The proposal was not accepted by the government,' the agency claimed (4 November 1978). The article was picked up by *Panorama* (24 May 1987), which interviewed the ANIPE editor nine years after the event. 'There was no reaction and silence is always a response worth reflecting on,' Livio Ricci told the magazine.

What is remarkable about all these strange claims is that they come from a fairly wide pool of people, many of them in contact with one another and some undoubtedly in contact with the secret services and therefore in a position to be well informed. They are surprisingly consistent, with certain themes recurring over and over again. It is possible of course that false information was passed from one person to another within the pool or that they were all part of a determined conspiracy to muddy the waters of the Moro affair. This is unlikely, though, as there is objective evidence to back many of their assertions. Finally, a number of people who unquestionably did not belong to this pool have come to share their suspicions. Some of them are former members of the Red Brigades.

Notes

1 Martin Brown (Brown's nephew) to the author, 1987.
2 Umberto Cecchi, *La Nazione*, 14 June 1986.
3 P2 Commission, Allegati alla Relazione, Vol. 7, Tome 18, Rome, 1987, p. 454.
4 Ibid., p. 522.
5 Licio Gelli to the author, 27 June 1989.
6 P2 Commission, Allegati alla Relazione, Vol. 7, Tome 18, Rome, 1987, pp. 502-3.
7 Ibid., pp. 911–12.
8 Elda Colasanti Semerari to Bologna magistrates, 19 January 1985.
9 Pietro Calderoni, *Servizi Segreti*, Tullio Pironti, Naples, 1986, p. 191.
10 Franco Coppola, *La Repubblica*, 21 May 1985.
11 Carlo Semerari to P.M. Libero Mancuso, Bologna, 30 December 1984.
12 Franco Ferracuti to the author, 22 June 1989.
13 Letter from US embassy to Rome police, 16 December 1975.
14 G.I. Giorgio Floridia, Ordinanza di scarcerazione di Ronald Stark, Bologna, 11 April 1979.
15 Ibid.
16 Marcella Andreoli, *L'Europeo*, 17 January 1983.

17 Giorgio Floridia, op. cit.
18 Maurizio De Luca and Mimmo Scarano, *Il Mandarino è Marcio*, Editori Riuniti, Rome, 1985, p. 118.
19 Ibid., p. 117.
20 Ibid., p. 121.
21 Giovanni Cerruti, *La Repubblica*, 20 October 1978.
22 Report of the Moro Commission, Rome, 1983, p. 144.
23 Ibid., p. 144.
24 Giuseppe De Lutiis, *Storia dei Servizi Segreti in Italia*, Editori Riuniti, Rome, 1984, p. 172.
25 *Corriere della Sera*, 29 November 1988.
26 Maurizio De Luca and Mimmo Scarano, op. cit., pp. 119–20.
27 IRS Report on The Brotherhood of Eternal Love, Los Angeles, 12 December 1973, p. 9.
28 Maurizio De Luca and Mimmo Scarano, op. cit., p. 117.
29 Ibid., p. 123.
30 Umberto Cecchi, *La Nazione*, 15 June 1986.
31 Raffaele Cutolo to G.I. Carlo Alemi, Bellizzi Irpino prison, 19 December 1986.
32 Gianni Flamini, *Il Partito del Golpe*, Vol. 4, Tome, 2, Bovolenta, Ferrara, 1985, pp. 569–70.
33 Gianluigi Melega, *L'Espresso*, 11 February 1979.
34 Ernesto Viglione to G.I. Ferdinando Imposimato, Rome, 6 February 1979.
35 Ernesto Viglione to G.I. Francesco Amato, Rome, 30 March 1979.
36 Pasquale Frezza and Ernesto Viglione to G.I. Francesco Amato, Rome, 9 March 1979.
37 Sergio Flamigni, *La Tela del Ragno*, Edizioni Associate, Rome, 1988, p. 267.
38 Vittorio Cervone, *Ho Fatto di Tutto per Salvare Moro*, Marietti Editori, Turin, 1979, p. 66.
39 Maurizio De Luca and Mimmo Scarano, op. cit., p. 254.

[16]

MORE VALUED
THAN MORO?

It is futile to speculate on whether or not Moro might have been
saved if the government had been prepared to meet some of the
terrorists' demands. Despite the existence of secret contacts
between some of Moro's friends and his captors, the bulk of the
government seems to have remained firmly opposed to negotiations. It
was their firm attitude that drove Moro to write his desperate appeals
from prison, reminding his erstwhile colleagues of previous occasions
when a more flexible approach had been preferred. In April 1989,
Licio Gelli gave a television interview in which he suggested that Moro
might well have been saved, that those who sought his release came
close to achieving their aim but were ultimately thwarted because a
part of the government did not want Moro freed. Gelli's claim,
delivered with an insinuating smile, seems to echo the allegations
made by Pecorelli, Giovanniello and others. It also coincides with the
testimony of Eleonora Moro, who claimed in court that action was
taken to block mediation efforts by the International Red Cross and
by Pope Paul VI. She said she had spoken personally to the pontiff,
who was a long-standing friend of her husband's. 'He told me he
would do everything possible and I know he tried, but he found a lot of
opposition.' Red Cross efforts, she said, were similarly thwarted. 'It
seemed in the beginning that something could be achieved, but all of a
sudden. . . I don't know who intervened to block the negotiations.
Somebody told the Red Cross that Italy did not appreciate its efforts.'[1]
Moro himself had his own suspicions as to who might be behind the
government's policy of rigour. 'Is there perhaps an American and
German recommendation behind the decision to stand firm against

me?' he asked in one of his letters from prison.[2] Moro's intuition was subsequently confirmed by the admission of Cossiga's American adviser Steve Pieczenik, at least in regard to his own role.

Whatever vacillations and secret talks there may have been, the impression that emerges at the end of the day is of a government determined to resist the Red Brigades' blackmail and strongly supported in this policy by the PCI. The only government party to break ranks on the issue was the Socialist Party. This is why the government's more flexible attitude to subsequent terrorist kidnaps seems all the more grave and inexplicable. A government that was prepared to sacrifice the life of one of Italy's most influential political figures was ready to negotiate with the Red Brigades for the release of other relatively minor figures. In one case the circumstances of the negotiations and the deal finally reached were of such a disreputable nature that those who participated have been forced to deny the evidence and the episode has gone to swell the armoury of Italy's legion of political blackmailers.

The first kidnap to put the government's policy of firmness to the test came in Rome on 12 December 1980, with the seizure of Giovanni D'Urso, a magistrate working on prison administration at the Justice Ministry. The Red Brigades campaign concentrated on improving the lot of the organization's imprisoned members. Just before Christmas the government announced its intention to close the tough maximum security prison on the island of Asinara, off the north coast of Sardinia. This had been one of the Red Brigades' demands and government insistence that the decision had been taken even before D'Urso's kidnap did little to salvage appearances. On 15 January 1981, D'Urso was released and there was a widespread perception that the authorities had bargained for his freedom.[3]

It was during the D'Urso kidnap that the role of Red Brigades leader Giovanni Senzani first came to light. Senzani, an academic criminologist and one of the few Red Brigades members with a genuine intellect to be identified, was challenging Moretti for control of the terrorist organization. While Moretti saw the Red Brigades as a warrior élite blazing a trail for the rest of the population to follow, Senzani's views were closer to those of Negri and Autonomia Operaia, believing there was room for all the disenchanted, including common criminals, in the ranks of the revolution. It was Senzani who ran the D'Urso kidnap, currying favour with the imprisoned BR leadership by involving them in decisions and setting an improvement in prison conditions as his principal objective. Conveniently for him, Moretti was arrested in Milan on 4 April 1981, leaving the road open for him to dominate the last stage in the Red Brigades' history as a serious challenge to the state. Under Senzani the image of a once idealistic organization would become seriously tarnished: utterly merciless and dabbling in a sinister dalliance with organized crime and the secret services. Extraordinarily, the man running the D'Urso kidnap chose to deliver the text of a Red Brigades interview and of D'Urso's interrogation to two journalists from *L'Espresso* in person. The journalists were aware of his identity and one of them ultimately revealed it to the police. Senzani's decision to run this unnecessary risk reveals either an astonishing faith in his own immunity or incredible stupidity.[4]

Suspicions about Senzani's true role abound. Born in 1940, he was a squat, thick-set man with dark hair and usually sported a beard or moustache. He has been identified as 'Blasco', depicted in a comic strip published by the extreme left magazine *Metropoli* in May 1979 as the man who brought the order for Moro's execution to the Rome column of the Red Brigades. His criminology studies led him to travel extensively and appear to have given him almost unrestricted access to Italian prisons. In 1971 he was working at a cultural centre in Torre del Greco near Naples, heartland of the Camorra faction controlled by Raffaele Cutolo. In 1974 he won a research grant to study at the University of Berkeley in California, where he remained until 1975. Interestingly enough, these were the years that the predominant colour of Italian terrorism was changing from black to red, as General Miceli had so accurately predicted. In 1979 he was suspected of membership of the BR 'Tuscan Revolutionary Committee' and arrested by Florence magistrates but released for lack of evidence. He is suspected of having selected three magistrates working on prison reform for assassination. Girolamo Minervini, Gerolamo Tartaglione and Alfredo Paolella were all murdered by left-wing terrorists. Tartaglione and Paolella were shot dead in 1978, the first by the Red Brigades and the latter by Prima Linea. Minervini was killed by the BR in 1980. They were all committed reformists and they had all attended a conference of criminologists in Lisbon where Senzani had also been present.[5]

But the real cloud overshadowing Senzani's career is that of his ambiguous relationship with the secret services. Numerous witnesses have alluded to this, among them Arrigo Molinari, deputy Genoa police chief in the late 1970s. It was Molinari whose testimony about the links between Licio Gelli and the US embassy in Rome was reported by *L'Espresso* and then, as we have seen, commented on by the embassy in a somewhat lame cable to the State Department. Molinari claimed he had joined the P2 lodge in 1978 in order to gather intelligence on the Red Brigades. 'Through P2 we hoped to discover BR cells. We knew that Senzani was recruiting among students and professors under the guise of helping prisoners' families.'[6] Molinari said he had been able to identify three Red Brigades members, including Senzani, with the assistance of William Rosati, a leading P2 member from the Genoa area.[7] Given P2's association with the right, it is surprising that a senior police officer should consider it worth joining the lodge in order to glean information about the Red Brigades and curious that one of the terrorists he was able to track down through the lodge should turn out to be Senzani. According to Molinari, Senzani was 'definitely in contact with representatives of SISMI'[8] and had enjoyed the protection of the authorities, who suppressed police reports on his suspect activities, during his early years as a terrorist.

This allegation has also been made by former BR member Roberto Buzzati, who has described a meeting between Senzani and a secret service agent outside Ancona railway station on 8 June 1981. Based on Buzzati's description of the man's appearance, it has been suggested that he could have been General Pietro Musumeci, a member of P2 and of SISMI.[9] Senzani told Buzzati that the man was 'a KGB agent who was also involved with our secret services.' Buzzati considered it strange that Senzani should be in contact with a KGB agent. 'In our documents we always defined the Eastern countries as social-imperialists. But at that time we had manipulative relationships even with the Camorra and the *'ndrangheta*, following the principle that one could make a pact with the devil if that would further the revolution.'[10]

What adds weight to these allegations is the fact that Senzani let his apartment in Via della Vite in central Rome to Luciano Bellucci, an external collaborator of SISMI. Bellucci and Senzani had done their military service together in 1967 and had remained in contact subsequently, Bellucci occupying Senzani's Rome apartment while the latter was living near Naples and then in the United States.[11] After Moretti's arrest, Senzani inherited the BR leader's Parisian contacts: with the Hyperion language school and with Paul Baudet, a collaborator of the French Interior Ministry who posed as a left-wing subversive, further compounding the suspicions about Senzani's role.

Senzani's relationship with the security services is by no means straightforward. It was, after all, Senzani who organized the kidnap and cold-blooded execution of Roberto Peci, the brother of 'repentant' terrorist Patrizio. Roberto Peci was kidnapped on 10 June 1981, in his home town of San Benedetto del Tronto, and shot dead in a ruined farmhouse outside Rome some fifty-three days later. He was put up against a wall beneath a placard reading 'Death to traitors' and the Red Brigades actually recorded his execution on film. This ferocity was justified by the group as a means of discouraging other captured terrorists from following Patrizio Peci's example and collaborating with the authorities and by their claim that Roberto Peci had himself betrayed the names of a number of terrorists from his area to the police. Some have even suggested that Senzani's ruthlessness may have been prompted by a conviction that Patrizio Peci's betrayal went beyond that of merely collaborating with the police after his arrest, and they have seen this episode as indirect proof that Patrizio had been an infiltrator in the terrorists' ranks from an early stage, perhaps the infiltrator referred to by Caprara and Gelli. If this were true, it would be hard to see Senzani as an agent of those same security services that had allegedly manipulated Peci. It is by no means easy to discern the loyalties of a man like Senzani, embroiled as he was in a game of mutual blackmail and manipulation with the secret services.

Where Senzani's role reaches its moral nadir is in his direction of the kidnapping of Ciro Cirillo, a Christian Democrat local politician from Naples. Cirillo, a regional councillor, was a representative of Christian Democrat power at local level, based on clientelism and corruption. He represented, in short, the soft underbelly of the great white Christian Democrat whale, to borrow an image often used by Italian journalists to describe the party. It is therefore extraordinary that Christian Democrat leaders, who stood firm against Red Brigades demands when one of the party's most influential politicians was kidnapped only four years earlier, should have been prepared to negotiate for the release of so modest a figure as Cirillo. What makes the contrast all the more striking is that it appears that they were prepared to do a deal of indefensible cynicism in exchange for Cirillo's life. Cirillo was seized by the Red Brigades on 27 April 1981. His bodyguard and driver were shot dead and his secretary wounded as he was snatched from the garage beneath his home. He was released after eighty-nine days in captivity, on 24 July, following the payment of a ransom of 1.45 billion Lire (£850,000) to the BR and of 2 billion Lire (more than £1 million) to the Camorra as a reward for its mediation efforts.[12] The money was raised by the Cirillo family and by party supporters on the understanding that those who contributed would be in line for compensation when the government awarded contracts for reconstruction work resulting from the 1980 earthquake in the Naples region.

Negotiations for Cirillo's release were handled by the secret services, with help from local politicians and members of the Camorra. Businessman and secret service collaborator Francesco Pazienza also played a leading role, regularly accompanying the negotiating team that trooped off to visit Camorra boss Raffaele Cutolo in his prison cell at Ascoli Piceno. Cutolo was considered to be an ideal mediator, given the pervasive power of the Camorra in the Naples area and the organization's desire to bring the police emergency to an end so that it could get back to its normal illicit activities. Under the protective mantle of the secret services, the motley assortment of negotiators had no difficulty in gaining unrestricted access to the lax prison where Cutolo was being held. SISMI officers General Pietro Musumeci and Colonel Giuseppe Belmonte were also prominent in the affair. A Justice Ministry report refers to links between the secret services, the Camorra and P2 initiating at this time and continuing subsequently.[13] As we have seen, there is every reason to believe that such links had been forged much earlier, perhaps at the time of the Moro kidnap. Among those to call on Cutolo was his right-hand man Vincenzo Casillo, himself a fugitive from justice, and who Cutolo has claimed had been working for the secret services since 1978.

Grave though it was that representatives of the state should agree to large cash payments to the Red Brigades and the Camorra, there were other even more sinister aspects to the deal. According to one of Cirillo's BR guards, the Camorra offered the Red Brigades, on behalf of interested Neapolitan politicians, not only money but 'a list of names and addresses of Neapolitan magistrates. We also learnt that the Camorra had offered to carry out attacks on magistrates selected for them by the Red Brigades.'[14] The claim is supported by a document written by Senzani and later found in a BR base in Rome. It too refers to a cash offer for Cirillo's freedom. 'Naturally it's Cutolo who makes the offers, adding the possibility of the future liberation of one of our companions, an arms consignment and a number of operations to

[330]

eliminate local cops. The tone with which the offers are made is not provocatory but of the following tenor: he (Cirillo) is certainly a pig. He deserves to die. But for our general interests and specifically for our building interests, we would prefer it if a solution could be reached that was beneficial to everyone.'[15] The document was described by Judge Imposimato as being 'of indisputable value as evidence'. Its implications were also accepted by a parliamentary committee which investigated the role of the secret services in the Cirillo affair. The committee's report described how the operation to secure Cirillo's release ended up with 'the payment of a large ransom to a terrorist group which would have used it to continue its attack on the state, with the offer by the Camorra to the Red Brigades to carry out a number of operations to eliminate magistrates and policemen and with other rewards to the Camorra mediators'.[16] One of those who participated in the negotiations, businessman and Pazienza associate Alvaro Giardili, has illustrated the value of Camorra assistance. He told magistrates that Cutolo's followers had threatened the Red Brigades that they would kill a hundred people, both members of the terrorist organization and their relatives, if the BR killed Cirillo. Given the military strength of the Camorra, this was not a threat to be taken lightly.[17]

The utter cynicism of the whole operation is highlighted by evidence from Cutolo himself. He told magistrates that he had relayed a message from the Red Brigades to the negotiators that they would consider releasing another of the hostages they were holding at the time, Giuseppe Taliercio, the director of a chemical plant near Venice, in exchange for the publication of certain documents in a German newspaper. The negotiators replied that '"they couldn't give a damn" about Taliercio's life but they just wanted me to deliver Cirillo as soon as possible'.[18] Taliercio was subsequently murdered by his captors. On the very day of Cirillo's release, a common criminal named Luigi Bosso, who had joined the Red Brigades in prison and had participated in the negotiations for Cirillo's freedom, was released from jail for lack of evidence. Journalist Paolo Guzzanti commented bitterly on the whole affair: 'So Cutolo had the power to release people from prison. If one thinks of the rigour with which an exchange of prisoners or concessions of any kind were refused at the time of the Moro kidnap, one feels like weeping. The facts of the story constitute a diabolical puzzle, a punch in the stomach to all civilized consciences.'[19]

It is therefore not surprising that those politicians who have been named as participating in the negotiations have been keen to distance themselves from the affair as far as possible. 'If the official policy of the [Christian Democrat] party was one of firmness, in reality there were people who operated to obtain Cirillo's freedom through the mediation of Cutolo and negotiations with the Red Brigades,' observed Examining Magistrate Carlo Alemi.[20] One of the names to crop up most frequently is that of Flaminio Piccoli. Alemi wrote: 'Piccoli, for example, has always maintained that he never went beyond seeking information that might lead to the identification of the prison, but a signed card from him ends up in the hands of Cutolo in prison and the explanations of the former Christian Democrat party secretary are by no means convincing.'[21] Piccoli's explanation for his dealings with Pazienza, in particular, seem somewhat lame. He told the magistrate that he had discussed the kidnap with Pazienza, who had said he might be able to pick up some useful information from his contacts in Naples, but that Pazienza had never mentioned Cutolo or the Camorra. 'Given the reputation that Pazienza had at the time, I had no reason to imagine that he might be in contact with such people,' he said.[22] This seems excessively naïve. Pazienza was unlikely to be able to identify Cirillo's prison by seeking information exclusively from respectable, law-abiding citizens. The parliamentary committee was altogether more realistic. 'A kidnap in Naples of someone of the importance of Councillor Cirillo not only could not have been carried out but could not even have been conceived without contacts with the Camorra. . .'[23] It is hard to believe that Piccoli was incapable of reaching this elementary judgement. In 1985, Piccoli's account of the affair received confirmation from a surprising quarter: one of Cirillo's kidnappers wrote to Piccoli from prison to say that the ransom paid had been the result of 'a direct and exclusive contact between the Red Brigades and Cirillo's family'. There had been 'no approach and no compromise made by the Christian Democrat Party'. As journalist Sandra Bonsanti has pointed out, this providential missive coincided with Piccoli's launch of a campaign for a reconciliation between the state and the scions of terrorism.[24]

Another Christian Democrat leader to be named in connection with the negotiations is Antonio Gava, a powerful Neapolitan politician who was Interior Minister in 1989. According to Cutolo, his henchman Casillo told him that he had accompanied Gava on a visit to Ascoli prison but that they had been unable to enter because there were too many journalists about.²⁵ Gava, on the other hand, insists that he knew nothing of the negotiations because of his position in the government and his 'conviction that the institutions could not and should not give in to the blackmail of the Red Brigades'.²⁶ But according to the testimony of Alvaro Giardili, he and Pazienza had met Gava to discuss the Cirillo case and had also made it clear that they were interested in winning government contracts for earthquake reconstruction. 'Gava went aside with Pazienza to discuss the Cirillo question. . . Pazienza told me that he had asked him to collaborate in saving Cirillo's life,' Giardili told the magistrates. Again Gava firmly denied this: 'I never went aside with Pazienza, I never spoke to Pazienza about the Cirillo kidnap. It was news to me that Pazienza had been involved over Cirillo.'²⁷ One has a choice between the word of a minister and that of a number of convicted criminals. The evidence seems to support the criminals.

When he was released, Cirillo was picked up by a traffic police patrol car, which was ordered to bring him in to police headquarters. The car had driven only a short distance when it was stopped by three other police cars whose occupants immediately purloined the kidnap victim and drove him to his home. There he was visited by Gava and other political colleagues, while magistrates who came to interrogate him were not allowed access to him.²⁸

Following Cirillo's safe release, the secret services cancelled all record of their involvement in the affair. SISMI officers told the parliamentary committee that this was because the secret services do not keep a record of their unsuccessful operations. They were not believed and, in any case, it is absurd to claim that the Cirillo operation was not a success.²⁹ Documents proving the involvement of senior Christian Democrat politicians in negotiations with the Camorra and the Red Brigades were found by police in Cutolo's home. These later disappeared and the head of the Naples police and another senior officer were accused of suppressing them. More alarming still was the fate that befell the head of the Naples Flying Squad, Antonio Ammaturo. He had been investigating the background to the Cirillo case, without informing his boss, the police chief. His sister testified that Ammaturo was demoralized and worried because of the results of his delicate investigation, while one of his close colleagues told magistrates that Ammaturo had told him that Gava and other Christian Democrat leaders had been involved in the efforts to secure Cirillo's release. 'I have finished, it's very grave,

Naples will tremble. I have sent everything to the [Interior] Ministry: be careful as I have sent you a copy of the report in the post,' Ammaturo told his brother. The report sent to the Interior Ministry has never been traced, nor did his brother ever receive his copy of it.[30] The head of the Flying Squad was murdered by the Red Brigades on 15 July 1982. The implications are particularly sinister when one remembers the Camorra's offer to assassinate Red Brigades targets as part of the deal to secure Cirillo's release.

The sensitivity of the whole affair was emphasized in a candid comment from the American consul in Naples to the State Department in July 1982. 'We will continue alert to any evidence that may emerge to link the Red Brigade [sic] with organized crime. Should such a connection emerge the GOI [government of Italy] may finally be forced to the drastic measures required to bring the mafiosi of Naples under some control. On the other hand, the reportedly wide political connections of the organized criminal element of Naples could, in the event of a proven Red Brigade/Camorra link, create some devastating repercussions in the government of this country.'[31] The implication is clear, not only that the failure to control crime in Naples resulted from a lack of political will, but that the BR/organized crime connection was a potentially explosive issue for the government, because sectors of the government were themselves linked to organized crime. This goes some way to explaining the reticence and mendacity of some of the Christian Democrat politicians questioned about the affair. It may also explain why a Naples assize court in 1989 reached the astonishing conclusion that there had been no secret negotiations between the secret services, Camorra and BR. The only person guilty of serious wrong-doing, the court found, was Raffaele Cutolo, who had tried to extort favours out of the state.[32] Significant sectors of the Italian press described the court proceedings as a farce.

If the Christian Democrat leadership comes out of the Cirillo affair with little honour, so do the Red Brigades. We have already mentioned the striking contrast between the fate of Moro and that of the mediocre Cirillo. While from the revolutionary's point of view it may be all very well to extort large amounts of money from the Christian Democrat Party, negotiating with the secret services and the Camorra is altogether another matter. Even if it was Senzani's intention to do the manipulating, the chances were that he would end up being the puppet of forces far more powerful than himself. Nor is it reassuring to note the blithe fashion in which he explained away the myriad suspicions that surround the Cirillo case. 'On the Cirillo affair I must make it clear that the plots that are constantly emerging are of no concern to me and of no concern to revolutionaries or to the Red Brigades,' he told journalists during a pause in a trial in Florence in 1985. 'The forces of the revolution have never sought or wanted mediators. These conspiracies are not our problem.'[33] This denial of the amply documented facts can only increase the doubts about Senzani's role.

Cutolo too has made his own contribution to the climate of suspicion. He told magistrates that he had come to the conclusion that 'the Cirillo kidnap was only apparently the work of the Red Brigades, who were just pawns manoeuvred by forces that were greater than them. It was all part of a political strategy devised by sectors of the Christian Democrat Party, of the Italian secret services and, behind them all, of the CIA.'[34] The Camorra boss claimed he had been told this, in particular, by one of the SISMI negotiators. One might be tempted to dismiss this view as fantasy or wilful disinformation, but considering the many twists in the Cirillo tale, that would be rash. Cutolo had been strategically placed at the point where the secret services, terrorism and organized crime met and mingled. If all these forces had been manipulated as part of a complex political game, the Camorra boss was likely to know it. And the knowledge would become a useful bargaining chip in his own political game.

Another Red Brigades kidnap that contrasts starkly with the Moro affair is that of General James Lee Dozier, snatched from his home in Verona on 17 December 1981 by a group of terrorists disguised as plumbers. The abduction of the highest-ranking American officer in NATO's southern Europe command prompted the largest manhunt in Italian history, larger even than the search for Moro. This time, of course, the Americans were prepared to help. US Ambassador Maxwell Rabb actually had to spend much of his time turning down offers of assistance from Washington, which wanted to flood Italy with military experts and FBI agents.[35] A stark contrast indeed with the CIA's blank refusal to lift a finger for Aldo Moro. The efforts were successful and on 28 January 1982 Italian police stormed an apartment in Padua and released the hostage unharmed. Dozier had been kept in a small tent inside the apartment with rock music blasting into his ears from headphones so as to isolate him completely from his surroundings. His release spelled the beginning of the end for the Red Brigades as a rapid succession of arrests wound up the remnants of what had been one of Europe's most fearsome terrorist organizations.

There are a number of conflicting accounts as to how Dozier's prison was identified and the contradictions between them have never been fully resolved. According to the official version, the success was achieved by good, dogged police work, the breakthrough coming after the arrest of one of the terrorists who acted as a driver during the kidnap. His name had been provided, according to this account, by the brother of arrested BR member Michele Galati.[36] But Galati himself, as we have seen, had already been collaborating with General Dalla Chiesa and it is not impossible that he was the original source of the information leading to the discovery of the prison. Galati has claimed, during interrogation by an Italian magistrate, that he actually warned Dalla Chiesa in October 1981 of the existence of a plan to kidnap a senior US officer based in the Veneto region. In January 1982 he complained to Dalla Chiesa that insufficient weight had been given to his warning. 'The general replied that he had warned the appropriate authorities of the danger,' Galati said.[37] If this is true it seems extraordinary that more effective measures were not taken to protect Dozier.

There are other possible explanations, however, of how the investigators may have succeeded in tracking down Dozier's prison. Numerous BR members had been arrested in the period leading up to Dozier's release; ten terrorists, including Senzani, had been captured on 8 January. The circumstances of Senzani's arrest have themselves given rise to doubts and suspicion. The left-wing newspaper *Il Manifesto* (12 January 1982) speculated that the BR leader may have decided to give himself up to the police: two of his associates had been arrested in Rome a week earlier but despite the fact that they knew the addresses Senzani was using, the ex-professor of criminology remained in Rome. Alternatively, the paper suggested, he may have been betrayed to the police by a foreign secret service, possibly Mossad. This ties in with the comment of Amos Perlmutter, editor of the US magazine *Strategic Studies*, that Italy owed Israel a considerable debt of gratitude for its help in the eradication of Italian terrorism. Perlmutter claimed that Mossad had played a crucial role in the rescue of General Dozier.[38]

What is certain is that during the Dozier kidnap Senzani tried to make contact with the terrorist cell holding the general, with a view to taking over control of the operation himself. It is therefore quite possible that it was his arrest that constituted the crucial breakthrough in identifying Dozier's prison. Perhaps to distract attention from this possibility, a number of colourful alternative accounts, probably containing a considerable element of truth, have been leaked to the press by the security services in the US and Italy. Most notable of these was the story published by *Time* magazine on 28 February 1983, claiming that Dozier had been located with the assistance of the Mafia, enlisted for the purpose by SISMI and the CIA, with the help of contacts in the American Mafia. The story is highly plausible, given the history of collaboration between the secret services and the underworld in connection with terrorism and the recent precedent of the Cirillo affair. It is likely that Pazienza had a part in the leaking of the story and interesting to note that one of the US Mafia middlemen was Alphonse Bove, named only as The Fat Man by *Time*. Bove, like Pazienza, had also played a role in the negotiations for Cirillo's release the previous year. Shortly after publication of the *Time* article, Pecorelli's successor as editor of *OP*, Paolo Patrizi, boasted to me that his news-sheet had actually scooped *Time* on the story. He showed me a detailed *OP* reconstruction of the Italian secret service role in the whole operation, naming secret service officers and describing the content of their phone calls. When I returned to the *OP* offices some years later to try and retrieve a copy of the article, the crucial issue of the news-sheet was missing; a fact that occasioned no surprise on the part of the *OP* staff. Clearly the original article had been deemed excessively indiscreet and had simply been removed from the archives. It seems rather unlikely that the secret services would have leaked a potentially embarrassing story to the press – the use of the Mafia to locate Dozier's prison – unless they were afraid that an even more embarrassing truth might come out.

The Dozier kidnap is one of the few episodes where there seems to be convincing evidence of contact between the Red Brigades and Eastern Bloc secret services. The organizer of the Dozier operation, Antonio Savasta, has spoken of an approach from the Bulgarian secret services with an offer of weapons and money in return for an opportunity to question Dozier. The offer was relayed by Luigi Scricciolo, an official of the socialist-controlled UIL trade union, via his cousin Loris Scricciolo, a member of the Rome Red Brigades column. A meeting between the latter and a Bulgarian agent was to have taken place at a Rome cinema but for some reason the Bulgarian failed to appear. Savasta was unable to give any details of subsequent contacts with the Bulgarians as he was arrested at the same time as

Dozier was freed. The Moro Commission described this affair as a first alarming exception to the Red Brigades' policy of total independence from foreign organizations, although, according to Savasta, the Red Brigades had decided to accept the Bulgarian offer of assistance while offering nothing in return.[39]

Even this episode may be somewhat more complex than at first appeared. Gelli's address book, confiscated from his office at Castiglion Fibocchi, contains the name of another Loris Scricciolo, a socialist Member of Parliament and a second cousin of the Red Brigades terrorist of the same name. Also listed was Piero Scricciolo, a businessman living in Arezzo and Luigi Scricciolo's uncle. Both had been members of P2. Moreover, Luigi Scricciolo, the trade unionist who put the Red Brigades in touch with the Bulgarian secret services, was in regular contact with the American embassy in Rome, calling on officials there almost every week.[40] It would therefore appear that the Scricciolo family could provide a potential bridge between P2 and the CIA on the one hand and the Red Brigades on the other. Official investigations have produced no evidence of this, but it is quite possible that the authorities preferred not to find it.

Dozier's rescue marked a crucial turning point in the war against the Red Brigades. Many terrorists were already in prison at the time of the general's kidnap as a result of information provided by an increasing number of 'repentant' terrorists following the example of Patrizio Peci and collaborating with the police in exchange for reduced sentences. After Dozier the process accelerated, with recalcitrant terrorists being encouraged to talk by police torture. Dozier's jailers, one of whom was holding a pistol to the general's head when the police burst into their Padua apartment, have given detailed and convincing accounts of the violence to which they were subjected following their arrest. Policemen involved in the rescue operation were convicted of using torture on them at a trial in July 1982 but were later acquitted on appeal.[41] The demise of the Red Brigades has been summed up by political commentator Giorgio Galli: 'The armed party was defeated when, having been infiltrated via the underworld, it compromised the prestige of the establishment in the eyes of their American ally by kidnapping an officer of the US Army. Having arisen from the left it had been allowed to operate in order to discredit the left.'[42]

Notes

1 UPI, Rome, 19.05, 19 July 1982.
2 Moro Commission, Relazioni di Minoranza, Rome, 1983, p. 96.
3 Giorgio Galli, *Storia del Partito Armato*, Rizzoli, Milan, 1986, pp. 237–9.
4 Antonio Padalino, *Panorama*, 26 January 1981.
5 Ibid.
6 *Panorama*, 13 August 1984.
7 Arrigo Molinari to G.I. Ernesto Cudillo, Rome, 9 November 1981.
8 *La Repubblica*, 29 August 1986.
9 Sergio Flamigni, *La Tela del Ragno*, Edizioni Associate, Rome, 1988, p. 179.
10 Silvana Mazzocchi, *La Repubblica*, 4 September 1986.
11 *L'Espresso*, 29 January 1984.
12 Marcella Andreoli, *Panorama*, 12 March 1989.
13 Quoted in Report on the Cirillo Kidnap by the Parliamentary Committee on the Secret Services, Rome, 1984, p. 18.
14 Sandro Acciari and Pietro Calderoni, *L'Espresso*, 19 February 1984.
15 Ibid.
16 Report on the Cirillo Kidnap by the Parliamentary Committee on the Secret Services, Rome, 1984, pp. 16–17.
17 *L'Espresso*, 29 January 1984.
18 Pietro Calderoni, *L'Espresso*, 13 December 1987.
19 Quoted in Giorgio Galli, op. cit., p. 260.
20 Giuseppe D'Avanzo, *La Repubblica*, 29 July 1988.
21 Ibid.
22 Sandro Acciari and Pietro Calderoni, *L'Espresso*, 30 July 1984.
23 Report on the Cirillo Kidnap by the Parliamentary Committee on the Secret Services, Rome, 1984, p. 9.
24 Sandra Bonsanti, *La Repubblica*, 13 September 1988.
25 Pietro Calderoni, *L'Espresso*, 13 December 1987.
26 Marcella Andreoli, *Panorama*, 12 March 1989.
27 Sandra Bonsanti, *La Repubblica*, 11 September 1988.
28 Antonio Padellaro, *Corriere della Sera*, 8 September 1988.
29 Report on the Cirillo Kidnap by the Parliamentary Committee on the Secret Services, Rome, 1984, pp. 19–20.
30 Sandra Bonsanti, *La Repubblica*, 13 September 1988.
31 Telegram No. 001641 from US Consul Naples to Secretary of State, Washington, July 1982.
32 Ermanno Corsi, *La Repubblica*, 26 October 1989.
33 *Il Mattino*, 1 November 1985.
34 Pietro Calderoni, *L'Espresso*, 13 December 1987.

35 *Time*, 28 February 1983.
36 Giorgio Galli, op. cit., p. 283.
37 Michele Galati to P.M. Carlo Nordio, Venice, 4 February 1982.
38 Giorgio Galli, op. cit., p. 281.
39 Report of the Moro Commission, Rome, 1983.
40 *L'Espresso*, 13 March 1983.
41 Giorgio Galli, op. cit., p. 288.
42 Giorgio Galli, 'Per una Storia del Partito Armato', Special Report, *Panorama*, 12 November 1984, p. 159.

[17]

TIME FOR *GLASNOST* IN THE WEST

I T seems appropriate that the kidnap of an American general should mark the first comprehensive defeat for the Red Brigades and the moment when their organization ceased to constitute a serious threat to Italian society. By 1982 political circumstances no longer required their presence on the scene. The Communist Party had proved itself in the hour of crisis to be a democratically reliable force. Even better, it had embarked on a process of slow but inexorable electoral decline. The insecurity caused by terrorism and the particularly damaging consequences of left-wing terrorism had deprived the party of the chance to form a genuinely alternative government in 1976, when power was almost in its grasp. And left-wing terrorists had robbed the party of its opportunity to share power through consensus with the Christian Democrats when the Red Brigades kidnapped and murdered Aldo Moro in 1978. By the time of the Dozier kidnap, the PCI was no longer a threat to the centre parties and the Red Brigades could safely be reduced to a marginal, maverick force, capable of the occasional sporadic political assassination but without even the illusion of a long-term, realizable political goal.

Italian public opinion is still far from ready to accept this kind of political analysis and will probably always remain deeply divided on the subject of the country's terrorist years. But a number of leading members of the Red Brigades have begun to discuss these theories and are now convinced that their struggle was exploited by conservative forces to block political change in Italy. Foremost among them is BR founder Alberto Franceschini, who formally dissociated himself from the armed struggle in February 1987 and is now engaged in cultural work during day-release from prison. 'One thing that has always struck me is the length of time that the Red Brigades lasted,' he told me. 'We were the only revolutionary organization in an advanced capitalist country that has lasted over the years. I used to think that this meant that Italy was a country ripe for revolution.' Franceschini no longer harbours such illusions and is convinced that the police could have wound up the organization in 1972 after Pisetta's revelations and again in 1976. 'I had the impression that the *carabinieri* could have arrested us whenever they wanted to but they never went the whole way.' The purpose of this official leniency is now clear: 'Our activities were destabilizing; those who used us did so in order to achieve a stabilizing effect, so that there should be no change in Italy, to maintain the exclusion from power of the Communist Party and of the left. We were acting to bring about change and those who used us did so to prevent change. It's a paradox, absurd, incredible.'

Franceschini is convinced there are a number of obscure holes in the history of the Red Brigades, the most mysterious of all being the Moro kidnap. 'It's difficult to say who was responsible for it. The answer will probably never come out. The question is whether there is a desire to discover the truth among Italian politicians, who tend to prefer compromise to the truth. More will come out, but we will probably never get right to the bottom of it; perhaps in fifty years' time when our [the Red Brigades'] history no longer has any bearing on Italian politics. For the moment the affair is too sensitive.' For many years Franceschini refused to contemplate such notions and his words amount to an admission of the most comprehensive defeat possible of the cause for which he fought over four years and which has already cost him more than fifteen years in prison. If one of the most influential members of the early Red Brigades and a man of considerable integrity can bring himself to voice these suspicions, it is hard to see how the bland official reconstructions of the Moro affair can survive intact.

Franceschini is distrustful of erstwhile companions who partici-pated in the Moro operation and have never spoken out about it or have actually contributed to the official version. During the course of conversations in jail, Prospero Gallinari (who has remained silent) and Antonio Savasta (who collaborated with the authorities) both privately led Franceschini to understand that the BR base in Rome's Via Laurentina had been Moro's prison. 'When Savasta told the magistrates it was Via Laurentina that was immediately confirmed by the Interior Ministry,' Franceschini said. He added that he had never asked Gallinari about the base and was embarrassed when he was told, in breach of Red Brigades 'need to know' rules of confidentiality. Franceschini had the impression he was being provided with information that could one day enable him to corroborate the Red Brigades' account of its affairs, an account he did not believe.[1] It has now been established that Moro's prison was not in Via Laurentina.

Another person who does not believe the official accounts of the Moro affair is Moro's daughter, Maria Fida, a Christian Democrat senator. 'The lack of clarity on the Moro affair and the guilty consciences that exist about it create a permanent stumbling block in Italian politics,' she said. 'Those who are in a position to clarify what happened either do not want to or are not free to do so. I have no desire for it to be clarified because I know that's not possible.' She is angry that not enough was done to save her father. 'Absolutely nothing was done. There were no negotiations; various attempts to negotiate were nipped in the bud.' She believes that anyone trying to understand the Moro case should start from 1964 (the year of General De Lorenzo's attempted coup). 'The Red Brigades are a sector of Italian political life that is not representative of the forty years during which my father was active in politics. For as long as I can remember papa was always surrounded by threats, against him and against us. My father tried to ensure that political conflicts found their expression in Parliament. It is ironic that he should then himself be killed by this blind violence.' She summed up her attitude to the official reconstruction of her father's kidnap and murder: 'I would tend to be among those who doubt it. I believe there is a fear of what we, the family, might say to be the truth, even if it turned out not to be.'[2]

These doubts about the Red Brigades' handling of the Moro kidnap are angrily rejected by many of the imprisoned members of the organization, particularly those who have refused to recant and continue to believe in the justice of their revolutionary struggle. Almost all have now come to recognize that there is precious little prospect of victory. Among these are Prospero Gallinari and Francesco Piccioni whom I spoke to in the defendants' cage during a pause in the 1989 trial of the Red Brigades for armed insurrection against the state. They were ultimately acquitted, as the court decided that their organization had never been remotely capable of over-throwing the state. Many observers saw the verdict as a way of keeping the door open for an amnesty or the selective reduction of sentences for imprisoned terrorists who renounced the armed struggle. Gallinari is a thin, grey-haired man. He was wearing silver-rimmed glasses and appeared remarkably courteous and mild-mannered for someone who was once one of the most feared members of his terrorist organization. He is also the man who is officially thought to have killed Moro, though he will not comment on this, and there is reason to doubt it. Piccioni, in contrast, is a bluff, heavily built and seemingly jovial character.

Gallinari dismissed suggestions that the Red Brigades might have been manipulated by Italian or foreign secret services during the Moro kidnap. 'That's absolutely false. Moro was kidnapped by the Red Brigades, a communist organization that has always worked independently. There are no dark pages in the Moro kidnap or in all the history of the Red Brigades,' he said. 'I don't accept the argument that our activities moved the political centre of gravity in the country to the right.' He also rejected the suspicions about the role of the Hyperion language school and the suggestion that it had been run by the CIA. 'It was a logistical and survival centre for our people. There are masses of rumours about us that have simply been invented.' Gallinari had no qualms about the decision to kill Moro, while expressing respect for the way in which Moro conducted himself during his imprisonment. 'Moro was tried and condemned for everything he had done. Today he is portrayed as the greatest democrat in the country, but two years before his kidnap he was the politician whom the people most hated. He was not the greatest thief in the land but he ran the country in a particular way. The historic compromise was a trap for the Communist Party.'

This view of the historic compromise as a trap was reiterated by Piccioni. 'The PCI found itself supporting the government's political programme, which involved sacrifices on the part of the people, and which was eroding the social basis of the party's consensus.' Piccioni was unrepentant about his choice of the armed struggle: 'Our only error was not to win.' Nor would he accept that there had never been any prospect of a revolution in Italy. 'The international situation was very different in the 1970s. There wasn't the stability there is now. There was a crisis of American imperialism, so one couldn't rule out the possibility of Italy leaving the US sphere of influence,' he said.

'Popular protest even caused de Gaulle to totter,' added Gallinari. Like Gallinari, Piccioni firmly rejected the notion that the BR had colluded with either organized crime or the secret services during the Moro kidnap, when I asked him about the role of underworld forger Toni Chichiarelli in the affair. 'These people were working for the state. They couldn't have had any contact with the BR. All these rumours were created in order to reduce the history of the Red Brigades to something suspect. In practice, it is the only clean bit of history this country has.'[3]

Piccioni may be somewhat overstating his case. Nevertheless, if the unpalatable truth that emerges from this investigation is to believed, an explanation must be found for why so many former BR members, many apparently in good faith, reject the idea of secret service interference in the activities of their organization. One possibility is that they are lying, to cover up for their own responsibilities or because they fear for their lives. Another is that they genuinely believe their own denials but know only a small part of the overall reality. Yet another possible explanation is offered by Alberto Franceschini, who spoke of his own difficulties in coming to terms with the idea that the revolutionary struggle may have been exploited by conservative forces. 'If I had realized this while I was still in prison [full time] I would have committed suicide. This is why Curcio [whose personal integrity is widely accepted and who is still a full-time prisoner] refuses to entertain such ideas,' he told me.

Franceschini is deeply suspicious of the role of the Hyperion language school and of its forerunner, the Superclan, in the story of left-wing terrorism. He is critical of Mario Moretti for having maintained contacts with the Hyperion without informing the imprisoned members of the Red Brigades leadership. 'He knew of the difficulties we had had with the people from the Hyperion. He should have told us. At this point I believe that he was always in touch with them. Moretti never told us he had been a member of Superclan. He always said he couldn't stand the Superclan people. If it should emerge that he had been in contact with Superclan that would be extremely grave.' This is precisely the claim that has been made by a number of repentant terrorists and there is little reason to doubt their word. Hyperion member Corrado Simioni has aroused particular suspicion among those who have begun to question the whole history of red terrorism. 'He had a bad reputation, many people warned one to beware of him,' Franceschini said. 'He told us about his work for USIS in Munich, perhaps in order to cover himself. And there was another rumour going around in the far left that he had been in contact with [right-wing bomber Giovanni] Ventura in the late 1960s.' Professor Robert Kupperman, a terrorism expert from the Georgetown University Centre for Strategic and International Studies (CSIS), registered a similar reaction on hearing a potted biography of Simioni. 'He sounds like an agent for the Agency, but I don't know,' he told the author.[4] Kupperman was, after all, merely stating the self-evident.

Franceschini also has doubts about the role of Prospero Gallinari, though he retains considerable respect and affection for him. 'Gallinari was in Superclan and he may have been another infiltrator in the Red Brigades on their behalf. He is a typical Stalinist: he would be capable of killing his own mother if they told him to do it. But I am convinced that Prospero is a comrade. He still probably believes that the Superclan people were real revolutionaries.' Franceschini has greater difficulty in judging Moretti's role but ultimately comes down to the view that the two of them may have been manipulated by other smarter operators and ended up by unwittingly serving reactionary interests. 'He [Prospero] and Mario are not agents. They are convinced BR members.' But he has few doubts about the manipulative role played by the Superclan/Hyperion group. 'They were just the people to do it. Superclan's plan was to direct all the groups of the far left. One of their people who collaborated with the magistrates said they had a couple of people infiltrated into the Red Brigades and a couple in Parliament. Their plan resembles that of P2, creating an informal [political] party within the left. They played the role of the so-called "third level" of the Mafia. They were the Cupola [the governing body of the Mafia].'

Franceschini endorsed Judge Calogero's theory of a secret intelligentsia, identifiable at least in part with the Hyperion group, pulling the strings of Italian terrorism. 'Effectively, Calogero was right. He's a judge whose career has been destroyed because of it.'[5] Calogero's view also receives authoritative confirmation from General Carlo Alberto Dalla Chiesa. A declassified State Department cable from 1981 reports on a pre-broadcast viewing of a television interview with the general. 'Dalla Chiesa suggested that Toni Negri, the jailed intellectual whose guilt or innocence of terrorist activity has been heatedly debated, was part of the brains of the Red Brigades, whereas BR founding father Renato Curcio fell into the category of executioner [soldier].'[6] The precise relationship between Negri and the Red Brigades has never been fully clarified and most BR members claim their organization rebuffed Negri's attempts to take it over. Dalla Chiesa's revelation that he considered Negri to be 'part of the brains of the Red Brigades' is a powerful endorsement of Calogero's interpretation, which does not necessarily require Negri to be the overt or even generally accepted leader of the BR.

More sensitive still is the suggestion made by Robert Kupperman of CSIS that Negri may have been a US intelligence asset all along. '[CIA director of counter-espionage James] Angleton made the allegation – not to me, so it's only hearsay – that Negri was an FBI plant.' This is astonishing corroboration from within the American intelligence community of the view put forward by Mino Pecorelli in his *OP* article on Negri. Kupperman also referred to tension between the CIA and the Italian secret services during the 1970s. 'The FBI guy [at the Rome embassy] ended up being the conduit for a lot of stuff that should have been handled by the CIA,'[7] he said. Officially, the FBI does not operate outside the United States except in exceptional circumstances and at the invitation of foreign governments. In practice, it is quite possible that the FBI was actively involved in penetrating European terrorist organizations and running operations about which the Rome CIA station might well have had qualms. It is likely, in any case, that Negri would have come to the Bureau's attention during the course of his numerous visits to the United States, where he frequented members of the US Workers' Autonomy movement and the left-wing magazine *Zero Work*. The latter organizations would undoubtedly have attracted the attention of the FBI.

It is worth remembering, in this context, one of the comments made in the recommendations of the Pike Committee Report. 'The committee hearings on the FBI documented the problem of inform-ants turned *agents provocateurs*. Informants are necessary; the use of *provocateurs* is totally contrary to principles of decency and honesty. One of these *agents provocateurs* was William Lemmer, who worked in Florida as an informant for the Bureau. Lemmer infiltrated the Vietnam Veterans Against the War and became one of the most active members of the chapter. As such, he allegedly suggested violent means of expressing VVAW disagreement with the country's Vietnam war policy. This kind of activity, directed by the Nation's foremost law enforcement agency, is plainly and starkly wrong.'[8]

If the FBI could be involved with *agents provocateurs* at home, it is not hard to imagine it doing the same thing abroad. There would have been considerable advantages in running the most secret covert operations through an organization not normally thought to operate overseas. According to police official Federico D'Amato, 'The CIA distrusted Gelli but he had a connection with the FBI.'[9] D'Amato's assertion, if true, would be highly significant, particularly in the light of Angleton's allegation about Negri and Kupperman's suggestion that the FBI had taken on work in Italy that should normally have been handled by the CIA. D'Amato was certainly in a good position to know, having himself collaborated with the CIA over many years and with his name featuring on the P2 membership list. In reality, Gelli himself seems to be reconciled to being thought of as an agent of the CIA. In October 1990 he went to the small town of Riolo Terme to collect sixth prize in the local poetry competition. A journalist at the ceremony asked him if he belonged to the CIA. 'No,' he replied, 'but if I keep hearing it said, I will end up believing it myself.' (*Corriere della Sera*, 22 October 1990.)

According to the State Department cable, General Dalla Chiesa's television interview contained further enlightening comments. 'Asked about foreign terrorist influence, Dalla Chiesa said he could not answer beyond saying that as long as there exist powerful, opposed superpowers, it would be absurd to think that the respective secret services are not seeking theatres in which economic and military strategies could be carried out. . . On the terrorist campaign itself, the general hinted at "political responsibilities", noting "as a soldier, I can say that one rule has not been applied: that of exploiting one's success."' A year and a half later, Dalla Chiesa would be dead. It is not unreasonable to assume that his inside knowledge about which superpower's secret services had been most active in Italy and which Italian politicians had prevented him from exploiting his successes against the terrorists may have had something to do with his murder.

If overall responsibility for the strategy of tension rests with the United States, a great burden of guilt must be born by the Italians, without whose willing participation the country's terrorist ordeal would never have come about. It was, after all, a young generation of Italians which took to political violence like ducks to water. For a significant minority, the hundreds who took up arms and the thousands who supported them, a pistol became an everyday fashion accessory and the destruction of human life almost a trivial occurrence. Though Italy has a long tradition of political violence, the period that became known as 'the years of lead' saw a quite unprecedented, as well as unnecessary, slaughter. A decade later, the levels of political violence prevailing in the 1970s and the motivations behind it seem incomprehensible, light years away.

Equally guilty were the Italian politicians who managed and exploited the strategy of tension, descendants of the men who built the Roman empire proving themselves willing vassals in the making of a new colonial Italy, a troubled outpost of the US empire. Some of those politicians are now proposing to bring the country's terrorist season to an official close by finding a political solution to the problem of the 'political prisoners'. The idea of an amnesty, or much reduced sentences, for imprisoned terrorists is being put forward. Many of those who support the proposal are motivated by genuinely humanitarian considerations and Italy's penal system is, as a result of their efforts, in some respects surprisingly compassionate and civilized. But the inevitable consequence of the amnesty scheme is to remove any incentive for imprisoned terrorists, of right or left, to offer information to the authorities in exchange for a lighter sentence. The message to the prisoners is clear: wait quietly for your release. As a result, the many gaps in the history of terrorism are unlikely to be filled. It is worth remembering, in this context, Pecorelli's remarkable prediction that a great amnesty would arrive 'when national pacification has been completed'. Its effect would be to 'cleanse all and consign all to oblivion', thus rewarding the Red Brigades who had provided cover for the 'people whom they believe to be their occasional allies' and who had carried out the Moro kidnap.

The Italian Communist Party must bear some responsibility too for the political violence of which it was itself the principal victim. Many of the Red Brigades began their political life in the party's youth wing, and some party members, who never embarked on terrorism themselves, clung to their revolutionary aspirations long after they had become an historical anachronism. With a few notable exceptions, party leaders have been remarkably diffident in their denunciation of P2 and other related scandals. The impression is inescapable that some of the material that might cause embarrassment for government parties has become the subject of secret negotiations rather than of open political dialectic. If the PCI has become caught up in a web of reciprocal blackmail, it is possible that it is paying the price for the secret activities of its own revolutionary wing and of incautious contacts between some of its own leaders and Italian secret service bosses, possibly even of contacts with Gelli himself.

[349]

But the lion's share of the blame must go to those members of the Italian secret services who deliberately fostered terrorist violence, firstly by covering up for the right-wing bombers in the early 1970s and then by allowing the left-wing terrorists to have their head in the second half of the decade. The political exploitation of Italian terrorism was not the result of a seamless conspiracy. The conspirators were often divided by fierce factional rivalries and there were many in the police and secret services who opposed the strategy of tension and did their best to thwart it. Far fewer fragments of the story would have emerged if this had not been the case. But there can be little doubt that a conspiracy did exist and continued to function for more than a decade, that its ultimate purpose was to keep the Communist Party from power and that its ultimate guarantor was in Washington.

The manipulation of left-wing terrorism is a complex and controversial issue. Whether one takes the extreme view expressed by Gianfranco Sanguinetti that 'the BR are the state, that is to say one of its many armed appendages',[10] or the view that the far left was manipulated at arm's length into unwittingly serving the interests of the right, there can be little doubt that the activities of the left-wing terrorists ultimately played into the hands of the conservative conspirators. The truth probably lies somewhere in the middle. It is likely that the secret services had very few infiltrators within the ranks of the Red Brigades and may have exercised only a partial control over them. But the results were still excellent. From a secret service point of view, the exploitation of genuinely autonomous terrorists constituted the most sophisticated kind of covert operation and offered the added advantage of plausible deniability. At the same time, it seems likely that the secret services were able to exercise a more direct control at crucial moments in the Red Brigades' history. One has only to remember the attempts to infiltrate the left and provoke it to violence in the early 1970s, carried out in a somewhat crude fashion by secret service-controlled rightists, to realize that it is highly unlikely that the terrorism of the late 1970s and early 1980s could have remained entirely immune from secret service influence. This suspicion is reinforced by the sinister role of the Hyperion intellectuals, who exercised considerable sway thoughout the far left and in particular over the youth protest movements that gave rise to the Red Brigades.

Despite the traumatic results of the P2 Commission's investigation, when the Italian political establishment effectively put itself on trial, the P2 power network has never been completely dismantled. One of the reasons was that the political establishment was simultaneously defendant, judge and jury, and so had a natural interest in minimizing the sentence. The international implications of the conspiracy were also too disturbing to be fully aired in public. It is illuminating that Tina Anselmi, who as president of the commission genuinely sought to penetrate the secrets of the lodge, refused to discuss the subject when asked several times for an interview in 1989. Licio Gelli, in contrast, was happily receiving the world's press at his luxury Tuscan villa and lecturing them on the unjust political persecution he had suffered. It was certainly not the P2 boss who gave the impression of being cowed or vanquished. After all, the government of the day was one that he had long advocated: based on an alliance between the Christian Democrats under Giulio Andreotti and Bettino Craxi's Socialists.

It is ironic that the United States, a profoundly democratic country and itself frequently the victim of international terrorism, should have played such an ignoble role in recent Italian history. There can be little doubt that much of the responsibility for what happened as a result of the strategy of tension rests with the United States. The strategy was aimed at keeping the Communist Party out of power in Italy. For the Italian secret services to have persevered with it for so long, it must have had the endorsement of NATO and of NATO's most powerful member in particular. Since the end of the Second World War the United States has exercised great and only gradually diminishing influence over the Italian secret services; it is unthinkable that those secret services could have been involved in major abuses and in collusion with terrorism for more than a decade without the approval of the NATO security establishment. It might be claimed that the intervention of the secret services averted a possible civil war and prevented even greater bloodshed but the argument is unconvincing. It fails to take account of the fact that under Enrico Berlinguer the bulk of the PCI was firmly committed to Western-style democracy. And it is hard to see how a strategy that cost the lives of many of the best and most honest servants of the Italian state, and included indiscriminate bombings against the public and the murder of Aldo Moro, could ever find justification.

The involvement of the United States in the strategy of tension is well illustrated by the close American ties of the P2 lodge. 'P2 was the bonding mechanism of the extreme right' and 'the social network of the security services', according to Professor Kupperman. 'Someone [from the US intelligence community] would have been assigned to Gelli, to cultivate him as an intelligence asset. I don't know who.' Membership of P2 was clearly a touchstone of Atlantic loyalty. As CIA collaborator Professor Ferracuti has explained, it was almost automatic for members of the secret services to be invited to join the lodge when they reached a certain stage in their careers. Kupperman, who worked as a consultant to the Italian secret services on a number of occasions in the early 1980s, found that many Italian officers used their membership as a guarantee of their reliability. 'I met many military and intelligence officers who openly told me, a complete stranger to them, that they were members of P2. They would say: "You can trust me, I am a member of P2."' Kupperman's candour contrasts with the discomfort and reticence displayed by former CIA director William Colby when I questioned him about the US connections of P2 members Michele Sindona and Licio Gelli. He appeared not to have even heard of Gelli, despite the fact that the P2 boss has undoubtedly been a US intelligence asset since the end of the war and despite the fact that Colby had served with the CIA in Italy in the 1950s and then been director of the Agency in the 1970s. The FBI must have been extremely jealous of their asset if they concealed his very existence from the CIA, as Colby's apparent ignorance would imply. The State Department also appeared to be uncomfortable about addressing US-P2 relations, turning down a request for an interview about this and other issues with the lame excuse that there was no one on the Italian desk who had been there long enough to answer my questions. It was almost as though the US government kept no records and was unable to give an account of its activities stretching back more than five or ten years. The reality, it would appear, is that it can give no convincing explanation for the close relationship that once existed between the US government and its intelligence agencies and extremely unsavoury individuals such as Sindona and Gelli.

It is clear that the United States did not just operate in Italy through proxies such as the Italian secret services and the P2 lodge but was also directly involved in highly sensitive covert operations. Negri's involvement with US intelligence, the Hyperion language school and the secret CIA-PLO deal to provide the Red Brigades with weapons are but a few examples. Most sensitive of all is the role of US intelligence in the kidnap and murder of Aldo Moro. Unquestionably, the United States was opposed to his policy of accommodation with the PCI and had an interest in his removal. Unquestionably, the CIA refused to help in the search for his prison. Even Colby expressed surprise at this, while remaining sceptical of its veracity. 'If an allied country had its Prime Minister kidnapped we would do everything we could to help. Perhaps we didn't have anything useful to offer. I find it hard to believe that we refused to help.'[11] Whether US intelligence agencies were directly involved in some way in Moro's kidnap, as Martin Brown claimed, remains, for the moment, an open question.

The exact role of the different US intelligence agencies in Italy is also by no means clear. Certainly, the CIA was not the only agency to be actively involved in Italian affairs. The dispute between the CIA and Ambassador Martin over the latter's funding of General Miceli reveals that the Agency sometimes took a doveish line towards Italy in contrast to the hawks elsewhere in the government. According to some, the State Department secret service, the Bureau of Intelligence and Research, often adopted a more ruthless approach than the CIA. As we have seen, the FBI was allegedly in contact with both Negri and Gelli, and Gelli's sending of an Army Field Manual into Italy was presumably intended to imply that the Defence Intelligence Agency (DIA) had played some role in the destabilizing of the country. It also suggested that the US may have adopted a South-east Asian approach to Italian communism. What may, or may not, have been appropriate for combating communism in Vietnam was certainly inappropriate in Italy. The threat of the PCI to the democratic order in Italy has consistently been overstated, while the party's progressive distancing of itself from its revolutionary roots passed virtually unremarked. The question inevitably arises whether US and Italian intelligence officials may have deliberately over-emphasized the communist threat in order to give themselves greater power and greater leeway for their own manoeuvres. Italian political parties of the centre and right had a similar interest in stressing the communist menace when appealing to the US for financial assistance. Perhaps the best indication of the damage caused to the PCI by terrorism and the party's commitment to the democratic order can be seen in its expenditure on anti-terrorism propaganda, which outstripped that of any other party. In the two decades from 1969 to 1988 the PCI spent 20 billion Lire (more than £10 million) on the propaganda war on terrorism, compared to only 15 billion spent by the DC.[12]

Another former member of the Red Brigades to harbour doubts

about the manipulation of Italian terrorism is Massimo Gidoni, a wealthy psychiatrist from Ancona, who participated in the kidnap of Roberto Peci and took Mario Moretti on his 1979 gun-running mission to Lebanon on his yacht *Papago*. Significantly, this was one of the mysterious PLO arms consignments, the bizarre background to which we have already examined. In Cyprus the two met a man who Moretti said was a representative of a Palestinian group but who struck Gidoni as being surprisingly pale-skinned for an Arab. It was this man who provided them with the co-ordinates for their rendezvous off the Lebanese coast. As skipper, Gidoni found that the whole journey went surprisingly smoothly: too smoothly, he would later come to think.

Gidoni voiced his suspicions about Moretti, whom he had previously considered to be 'a good comrade and a friend', in an interview from prison with *Panorama* magazine (17 July 1988). 'People are now talking about a two-tier Red Brigades organization and I can't understand his behaviour, this refusal to clarify his position, even if only internally. I can understand the logic of refusing to deal with institutions and that's why I can't understand him when he agrees to go on television and continues to give explanations that are . . . not completely believable for anyone.' Gidoni described his reaction to the murder of Roberto Peci and the sense that something irreparable had happened in his own life as a result. He then added a comment that indicates that he too harboured suspicions about the true role of Peci's brother Patrizio: 'Immediately afterwards I thought that if that was the way it had turned out something important must have happened, that perhaps something serious to do with Patrizio Peci had been discovered.' The implication is that the Red Brigades may have become convinced that Patrizio had been an infiltrator all along: thus their ferocity towards his brother. Like Franceschini, Gidoni said he had joined the armed struggle in order to change the world but subsequently found that he was achieving exactly the opposite effect. 'I have often put this question to the older comrades: "If you know the truth then tell me, so at least I'll know which window to go to to collect my pension: whether it will be marked Red Brigades or Italian or foreign secret services."' 'It's obviously a joke,' commented the interviewer, 'but full of bitterness.' The truth may be bitter for ex-members of the Red Brigades but it is still more so for their wholly innocent victims.

Following the discovery of Moro's handwritten documents behind a panel in the Red Brigades base of Via Montenevoso in October 1990, Rome magistrates opened an investigation into the possible existence of contacts between the BR and Italian or foreign secret services. One of the magistrates, Franco Ionta, had specifically ruled out such a hypothesis in a report he had concluded not long before. He has been assigned an escort of ten bodyguards in view of the highly sensitive nature of his inquiry.

The recent revolutionary changes in Eastern Europe have altered the political geography of the globe and may have removed the last vestiges of the Cold War. As a result, the Cold War requirement that the PCI be permanently excluded from power in Italy should also fall. The PCI itself has decided to reflect its true social democratic identity by dropping the word communist from its name altogether. In October 1990 it was renamed the Democratic Party of the Left (Partito Democratico di Sinistra). PDS does not have much of a ring to it, however, and most people continue to refer to the party as the PCI ('pee-chee'). It is understandable that at a time when the superpowers were engaged in planet-wide competition and conflict, the role of the PCI, with 30 per cent of the electorate behind it and in a country as apparently unstable and socially divided as 1970s Italy, should have caused acute anxiety. But it was a major error to assume that the threat from Italian communism bore any resemblance whatever to that from Korean or Vietnamese or Soviet communism. Italian communism was a much more moderate and homespun affair.

It is clear that in the course of pursuing the conflict in Italy, the United States resorted to a number of tactics that it could never publicly justify, that negated the fundamental principles of Western democracy and involved the abandonment of the moral high ground in its ideological battle with the Soviet Union. There is no suggestion that this course was lightly or unthinkingly embarked upon, but it was the result of serious errors of judgement, both in exaggerating the perceived threat and in failing to select an appropriate response. Probably the United States' gravest blunder was the decision to ally itself with the unpresentable Sindonas and Gellis of the Italian scene, who will continue to cause the US government embarrassment long after they have all gone to their graves. As the Iron Curtain is rung down across Europe, it is perhaps time to examine the beam in our own eye and to practise a little *glasnost* in the West.

Notes

1 Alberto Franceschini to the author, 28 July 1988.
2 Maria Fida Moro to the author, 2 August 1988.
3 Prospero Gallinari and Francesco Piccioni to the author, 15 June 1989.
4 Prof. Robert Kupperman to the author, 7 December 1989.
5 Alberto Franceschini to the author, 3 October 1989.
6 Cable from US embassy, Rome, to Secretary of State, Washington, No. 5888454, Recent Developments Concerning Italian Terrorism, February 1981.
7 Prof. Robert Kupperman to the author, 7 December 1989.
8 Recommendations of the Final Report of the House Select Committee on Intelligence, Washington, 11 February 1976, p. 12.
9 Federico D'Amato to the author, 8 October 1989.
10 Gianfranco Sanguinetti, *Del Terrorismo e dello Stato*, Milan, 1980, p. xv.
11 William Colby to the author, 4 December 1989.
12 *Corriere della Sera*, 5 April 1988.

POSTSCRIPT

Since completing the book, the disconcerting series of acquittals in right-wing bombing trials has continued virtually uninterrupted. On 5 March 1991 the Court of Cassation quashed a Florence appeal court's guilty verdict on Pippo Calò and his associates for the Christmas 1984 train bombing. The court ruled there was insufficient evidence to convict Calò and ordered a new appeal court hearing. Some three weeks later, on 28 March, a Florence assize court sentenced MSI deputy Massimo Abbatangelo to life imprisonment for his alleged involvement in the bombing. The neofascist parliamentarian was accused of supplying part of the explosive used in the bombing to co-conspirators in the Neapolitan Camorra. The chances of the verdict being confirmed on appeal are slim, however. Abbatangelo's alleged accomplices in the Camorra have already been definitively acquitted.

On 4 April a Bologna appeal court quashed the life sentences on two neofascists, Mario Tuti and Luciano Franci, for the 1974 Italicus bombing. These verdicts appear to follow the now established pattern of terrorist bombings going unpunished and call into question the fascist label that has been attached to them. President Cossiga recently went so far as to apologize to a representative of the MSI for having publicly attributed the Bologna station bombing to the far right. The verdicts show up the true gravity of the judicial sabotage carried out over the years by the secret services and set the seal on the almost comprehensive failure of the judiciary to clarify the mysteries of Italy's terrorist past.

Investigations into Gladio do, however, appear to be making considerable progress. The crucial role of the United States in the genesis and running of the stay-behind network is becoming ever more plain. Magistrates have established that weapons for the gladiators were stored at the US military base of Camp Derby near Livorno and that numerous Italian right-wingers received military training at the base. It is also increasingly apparent that the true purpose of the organization was not to oppose an invasion of Italy by Eastern Bloc troops but to counter the internal threat of the PCI. The testimony of Peteano bomber Vincenzo Vinciguerra continues to be particularly illuminating. In an interview with *L'Espresso* magazine (4 April 1991) he emphasizes the anti-communist purpose of Gladio. 'I can say this from my own personal knowledge, given that members of this organization have carried out bombings and incited others to do so,' Vinciguerra told the magazine. He reeled off a list of twenty names of right-wingers who do not appear on the official Gladio membership list but who, he maintains, worked for the NATO organization. Vinciguerra described the gladiators as being inspired by 'a visceral anti-communism and an opportunism that meant they would stop at nothing.' The CIA has refused to permit the publication of the text of the original agreement setting up Gladio; an indication that its contents would still be viewed today as an unacceptable infringement of Italian sovereignty.

Rome magistrates are investigating the claim by Camorra boss Raffaele Cutolo that he was able to secure the release from the Red Brigades of Aldo Moro but that his offer to do so was turned down by political associates of the Christian Democrat leader. In a letter to the author, Cutolo said he learnt of the possibility of freeing Moro through a contact in the Magliana band. His willingness to discuss these matters was greatly reduced by the murder, in December 1990, of his twenty-eight-year-old son Roberto.

GLOSSARY

Autonomia Operaia, Workers' Autonomy, extremist left-wing organization

Avanguardia Nazionale (AN), National Vanguard, right-wing terrorist organization

Azione Rivoluzionarie, Revolutionary Action, minor left-wing terrorist organization

BR, Red Brigades, left-wing terrorist organization

CIA, Central Intelligence Agency (US)

CPM, Collettivo Politico Metropolitano, Metropolitan Political Collective, left-wing political organization

DC, Christian Democrat Party

DIA, Defense Intelligence Agency (US)

FBI, Federal Bureau of Investigation (US)

GAP, Gruppi di Azione Partigiana, Partisan Action Groups, left-wing terrorist organization

MAR, Movimento di Azione Rivoluzionaria, Revolutionary Action Movement, right-wing terrorist group

NAR, Nuclei Armati Rivoluzionari, Armed Revolutionary Cells, right-wing terrorist group

NATO, North Atlantic Treaty Organization

Office of Special Affairs (Ufficio Affari Riservati), political police department of the Interior Ministry

Ordine Nero, Black Order, right-wing terrorist organization

Ordine Nuovo (ON), New Order, right-wing terrorist organization

OSS, Office of Strategic Services, forerunner of the CIA

OVRA, Opera Vigilanza Repressione Antifascismo, The Organization for Vigilance and Repression of Anti-fascism, fascist secret police

Pace e Libertà, Peace and Freedom, right-wing association

PCI, Italian Communist Party

PLO, Palestine Liberation Organization

Potere Operaio, Workers' Power, extremist left-wing organization

Prima Linea, Front Line, left-wing terrorist organization
PSI, Italian Socialist Party
SID, Servizio Informazioni Difesa, Defence Information Service
SIFAR, Servizio Informazioni Forze Armate, Armed Forces Information Service
SISDE, Servizio per le Informazioni e la Sicurezza Democratica, Democratic Information and Security Service
SISMI, Servizio per le Informazioni e la Sicurezza Militare, Military Information and Security Service
Superclan, left-wing terrorist group
USIS, United States Information Service

INDEX

INDEX

Balzerani, Barbara, 263, 295
Banco Ambrosiano, 57, 68, 174, 203, 262, 302; fraudulent bankruptcy of, 64
Bani Sadr, Iranian President, 80
Barberi, Andrea, 75
Barbie, Klaus, 35, 68
Baudet, Paul, 328–9
Bellocchio, Antonio, 55
Bellucci, Luciano, 328
Belmonte, Colonel Giuseppe, 161, 330
Belsito, Pasquale, 301
Beltrametti, Eggardo, 41
Benedetti, Ermenegildo, 61
Beolchini, General Aldo, 37–8, 150
Berio, Duccio, 188, 189, 191, 192, 197–8
Berlinguer, Enrico, 18, 55, 113, 217, 222, 351
Bertolazzi, Pietro, 310
Bertoli, Gianfranco, 134, 152
Bilski, Jean, 301
Black Shirts Battalion, 50
Bocca, Giorgio, 208, 254, 258, 260, 272
Bogatyrëv, Petr, 179
Bologna station bombing (1980), 13–14, 40, 44, 64, 71, 76, 89, 105, 136, 142, 160–7, 170–3, 176, 194, 229, 257, 304–5
bomb attacks, 121–44, 160; Alto Adige, 121–2; Brescia (1974), 134–5, 136, 152; Christmas train (1984), 13, 160, 161, 173–7, 266–7; Italicus train (1974), 63, 135, 173, 267, 312; Peteano car-bombing (1972), 137–43, 153; Piazza Fontana (1969), 40, 41, 85, 94, 101, 122–3, 134, 200, 203, 205, 248, 276; Trento (1971), 122, 137; Ustica DC-9 crash (1980), 167–72; see also Bologna station bombing
Bonifacio, Francesco, 204
Bonisoli, Franco, 292
Bonsanti, Sandra, 332
Bontade, Stefano, 88
Bordoni, Carlo, 102–3
Borghese, Prince Valerio, 84, 90, 91, 95, 118, 160
Borghese coup attempt (Operation Tora Tora: 1970), 58, 90–9, 101, 107, 115, 117, 118, 133, 160, 248, 312
Il Borghese, magazine, 76–7, 294
Bosso, Luigi, 319, 331
Bove, Alphonse, 337
Bozzo, Carlo, 219
Braghetti, Anna Laura, 239–40

Brenneke, Richard, 78–9, 80–2
Brescia: Piazza della Loggia bombing (1974), 134–5, 136, 152
Breslin, Jimmy, 301
Brink's robbery (1984), 257–8, 259, 261, 266, 268
Brioschi, Anna, 281
Britain, 31, 34; freemasonry, 58; Labour Party, 18; secret services (MI6), 71, 130, 147; SOE, 30, 107
Brogi, Andrea, 63, 65
Brotherhood of Eternal Love, 309, 316
Brown, Martin Woodrow, conspiracy allegations of (CIA's involvement in Moro kidnap), 298–309, 314, 316–19
Brown, Martin, Jr, 317
Buda, Franco, 312
Bulgarian secret services, 337–8
Bureau of Intelligence and Research, US, 353
Buscetta, Tommaso, 96–7, 175, 265–6
Bush, President George, 79, 80
Buzzati, Roberto, 328
Buzzi, Ermanno, strangling of, 136

Cagol, Mara, 190, 222; death of (1975), 200–1
Calabrese, Luigi, 134
Calderone, Antonino, 97
Calò, Pippo, 174, 175–6, 226–8, 269, 357
Calogero, Pietro, 182, 185–6, 190, 193, 311, 346, 347
Calore, Sergio, 23, 135
Caltagirone, Gaetano, 85
Calvi, Clara, 57
Calvi, Roberto, 57, 105, 174, 203, 262, 302
Camorra, Neapolitan, 162, 173–4, 176, 177, 240, 266, 305, 318, 319, 327, 328, 330–1, 334
Camp Derby military base, Livorno, 170
Candido, magazine, 205
Cannizzaro, Colonel Rocco, 71
Cape Marrargiu (Sardinia), secret NATO training base (Gladio), 45, 151, 156, 157
Caprara, Massimo, 281–2, 283, 284, 307, 329
carabinieri (paramilitary police), 24, 25, 34, 35, 36, 59, 64, 91, 94, 98, 122, 127, 132, 153, 199, 201, 207, 237, 252, 310–11, 342; Borghese coup attempt,

Colli, Mauro, 111
Colombo, Emilio, 71
Colonna, Prince Prospero, 160
Committee for Democratic Resistance, 108
Communist Party, Italian (PCI), 13, 15, 16–19, 20, 26, 28, 30, 34, 51, 59, 61, 62, 75, 95, 98, 101, 112, 113, 132, 161, 166, 180, 181, 185, 186, 187, 188, 219, 264, 274, 282, 326, 349, 350; *doppiezza* policy, 17; effect of terrorism on support for, 15, 17, 22, 24, 341, 353; electoral decline of, 341; Eurocommunism of, 17, 113, 235–6, 351; extreme left's hostility towards, 182, 183; and Gelli, 51–3, 54, 60, 68, 70, 86; Moro's policy of 'historic compromise' with, 37, 182, 214, 215, 217, 219–21, 225, 230, 235, 341, 344, 353, 1948 elections, 31–3; name changed to Partito Democratico di Sinistra (1990), 355; Operation Gladio, 146, 148, 149, 153; revisionism, 26, 181, 182, 206; Soviet relations with, 18, 19, 20, 33, 235–6; US opposition to taking of power by, 16, 18, 19–20, 27, 28, 32, 214, 219–21, 235, 236, 351, 353, 355; wartime resistance, 30, 51–2, 53, 54
Concutelli, Pierluigi, 88, 136
Condo, Lieutenant-Colonel Giuseppe, 110
Connally, John, 86
Coppetti, Marcello, 51, 70, 229, 279–80; documents (on Gelli and Moro affair), 277–81, 283, 284, 288, 294, 301–3; list of racing drivers, 302
Cornacchia, Colonel Antonio, 247, 250
Corriere del Ticino, 165
Corriere della Sera, 14, 69, 75, 154, 167, 170, 188, 191, 193, 198, 229, 240, 282, 292, 293–4, 314, 348
Corsini, Giuseppe, 52, 53, 54
Corsini, Renato, 85
Cortini, Publio, 58
Cosentino, Francesco, 57
Cossiga, Francesco, 71, 78, 239, 313; Moro affair, 223, 238, 240, 241–2, 244, 245, 255, 287, 304, 305, 326, 357; and Moro's letter to, 271–3, 274; Operation Gladio, 147, 148–9, 150
Costanzo, Maurizio, 229–30

coup conspiracies, right-wing, 22, 25, 26–7, 28, 31, 35, 38, 62–3, 90–113, 121; Borghese plot (1970), 58, 90–9, 101, 107, 115, 117, 118, 160; De Lorenzo's 'Piano Solo' (1964), 28, 35, 36, 45, 92, 94, 139, 147, 149–50, 154, 155; Fumagalli's involvement, 110–13; 'Rosa dei Venti', 26–7, 58, 99–100, 101, 102, 110, 146, 151–2; Sindona's involvement in, 101–4; Sogno's plans, 107–10; US funding of non-communists, 114–18
Crawford, John, 315
Craxi, Bettino, 191, 290, 314, 351
CSIS (Georgetown University Centre for Strategic and International Studies), 346, 347
Curcio, Renato, 188–9, 190, 192, 198, 200, 201, 205, 206–7, 219, 222, 236, 256, 292, 295, 310, 311, 345, 346; arrest of (1974), 205, 206–7, 222, 237, 358
Cutolo, Raffaele, 265, 266, 318–19, 321, 327, 330–1, 332, 334, 335
Czechoslovakia, 18, 33, 81, 158

Dainelli, Luca, 275
Dal Bello, Luciano, 252, 260, 261–2, 263, 266
D'Alema, Giuseppe, 58
Dalla Chiesa, General Carlo Alberto, 207, 208, 237–8, 282, 283–91, 320, 336, 346–7, 348; Andreotti's relationship with, 288–90; assassination in Palermo of (1982), 286–9, 348; as head of *carabinieri* anti-terrorist unit, 237–8, 285, 288; and Mafia, 237, 286; Moro affair, 206, 237–8, 273, 278, 281, 283–91
Dalla Chiesa, Nando, 288–9, 290
D'Amato, Federico Umberto, 73–7, 84–5, 92, 94, 107, 118, 210, 280, 348
D'Ambrosio, Loreto, 129
Dante Alighieri, *Inferno*, 48
Dardani, Attilio, 55
D'Arezzo, Bernardo, 72, 228
'David' (Stark's friend), 308–9, 314–15
David, Jean Paul, 108
De Boccard, Enrico, 40, 41
De Chirico, Giorgio, 252, 262
De Felice, brothers Fabio and Alfredo, 94
De Gori, Giuseppe, 268–9
De Iorio, Filippo, 95

Leto, Guido, 34, 74
Lex, Matteo, 69–70
Libya, 70, 80, 81; plot to overthrow
  Khadafy government, 169, 170, 172
Ligas, Natalia, 202
Liggio, Luciano, 97
Lima, Salvo, 289, 312
Lockheed bribery scandal, 217, 274–5,
  278, 280
Loiacono, Alvaro, 215–16
Lombardi, General Luigi, 38
Lombardo, Carmine, 176
Loren, Sophia, 177
Lorenzon, Guido, 128
Lotta Continua, 134, 138, 139, 180
Lotta Continua, newspaper, 23, 122, 137,
  190, 283, 312
Luciano, Lucky, 31
Lucioli, Fulvio, 175
Lunetta, Gaetano, 97–8

MacArthur, General Douglas, 53
McFarlane, Robert, 80
Mafia, 31, 58, 78, 87, 88, 101, 103, 111,
  163, 175, 185, 201, 237, 240, 246, 260,
  304, 312, 316, 334, 337, 346;
  assassination of Dalla Chiesa by
  (1982), 286–9; Borghese coup, 96–8;
  Calabrian ('ndrangheta), 192, 215, 252,
  263, 265, 321, 328; Christmas train
  bombing (1984), 173–4, 176; Moro
  affair, 262–4, 265–6, 267; Sindona's
  Sicilian coup plan (1979), 103, 104
Magliana band, 163, 174–5, 177, 252;
  Moro affair, 240, 242, 266, 267–8;
  Pecorelli murder, 87, 88, 89, 162
Malagugini, Alberto, 197
Maletti, General Gianadelio, 77, 84,
  113–14, 124, 125, 126, 129, 130, 133,
  197, 199–200, 234
Malta, 16, 93, 167
Mancuso, Libero, 55
Manes, General Giorgio, 37, 39; death
  of, (1969), 39–40
Il Manifesto, newspaper, 336
MAR (Movimento d'Azione
  Rivoluzionaria), 111
Maradona, Diego, 106
Marini, Vincenzo, 263
Marolles, Colonel Alain de, 172
Martin, US Ambassador Graham, 59, 98,
  123, 353; CIA dispute over funding

with, 115, 116–17, 118, 353
Martini, Admiral Fulvio, head of SISMI,
  126, 158, 168–9
Marxism, Marxism-Leninism, 17, 26, 27,
  43, 180, 182, 194
Mastelloni, Judge Carlo, 193, 194, 195,
  196, 197, 314; Operation Gladio, 146,
  153, 154
Mattarella, Piersanti, assassination of
  (1980), 87, 88–9, 177
Mazzanti, Manfredo, Red Brigades'
  shooting of (1980), 202
Mazzola, Giuseppe, 200
Mears, John 215
Melega, Gianluigi, 322
Il Messaggero, newspaper, 163, 216, 258,
  259, 268, 281, 282–3
Metropoli, magazine, 184, 327
Miceli, Gaetano, 259, 327
Miceli, General Vito, 24–5, 27, 60, 70,
  74, 84, 92, 107, 113, 131–2, 133, 149,
  154, 199, 234, 244, 312, 313, 314;
  Ambassador Martin's funding of, 59,
  115, 116–17, 123, 353; arrested and
  charged with conspiracy (1974), 26, 99
Milan: City Council bombing (1972),
  163; Piazza Fontana bombing (1969),
  13, 23, 40, 41, 85, 94, 101, 122–31, 134,
  135, 141, 200, 203, 205, 248, 276;
  police HQ grenade attack (1973), 134;
  trade fair bombing (1969), 123; *see
  also* Via Montenevoso
Minervini, Girolamo, murder of (1980),
  327
Mino, General Enrico, 280
Mintoff, Dom, 16
Molinari, Arrigo, 68–9, 106, 327–8
Le Monde, newspaper, 172
Il Mondo, financial magazine, 37–8,
  102–3, 129, 252
Mondo d'Oggi, magazine, 84
Montebelluna documents, 128–9
Montedison petrochemical company, 164
Montgomery, Hugh, 128
Moretti, Mario, 190–1, 192, 198, 204,
  205, 219, 222, 241, 242, 243, 256, 263,
  284, 285, 293, 315, 326, 346; arrest of
  (1981), 192, 208–9, 327, 328; and arrest
  of Curcio and Franceschini (1974),
  190, 206–7; contacts with Hyperion
  language school, 191, 208, 328, 345;
  gun running mission to Lebanon